Cambridge Imperial and Post-Co[...]

General Editors: Megan Vaughan, Ki[...] Corpus
Christi College, Cambridge

This informative series covers the broa[...] [...]ploring
the recent developments in former col[...] [...]: found.
The books provide in-depth examin[...] [...]nentary
power structures encouraging the rea[...] [...]ational
and world history during recent centu[...].

Titles include:

Sunil S. Amrith
DECOLONIZING INTERNATIONAL HEALTH
India and Southeast Asia, 1930–65

Tony Ballantyne
ORIENTALISM AND RACE
Aryanism in the British Empire

Robert J. Blyth
THE EMPIRE OF THE RAJ
Eastern Africa and the Middle East, 1858–1947

Roy Bridges (*editor*)
IMPERIALISM, DECOLONIZATION AND AFRICA
Studies Presented to John Hargreaves

L.J. Butler
COPPER EMPIRE
Mining and the Colonial State in Northern Rhodesia, c.1930–64

Hilary M. Carey (*editor*)
EMPIRES OF RELIGION

T.J. Cribb (*editor*)
IMAGINED COMMONWEALTH
Cambridge Essays on Commonwealth and International Literature in English

Michael S. Dodson
ORIENTALISM, EMPIRE AND NATIONAL CULTURE
India, 1770–1880

Ulrike Hillemann
ASIAN EMPIRE AND BRITISH KNOWLEDGE
China and the Networks of British Imperial Expansion

B.D. Hopkins
THE MAKING OF MODERN AFGHANISTAN

Ronald Hyam
BRITAIN'S IMPERIAL CENTURY, 1815–1914: A STUDY OF EMPIRE AND EXPANSION
Third Edition

Iftekhar Iqbal
THE BENGAL DELTA
Ecology, State and Social Change, 1843–1943

Robin Jeffrey
POLITICS, WOMEN AND WELL-BEING
How Kerala became a 'Model'

Gerold Krozewski
MONEY AND THE END OF EMPIRE
British International Economic Policy and the Colonies, 1947–58

Sloan Mahone and Megan Vaughan (*editors*)
PSYCHIATRY AND EMPIRE

Javed Majeed
AUTOBIOGRAPHY, TRAVEL AND POST-NATIONAL IDENTITY

Francine McKenzie
REDEFINING THE BONDS OF COMMONWEALTH 1939–1948
The Politics of Preference

Gabriel Paquette
ENLIGHTENMENT, GOVERNANCE AND REFORM IN SPAIN AND ITS EMPIRE 1759–1808

Jennifer Regan-Lefebvre
IRISH AND INDIAN
The Cosmopolitan Politics of Alfred Webb

Ricardo Roque
HEADHUNTING AND COLONIALISM
Anthropology and the Circulation of Human Skulls in the Portuguese Empire, 1870–1930

Michael Silvestri
IRELAND AND INDIA
Nationalism, Empire and Memory

John Singleton and Paul Robertson
ECONOMIC RELATIONS BETWEEN BRITAIN AND AUSTRALASIA 1945–1970

Aparna Vaidik
IMPERIAL ANDAMANS
Colonial Encounter and Island History

Kim A. Wagner (*editor*)   .
THUGGEE
Banditry and the British in Early Nineteenth-Century India

Jon E. Wilson
THE DOMINATION OF STRANGERS
Modern Governance in Eastern India, 1780–1835

Cambridge Imperial and Post-Colonial Studies Series
Series Standing Order ISBN 978–0–333–91908–8 (Hardback)
978–0–333–91909–5 (Paperback)
(*outside North America only*)

You can receive future titles in this series as they are published by placing a standing order.
Please contact your bookseller or, in case of difficulty, write to us at the address below with
your name and address, the title of the series and the ISBN quoted above.

Customer Services Department, Macmillan Distribution Ltd, Houndmills, Basingstoke,
Hampshire RG21 6XS, England

The Domination of Strangers

Modern Governance in Eastern India, 1780–1835

Jon E. Wilson

First published in hardback 2008 and this paperback edition 2010 by
PALGRAVE MACMILLAN

Palgrave Macmillan in the UK is an imprint of Macmillan Publishers Limited, registered in England, company number 785998, of Houndmills, Basingstoke, Hampshire RG21 6XS.

Palgrave Macmillan in the US is a division of St Martin's Press LLC, 175 Fifth Avenue, New York, NY 10010.

Palgrave Macmillan is the global academic imprint of the above companies and has companies and representatives throughout the world.

Palgrave® and Macmillan® are registered trademarks in the United States, the United Kingdom, Europe and other countries.

ISBN: 978–0–230–57453–3 hardback
ISBN: 978–0–230–27915–5 paperback

This book is printed on paper suitable for recycling and made from fully managed and sustained forest sources. Logging, pulping and manufacturing processes are expected to conform to the environmental regulations of the country of origin.

A catalogue record for this book is available from the British Library.

A catalog record for this book is available from the Library of Congress.

10   9   8   7   6   5   4   3   2   1
19   18   17   16   15   14   13   12   11   10

Printed and bound in Great Britain by
CPI Antony Rowe, Chippenham and Eastbourne

for Elaine

Contents

List of Map and Illustrations   viii

Preface and Acknowledgements   ix

Abbreviations   xi

1   Introduction   1

2   Comparing Eighteenth-Century Polities   19

3   Crisis, Anxiety and the Making of a New Order   45

4   Colonial Indecision and the Origins of the Hindu Joint Family   75

5   Governing the Power of Proprietors   104

6   The State as Machine and the Ambivalent Origins of Colonial
    Utilitarianism   133

7   Indian Liberalism and Colonial Utilitarianism   161

8   Reflections   182

Notes   195

Bibliography   223

Index   238

List of Map and Illustrations

Map

1 Map of Bengal and Bihar xii

Figures

3.1 The Judge's House at Dinajpur, watercolour, *c.*1790–1800, BL
Add.Or. 3199 68

5.1 Page from Quinquennial Register, 1799, Rangpur District
Record Room 110

5.2 Revenue Survey Map, 1858–1859, sheet 2, circuit 11, Rangpur
District Record Room 130

Preface and Acknowledgements

This book challenges the claim that European attempts to dominate the rest of the world were part of an intellectually coherent project. In the last few years that claim has been made forcefully by scholars wishing to 'make empire whole again', as Madhavi Kale puts it, whether they are critical or supportive of empire.[1] The book criticises such accounts by showing how colonial practice produced strange and deeply ambivalent forms of thought that nonetheless became fundamentally intertwined with the practices and concepts of modern European politics. Britain's first modern state emerged in Bengal, it argues, but it suggests that it was the indecisive and ambivalent character of colonial political thought that marked its modernity more than anything else. Instead of using artificially constructed canons of 'western' political theory, it attempts to find a more historically realistic vocabulary for discussing both Western and non-Western political practice. That vocabulary needs, above all, to be able to explain why highly abstract forms of 'theory' had more purchase over practical life in some contexts more than others.

Consequently, the following chapters are indebted to my own immersion in the real world of political and institutional practice in different locations: as a councillor in the London Borough of Waltham Forest between 2002 and 2006; as an academic at King's College London; and as a close observer of Indian and in particular Bangladeshi politics; I would like to thank friends and colleagues in each place. Publication of this book was made possible by financial support from a number of institutions: the American Social Science Research Council, the Arts and Humanities Research Board and later Arts and Humanities Research Council, ASAF Foundation in Dhaka, the British Academy, Scouloudi Foundation at the Institute of Historical Research, Humanities School of King's College London, Oxford University Beit Fund, St Anthony's College Stahl Fund and St Hugh's College Oxford. I am grateful to the British Library for giving permission to reproduce a number of images.

Research was conducted at archives in Britain, India and Bangladesh. Without exception archivists in each place have been efficient and helpful. But in particular I would like to thank Professor Sharif Uddin Ahmed, until recently Director of the National Archives in Dhaka. Historians of Bengal are indebted to him for having run one of the best organised, most dynamic and most ambitious archival repositories in the world. Professor Ahmed and many others have ensured that Dhaka has been a hospitable second home over the last few years. I hope this book and future work begins to return their generosity.

Working with Talal Asad in New York sparked many of the initial ideas that were later developed in these pages. Over the years since then, Talal has been an acute critic and interlocutor. David Washbrook supervised the dissertation that this book grew out of, and has been a source of support since. Since examining the doctoral thesis this book grew out of, Chris Bayly has offered constant engagement and an endless source of advice. Three friends have been constant intellectual allies, collaborators and sparring partners, helping shape my thinking the most over the last decade: Shruti Kapila, Iftekhar Iqbal and Laura Roush. Hussein Agrama, Talal Asad, Chris Bayly, Jim Bjork, Michael Dodson, Carrie Gibson, Shruti Kapila, Elaine Lester, Michael Lobban, Maleiha Malik, Benjamin Page, Javed Majeed, Andrew Sartori, Adam Sutcliffe and Tim Wilson commented on chapters; Nandini Chatterjee, Iftekhar Iqbal, Robert Travers and Nick Wilson read the entire manuscript. Their very detailed engagement has made it much better than it would have been otherwise. In addition, comments from or conversations with Rushanara Ali, Claire Anderson, Duncan Bell, Ujjayan Bhattacharya, Ritu Birla, Rajat Datta, Faisal Devji, Andrew Dilley, Richard Drayton, Serena Ferente, Durba Ghosh, Catherine Hall, Joanna Innes, Sirajul Islam, Ayesha Jalal, Ruby Lal, Ian McBride, Nuru Huda Monsur, Andrew Porter, Emma Page, Paul Readman, Sarah Stockwell, Mohammed Tabishat, Richard Vinen, Rupa Viswanath and Tim Wilson were significant, sparking many of the ideas in the pages below. I am grateful to Naomi Hossein, Alfaz Hossein, Kathy Hossain, Dipu Moni, Nurul Huda Monsur, Tawfique Nawaz, Tawquir Nawaz, Deepavali Nawaz, Iftekhar Iqbal and Rizwana Siddiqua for making Dhaka a second home for so many years. The corridors of King's College London history department are amongst the most intellectually stimulating places I know. I'd like to thank colleagues and students there, particularly participants in my third-year class 'The Making of the Colonial Regime' during the last two years. Richard Drayton's enthusiasm for this book led to its publication by Palgrave Macmillan; I'd like to thank Richard, Michael Strang and Ruth Ireland for making the process of publication so easy. My family, Dot Wilson, Rod Wilson and Tim Wilson have been a source of immense support and intellectual excitement. Elaine Lester has changed my life in ways I could never imagine; I have her to thank for everything.

March 2008

Abbreviations

Add Mss	Additional Manuscripts, British Library
BJC	Bengal Judicial Consultations
BL	British Library
BRC	Bengal Revenue Consultations
CoD	Court of Directors
CRO	County Record Office
CSSH	*Comparative Studies in Society and History*
DR	District Records
FWIH	*Fort William-India House Correspondence* (22 vols, Delhi, 1949–1985)
HCSP	*House of Commons Sessional Papers of the Eighteenth-Century, 1715–1800*
IESHR	*Indian Economic and Social History Review*
IOR	India Office Records, Asia, Africa and Pacific Collections, British Library
MAS	*Modern Asian Studies*
Mss Eur	European Manuscripts, Asia, Africa and Pacific Collections, British Library
NAB	National Archives of Bangladesh
n.p.	no page numbers
PP	*Parliamentary Papers*
PRO	Public Record Office manuscripts, National Archives, London
SDA	*Sadr Diwani Adalat* (referred to by British officials as the Sudder Dewanny Adawlut)
WBSA	West Bengal State Archives, Kolkata

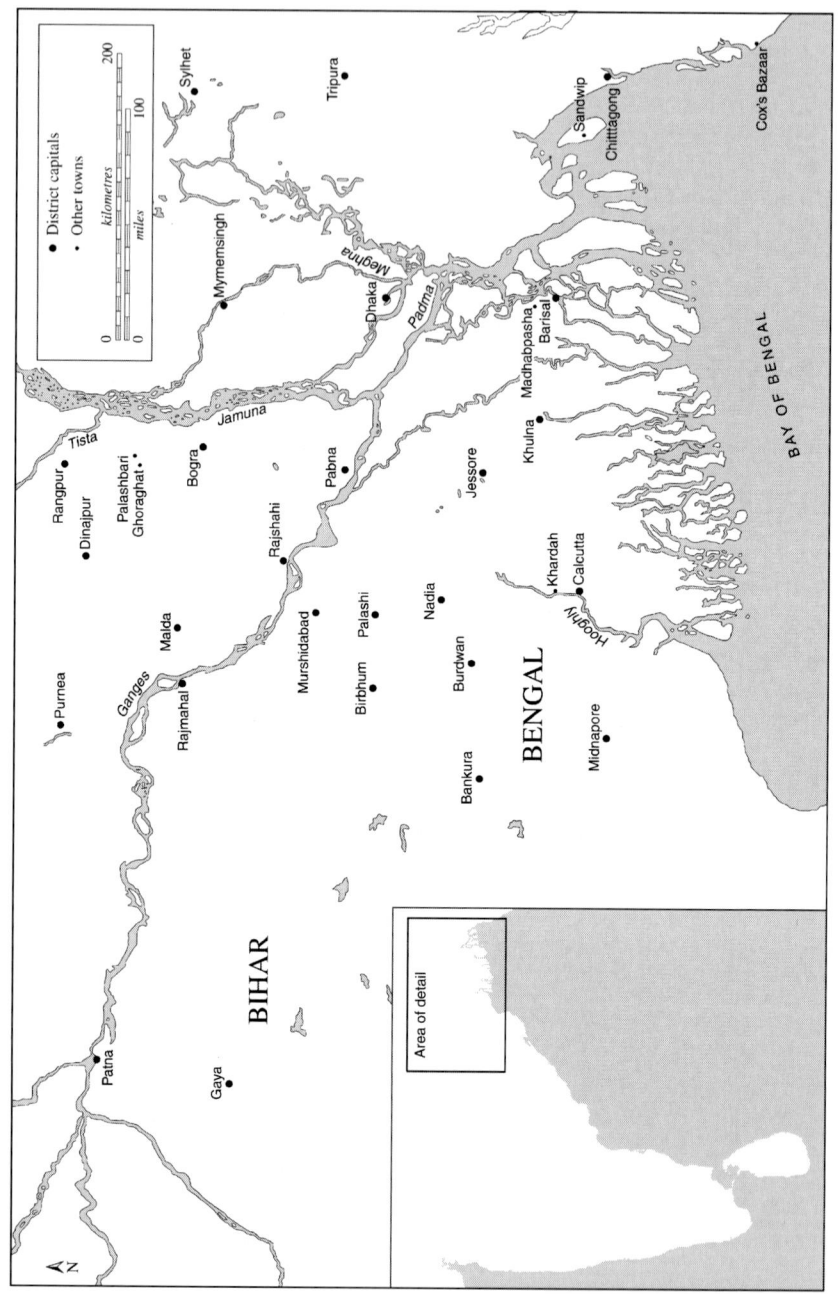

Map 1 Map of Bengal and Bihar.

1
Introduction

Modern states treat their subjects as strangers. But in many places in Europe and Asia, before the late eighteenth century, governance was based on a model of familiar relations between ruler and ruled. Early modern commentators wrote as if personal familiarity was an important aspect of political conduct. In this idiom governance was regarded as a form of face-to-face exchange in which rulers needed to constantly gauge the people's affection to them. The visibility of the prince and the possibility of coming into his presence were crucial to South Asian politics before British rule. The most important treatises on politics and ethics in early modern India were concerned with the skilful balance between persuasion and chastisement needed to maintain the affection and awe of the population.[1] The same was true in Europe, for writers as different as Baldassarre Castiglione and Niccolo Machiavelli, Thomas Hobbes, William Paley and Edmund Burke, all of whom saw the relationship between ruler and ruled as a process of continual interaction based on familiarity between the two.[2]

Many of the regimes that emerged across the globe in the nineteenth and twentieth centuries were different. They treated their subjects as unfamiliar beings who needed to be ruled using techniques of governance that did not presume prior familiarity. The inhabitants of those states were subject to grand strategies, objective forms of statistical knowledge and abstract codes of law. Though they often spoke of the need for rulers to be sympathetic to the welfare of the governed, few were concerned with the degree of affection existing between ruler and ruled.

Such modern regimes act on their subjects in two ways as noted by the German sociologist Georg Simmel in his 1906 essay on 'The Stranger'.[3] Not being connected 'through established ties of kinship, locality, and occupation' to those they rule, strangers adopt an attitude of objectivity which is passive and detached. Simmel noted that '[o]bjectivity may be defined as freedom: the objective individual is bound by no commitments which could prejudice his perception, understanding or evaluation of the given'. But such freedom creates an unnerving, anxiety-inducing degree of uncertainty about

1

how to judge and what to do. As a result, modern governance is marked by indecision and ambivalence.[4]

Secondly, the stranger's objectivity 'finds practical expression in the more abstract nature of the [subject's] relation to him'. Modern states do not consider their subjects as unique, particular individuals, 'but [instead] as strangers of a particular type'. Rather than the complex, inter-subjective forms of ethical practice that constituted the early modern polity, the modern state attempts to govern its subjects with general, abstract rules.[5]

This book examines the emergence of such a modern form of governance in colonial Bengal, showing how the characteristics Simmel noted became central to British rule in India. Bengal was the first large area of territory that came under the direct rule of the English East India Company. During the seventeenth and eighteenth centuries, its people were governed in a heterogeneous series of regional and Indian-wide sovereignties, including both the Mughal empire and a patchwork of local principalities. Taking advantage of a complex set of revolutions in Bengali politics, by the mid-1760s the Company established a form of political authority backed by military power. To begin with, though, British rule was rooted in familiar networks of friendship and enmity that extended from the provincial capital in Murshidabad, to Calcutta and London. This book shows how a dramatic rupture occurred in the culture of politics in Bengal from the mid-1780s onwards, as a crisis in Britain's worldwide empire intersected with the unstable politics of war, revenue collection and British governance in India. The response, over the next 50 years, was the emergence of a form of governance in British-ruled India that treated its subjects as strangers for the first time.

That style of administration was very different from the way people had been ruled in mid-eighteenth-century Bengal. But it also differed from the style of governance at home in Britain, where for the most part political leaders continued to encounter their subjects as familiars, often as friends or enemies. In Britain, strangeness did not characterise the relationship between state and society, or government and population as a whole.[6] By contrast, India's British rulers were preoccupied with the administration of new abstract types such as the Indian landholder, the peasant proprietor or the Hindu widow, categories whose genealogy will be charted in the pages below. So whilst English land law continued to be based on the heterogeneity of uncodified local rights, the British state in Bengal tried to define a single general type of propertied subject in written rules; a type often referred to with the word 'landholder' or *zamindar*. Although the families from which the British collected revenue remained changed little from the 1810s, British officials rapidly moved from one conception of the rights of the landholder to another. Without sustained engagement with Bengali ways of life, officers suffered from exactly the kind of anxious intellectual freedom that Simmel discussed.

In part this book tells the story of the official mind that ruled Bengal between the 1780s and the 1830s, a set of mentalities very different from those which governed Britain or imperial politics in the metropolis.[7] It shows how colonial thought came to be dominated by an obsession with the search for general, abstract rules, which could be applied mechanistically by an authoritarian state. That cluster of ideas and instincts might be referred to as colonial legal posivitism; it could also be described with Bernard Williams' term 'government house utilitarianism', a phrase referring to the practical political philosophy of an elite with an abstract and idealised definition of public welfare not shared by the population at large.[8] Revising many of the arguments of Eric Stokes' *English Utilitarianism and India*, the following chapters nonetheless offer a genealogy of this utilitarian governing mentality in a colonial environment. But they also suggest that such a genealogy needs to explain how a rule-based approach to human interaction diffused itself amongst sections of Bengal's elites. As the final chapter of the book illustrates, the very idea of Indian 'society' articulated by Calcutta-based Indian intellectuals in the first half of the nineteenth century was in part dependent on these strands of colonial thought.

The book places the process of colonial governance occurring in the specific location of late-eighteenth- and early-nineteenth-century Bengal within a broader context, examining its relationship to an enduring story about changing practices of governance told by philosophers and historians interested in other parts of the world. Historically-minded philosophers from Max Weber to Michel Foucault and beyond, as well as conceptually-minded British historians such as Oliver MacDonagh and Eric Stokes, argue that a dramatic transformation in the ideologies and practices of government occurred in Europe in the eighteenth and nineteenth centuries, which went on to have an extraordinary impact on the rest of the world. Each explained the emergence of modern politics and the modern state in very different ways; but their concerns overlap. They note that the modern forms of governance which had come into existence in nineteenth-century Europe shared an attempt to target populations with general categories and rules, supposedly for their own welfare; to create permanent and hierarchical agencies to produce and enforce those norms; and to produce new ideas about how to manage the frontier between society's autonomous self-regulation and the intervention of the state: in other words, they were characterised by governmentality, bureaucracy and liberalism.[9] And from Eric Stokes to Partha Chatterjee onwards, scholars concerned with the colonial transformation of Asia examine the process and implications by which these ideas and practices were transported from Europe to the colonial world.

This book is influenced by these arguments about the emergence of political modernity in Europe and the rest of the world. But it suggests that attention to the early history of colonialism in Bengal allows them to be reworked in two respects. First of all, the book shows how the emergence of new forms of governance occurred from the anxious, insecure attitude to Indian society which politicians and administrators had during these years; they did not develop from a confident desire to transform South Asia or impose a coherent political ideology rooted in the continuities of European intellectual history upon the rest of the world. In particular, the following chapters suggest that colonial Bengal's political modernity needs first of all to be rooted in the complex set of responses to a complex, multi-layered series of imperial crises that occurred within British rule in Bengal in the late-eighteenth and early-nineteenth centuries.

Secondly, the book suggests that events and processes outside Europe were central to the making of modern forms of rule in Asia and elsewhere, including in Europe itself. The colonial regime that developed in Bengal was not the product of the centrifugal flow of ideas or practices from metropole to colony; centripetal forces, in which concepts and practices flowed from the 'periphery' to the imperial 'centre', were more important. Many characteristics of 'British' political modernity emerged in colonial India before they occurred in Britain itself. A positivistic conception of law as the command of the sovereign developed first in India, as did a mechanistic idea of the state, and a perception, shared by rulers and subjects, of the population as a body of people united by a common culture, not merely common allegiance to political institutions. None of these were significant in Britain before the colonial encounter.

I

The beginning of these processes was noted by one Indian observer of British rule. Writing in 1784 about the revolutions that had occurred in the province of Bengal since the decline of Mughal power, Ghulam Hussein Khan Tabatabai (*c.*1727–1797) noted the 'declining state of the country'. He had spent most of his life moving through India in the service of the Mughal regime, writing his *Seir Mutaquerin* ('View of modern times') 20 years after the British had begun to assert their political dominance in India for the first time. From the early 1760s his career and income were bound to the fate of the Company in the eastern province of Bengal.[10] Despite these long-standing colonial connections, Ghulam Hussein's work emphasised the British role in the process of decline. After observing their government for two decades, Ghulam Hussein was clear that Bengal's new rulers were 'quite alien to this country', 'strangers to the methods of raising tribute, as well as to the maxims of estimating the revenues or of comprehending the ways of tax-gathering'. Ghulam Hussein differentiated the practice of the British from India's pre-colonial Mughal rulers. The Mughals had 'lived among their people'. The British, by contrast, exchanged information with Indian subjects without effectively imbibing Indian ways of life. They hid themselves away in their own world of institutions and ideas rather than effectively engaging with the population they ruled.[11]

Ghulam Hussein believed the strange relationship Britons had towards Indian society had something to do with the way they used writing. British rule seemed rooted in the physical exchange of written words between the officers of the East India Company. It was, he said, 'a standing rule with them',

> that whatever anything remarkable they heard from any man versed in business, or even from any other individual, was immediately set in writing in a kind of book consisting of a few blank leaves, which most of them carry about, and which they put together afterwards, and bind like a book for future use.

The Company's officers were constantly 'endeavouring to engage [Indians] in conversation, especially upon the politics of the country'. But those conversations did not consist of a proper dialogue. Ghulam Hussein continued,

> so soon as an Englishman could pick up anything relative to the laws or business of this land, he would immediately set it down in writing, and lay it up in store for the use of another Englishmen.

'Matters have come to such a pass', he argued,

> that the Books and Memorandum composed by the English ... have come to be trusted as so many vouchers; whereas they are only some faint idea of the exterior and bark, but not the pith or real reason of these institutions.[12]

The texts the British produced were signs empty of significance. Written by a class of officials who saw themselves as strangers to India, Ghulam Hussein argued, they contained knowledge of a kind but not the wisdom that came from familiar forms of interaction which could effectively guide action.

One metaphor stands out in Ghulam Hussein's account. The Mughal official described how officials engaged with Bengal's population as if they were 'pictures on a wall'.[13] British officials encountered their subjects as static objects of scrutiny, whose lives were governed by stable patterns and structures that could be represented objectively, like a picture, from a distant perspective. The problem, Ghulam Hussein suggested, was that British officers rarely perceived themselves as active participants in the everyday lives of those they governed. One of the major themes of this book is the way Company officials maintained an estranged relationship from Indian society, avoiding interaction that would have enabled them to engage in the tactical game of Indian politics on its own terms.

Ghulam Hussein's history of British rule in India was interested in practices, affections and experience. The Indian nobleman thought the British
were strangers because they did not embody the habit and skill proper to a
ruler and had not learnt the forms of conduct that allowed the sovereign to
'inquire into the characters and tempers of men' and govern each accordingly. For him, intelligence was not purely cognitive or primarily linguistic.
Ghulam Hussein inhabited an Aristotelian early modern world in which
good governance depended on the cultivation of practical virtues through
training, experience and personal forms of familiar interaction rather than
the possession of abstract knowledge.[14] Governance was an inter-subjective
form of ethical practice that could not be adequately described with written
rules. From within a practical tradition that valued the ruler's ability to make
'personal inquiry into the circumstances of his suitors', the aloof perspective
the British adopted appeared strange.

Two centuries or more after Ghulam Hussein wrote, scholars tend to critically examine colonial representations and discourse rather than look at
institutions or practices when they discuss the British regime in India. Following the publication of Edward Said's *Orientalism* in 1978, many have
noted how the British represented India as inferior, backward and unchanging, then shown how Indians resisted by imagining themselves differently
afterwards.[15] Others explain the introduction of European ideas about politics and economics to the subcontinent, illustrating how new, modern
notions of the state, civil society and market economics transformed (or
did not transform) Indian society.[16] Underlying these trends in the history
of colonialism is the assumption that humans are fundamentally representa-
tional beings, whose ability to use language to construct coherent concepts
of the world in their minds is the most important factor in determining
how they engage with the world in practice. The problem with this kind of
cultural history is that it does not explain why an instance of discourse or
a form of representation occurs at a particular place at a specific point in
time; nor does it help understand where that discourse comes from.[17] All it
offers is a static account of the attitudes Europeans had about Indians written
in particular texts, which remain unconnected to an understanding of the
power relations that led them to be articulated, the purposes they were put
and the instruments which used them at a particular moment in the flow
of time.[18] What is missing is an interpretation of the historical process by
which a particular form of discourse comes into being and then has an effect
on the world around it; of the relationship between the general categories of
discourse and the events within which they occurred.

In part, the following pages offer an account of the ideas and discourses
of governance that the British in the early colonial period used to govern
in the province of Bengal. The book pays special attention to the texts
through which the process of colonial governance, in particular the governance of property, was conducted. But the analysis here concerns the forms

of experience, practice and instinct that led British officials and their Indian interlocutors to use texts in a particular way to begin with. That experience was defined by the complex set of practical purposes which colonial officials in Bengal tried to fulfil; much of the time, it was driven by the often-rootless effort of officials to find categories and concepts that allowed them to practically understand what it was they did when they acted to fulfil those purposes. British rule in early colonial India was underwritten by an anxious search for semantic coherence. The argument here is that that search was one of the most important forces shaping the development of politics in colonial South Asia, in particular in creating a transformation or rupture in political practice and thought.

II

As has already been noted in this chapter, the rupturing force of colonialism can be associated with a number of concepts: capitalism, utilitarianism, bureaucracy, governmentality and, most recently, liberalism. The argument here is influenced by a recent emphasis on the close relationship between liberalism and empire in a number of recent works: in particular within the writing of C.A. Bayly, Uday Singh Mehta, Jennifer Pitts and Andrew Sartori.[19] As Bayly reminds us, liberalism comes in many different guises. Some varieties are historicist and intrinsically sceptical about the virtue of abstract forms of social analysis. But in the form that scholars have referred to it in their discussion of colonialism recently, liberalism tends to be characterised by its use of abstract or universalistic modes of thought, and its suspicion about the role of particular concrete situations or practical traditions in providing grounds for political action and thought.

Such, at least, is the way Uday Singh Mehta defines colonial liberalism in one of the most important books published in the last few decades in the field. Mehta suggests that the nineteenth-century liberal rhetoric of James and John Stuart Mill was marked above all by its sense of detachment from, and unfamiliarity with, the world it analysed. Liberalism's unfamiliarity with real life allowed it to 'compare and classify' different societies, constantly judging what it actually saw against an abstract set of normative standards, giving it an 'urge to dominate the world' as a consequence. Mehta finds this link between abstract universalism and the urge to both conceptually and materially dominate the world in British political thought from John Locke onwards. He contrasts the arrogance of imperial liberalism with the attention to the particularity of concrete situations and emphasis on lived experience found in the writings of the British politician Edmund Burke in particular.[20]

The argument of this book is strongly influenced by Mehta's work. The difference, however, lies in the concern here with the relationship between the complex, situated practice of colonial power and liberal ideas. Because

Liberalism and Empire does not locate the emergence of colonial liberalism within specific institutions or particular forms of life, its argument neglects the important role the anxieties and limitations of colonial practice had on liberal thought. Mehta suggests that British thought about ruling the empire had 'the quality of confidence, inner certainty, and the perspective from which unhindered judgements can be issued'.[21] Paying more attention to the practical situation of colonial liberals allows one to see how their thought was rooted in an intellectual context that was much less sure of itself than Mehta and others suggest.

So, officials in the subcontinent did not think that British rule in their Indian territories was safe even after the defeat of the Maratha polity in 1818; attention to the persistent and often rather anxious emphasis British officials placed on the need to expand the range of force at the Company's disposal until deep into the 1830s makes that much clear.[22] James Mill's *History of British India*, perhaps the founding text of imperial liberalism, was written in the anxious years of the Napoleonic Wars, when many in Europe and India feared the demise of the British state. As Chapter 6 argues, Mill's brand of colonial utilitarianism was as much a response to the anxious experience of colonial administration in these years as it was the product of confident metropolitan theory. The two 'reforming' Governor-Generals of the period, Cornwallis (1786–1793) and Bentinck (1828–1834), were sent to India to cut costs and curtail expensive wars. Land revenue in Bengal began to stabilise only in the 1810s; the Company's expenditure continued to exceed its income into the 1830s. If this was the 'Age of Uncertainty' in domestic British politics, as David Eastwood suggests, it was doubly so in the world of colonial governance.[23] Colonial utilitarianism and with it what Andrew Sartori calls the language of 'liberal abstraction' were formulated in India to overcome or circumvent the complex resistance of an intractable real world that from a British point of view often seemed impossible to understand or rule.[24]

Throughout the late-eighteenth and early-nineteenth centuries new forms of governance occurred both as India's colonial governors struggled to produce money and meaning from worlds of economic and social interaction they found unfamiliar, and as colonial subjects tried to make sense of being dominated by strangers. In the process, each created ideas that were very different from those that dominated political life in Britain or pre-colonial Bengal. The practice of British colonial existence in the subcontinent produced a sense of anxiety about these differences and about Britons' inability to be 'at home' in India, as Ranajit Guha puts it. These anxieties dramatically shaped the character of colonial rule.[25] Throughout the period examined in this book, the colonial state remained an unstable, restless entity, never quite certain what it was doing, how it should act or whom it was acting for. But such ambivalence should not be written off as a sign of colonial weakness, though;

it had very significant, often transformatory effects. As the work of Homi K. Bhabha emphasises, ambivalence was an unconscious source of colonial power.[26]

III

The rest of this introductory chapter develops some of the methodological and theoretical concerns that underpin the argument, looking first at the relationship between practice and thought, secondly at the strangely neglected role of time and temporality in studies of the colonial state. Readers concerned more with the historical argument than theory might want to skip to the next chapter; the methodological suggestions made in this section are implicit throughout the rest of the book. Together with the empirical material in the chapters which follow, they provide a framework for situating concepts and categories in the context of the constantly moving flow of colonial action, reading the published voice of the colonial state alongside and against the record of interactions and transactions from which that voice emanated.

Such an approach relies on an understanding of political thought that does not begin with abstract forms of thought itself. Thought is always rooted in particular material and institutional situations. Writing and speech are produced in contexts structured by interactive forms of experience that cannot be expressed in purely abstract conceptual terms; there is no such thing as pure discourse, nor can the historical meaning of concepts be properly understood if placed in the context of nothing but other concepts. The varieties of political thought occur within worlds of action and interaction that their authors cannot fully control nor, more importantly, comprehend, so meaning can never be reduced to intention alone.[27] It is impossible to separate the structure of thought from the active contexts that produced it. 'Theory does not express, translate or serve to apply practice, it is practice', as Michel Foucault suggested. Or as Martin Heidegger put it, 'thinking acts insofar as it thinks'.[28]

The linguistic or discursive turn which colonial and South Asian history, along with other disciplines, has taken since the early 1980s has partly been associated with the influence of continental European philosophy, in particular perhaps the work of Michel Foucault. Yet this same intellectual heritage contains resources to critique an over-emphasis on the role of language or discourse. The 'discursive formations' that Foucault discussed were not unified by unitary concepts or stereotypes, nor concerned with a single object; they represented intellectual techniques embedded in specific institutions that oriented subjects to the world in very practical ways.[29] But there are limits to the Foucauldian approach. Even if it shows how discourse is an effect of both intellectual and institutional power, Foucault's genealogical method presents thought as something that is never baffled by its inability to construct stable forms of meaning; systems of thought succeed one another without any crisis in between. Foucault's work does not offer a conceptual guide for explaining how concepts and categories emerge from the anxiety and uncertainty of experience as much as the successful exercise of the will to power. For a more practically-oriented approach to political thought, Foucault's work needs to be supplemented with reference to the philosopher who influenced Foucault's generation of theorists the most, Martin Heidegger.

For Heidegger, understanding comes first of all from the non-speculative practical relationship people have with the world as they go about their everyday lives, the way they engage in particular projects and try to achieve particular purposes. Heidegger uses the German word *verstehen* ('understanding') in a way that does not only imply abstract cognition, but includes the forms of unreflective practice often described with terms such as 'know-how' or 'skill', as well as the way sensations are responded to instinctively.[30] From Heidegger's point of view, the things and people subjects come across in the world are not initially encountered as objective entities present for detached, speculative observation, nor are they part of a mental discourse. So, the notebook which Ghulam Hussein Khan's British official picked up would not primarily be perceived *as* a 'notebook' with the attributes of notebook-ness about it; nor was the abstract representation of the Indian landholder whose words the official transcribed in the book present in the mind of the official beforehand either. Instead, the official just picked up the notebook in order to write down what his interlocutor said, in order to work out how much revenue a landholder needed to pay. Before being an object of thought they each were objects of use. Objects or concepts such as these are what Heidegger calls ready-to-hand in a world of purposive action that precedes reflection, a world that subjects practically 'grasp in advance' before they reflect cognitively upon it.

For Heidegger, '[t]he ready-to-hand is always understood in terms of a totality of *involvements*', which always already exists before an individual action.[31] The existence of the notebook, for example, in a revenue office makes no sense without the act of writing about Indian revenue-payers it was printed for, which in turn relies on the complex purposes underpinning the British presence in the subcontinent, most of which are not represented in any place in abstract terms. Of course, Heidegger notes that people do have concrete thoughts, and can speculate abstractly about things 'as they are' rather than merely as they are used. But this more abstract way of thinking is always derived from an unreflective understanding of the network of possibilities and encounters in which objects and concepts are first practically encountered. From this point of view, to write a history of colonial discourse one cannot merely consider the ways in which people have 'represented' India in an abstractly conceptual form, nor think about the 'ideologies' which were supposed to have guided them. More importantly, one must examine the practical, often unspoken purposes that made particular written texts and descriptions about India meaningful (and here to be meaningful is to be useful) or meaningless at different points in time. Those purposes were often not present as a conscious intention in the mind of the actor before they performed an action.

The aims and purposes that officials were involved with in early colonial Bengal were many. They included the Company servant's desire to make enough money to return home wealthy, the demand for a stable source of revenue for the East India Company, to limit risky encounters with local inhabitants or reduce the amount of paperwork which had to be faced, all of which encompassed a certain set of conceptual and practical conditions, and involved the deployment of forms of knowledge to be achieved. On occasion the following chapters use terms such as 'colonialism' or 'the process of colonial rule' to describe the complex collection of interactions and purposes that clustered around the process of British governance in Bengal. Nonetheless such a heterogenous collection of purposes were not driven by a single dynamic; nor were they undergirded by a single ideology, although they did produce a particular style of thought. Not only did different purposes drive different elements within the colonial 'state' at any one moment, the characteristics of colonial governance changed significantly, as the meaning of terms such as 'Company servant', 'landholder' and even 'government' were transformed between the years that circumscribe the period covered in this book.

The multivarious purposes that British officials attempted to fulfil in Bengal allowed them to interact with the similarly diverse purposes behind the actions of their Indian subjects in complex ways. Sometimes, where the purposes of each coincided, mutually meaningful dialogue occurred. More usually the colonial encounter was governed by the estranged and aloof approach noted by Ghulam Hussein Khan. Sometimes interaction occurred in acts of violence. Where an aloof and distinctively colonial relationship emerged between Europeans and Indians this was often simply because British officials and their South Asian interlocutors were trying to do two incompatible things: a landholder's desire to maximise his or her income or achieve greater autonomy clashed with the Company's demand for more resources; a political leader's attempt to retain the affection of his or her tenants working against the British attempt to adjudicate a property dispute, for example. This was not an encounter between interlocutors or antagonists who fully knew their own minds, who were able to satisfactorily realise their conscious or unconscious strategies at any one point in time. Instead of seeing the interaction between Britons and their South Asian subjects as a clash between predetermined subjectivities guided by abstract predetermined cultural representations or intentions (as a clash between the colonial state or Europe's 'modern regime of power' and Indian 'society' or 'culture', for example), the following chapters narrate the contingent fashion in which these aims interacted with one another to produce unexpected effects.

The most important, unifying phenomenon that any historical account of these complex interactions has to explain is the emergence of the colonial regime's peculiarly abstract, objectivising style of thought. Why, despite the chaos and complexity of colonial and Indian forms of life, were British officials ruled by the instinct to classify and generalise on such a large scale? Why was their response to uncertainty and ambivalence to produce general textual rules? Why did Indian elites follow suit, and define their own subjectivity with general social categories too?

The emergence of this peculiarly objectivising style of thought is a theme that will be addressed in detail in the chapters that follow through an empirical study of the archive of everyday, often local colonial administration and encounter. But the way Heidegger discussed human action helps frame this discussion. Heidegger noted that things are perceived as objective entities when they lose their place in the practical projects that people are trying to fulfil, as when a tool breaks, or perhaps a particular colonial category does not work in the course of revenue collection, for example. What the Oxford philosopher John Austin would have called an infelicitous performance forces the observer to ask what went wrong, and adopt a more detached approach and objective attitude to the situation. Only at the point when something loses its place in the network of active relationships, with 'the discontinuance of a specific manipulation in our concernful dealings', does it become an object of theoretical knowledge.[32] It is only when it is no longer of direct use that something is seen as an object with abstract properties, which obeys general rules for example. In colonial Bengal, abstraction and objectification did not occur as the result of the colonial regime's successful exercise of the will to power or knowledge; they were processes emerging from practical semantic crisis, in which concepts and practices could no longer be taken for granted as working in an unreflexive fashion.

In this process though, the object was not simply removed from its previous practical context. Examined in a more abstract fashion it was quickly placed in a different, more 'scientific' practical environment governed by the unreflexive manipulation of 'ready-to-hand' objects nonetheless. Theory, in other words, depends on a non-theoretical element or practical world: on non-theoretical practice. 'Even in the "most abstract" way of working out problems and establishing what has been obtained, one manipulates equipment for writing, for example.'[33] In colonial Bengal, an abstract frame of thought produced not only a peculiar colonial discourse but its own practical institutions too.

Humans have always objectivised in this way. Writing in the second and third quarters of the twentieth century, Heidegger nonetheless noted that estranged ways of thinking which treated objects and people outside familiar, practical contexts had only been institutionalised within bureaucracy, academia or the market in recent times. Heidegger criticised his own age for its tendency to understand the world as a picture, comprehending human existence through 'the representedness of beings', as if the world were a static object of scrutiny existing outside the observer, rather than a practical network of active involvements and encounters.[34] There is something uncannily Heideggerian about Ghulam Hussein Khan's suggestion that Company officials perceived Indians 'like pictures on a wall'. Perhaps this should not surprise us. In different ways, both Heidegger and Ghulam Hussein were heirs of an Aristotelian tradition that saw thought as the result of purposive practical action, not static, disembodied abstract reason.[35]

Ghulam Hussein's account of Britons' treating Indians 'like pictures on a wall' can be read as a description of the way British unfamiliarity and semantic uncertainty was followed by colonial disengagement and the production of far more abstract categories of thought. Later chapters of this book show how the kind of aloof relationship with Indian practice which Ghulam Hussein described produced the objectified categories of the colonial state, the Indian landholder and even Indian society in the early nineteenth century. But the British objectification of India was always shaped by an engagement with an Indian world that was itself continually changing and responding. Colonial governance was a process in which the colonial gaze was continually shifting focus in order to follow the fluid patterns of Indian social practice. Social objects moved rapidly between different frames of reference, as interpretative contexts were created to make sense of phenomenon that began to appear unfamiliar, were briefly understood with the construction of short-lived systems of colonial knowledge, only to move out of focus again of their own volition in their confrontation with colonial institutions. The result of this process was the transformation of the logic of British rule in India in a relatively short space of time; particular arguments went in and out of fashion very quickly. What remained consistent, however, was the state of restless unease in which colonial thought occurred.

IV

This book argues that time needs to play a more important role in the study of colonialism, for two reasons. Most obviously, historical time offers an analytical axis on which the specific character of colonial events needs to be plotted. The actions which made up colonial political culture occurred as a response to actions which occurred at specific past historical conjunctures. The new colonial political landscape which emerged by the mid-nineteenth century can be properly understood only if it is seen as the result of a dialectical process of change over time; as the consequence of a complex process of encounter and response, in which the thought and action of one subject emerges in retort to the subjectivity and actions of others at a previous particular moments.[36] For example, the colonial state that came into existence by the 1830s emerged as a response to the colonial regime which existed in the 1790s; Indian arguments about the self-sufficient nature of Indian society developed as efforts to negate prior colonial conceptions of the centrality of British courts to stable Indian law.

But time is also phenomenologically important to the way political actors experience their lives. How a subject understands the way past, present and future relate to one another is an essential element of their political practice. Whilst the objective structures of colonial governance and Indian social practice changed, the subjective temporal structures within which political life was lived dramatically altered under colonial rule too.

A new concept of the identity and purposes of the state emerged in colonial Bengal in the years under discussion. This novel conception involved a new subjective understanding of the relationship between politics and time. The state is a difficult thing to think about. Scholars often try to define it at the outset, treating it as the supreme agent of authoritative power, as 'an entity, function or relation' with the theoretical potential (if not always the actual capacity) to effect dramatic change.[37] In so far as this book is concerned to trace the genealogy of an idea of the state as an entity with capacity to cause transformative effects in this way, beginning with a definition such as this will not do. Criticising the use of such definitions before engaging in historical analysis of really existing states, a number of scholars have begun to examine the way the state is represented in everyday life in the last few years; Akhil Gupta's work is an important reference here. 'Foregrounding the question of representation', Gupta uses evidence from present-day north India to suggest that in fact the state is 'conceptualised in terms far more decentralized and disaggregated' than is often thought.[38]

Gupta's analysis of the complex ways in which concepts of the state resonate in the lives of ethnographic subjects or historical actors rightly abandons any abstract definition of 'the state' at the outset. It allows one to engage in the kind of analysis undertaken in this book, and plot changes in everyday understandings of statehood over time. But what is missing from Gupta's approach is any sense of the relationship between how people understand the state in relation to their own internal consciousness of time. Gupta notes that the late-twentieth-century north Indians whose attitudes he discusses in his research believed the state was undisciplined, disordered and vulnerable to corruption: from this perspective it appears a more coherent entity than social scientists previously thought. Yet Gupta's account makes clear that their sense of chaos in the present was articulated as part of a rhetoric which insisted that the state needed to act in a coherent and systematic way in the future. A sense of the lamentable state of things in the present was contrasted with a view of what the state *should* have been in the past, or *might* be in the future. A normative idea of the state as an entity able to effectively enforce a single bureaucratic will upon society as a whole was projected onto other (past or future) moments of time, and contrasted with the degenerate present. This notion relied on an understanding of political time that presumed that the future would be (or at least should be) dramatically different from the present. It is precisely such a modern conception of state-time that later chapters of this book trace in early colonial Bengal.

The argument here is indebted to Talal Asad's discussion of modern politics in general. Asad notes that many scholars argue 'modernity' should not be used as a noun to describe a set of objects that actually exist, because 'contemporary societies [just like modern states] are heterogenous and overlapping' rather than being structured according to a single, consistent logic. But Asad suggests such critical scholars ignore the fact that '[a]ssumptions about the integrated character of "modernity" are themselves part of practical and political reality'. Most importantly, they forget that the idea that modernity is a coherent condition that can be achieved (even if it cannot in reality) 'direct[s] the way in which people committed to it act in particular situations'. 'Modernity', just like the modern state, is not a 'totally coherent object' or condition which exists in the present. It is a state of affairs which people try to bring into existence in the future, 'a *project* – or rather, a series of interlinked projects – that people in power seek to achieve'.[39] This book nuances Asad's argument by suggesting that the 'project' of modern statehood emerged from political and semantic crises occurring in colonial South Asia: it was not an export of European society. In other words, the project of colonial state-formation was structured by prior British perceptions of the failure of governance in India. But like Asad, this book suggests the modern colonial state was not something that was merely described or 'represented' in a static fashion by contemporaries. When it was written about, it was situated in a story about a future-oriented project of state-formation, in which human action relied on a complicated sense of the relationship between past, present and future.

In Bengal during the first third of the nineteenth century, British officials criticised India's present-day state by comparing it with a future in which every action would occur according to general written rules. As time passed, that future never came into existence. For colonial officials, the state was subject to continual reform. Changes happened, but the ordered society which state action was expected to produce never quite came into being. The edgy, restless and forever unsatisfied character of governance was one of the most important attributes of the modernity of the colonial regime; this characteristic continued to mark the subcontinent's post-colonial regimes as well. However different they might have been in other ways, their aloof disconnection from the political relations of their own present time meant that India's modern governors from Lord Teignmouth to Jawarharlal Nehru and Sheikh Mujibur Rahman shared the same constant mood of restlessness. Each was continually critical of their own present-day, trying to either produce a better future, recreate a golden past or sometimes both; but never able to reach a satisfactory, stable state of affairs. As Zygmunt Bauman notes, modernity is 'an obsessive march forward – not because it always wants more, but because it never gets enough; not because it grows more ambitious and adventurous, but because its adventures are bitter and its ambitions frustrated'.[40] In British-ruled Bengal, the fractious vicissitudes of the colonial encounter created a restless, future-oriented, but continually frustrated way of dealing with time.

V

The chapters of this book tell a story about change in colonial India in which the British engagement with Indian social and political practice plays the most important part. Consequently, Chapter 2 offers a comparison of the practice of politics in pre-colonial India and Britain in order to suggest that each belonged to a simultaneous and comparable eighteenth-century world, and dispel the idea that 'Britain' or 'Bengal' were irreconcilably different at that point in time. Recognising Eurasian comparisons and similarities makes it impossible to see the intrusion of Europe into Asia as the cause of colonial change; it focuses the attention of scholars wishing to explain the transformation of Indian politics under colonial rule on the specificities of this particular colonial encounter. Chapter 3 examines these processes by tracing the emergence of an increasingly estranged, distant orientation to Indian social practice from the 1780s. The imperial crises of that decade did not merely threaten political and economic institutions. The chapter argues that Britons in India also experienced a crisis of meaning, in which their very ability to make sense of themselves in the subcontinent seemed in doubt. It suggests that Lord Cornwallis' 'permanent settlement' and new constitution of 1793, often treated as the birth of the modern state in Bengal, emerged as a response to this crisis.

Chapters 4 and 5 explain the practical roots of the varieties of legal positivism that developed from different local situations in Bengal. They show how the crisis of colonial experience affected governance in the practical locations of the district courthouse or revenue office, going on to explain how they led to the emergence of a British belief in the need to govern with abstract general categories and to codify law. After the permanent settlement, British officers failed in their efforts to comprehend the plurality of Indian social forms from the aloof perspective of the colonial regime's stranger-state. These chapters explain how two categories emerged from this process of objectification; the 'Hindu family' and the 'Bengali landholder' were constructed as a consequence of that failure. Chapter 6 moves back to the colonial metropolis, looking at the vocabulary of governance and statehood in Calcutta during the first third of the nineteenth century. The chapter shows how new ideas about the machine-like conduct of the state originated in early-nineteenth-century Bengal. These ideas emerged as part of an attempt to overcome the chaos and uncertainties of everyday colonial rule described in previous chapters. Specifically, the chapter rethinks the relationship between the *English Utilitarians and India* with the suggestion that colonial reforms of the 1830s were efforts to find semantic coherence in what, for British officials, seemed an uncertain colonial world, wracked by the difficulty of making sense as much as collecting revenue. The mechanistic vocabulary of utilitarian political thought offered officials a way of producing stable categories of governance by using the powers of the state to create new forms of knowledge and new forms of law.

Chapter 7 examines the Indian use and critique of the colonial regime's new rules. It looks at the way men such as Rammohan Roy, a man whom C.A. Bayly calls 'the first Indian liberal', challenged the state's emphasis on the need for a dramatic reconstruction of Indian thought and law. In doing so, the chapter suggests that they constructed a conception of Indian 'society' governed by a temporal dynamic different from that which ruled colonial concepts, but which nonetheless viewed Indian practice from the aloof sociological perspective of the stranger nonetheless. Like its cognates in colonial discourse, these Indian arguments rested upon a critique of the disordered present-day, and the projection of order and coherence onto another time, for example, the distant past rather than the long-awaited future in the case of Rammohan and Bhabanicharan. But as the book's concluding remarks show, whether they were based on the projection of a better society onto the past or future, British and Indian forms of colonial discourse were able to create stable forms of meaning only by producing utopian accounts of South Asian life.

This book is concerned to explain historical change. As such, it relies on a narrative about the consequences of human actions. But it does so by trying to avoid reducing the story of early colonial politics to a narrative about the effects of a single subject, whether a particular group of individuals or an unconscious force like capitalism, the colonial state, the 'modern regime of power' or indigenous Indian society. There is nothing in the logic of historical narrative that forces it to be the story of the actions of a single subject, indeed quite the reverse: where scholars attribute social or political change to over-simplified abstract forces, the necessarily complex character of narrative writing is denied. Narrative forms of history-writing do not need to celebrate the supposed self-present rationality of a subject of history such as the 'Indian nation' or 'the colonial state'. Historical narratives can tell stories that are tragic as well as successful, illustrating the wide gap that often exists between consciousness and action, and the inability of agents to control events, in particular how historical actors usually fail when they attempt to insist that social change is the effect of a single subject.

Even so, historical narratives are constructions in which a later writer offers their attempt to understand events in ways contemporaries did not necessarily comprehend them. One purpose of this book is to impose order and meaning on events that seemed random and chaotic to the actors who experienced them. 'Stories are not lived but told', as Louis O. Mink put it.[41] Like all forms of narrative this book assumes the past can be understood as a linear sequence of events, when this may not be how things were perceived at the time. Historical narrative is a necessarily teleological form of writing, in that the reader is 'pulled forward' with a sense of what Paul Ricoeur calls 'direct-edness'; in this book, the direction is provided by the colonial search for meaning in an uncertain world, and the process which led to the emergence of a particular conception of the colonial state and Indian society.[42] If it does not necessarily imply that historical transformation is the work of a single subject, using narrative to explain change over time has the danger of reify-ing the 'before' and 'after', presuming that a stable state of affairs has been reached by the terminal date of the story. This book might legitimately be criticised for presenting an overly stark opposition between the early mod-ern political culture discussed at the beginning and the modern forms of political argument and practice outlined at the end: for the way it presumes the complete transition from one to the other occurring in the period under discussion. Perhaps these might be seen as the fictional elements necessary for the successful exercise of the historian's craft. But rather than abandon-ing such a useful tool of historical explanation, its author believes it is better to accept the limitations of one's craft, and see history as a form of analysis that needs to exist alongside other forms of social and political analysis and action.

2
Comparing Eighteenth-Century Polities

In a lecture delivered in 1917, the Bengali historian and sociologist Benoy Kumar Sarkar argued that modernity was a late arrival to Europe. Sarkar described his own present-day as 'an age of Pullman cars, electric lifts, long distance telephones, zeppelins and "the new woman"'.[1] When they compared Asia and Europe, he noted, 'Eur-American scholars seem to assume that these have been the inseparable features of the Western world all through the ages', even though 'some of these were not known to their grandfathers, and others even to their fathers'. Modern political ideals such as democracy and the modern state, just like telephones and lifts, were almost as recent newcomers to Europe as they were to Asia.[2]

Sarkar's point was that exaggerated claims about the difference between East and West were maintained because Westerners attributed a spurious continuity to the patterns of European thought. In fact though, '[t]he people of Asia from Chandragupta to Kanghi would not have found any fundamental difference in Europe from Pericles to Frederick the Great'. Modern politics, like modern technology, transformed Europe and Asia at roughly the same moment, only a short period of time ago.

Despite almost a century of scholarship since Sarkar's attempt to place modern Asia on the same conceptual map as Europe, the history of both western and non-European worlds still relies on extravagant claims made on behalf of the continuities of European political thought. Even the most contextual historians of political ideas argue that it is useful discussing the extent to which 'our' modern ideas of the state or political society had their foundations in the political thought of Renaissance Italy or seventeenth-century England or France.[3] Applied to studies of the relationship between Europe and the rest of the world these perspectives presuppose that, until colonialism brought the two societies into contact, India and Britain had irreconcilably different political traditions.[4] From this point of view, the absolute authority of the modern state and the creation of a separate sphere of civil society based on private property were aspects of European political thought that did not occur in pre-colonial India, but were introduced in the cataclysmic process of colonial transformation. Although scholars have recently begun to compare the political economy of different parts of Eurasia, when it comes to political practice and political thought, pre-colonial Europe and South Asia are still seen as being very far apart. Space seems to be a far more important rupturing force than time.[5]

This chapter examines similarities between the politics of Britain and Bengal in the second half of the eighteenth century to show that these perspectives are misleading. The focus is on the way political actors in each place understood their conduct in the eighteenth century. Although eighteenth-century Britons and Indians spoke different languages, the chapter shows that they did not understand politics using incommensurably different concepts and categories. Each inhabited hierarchial yet intensely participatory political societies. In both places, politics occurred in an historicist mood, in which a continually-present past provided the legitimacy for political action. But politics relied on political actors' skilful negotiation within dynamic and contestatory public cultures in which authority was continually displayed and subject to challenge. In both societies, political practice was, therefore, a tumultuous exercise. Until the second or third decades of the nineteenth century, many suggested the British were an 'ungovernable people'.[6] British observers and Indian elites described Bengal's highly mobile and highly articulate eighteenth-century population in a similar way: words such as 'vexatious', 'contumate' and 'rebellious' pepper British discussion, many of them reflecting the English translation of Persian terms. In fact, these terms could be used both to describe characteristics of the subjects of British rule and irksome European Company officers.[7] Such descriptions were possible because abstract rights, written laws or bureaucratic regularities mattered less than practical skill in managing historically continuous political and social relationships that, nonetheless, occurred in a number of different public spheres. In Britain and Bengal, politics was rooted in the need to manage subjects who had complex actions and intentions of their own. Each could, and occasionally did, see the other as belonging to a familiar political world.[8]

Colonial rule did not constitute a clash of cultures; this chapter shows instead that the political worlds of eighteenth-century Britain and Bengal were less different from one another than each was from the idioms of governance that emerged in colonial Bengal by the middle of the nineteenth century. Such an argument allows one to begin asking why, despite possible points of connection, Britain's colonial officials saw themselves as strangers to India, and why they began to believe that their purpose was to act upon a society which they believed was dramatically different from their own.

I

The story of Maharaja Harishchandra circulated widely in early modern Bengal. The tale concerned a king who lived in the north Indian city of Ayodya. Harishchandra was asked by the Brahmin ascetic Visvamitra to renounce his worldly power and goods, which he did. Harishchandra was given a series of humiliating tests in order to prove his worth; he was asked to murder his son and sell his wife, for example. Having proved his virtue, the king ascended to heaven. The story occurs in the *Mahabharata* and has been retold in a range of Indian languages until the present day, often in order to teach 'noble lessons in morality'. A highly moralised version of the story provided the subject of the first Indian feature film in 1917. M.K. Gandhi suggested that Harishchandra was a model for his own life from a very early age, his simple living and renunciation providing an important example.[9]

But in the story as it was told in Bengal in the eighteenth and early nineteenth centuries, Harishchandra's public political skill mattered more than his private morality. The text emphasised the king's practical duty towards his subjects; renunciation was not the most important part of the story as it was told before the late eighteenth century. Those duties forced Harishchandra to act in a benevolent yet conspicuously powerful way.[10] At the close of the narrative, the king refused to go to heaven unless his subjects came with him too. 'A king is a king because of his subjects (*praja*) as well as because of sacrifice and birth and deeds. Whatever worthy deeds I have performed I have performed because of them', not from a sense of duty inspired by a belief in the need to follow divinely inspired rules.[11] This notion of earthly, reciprocal duty was present throughout different strands of early modern Indian thought. As Muzaffar Alam points out, early modern Muslim political theorists often argued that 'the world is better served by justice without Faith/than by the tyranny of a Faithful king'; worldly justice, and the approbation of subjects were the standards by which a king should be assessed.[12] In the same way, the early modern tellers of the Hindu parable of Harishchandra argued that duty to subjects could be more important than divine obligation.

A generation ago, scholars traced an Indian concern with the 'duties' or *dharma* of the monarch to a pre-colonial Indian belief in a static, theological cosmic order that defined roles rigidly, and left no room for the individual activity of the ruler or subject. As V.S. Naipul once put it, India was 'a world in which men were born only to obey rules'.[13] Harishchandra's story offers an opening into a situation that was more turbulent. Bengal's pre-colonial rulers believed that their duties involved negotiation with subjects who had complex wills and intentions of their own. They emphasised hierarchy, in so far as the king ruled and others followed. But that conception incorporated the active, sometimes rebellious role of subjects, of *praja* or *raiyat*, who had a clear and active sense of participation in the political world they inhabited.

Harishchandra defined the duties of the ruler (*rajadharma*) as threefold: 'the role of a righteous king, a king who knows his proper path is giving gifts, protection of his subjects, and making war'. This triple definition of the duties of kingship was an early modern cliché, repeated many times by both Hindus and Muslims in India's literature on the proper conduct of rulers. It overlapped partially with the fourfold Sanskrit formula for over-coming an enemy: *sama* (persuasion), *dana* (gift-giving), *bheda* (sowing dissent) and *danda* (force). These were present in ancient texts such as the *Manu-smriti*, but were also widespread in eighteenth-century political literature.[14] Harishchandra's threefold scheme consisted of a number of moral acts ordained to ensure the continued existence of a harmonious, balanced polity. Like the far more instrumental Sanskrit scheme they were also tactical moves which the ruler made to advance his own self-interest and continue in power. Each was designed to ensure the deference of subjects who had choices. If the king could not persuade them of the virtue of his acts, they would rebel or move and defer elsewhere, and be the agents of 'fate' in making the king's *rajya* (state) collapse. Because his subjects had minds and intentions of their own, Harishchandra needed to constantly act, to persuade and supervise, entice and chastise to ensure that present-day polity survived.

II

Eighteenth-century Bengal had no kings as powerful or virtuous as the mythical Harishchandra. Its subjects inhabited a complex, hierarchical network of connections based on the continual action of both rulers and ruled. The need for rulers to cultivate the affection of their subjects leads the historian Rajat Ray to suggest that eighteenth-century Indians were united by what he calls 'communities of sentiment'.[15] Ray's phrase captures an important aspect of early modern Indian political discourse. Persuasion and affect played a significant role in the canons of early modern Indian political thought, in both Persian-language political ethics and the vocabulary of Sanskrit jurisprudence and statecraft, for example. Sentiment and 'intuition' were significant in the *akhlaq* literature that Muzaffar Alam discusses in his recent study of early modern Muslim political thought in India.[16] The vocabulary of affect was central to the work of the seventeenth-century Iranian philosopher Sadr al-Din al-Shirazi (more commonly known as Mulla Sadra), an influential figure in eighteenth-century India who certainly influenced Ghulam Hussein Khan.[17] The *Akhlaq-i-Jalali*, a work written by an earlier scholar, Jalal al-din al-Dawani, was read widely in eighteenth-century India, and also emphasised the importance of sentiment in maintaining political connections. Al-Dawani argued that 'the perfection of men' depended on 'association and concord, which can only be realized by affection and unanimity'.[18] Within the very different Sankritic intellectual tradition, compassion and the ability to experience the world in a sympathetic mood were important in juristic and aesthetic thought, and significant in descriptions of the personality of great rulers.[19] As C.A. Bayly argues, throughout India sentiment was taken seriously in the practice of everyday politics as Mughal emperors and Hindu and Muslim little kings stationed new-gatherers and opinion collectors throughout the towns and markets of their realm to ensure a ruler's authority rested upon the 'moral suasion' of the population.[20]

The *akhlaq* literature mentioned above was concerned mostly with the relationship between the Mughal regime and its subjects. But most of Bengal's population had a more significant relationship with smaller units of authority, units that can be described either as landed estates (*zamindaris*) or little kingdoms (*rajyas*). These domains were ruled by men and women described as landholders (*zamindars*) or kings and queens (*raja* or *rani*), although other terms were used as well. Bengal's little kingdoms ranged in size from the massive Burdwan *raj*, which paid between Rs 15 and 20 crores (Rs 1.5–2 million or £75–100,000) in revenue to the *diwan* (Mughal provincial ruler) in the 1760s, to smallholdings that contributed less than a Rupee. Above this patchwork of petty principalities lay the theoretical authority of Mughal and (from the 1760s) East India Company sovereignty, entities whose own ruling ideologies were aimed at reducing the power of local principalities, but which were rarely able to govern without relying on local authorities in some form. Larger *zamindars* and tax farmers used a range of tactics to bargain with provincial rulers. By the middle of century they or revenue-farmers (*ijaradars*) signed leases for between one and three years at widely varying rates of revenue which allowed them to retain the option of reducing their payments in future years, and thus a large degree of independence. Until the 1790s, 60% of Bengal's revenue was paid by its 15 largest semi-independent estates.[21]

The first kind of action that Harishchandra described, gift-giving, was crucial to the preservation of the local polity, and the exercise and maintenance of this local authority. First of all, *zamindars* and regional rulers sought deference from their subjects and enshrined their local authority by recycling the revenue they received, and giving to local institutions and residents as well as conspicuously providing food for the poor and for the general population on particular occasions.[22] Those who subjected themselves assumed they would get something in return: the lord needed to give back. Just as English country gentlemen or city magnates portrayed themselves as the beneficent patrons of local religious and educational institutions to maintain their authority, Bengali landholders conspicuously endowed places of worship, shrines dedicated to local *pirs* or Muslim holy men and educational establishments, as well as making endowments for pilgrimages to Mecca, Kashi (Benares) and to support the poor; the *Nizamat* at Murshidabad, the sovereign with ultimate authority in post-Mughal Bengal, did the same.[23] Patronage was the main way in which literature and learning were supported. Just as in pre-romantic England, public intellectuals were conscious of their dependence on complex networks of friends and patrons for their work to be produced.[24] The poet Bharatchandra (1712–1760) and 'reformer' Rammohan Roy (1772–1833) came under the patronage of the *raja* of Burdwan at one time or another, although Bharatchandra had to leave over disagreements about property with his master. In some ways, it was Rammohan's later independence from patronage that marked the distinctiveness of his role in Bengali public opinion; these aspects of his career will be discussed in Chapter 6. The career of Jagannatha Tarkapancanana, a jurist, discussed in more detail in Chapter 4, and the later career of Bharatchandra were supported by the nearby Raja Krishna Chandra of Nadia.[25]

Overall, gift-giving probably accounted for between 5 and 15% of the income of each landed estate. More than a tenth of the total cultivated area of one of the few villages whose accounts historians have was allocated to support local institutions such as mosques, temples and pilgrimages in the 1780s; a quarter of the land of Rangpur district as a whole was demarcated to pay for local religious and civic institutions in addition to remunerating village officers. Similar figures were reflected elsewhere.[26]

The persuasive act of gift-giving occurred most frequently when there was the greatest unrest. It seems that mosques and Hindu temples were more likely to be built in times of rural turmoil, when rulers needed to work hardest to maintain local allegiances; perhaps the uncertain economic and political conditions of the last quarter of the eighteenth century and early years of the nineteenth explains the spate of new buildings constructed in those years.[27] Most of the Hindu temples built during this period were dedicated to *sakti* or *saivite* deities, reflecting a concern by rulers to articulate a sense of power and local dominance, rather than the meeker virtues associated with *vaisnava* worship.[28]

Despite the existence of similar forms of patronage in Britain, British officials in Bengal found Indian 'charity' difficult to understand.[29] Official difficulty in understanding practices that would have been perfectly comprehensible in England, together with a clear Bengali sense of the instrumental purposes behind their largesse, is illustrated by an exchange that occurred in Rangpur district. A British Collector examined the accounts of the estate of Idrakpur in 1793, and suggested that the amount spent on feeding the poor and supporting Hindu and Muslim religious institutions was extravagant. The landholder, Gokul Nath Ray, objected strenuously to this attempt to curtail his spending. As the Collector put it,

> on being questioned concerning this article, he [Gokhal Nath] replied that the Ryots said they should have no confidence that he would treat them well if he refused it

and as a result would all run away. In Gokhal Nath's description giving was an instrumental act intended to support the *zamindar*'s own authority, and the Company's revenue would suffer if it were taken away. Raja Tejchandra of Burdwan made a similar point when British officers questioned his endowment of land rent free to Brahmins and other local elites. The *raja* argued that if *zamindars* 'could prevail on men of Rank to stay in the District it would greatly help cultivation'.[30]

The second action described by Harishchandra, 'protection', was another tactic used by Bengal's little kings and queens to produce the deference of their subjects. The need for landholders to protect their tenants and subjects from the vicissitudes of fortune, especially fluctuations in climatic or economic conditions, was central to eighteenth-century political rhetoric and practice. Cultivators insisted on reductions in the rent paid throughout the year, and on donations of cash and seed-grain, both of which were paid back in some measure at the end of the year. In Rangpur in 1783, landholders were forced to offer discounts to their tenants amounting to 18% of the total revenue due to be paid to the Company in 1781–1782, and 29% at the beginning of the following year.[31] As one little queen, Rani Bhawani, wrote when faced with drought in 1775, 'I am a zamindar, so was obliged to keep the ryots from ruin and gave them what ease I could by giving them time to make up their payments.'[32] Protection was offered through loans and reductions in rent that allowed peasants to survive uncertain conditions. But it also involved Harishchandra's third kingly action, the waging of war and use of force more generally. Landholders used coercion to protect their own subjects from the depredation of others, whether marauders attached to neighbouring states such as Assam, Bhutan or Arakhan, or rival landholders.

In many parts of Bengal, the ruler's ability to offer protection and gain the trust or confidence of his or her tenants was often expressed with the word *zimma*. *Zimma* was a term deriving from the Persian word *zamn*, signifying suretyship or sponsorship.[33] Protection, however, was always a two-way process. Peasants who wanted to escape from the rule of one *zamindar* sought the *zimma* of another. In many parts of late eighteenth-century Eastern Bengal, *zimmadars* (holders of trust or responsibility) were individuals who had built up a financial interest by acting as the agent for cultivators and smaller, less well-represented landholders in their negotiation with superior *zamindars* and the government.[34] Elsewhere, especially in the south-eastern district of Bakarganj, *zimmadari* estates were built when peasants transferred their allegiance from one landholder by 'placing themselves under the *zimma* of another'. Henry Beveridge noted this when he suggested that in most parts of Bengal 'ryots run away when too much trampled on; in Bakarganj they go to a zimmadar'.[35] Not surprisingly, the situation resulted in tension and sometimes violence between landholders competing for the allegiance of tenants.[36]

The landholders' use of these various idioms to persuade the rural population to submit to their authority occurred in a context where labour was relatively scarce compared to land and peasants had choices. One of the first things the East India Company's British officials noticed on their arrival in Bengal was the amount of uncultivated land. In 1789, Lord Cornwallis complained that a third of the land of Bengal was waste, consisting of 'jungle inhabited only by wild beasts'.[37] In 1790, 10% of land in the village of Radhanagar in Rangpur district was uncultivated, a figure that does not include vast tracts of waste ground outside the village's borders.[38] Even as late as 1855, more than 10% of the cultivable land of the district was not being ploughed.[39] Throughout Bengal, uncultivated land was plentiful until the last years of the nineteenth century.[40] In this demographic environment peasants had choices, the most important being migration. When, in 1783, peasants in Rangpur felt they had been treated badly by their local rulers, they submitted a petition to the British Collector that ended in the following words: 'You are head of one country, we have a thousand countries to go to, You are Chief, we are Ryotts [subjects], you will therefore order us Justice'.[41] With this statement the *raiyats* acknowledged their deference to the British Collector's authority. But their submission was conditional on the official's ability to act justly towards them. If Richard Goodlad, the Collector, did not 'order justice' and act as a good, benevolent local ruler, the *raiyats* would move to another country where they would be treated better. Where they were not 'treated well', authority suffered and estates fell into rapid decline. In the 1780s and 1790s, Idilpur, a once prosperous little kingdom to the south of Dhaka, was wracked by internal dissension as the family members who controlled it argued vehemently amongst themselves. Unable to project an image of their authority to protect their subjects, most cultivators left to find more profitable fields elsewhere. The need for protection predominated over the attraction of this highly fertile, alluvial soil. By 1797, only one-eighth of the cultivable land in the district was still being cultivated.[42] If their fortunes worsened peasants would rather 'fly to another part of the country' than 'sell their plough and cattle to pay their rents', as the Raja of Nadia put it in 1791.[43]

Demographics intersected with political practice so that peasant mobility played a key role in determining the shape of local institutions. At the end of each year, landholders assumed that a proportion of their tenants would move elsewhere. *Zamindars* frequently complained that their peasants had all run away.[44] Landholders and their agents could not assume that their subjects would cultivate the same plot of land from one year to the next. Local politics was governed by a short-term process in which peasants bargained to find protection, and rival magnates outbid each other to attract cultivators onto their estates, and so allow their polities to survive. In 1770 the British officer J. Grose argued that it had been a 'universal and pernicious custom' for landholders 'to entice the ryots [*raiyats*] from other parts'.[45] These attempts by landholders to persuade occurred in a world in which peasants were effective at using forms of collective mobilisation to enforce their demands. Far from being a product of later forms of mass politics, the rent strike, what from the 1860s was referred to as *dharmaghat*, was a common tactic when landholders refused to agree to their terms in the eighteenth century.[46] It was usually accompanied by a mass gathering of peasants near the seat of local political and economic power, and the collective, although usually symbolic, display of force. Joseph Sherburne, the Collector of Birbhum district in western Bengal noted that it was

> an almost annual custom for the Ryots [cultivators] . . . to assemble in arms in the months of Augun and Poose [at the end of the year] and put a stop to the Collections till they have brought the farmer to terms.

In 1792, collective organisation forced the Raja of Birbhum to sack his own choice of agent and appoint the *raiyats* nominee in his place, 'much to the chagrin of the Collector'.[47] These actions were instances where peasants had a strong sense of being able to use their collective power to negotiate the terms by which they submitted to the local polity. A passage from the poet Krsnahari Das's poem about the Rangpur rebellion conveys this sense well. During the rebellion

> [t]he *diwan* [revenue officer] said, *raiyats* can do anything. They can raise someone to heaven, or throw him down to death. The *raiyat* creates the kingly authority of the lord. All the gold bangles you see are their doing.[48]

Certainly, deference and a hierarchical sense of obligation mattered in this way of viewing political relationships. The historian Gautam Bhadra suggests that '[i]n the consciousness of the peasant, the king or lord was duty-bound to look after him'.[49] But, in eighteenth-century Bengal, this sense overlapped with the subject's clear conception of the active role they had in constituting the authority they submitted themselves to, often being able to force landholders to obey their duty.

Alongside migration then, peasant rebellion was a common phenomenon in late-eighteenth-century Bengal. Uprisings of one sort or another occurred throughout much of North Bengal as well as Birbhum, Bakarganj, Chittagong, Comilla, Mymemsingh and Sylhet districts during the 1780s alone. The period saw groups of *fakhir* and *sannyasin* moving throughout the countryside between and beyond particular local regimes.[50] For the most part these instances of 'rebellion' consisted of efforts by peasants to bring their rulers 'to terms', not overturn the local social order. Large uprisings occurred when cultivators were denied the chance to negotiate, when elites tried to stop peasants from moving, for example. The famous Rangpur insurrection or *dhing* of 1783 only escalated when the peasants' attempt at negotiation was met by the East India Company's deployment of its troops. Where local notables were willing to concede to the rebels' terms and reincorporate them back into the polity, rebels returned home. This happened in some districts in Rangpur. The insurrection begun by Chakma peasants on the frontier of Company territory to the east of Chittagong came to an end when the Chakma *raja*'s claims were partially recognised, initiating a process of negotiation and resistance between the sedentary state and mobile Chakma polities which continued for the next 200 years.[51]

Raiyats articulated their active role in constituting the local social order most vocally in areas where population density was lowest and the dynamism of Bengal's riverine landscape the greatest: in districts such as Bakarganj and Dhaka to the south, and Rangpur, Dinajpur and Birbhum to the north; now all districts in Bangladesh. Throughout the late eighteenth and early nineteenth centuries these were by far the most prosperous places in Bengal.[52] Further west, in more highly populated areas such as Burdwan and Bankura, peasant action played a significant role in structuring local social relations, but allowed the emergence of more stable and less prosperous political hierarchies.

III

Ideas about peasant action were important in eighteenth-century Bengali political thought; but the region's elites perceived the political structures they inhabited in other ways as well. Bharatchandra's description of Burdwan in the *Vidya-Sundera* and Dewan Manulla Mandal's discussion of a little king from Dinajpur in his *Rajadharma* allowed little room for peasant action.[53] From these points of view, the landholder's patronage of civic and religious establishments was a way of ritually embedding authority that was not supposed to depend on their subject's consent even though, in practice, these representations were a way of producing it. To complicate matters further, local narratives which described the power of little kings and queens coexisted and conflicted with a narrative about the absolute authority of the Mughal empire, which perceived landholders, not peasants, as unstable forces of insurrection. These conceptions were central to the self-image of the *Nizamat* regime, and dominated the Mughal heartland of north-west Bengal in particular. Here they were articulated by former members of the Mughal service gentry such as Ghulam Hussein Khan who looked back to mythical days of Mughal splendour in which *zamindars* and other intermediaries were supposed to have been kept in their place.[54]

A number of different, mutually incompatible idioms and traditions intersected and battled with one another in the competitive effort of landholders and peasants to understand and describe political action of various kinds. Throughout though, the role of local negotiated forms of affective connection in the making of Bengal's complex polity made the production of general rules or norms, or the establishment of unitary points of legitimate authority, impossible. Bengal's political languages emphasised the importance of particular moments of encounter between ruler and subject, in which ethics and self-interest intertwined, instead of abstract conceptions of right or justice. As a result, eighteenth-century Bengal did not possess a single set of 'juridical' institutions. Instead, petitioners appealed to a variety of different political authorities, from village notables, landholders, Hindu *pandits* and Muslim *qazi*s, to the officers of the Mughal or British regime, each of which claimed to adjudicate according to its own sense of the local public good. Throughout these overlapping institutions, publicity was key: a complainant could have a transaction or decision nullified if it occurred in private or secret. Each had its own intellectual traditions and logic. Many employed juridical experts trained at institutions of higher learning such as the Nabadwip *tols* (schools which taught Sanskrit logic and law) or Hughli *imambara*.[55] Legal education was based on the process of reading and commenting on prior ethical and juridical works, applying the arguments of a text produced in the past to the present situation. Throughout early modern Bengal's various schools of ethics and jurisprudence, there was a strong sense of the importance of interpretation, and the need to connect the maxims of particular authors and commentators to specific ethical contexts. In practice, the process of adjudication was rooted in the local politics of affection and negotiation, what C.A. Bayly calls 'a sense of the neighbourhood', and needed to take account of the contingent dictates of 'locality, loyalty and authority' rather than the attempt to apply general rules.[56]

In this context, the functions performed by the modern state (maintaining order, paying for local public institutions, adjudicating civil disputes, raising revenue, providing a basic level of subsistence for those in need) occurred at different levels within a complex web of institutions that criss-crossed rural society. If the category of the 'state' has any validity in describing the practice of rule in eighteenth-century Bengal at all, it should be used to describe the network of relationships that linked rural non-elites (peasants, traders and so on), local landholders and the *nawabi* or British regime.[57] Mughal or British sovereigns sometimes claimed a general form of absolute authority, from the 1720s to 1770s at least, but they could only act with and alongside the authority of the province's landholder-princes and other local social forces, rather than imposing their own distinctive will on Bengal's social world. Similarly, 'social' categories such as kinship, regional and linguistic identity were not concepts used to carve out a separate sphere of society (*samaj*) that was distinct from the realm of political practice or the state.[58] Rather than being a matter of what people did within static, highly differentiated institutions such as the state or the different segments of Indian society, political conduct in eighteenth-century Bengal involved the art of building and maintaining relationships in a highly mobile environment where the boundary between political and non-political action was impossible to define. Political practice was a kind of action inseparable from social life.

IV

A superficial analysis might lead one to suspect things were different in Britain. If Bengal's political society was clearly constituted by a complex network of overlapping public institutions, Britain had its Parliament, excise officers, landed estates and law courts, all of which seem to provide the basis for a less flexible conception of the structure of political action. Historians often emphasise Britain's difference when they suggest that the East India Company introduced a conception of state authority to the subcontinent unknown to pre-colonial India.[59] That conception is said to have been reliant either on the sovereignty of Parliament, something supposed to have expanded in the late seventeenth or late eighteenth centuries, or a canon of British political thought emphasising the existence of stable principles of political legitimation to justify the existence of a unitary point of sovereign power, Hobbes and Locke's very different contractual theories of obligation, for example. Locke, of course, is supposed to have invented the idea that civil society is a realm of social activity separable from the state.

These impressions are illusory. In eighteenth-century Britain, political practice was rooted in practical skill and complex, contingent networks that the British were reluctant to codify. The eighteenth-century British polity consisted of a series of 'communities of sentiment' as much as Bengal's did. Nineteenth-century Europe's most celebrated theorist of the state, G.W.F. Hegel, noticed this. In a brief essay on English politics (Hegel did not mention Scotland or Wales) he lamented the absence in Britain of abstract political thought. Discussing the 1831 parliamentary reform bill just before he died, the German philosopher suggested that the bonds of the English political class were created through a continual whirl of 'family connexions, political conversations and speeches at dinners' as Hegel put it, 'the endless and world-wide exchange of the political class, even the social gadding about to country seats, horse-races, fox-hunting &ca.'. Political practice was inseparable from social life. Consequently, Hegel complained, no stable principles seemed to guide the actions of the English state. Hegel noted that governance in Britain was scattered between countless local authorities that each had their own rights, privileges and authorities. 'The Constitution of England' he argued, 'is a mere complex of particular Rights and particular privileges'. The country was ruled by an 'inherently disconnected aggregate of positive provisions', not a system ruled by a single, rational logic. 'These arrangements, based on particular interests', Hegel complained, 'render a general system impossible'. Hegel believed the difference between Britain and continental politics occurred because the British were incapable of objectifying their interpersonal relations with general categories such as civil society or the state. As a result, England was 'so remarkably far behind the other civilised states of Europe' because there, 'the governing power lies in the hands of those possessed of so many privileges which contradict a rational constitutional law and true legislation'.[60]

Hegel's voice was absent from the British political world until the late nineteenth century.[61] But had they engaged with Hegel's views British commentators in the first half of the century would have argued that it was chimerical to separate the process of government from the connections and personalities that it relied upon. The art of politics was an essentially social enterprise, depending on learning by experience the skill of social interaction proper to the ruler, not imbibing the kind of abstract categories Hegel articulated. The actions of 'men' were as important as the principles that guided the 'measures' they implemented. The character of the statesman mattered as much as the policies they were supposed to implement. The political actor needed to continually respond to contingencies that were unforeseen, and to alter his (or more rarely her) behaviour in order to retain the allegiance of followers or remain loyal to their patron.[62] None of these actions could be comprehended by the kind of 'general system' that Hegel proposed. Hegel would have criticised such an approach as inconsistent and arbitrary. But, as the anti-slavery campaigner, geologist and clergyman Thomas Gisborne explained in 1794, even the most virtuous form of political action involved a degree of inconsistency. When considering whether to support a man or not, the 'private gentleman' should not allow 'mistaken ideas of consistency to lead him to countenance the same person at a subsequent period, if the sentiments, which he then entertains of men and measures, make it his duty to throw his weight into the adverse side'. 'Duty' for Gisborne did not consist of the politician's obedience to general rules or abstract forms of right that endured unchanged through time. Instead it involved a contextual, situational sense of how to act rooted in the specifics of place and time that looks remarkably like similar discourses articulated in Bengal.[63]

Hegel and later radical critics of British politics may have believed that deferential forms of social connection prevented the existence of true freedom, but few eighteenth-century Britons felt the same. As J.G.A. Pocock argues, deference and freedom were complementary elements within eighteenth-century British political rhetoric. In a short but important article, Pocock argues that the early modern British notion of deference 'is a product of conditional freedom'. Deference involves 'the voluntary acceptance of leadership by persons not belonging to [the] elite, but sufficiently free as political actors to make deference not only a voluntary but a political act'.[64] The deference that a tenant showed to a landlord, or a political client to their patron, was very different from the exercise of domination that might characterise the relationship between a master and servant or slave. In theory at least, the tenant retained their ability to choose to whom they deferred.

Just as in eighteenth-century Bengal, political conduct in Britain involved the continual maintenance of affective connections between individuals occupying different places in the social hierarchy. The relationship between landlords and their tenants was a central component in the British state. The landlord's status as a leader of local society, often also a Justice of the Peace and Member of the Parliament, depended on the loyalty of his following.

Commentators were certain that consent and loyalty needed to be obtained by persuasion not force. Gisborne argued that,

> [t]o encourage a race of upright, skilful and industrious tenants is one the first duties of a private gentleman . . . Let him unite the votes of his tenants to his own by argument and honest persuasion . . . But let him not force their compliance by menaces of expulsion from their farms, or forfeiture of his favour.[65]

Tenants usually expected to support their landlord. But whilst doing so, they often articulated a spirit of independence which meant local politics was governed by what John Cannon calls a 'restlessness against local oligarchies', the same spirit which British officials called 'refractory' and 'contumacious' when they saw it in Bengali peasants.[66] Political representation in parliament and other bodies involved a process of negotiation between patrons and their clients in which elites did not straightforwardly have the upper hand. In Bengal, this kind of negotiation did take place in peaceful public institutions such as the *samaj* or *eka-jai* (caste council); as often it involved violent conflict between groups of retainers, or the use of patronage networks to ensure a large amount of evidence was presented in favour of a landholder in court. In Britain, similar processes occurred in the slightly less violent but equally 'corrupt' scene of parliamentary elections. Rather than representing a 'general interest' or an abstract conception of 'the people' as Hegel would have preferred, politicians in each case spent most of their time articulating particular interests in parliament or other public arena in return for local support. Parliament's task was to arbitrate and negotiate between the complex web of interests and connections that constituted the political community, rather than impose its general will upon society as a whole.[67]

As the historian Paul Langford argues, Britons used the concept of property to understand the web of interests and connections that constituted the British polity. Property had complex affective and political implications. The possession of private, landed property was supposed to bring public duties, including benevolence, patronage and local leadership. During the mid-eighteenth century many complained that the political class's endless 'gadding about' had become urban and global, taking them too far from the local communities they were supposed to rule, although Langford notes that a late eighteenth-century process of civic renewal emerged in response to such allegations. Property was not an abstract right that could be defined according to a general set of governmental classifications: in the eighteenth century, it was not something that could be disciplined and controlled by political power. Instead, property was a relationship, and a form of power, that actively constituted Britain's political society: '[n]ot many people expected the State to leave its mark on property. Almost everyone expected property to leave its mark on the State'. The contingent relationship between property and the polity made attempts to 'govern' land as difficult in Britain as they were in Bengal. A land registry, for example, was impossible because it would have made property subordinate to the classificatory and potentially arbitrary power of an administration. One M.P. suggested that the centralised registration of land would 'shake the ancient inheritance of England', and undermine the basis of the country's political society.[68] In both Britain and India, the inhabitants of rural society feared that any attempt to define the relationship between state and society in a written form would undermine the contingent, affective connections which sustained the polity community.

Unlike pre-colonial Bengal though, England, Wales and Scotland did have fairly stable juridical institutions. The greater immobility and density of both the population and its property were factors that allowed a hierarchy of law courts to have emerged in late-eighteenth-century England.[69] But even if institutions that were supposed to have absolute authority over the resolution of disputes existed, they occurred in an almost impossibly complex network of different juridical agencies: hundred boroughs and manorial courts scattered throughout the countryside along with the King's bench, Chancery, Court of Arches, Admirality and so on in London.[70] But this complex system's purpose was not to apply and enforce a set of general, governmental classifications upon the actions of propertied society. As Michael Lobban notes, the conduct of judges and lawyers was governed by shared 'customs of the court' rather than abstract, codified juridical norms and rules. The court decided cases with a complex range of adjudicative practices that needed to be learnt from experience, not by digesting rules. England's 'rule of law' consisted of the rule of a complex web of courts, not the government of society by a single set of rules.[71]

English law depended on the role of shared adjudicative practices able to neutrally uphold property rights rather than the judge's sense of sympathy for the litigant or accused. Sentiment was seen by eighteenth-century commentators as the basis of Britain's political order in other spheres though. Most famously perhaps, Edmund Burke linked property to the affective connections that bound men together within the polity. For Burke, society was held together by a 'mixed system of opinion and sentiment' in which property was absolutely central. In a passage beginning his discussion of the American War of Independence that is strikingly redolent of the language of Ghulam Hussein Khan, Burke argued that a ruler governed his subjects 'by a knowledge of their temper, and by a judicious management of it', not primarily by either force or law. The local connections that property sustained were 'the first principle (the germ as it were) of public affections', 'the first link in the series by which we proceed toward a love to our country and to mankind'.[72]

As the recent work of Emma Rothschild shows, Adam Smith was similarly concerned with the role of sentiment in guiding social and political action, most famously in his *Theory of Moral Sentiments*.[73] A.G. Megill notes that Smith's philosophical writings were underpinned by a concern with the 'connectedness' of otherwise discrete phenomena. For Smith, the purpose of philosophy was to remove a perception of the 'chaos of discordant and jarring appearances' by 'representing the invisible chains which bind together all these disjointed objects'.[74] In the *Theory of Moral Sentiments*, Smith argued that sympathy was the principle that connected individuals together in political society. Catherine Packham notes that Smith perceived society as a self-regulating mechanism ruled by sentient principles. Sentiment was one 'vital' force that regulated the actions of human beings.[75] Such a view intersected with Smith's scepticism about the powers of abstract reason in guiding the actions of politicians and legislators, which will be considered in a little more detail in the next chapter. Like Burke, Smith saw the state as something that was synonymous with political society: it was a complex organism, a network governed by the continual movement of individuals connected by sentiment and affect. It was not an abstract entity that could successfully impose its will or its governmental logic on the rest of the society.

Scholars interested in the transmission of ideas across the globe often treat the writings of Hobbes and Locke rather than Burke or this sentimentally minded Adam Smith as representative of the kind of British political thought that underpinned the actions of Britain's global polity overseas in the eighteenth century.[76] These two very different seventeenth-century political thinkers had an aberrant place in the ordinary currents of seventeenth and in particular eighteenth-century British political thought though. Each presented a theory in which sovereignty emerged from a contractual moment before which individuals or communities existed without subjection to a ruler; such a fictional story was widely criticised in the eighteenth century by Burke and Smith as much as other thinkers. As William Paley noted (and Hobbes perhaps understood) the idea of a popular assembly presupposed some form of subjection to authority, in order to discipline and form the group beforehand.[77]

What Paley and other eighteenth-century critics missed was that both Hobbes' *Leviathan* and Locke's *Second Treatise* were written to explain or justify how subjects needed to act in a highly aberrant moment of rupture and constitutional crisis: at least as interpreted from the late eighteenth century. In Hobbes' case this context was the British civil war and republic; in Locke's the political strife occurring from the exclusion crisis of 1680 and expulsion of James II from England in 1688. Hobbes and Locke each emphasised the need for the polity to be sustained by trust and some form of sentimental attachment between ruler and ruled. But as Ross Harrison has recently argued, each was written in confusing, tumultuous political times.[78] Given the dramatic collapse in civilised political relationships which they both felt they had experienced, each suggested that trust could only be restored in a radical moment of constitutional innovation in which an artificial state was constructed based from abstractly conceived human relationships and characteristics.[79] Hobbes wrote *Leviathan* in exile; Locke wrote the *Two Treatises* soon before he left for the continent himself.[80] Each proposed a radical reconfiguration of the foundation of political relations in a way that contemporaries immersed in British politics found very difficult to think; Locke's own awareness of the radicalism of his argument is indicated by the fact that he never publicly acknowledged authorship of the *Two Treatises on Government*, for example. Instead of adopting the kind of constitutional project Hobbes or Locke advocated, in practice Britons who stayed at home during these years restored the trust the polity relied on by allowing the sentimental connections of the British state to close over the rupture of civil strife, pretending that the relation between sovereign and *populus* could carry on exactly as before. The civil war was followed by a moment when the old order was simply restored, rather than the authoritarian rule of a new sovereign justified, as Hobbes desired. Similarly, the expulsion of the king in 1688 was quickly reinterpreted as James II's voluntary abdication, to prevent any sense that there was a constitutional crisis.[81]

Read in the eighteenth century then, Hobbes and Locke stand as peculiar figures, outside the dominant tendency for politics to incorporate crisis and opposition within an essentially historical language of legitimacy that emphasised the interactional inseparability of state and society, sovereign and subject *populus*.[82] Of course, throughout the period, political commentators articulated a sense of social division as much as the existence of a stable, organic hierarchy. But until the 1790s (often well beyond), the most critical voices were united by their bid for incorporation into the fluid framework of the 'body politic' not to reconstitute the 'state' as a whole on behalf of a resistant 'society'. Just as Bengal's eighteenth-century rebellions usually began when peasants tried to force themselves onto the negotiating table and play an active role in constituting the polity, in Britain, popular radicalism attempted to incorporate the disenfranchised into the networks of the polity, pumping new lifeblood into the sclerotic veins of power in the process. As Hegel complained, events such as the Reform Act of 1832 or popular movements such as Chartism were efforts to rebalance these complex participatory political relationships, rather than dramatically reconfigure the state in a rational way.[83] In doing so, they allowed British politicians to see political change as part of long lines of historical continuity.

V

The analysis offered in this chapter so far has been intended to deflect attention away from the usual questions historians ask about the extent and effects of the introduction of British thought to India. Instead, it forces one to pose a different problem: why the emergence of colonial governance could not have been more easily accommodated within the capacious idioms and practices of British statecraft; why, in other words, the exercise of the East India Company's sovereignty in Bengal came to be regarded as such a dramatic rupture in both British and Indian ways of practicing politics. The next chapter begins to answer that question. Before doing so, this chapter considers the relationship between political action and time in more detail.

Historians of South Asia frequently suggest that colonialism brought with it a new way of understanding time.[84] Often, these accounts presume the existence of a single modern way of understanding temporality introduced by the European intrusion into the subcontinent. That mode of understanding is supposed to tell the story of mankind's progression through what Walter Benjamin called 'homogenous, empty time'. It consists in the narration of the secular, future-oriented acts of men and women who belong to nations, cultures and communities united by their common characteristics, which occupy clearly delineated territories, and act collectively to produce a future which is irreversibly different from the present and past. For Partha Chatterjee and other scholars, this form of history first occurred in Europe. But as Walter Benjamin pointed out in the 1930s, and Talal Asad has argued since, many different ways of understanding historical time occurred in modern Europe itself. 'The French Revolution viewed itself as Rome incarnate', Benjamin noted, a moment of return to a long-gone time, as well as a break with the *ancien regime* of the more immediate past, for example.[85] Bengali works such as Mritunjoy's *Rajabali* which assumed that divine agency was a major principle of change were written at the same time British evangelicals argued that Napoleon was the agent of a providential Christian god who wanted to punish the British for their sinful role in the slave trade. As was the case in Bengal, these deeply theological points of view existed alongside other, seemingly more secular languages of historical understanding.[86]

Late-nineteenth- and early-twentieth-century Bengali historical narratives emphasised both the irreversible unfolding of historical time, and the agency of men and women situated in the present in producing a future that was dramatically different from the past. As elsewhere in nineteenth-century Europe and Asia, history-writing in Bengal was inseparable from self-conscious projects of 'national' revival, whether, like Benoy Kumar Sarkar, its authors wished to revive a coercive nationalist state, or argued that it should come from the social connections of national society (*samaj*) beyond the state instead, as Rabindranath Tagore suggested.[87]

These histories were different from eighteenth-century narratives in presenting a single large-scale subject as the agent responsible for the process of historical change. Earlier forms of temporal understanding offered complex and less deterministic ways of understanding the forces behind political action. Eighteenth-century narratives were not interested in explaining the march of progress, or the play of power, but nor did they show how political actors were locked in what Manu Goswami calls 'the absolute, qualitative time of patterned recurrence'.[88] Instead they described the way in which the actions of men and women influenced the fate, the survival or decline of the complex, hierarchial yet participatory polities of Bengal. In that respect, they were not wholly dissimilar to British histories written at the same time.

In his essay on 'Modes of political and historical time in early eighteenth-century England', J.G.A. Pocock considers the way 'people order their consciousness of public time'. Pocock differentiates between two forms of political temporality, which he describes as modes of 'continuity' and of 'contingency'. The first emphasised the continuous transmission of practices from the past into the present. Within this mode of thought, political action was concerned to maintain customary continuities. 'Custom' was something that could only be known by the fact of its transmission. It was '[f]ounded upon the individual's ability to recall and summarize his own experience and to presume its continuity with the experience transmitted to him as that of his ancestors'.[89] But custom was not something that could be abstractly or objectively defined. To define or codify custom would undermine its foundation in the continuities of experience. Of course, change occurred, even cumulative progressive change. But it was understood and legitimated within the habitual, customary modes of practice and experience that had been inherited from the past. This customary mentality involved a strong sense of the importance of political action, as institutions needed the continual action of subjects and rulers to be maintained. Acting in accordance with custom involved the skilful management of the relationship between juridical and political institutions and the heterogeneous flow of contingent events.

In Britain, this emphasis on the experiential transmission of customary practice was expressed most forcefully within juridical institutions, where it allowed the characteristically English disapproval of any attempt to abstractly define or codify the rights of subjects or rulers.[90] Outside the law, the importance of custom was articulated by others concerned with the dangers of abstract forms of political 'speculation' that attempted to model and create a radically different future. Such a conception underpinned Edmund Burke's thought. As Uday Singh Mehta emphasises, Burke believed political meaning itself was rooted in the continuities of practical experience.[91] Burke's diatribe against the French Revolution was based on his belief that any attempt to rationally remodel political institutions would annihilate the experiential forms of inter-generational connection that allowed stable forms of political meaning to endure.[92] Burke used a similar argument against the supposedly 'despotic' conduct of Bengal's Governor-General, Warren Hastings. In each case, custom and historical continuity offered an alternative to the rational foundations of political legitimacy that theorists such as Hobbes or Locke proposed.

The continuous, customary past provided an important basis of political legitimacy in eighteenth-century Bengal as well. 'Custom' and prescription were not alien principles to India's eighteenth-century jurists and political practitioners. Landholders and nobles employed genealogy as a principle to justify their political authority.[93] Élites often deliberately echoed archaic styles of architecture and writing to uphold their legitimacy.[94] In each case, it was an attempt to visibly project the polity's continuous existence from one generation to the next that gave them legitimacy. The holders of *zamindari* estates and preferential land grants in the late eighteenth century often spoke as if the mere fact of 'ancient' succession from the past justified an institution's continuity into the future: even if, as in the case of western Bengal's Burdwan *raj*, the estate came into existence less than a century before. In some places, families of ancient or *qadimi* forms of tenure were supposed to be entitled to preferential treatment as a matter of right.[95] As we will see in Chapter 3, when they were asked about 'local customs and usage' by the East India Company's judges, Indian litigants understood what the British were talking about, although the British were rarely able to make much sense of their answers. A similar emphasis on the importance of experiential continuity occurred amongst jurists. Indian jurists often saw the inherited experience of juridical practitioners as the foundation of authoritative judgement, although, unlike English lawyers, they believed experience was transmitted in a particular strand of scholarship or public discourse rather than an institution such as a law court. Hindu jurists often made reference to what was practised (in Sanskrit, *achara*) where the way to resolve a particular dispute was unclear.[96] In doing so, they referred to the continuous conduct of a community of scholar-jurists as the source of authority rather than to a positive, external source of law. All these various perceptions saw political action as something whose purpose was to maintain and continue the continuities of the past into the present. As in Britain, custom did not offer rigid roles or rules that limited the scope for political action, but defined the institution or community authorised to interpret present-day behaviour.

The emphasis on custom and experiential continuity existed alongside another way of perceiving the relationship between political action and time, a mode that was perhaps more dominant in Bengal than in Britain. This form of temporal understanding emphasised contingency instead of continuity, stressing – as Pocock notes – 'the unpredictable contingencies and emergencies which challenge[d] the human capacity to apprehend and to act'. This second way of thinking about time emphasised the inevitable degeneration of states and empires. Political conduct was a process of constant, tactical manoeuvring, in which political actors worked to prevent the polity – and their own authority – from collapsing in the face of fate and fortune. The future was not merely a continuation of the past; it was a threat, something that contained the seeds of decline. The task of the political actor was to act skilfully by stretching out the present as long as possible before inevitable degeneration. Perhaps Burke's great foe, Warren Hastings, emphasised this idiom in his political thought rather than the customary idiom which Burke emphasised.

Pocock associates such a conception with the tradition of civic humanist politics that stretches from Cicero to Machiavelli, but which had a powerful role in eighteenth-century British political discourse.[97] Within this political language, 'virtue' was the form of practical skill needed to prevent the 'degeneration' of the political community. Such a vocabulary informed the way British commentators spoke about the dangers of 'corruption', a significant category within late-eighteenth-century British political rhetoric. Corruption occurred when deference became dependence, when the political subject's ability to act independently and retain a mutually beneficial relationship with their superiors was replaced by submission to their every whim. From this point of view the corruption of the polity was inevitable. As Hume put it, '[t]here seems to be a natural Course of Things, which bring on the destruction of great Empires', a 'natural course' which occurred through the inevitable contact between the virtuous polity of Britain and the 'barbarism' or 'despotism' that lay elsewhere. Ostensibly, the task of politicians was not to expand into new territories, but secure and preserve what existed before.[98] The polity was protected by character, virtuous conduct and the skilful maintenance of the affective relationships emphasised in this chapter. In Britain, it was precisely these forces that some believed had defeated the Jacobite rebellion in 1745–1746. The uprising, which intended to replace George II with a Catholic king, was seen as a radical attempt to undermine the fundamentals of the British polity, Protestantism and property in particular. Many commentators used the rebellion to call for a renewal of patriotic, ethical governance, a 'reformation of manners' and a more concerted effort to incorporate virtuous local populations into the state through institutions such as the militia.[99]

Perhaps because of its more uneven, fluid political topology, this concern to ensure that the polity survived the vicissitudes of fortune was even more important in eighteenth-century Bengal than it was in Britain. Bengal's political communities were seen by Indians as highly vulnerable to fate: its little kingdoms, but even its more centralised forms of sovereignty such as the *Nizamat* and Mughal state. Fate was manifest in floods, drought, political strife or mass migration. Each polity would only survive its vicissitudes by the proper deployment of virtue and political skill. Here, one can draw parallels between the Jacobite rebellion and the war waged by Maratha cavalry on western Bengal between 1742 and 1751. Both occasions were moments of vulnerability, understood in some quarters as crises that threatened to undermine the basis of the state.

The Maratha invasion was led by Bhaskar Pandit, a man acting with the supposed sanction of the Mughal emperor. Unlike their Jacobite counterparts, the Marathas aimed to bring Bengal to terms, not overthrow its governing regime entirely. The Maratha actions occurred in the context of a process of continuous *fitna* or struggle which André Wink suggests was central to Maratha politics.[100] Claiming to be the agent of the Mughal empire, Bhaskar Pandit tried to force Bengal's *nizam* Alivardi Khan to acknowledge Maratha overlordship, and pay a significant sum of *chaut* or tribute. Alivardi assassinated Bhaskar Pandit at a conference organised to negotiate terms in 1744. But raids continued for almost a decade. Much of western Bengal's population fled to eastern regions such as Dhaka, Dinajpur and Rangpur. Consequently, Alivardi decided that the only way to save his polity from total ruin was to agree terms. In 1751 he abandoned the province of Orissa to Maratha rule, and paid 12,00,000 Rupees in *cauth* or tribute.

Scottish and English commentators often attributed moments of British political vulnerability such as 1745, the Seven Years War and later, the threat of Napoleonic invasion to a decline in good ethical conduct. The historical language that Indians used to discuss the Maratha incursions saw the vulnerability of the Bengali polity in similar terms.[101] In both Bengal and Britain, divine agency often intervened to ensure human beings with free will got their just deserts. In the *Maharashta-Purana*, written by the east Bengali poet Gangaram soon after the Maratha wars, the incursions were portrayed as the result of the increasingly sinful and ungovernable character of the people of earth, here equated with the population of Bengal. 'Day and night were spent in amorous sport, or in abusing others and doing injury to them'. Chaos and moral decline had disturbed the orderly passage of time: '[n]o-one knew what might happen at any time'.[102] Just like Bharatchandra, who wrote about the incursions in his *Annada-mangal*, Gangaram partially equated sin with decline in the worship of Hindu deities. Bharatchandra saw the Maratha raids as divine retribution for *nawab* Alivardi Khan's desecration of the shrine to the god Bhubanesvara in Orissa; Gangaram noted 'there was no worship of Radha and Krsna' in Bengal anymore. Coming from the more open and pluralist eastern part of the province, Gangaram equated 'sin' and 'vice' with political decline, lamenting in particular the increasingly loose relationship between Bengal and the Muslim, Mughal polity. In a narrative that demonstrates the complex intercalation of Indic/Hindu and Islamic/Persian elements in the political rhetoric of eighteenth-century Bengal, Gangaram suggested that Parvati, a Hindu deity, used Maratha raiders to force a Muslim province to submit itself to the authority of the Muslim Mughal empire. Eventually, it was the virtuous conduct of the *nawab* Alivardi Khan in the war, the moral rearmament of the Bengal *suba* and the fact that the *bargis* caused virtuous Brahmins and Vaisyas to flee which caused the gods to call a halt to the violence.

But some acts could not even be controlled by the gods. Gangaram noted that elephants rampaging in the midst of Maratha forces played a key role in one Bengali victory. The Marathas' inability to respond courageously to what Gangaram saw as an utterly random, contingent event was significant to their early defeat. Again, it was the human response to contingent events that governed the course of events. For Ghulam Hussein Khan Tabatabai on the other hand, the elephants rampaged as a result of God's will. The author of the *Seir Mutaquerrin* believed they represented the 'divine assistance' of 'the Almighty disposer of things'.[103] Even Ghulam Hussein believed providence favoured men who had choices, and who acted with virtue and skill though. Throughout his narrative, the *nawab* Alivardi Khan, the employer of Ghulam Hussein's family, was described as being rewarded for the virtue of his character. But reward came from different quarters, not usually the direct actions of god. Alivardi's courageous and virtuous deeds 'overjoyed the hearts of his subjects', and strengthened the support he gained from his subjects as a consequence. Nonetheless, for Ghulam Hussein Khan, the virtues of Alivardi and his close allies, their skill in managing 'friendship' with their subjects and allies and tactical ability to act in a devious way when necessary were unable to prevent the lineage they belonged to from declining. By 1784, when Ghulam Hussein was writing, Alivardi's 'illustrious house, which having risen in these very provinces to the summit of power, glory and riches, [wa]s now fallen and totally extinct'. The 'natural course' of events ensured that all states eventually fell victim to the entropic dynamic which ruled all political relationships.[104]

In the narratives of Gangaram and Ghulam Hussein, political history was the story of how people with choices needed to constantly adjust themselves to events that the rational powers of the human subject could not entirely calculate or control. For the most part, the actions of human beings determined the fate of states. They did so in the way they responded to uncertainty and fate, by manipulating the customary practices inherited from the past or managing the familiar connections that existed between friends and subjects in the present, rather than by projecting abstract, rational plans of progress or reform onto the future. Individuals were immersed in a world constituted by the particular actions needed to protect their livelihood or state at a specific time and place. They were unable to abstract themselves out of the flow of contingent time to act on events in order to produce a dramatically different future. Despite the predominance of present-centred or backward-looking ways of seeing the relationship between politics and time though, eighteenth-century political culture was dominated by willed, often seemingly wilful, human action.

VI

Differences existed within and between eighteenth-century Britain and Bengal. But the kind of comparative perspective followed here does not need to demonstrate that the same phenomena existed in different contexts, merely to show that a similar analytical vocabulary is useful to describe political culture in each place. As this chapter has shown, the political practice of Britain and Bengal was described – and can be described now – using a similar series of concepts. Nonetheless, as the next chapter argues, early colonial officials emphasised the strangeness and difference of India – increasingly so during the 1780s, 1790s and beyond. Why did individuals who understood their own political worlds in ways that were comparable believe they were strangers to one another? Far from being the result of a clash of cultures or fundamentally different ways of understanding politics, the next chapter shows how they were produced by the specific concatenation of forces that created the peculiar logic of colonial interaction in Bengal.

This chapter concludes with a story that shows how similar ways of understanding political action met to produce something quite different. Owing to what his mother called 'the vicissitudes of fortune' the *Raja* of Chandradwip in Bakarganj district, Durga Kuar Narayan, was forced to sell his estate at a public auction: Durga Kuar had not been able to pay the East India Company's revenue demand.[105] Alexander and George Paniotty, two Anatolian Greek merchants whose trading empire had been built by commerce between northern Bengal and Assam formally 'bought' the estate at auction. The Paniottys quickly found that paying cash to the Company didn't guarantee practical possession of the estate. Because they had patronised a range of religious and civic institutions and protected *raiyats* with money and force, Durga Kuar and his ancestors had established their centrality to local society. Despite their deed of sale, the Greeks found it impossible to break the sentimental bonds that bound Chandradwip's subjects to their previous rulers.

The Paniottys were interested in making a series of short-term tactical manoeuvres to shore up their power, not laying up and investing to improve the estate for the long term. 'We do not', they noted, 'purchase the Zumeendaree for after years, that it might be of use after our deaths'. They tried to enlist the East India Company on their side. The Paniotty brothers demanded 'vigorous methods' including the imprisonment of the *zamindar* and the deployment of troops in the estate to assert their power over the domain.[106] The British sent a few ineffectual armed officers into the countryside: men such as Fakhir Mohammed Chaprassi, who was defeated by the much greater force at the disposal of the *raja*. They also moved their district headquarters to the village of Barisal. Until 1814, the revenue Collectorate offices – and with them the Company's officials – were a week's boat journey up river in Dhaka. A subordinate office, visited occasionally by British officials, was situated 20 miles away at the village of Madhabpasha. The Company's law courts were scattered elsewhere. Madhabpasha and these other sites were in Durga Kuara Narayan's ancestral domain, the scene of his local economic and cultural authority. It was simple for him to use his local retinue to ensure decisions occurred in his favour. From there, it was easy for the former landholder to prevent the brothers from receiving rent. The village of Barisal, on the other hand, was situated on land that the Paniottys controlled. Moving the revenue office and judicial courts there would give them a better chance to visibly project their authority over events on the estate.

There was nothing characteristically Bengali about this controversy. The battle between the two settlements, Madhabpasha and Barisal, has parallels with disputes between rival towns in early modern England and the rest of Europe. Arguments about the sitting of judicial offices, turnpikes, canals, embankments, assizes, gaols, church courts and every other species of institution in Britain were a commonplace feature of the unruly fabric of eighteenth-century British political life. The battle for prestige and liveli-hood was messy, involving local landlords, nobles and frequently Parliament as well.[107] 'Central' forces of authority such as parliament or the Westminster courts were vigorously lobbied by participants in local disputes, pulled down into local battles for wealth and authority where there were no rules able to clearly determine whose side they should take. The response of central institutions was usually determined by personal relationship and political alliances, most importantly the beneficiary's ability to mass a large enough retinue of supporters in parliament or elsewhere, not abstract and objective standards of authority.

Despite these parallels, the Paniottys' anxious lobbying played a minor part in the creation of a colonial regime that attempted to create such abstract, objective standards. Eventually, the Company's hierarchy shifted most of its offices. Barisal was founded, as a new town, in 1801. Over the next two cen-turies, the settlement grew into an important administrative centre. By the late twentieth century, it had become one of the most important adminis-trative centres in Bangladesh and the capital of one of four of the country's divisions. But to begin with though, the town of Barisal was home to no one. John Wintle, the district judge, moved most of the offices in March, but Wintle had built a town without any inhabitants. Time was needed

> on account of the removal of the station, to enable the omlahs, vakeels and pleaders to erect habitations at the new Residence, and to give time for removing the prisoners, cutcheries, &ca.

It was only in October 1801 that the town's Indian administrative staff arrived; but none stayed for good. Throughout much of the nineteenth century (to some degree even to the present day) Barisal remained a place of only temporary residence, as officials returned 'home' to their scattered settlements whenever the court or revenue office's term was over.[108]

The town of Barisal was founded because the Paniottys believed they could appeal to the East India Company's obligations to its subjects, and manip-ulate their 'friendship' with British officers for their own benefit. But an action whose origins lay in the affective politics of eighteenth-century Ben-gal played its part in the creation of an administrative centre which acted very differently. Wintle, the district judge, had been appointed to the dis-trict in order to 'frame Regulations' that were supposed to improve the order and regularity of the government of the surrounding countryside. Rather than acting within the dynamic and uneven networks which constituted Bengal's eighteenth-century polity, those institutions were meant to govern stable forms of right that were supposed to be classified from the aloof, and objective perspective of the colonial regime. But as a result, they uninten-tionally placed existing ways of doing things on a new footing. This chapter has shown how sensibilities that underpinned the establishment of a new district capital in Barisal were not caused by the straightforward introduction of British ideas of governance to Bengal. Instead, the introduction of a radically different attitude towards government, political practice and time emerged from a complex set of events occurring in the 1780s and 1790s, which the next chapter will narrate.

3
Crisis, Anxiety and the Making of a New Order

A few months after Louis XVI was executed in France, the English peer Charles Cornwallis ended his seven-year term as Governor-General of Bengal (1786–1793). In the months before he left, Cornwallis transformed the British governance of India, putting in place a series of dramatic reforms in the East India Company's administration of revenue and law. The Company had possessed some form of sovereignty in Bengal after wielding military force and being given the *diwani* or office of revenue collection from the Mughal Emperor in Delhi in 1765. Yet British rule in the years before Cornwallis had been fluctuating and uncertain, dominated by what the historian Ranajit Guha calls 'empiricism and short sightedness'.[1] Sent to Bengal in 1786, Cornwallis was instructed by the Prime Minister William Pitt to introduce stability and solvency to the regime, ensuring that its government was 'speedily placed upon a good footing'; John Shore described the task as to 'introduce system and order where all before was disorder and misrule'.[2] Cornwallis enacted a series of rules for the guidance of the Company's officers that replaced existing regulations. His constitution separated the collection of revenue from the administration of justice, as separate judges and collectors were sent to Bengali districts from 1793 onwards. Most famously, in March 1793 Cornwallis' government fixed the amount of revenue which Bengal's Indian landholders, its *zamindars*, were supposed to pay the Company forever. For Ranajit Guha, whose 1963 *A Rule of Property* has dominated the interpretation of these events since, Cornwallis' aim was no less than to transform the Indian countryside into a capitalist society. Other historians have noted that the introduction of the Cornwallis system was a less dramatic attempt to 'stabilise a hereditary agrarian society', but nonetheless see it as a pivotal moment in British rule.[3]

The year 1793 is frequently seen as marking the beginning of the modern state, or at least the emergence of a consolidated colonial regime in Bengal. It is easy to overestimate the transformative effects of Cornwallis' regime. The

East India Company was not military dominant throughout India for another 25 years. The Cornwallis reforms did not immediately result in a more stable income or reduce the Company's debt, although they did allow the Company to borrow money more easily. The British relationship with landholders, the Company's main revenue payers, remained uncertain until the 1820s. Cornwallis' new regulations were mere guidelines for the conduct of British civil servants. The government did not provide a code of law or new set of rules to govern Indian society, nor did it attempt to introduce new forms of property rights. The permanent settlement certainly did not produce a new breed of capitalist landlord. If anything it consolidated the rural power of local gentries who were rising already; but its transformative reach was limited by ecological and demographic forces that prevented British policy from having an unmediated impact on agrarian society until the late nineteenth century.[4] Later chapters of this book show how the attempt to create new, codified rules in the early nineteenth century occurred as a response to the perceived failure, not the success, of Cornwallis' approach. To begin with, the new judicial system resulted merely in a massive backlog in court cases. In Bengal itself the 'Bengal system' was revised significantly to remedy these various 'evils' during the next 30 years. In other parts of India and in London it rapidly became the object of sustained critique.

If claims about the origin of India's modern colonial state in 1793 are exaggerated, Cornwallis' new constitution involved a significant and self-conscious rupture with earlier styles of governance nonetheless. What was distinctive about Cornwallis' regime was its conscious effort to produce a break with the past. As Robert Travers has recently shown, debates about the British governance of Bengal before Cornwallis were disagreements about the uses of Indian history, as officials argued about different interpretations of a purported Mughal ancient constitution.[5] Custom mattered to the officials who surrounded Cornwallis in so far as it provided the basis of property rights in the present. But the institutions which Cornwallis' officials constructed to govern Bengali society abandoned any claim to being based on historical precedent. Cornwallis' constitution consisted of what the House of Commons' 1813 *Fifth Report* into East Indian affairs called 'a new order of things'.[6]

This desire to innovate was not the confident articulation of coherent ideas expressing Britain's will to transform Bengal, nor the expression of Enlightenment principles as Guha and historians since have argued. Instead, this chapter shows that it was a response to two crises. First of all it occurred as an attempt to 'secure' an important site of British global power amidst imperial collapse elsewhere by creating a stable relationship between the sovereign and the largest group of revenue-payers, Bengal's *zamindars*. The near collapse of the Company's solvency was a necessary condition for the emergence of a new style of rule between 1786 and 1793, but this dynamic was not sufficient to explain the dramatic nature of the change. Cornwallis' new constitution was a response to a crisis in British officials' ability to engage with Indian society and history in a meaningful way as well. This chapter begins by looking at the Company's military and financial disaster, but moves on to show how Britons in Asia experienced a crisis of meaning. The second section shows how, in the 1780s, colonial officers began to be sceptical about their ability to develop useful knowledge by directly experiencing the historic continuities of Indian society. The 1780s saw officials' private disorientation at being strangers a long way from 'home' in India converge with the discourse of colonial governance to influence the structure of the official mind and character of the East India Company's regime in Bengal.

In an essay entitled 'Not at Home in Empire' published in 1997, Ranajit Guha himself notes that the academic discussion of colonial India has tended to ignore the pervasive mood of colonial anxiety experienced and articulated by imperial officers. Instead he suggests that scholars have presented colonial officials as men enthusiastically committed to an ideologically coherent imperial project. Colonial historiography 'creates an image of empire as a sort of machine operated by a crew who knew only how to decide but not to doubt, who know only action but no circumspection, and in the event of a breakdown, only fear and no anxiety'.[7] Instead, Guha discusses the way European colonial officials articulated their inability to be 'at home' in the subcontinent, using the term 'anxiety' to describe their unsettled state of mind. Drawing on the philosophy of Søren Kierkegaard and Martin Heidegger, Guha defines anxiety as a general, inchoate sense of disconnection from the world. The colonial situation gave colonial officials in India a perception of 'the immensity of things in a world whose limits are not known'. For British officials, colonial India had, to quote Heidegger, become a 'world [that] has the character of completely lacking in significance'.[8] British officials in late eighteenth-century Bengal saw government as an uncertain enterprise, marked by exactly the kind of mood that Guha describes. As this chapter argues, the 'new constitution' of 1793 was an unsuccessful attempt to suppress those anxieties.

II

C.A. Bayly suggests that 'the 1770s and 1780s were a British recessional'. During these years the 13 American colonies were lost in war and British-ruled India seemed riven with corruption, mismanagement and was continually defeated by Indian powers in expensive battles.[9] The end of this period, the last years of Warren Hastings' period as Governor-General (1772–1785), were dominated by the East India Company's involvement in difficult wars in India, and accompanying financial strife. Between 1779 and 1782, British armies were defeated in both the south and west, by the state of Mysore and the Maratha confederacy, although the Company regained some of their losses in each case. Already fighting in the Americas, the involvement of

France on the ex-colonial side threatened to turn the American War of Independence into a global conflict. A French expeditionary force arrived in south India in January 1781, an event that gave the British serious anxiety about the survival of their power on the Indian subcontinent. In reality the relatively insignificant French threat was driven from South Asia quickly; British fear of France in India reappeared intermittently until the defeat of Napoleon. The treaties of Salbai and Mangalore, signed with the Marathas and Mysore in May 1782 and January 1784 respectively, restored the disposition of power on the Indian subcontinent before these wars. The terms of the peace were condemned by those in London who hoped they would find 'in the East Indies a recompense for all [British] losses in the west'.[10] Officers stationed in the subcontinent saw it was a necessary but uneasy truce.[11]

But in the middle of the 1780s the British exchanged geopolitical uncertainty for financial insolvency. Bengal, whose revenue the East India Company had collected since 1765, was required to bear the costs of battle. By the time the peace of Mangalore was signed at the beginning of 1784, payments from Bengal's treasuries to armies stationed at Bombay and Madras meant the Company in Bengal owed more than three *crore* Rupees (£3 million) to creditors, almost half of which were unpaid treasury orders. In total, almost Rs 2.5 *crore* (£2.5 million) was remitted to the Madras presidency alone from Bengal between 1781 and 1784.[12] Warren Hastings had hoped to pay back the Company's debt in Bengal before returning to England at the beginning of 1785, but the Bombay and Madras presidencies continued to draw on Bengal's finances to pay for military expenditure, as conflict with Mysore and the Marathas seemed likely to recur.[13] Hastings attempted to raid the treasuries of subordinate allies, acting against the Raja of Benares in 1781, then journeying to Lucknow to broker an agreement with the Nawab Wazir of Awadh the next year. Again though, the situation barely improved.

The late arrival of the monsoon rain in Bengal in 1784 led some to expect food scarcity on the scale of the devastating famine of 1769–1770, but it was the shortage of cash that plagued the minds of Europeans. By November of that year, the pay of the Company's Indian and British troops was substantially in arrears, and official salaries were being withheld. Indian bankers refused to lend 'knowing that they are unlikely to get the interest due on their bonds'. The Company was unable to purchase the goods it needed to export to remain solvent in London. One official, L. Archdekin wrote that the Company was insolvent, its credit 'absolutely *ruined*', lamenting 'our Poverty, distress, and visible decline'.[14] The Company's bonds were 'useless paper', being discounted at more than 40%. John MacPherson, the man who administered Bengal whilst Hastings was away in Lucknow and temporarily succeeded him as Governor-General in 1785, noted that the Company's 'treasury was drained, and every means of raising money by loan, by annuities, by partial remittance had been tried'. 'Such', MacPherson noted 'was the crisis at which it was my destiny to become one of the members of the superior government of India'.[15]

From 1783 to 1785 the language of crisis became commonplace to describe the East India Company's situation. In the eighteenth century the word 'crisis' didn't have the same negative consequences it does now, merely referring, as Samuel Johnson's *Dictionary* put, to 'the point in time at which any event comes to its height'.[16] In its ordinary usage, a crisis didn't call out for a particular kind of response. Sometimes it was dealt with by doing nothing, waiting until the high point of an illness had passed, for example. Yet when they spoke of crisis in Bengal during the 1780s, British politicians and imperial officers used the word to justify decisive action. In Britain, the sense of financial crisis began to intersect with a heightened concern about Indian affairs, and a new sense of the need to intervene and regulate the Company's affairs. The returned Company officer Sir Richard Sullivan described the situation as a 'crisis at which India matters are become such a serious concern of this nation'.[17] Literally, India was a 'concern' in 1784 because the East India Company's recovery was dependent on intervention from the British state, in particular a drastic cut in duty on tea imported from Canton, allowing the Company to expand its revenue at possible cost to the British Treasury. Since 1767, the Company had repeatedly been bankrolled by the British state.[18] More than previous moments though, the mood of crisis in the early 1780s encouraged a critique of the character of British politics in India and drove a wave of parliamentary and ministerial intervention into 'Indian affairs'. It impelled the appointment of Cornwallis as Governor-General and the demand for reform in Bengal. To understand that process one has to step back and consider the regime of Cornwallis' predecessor, Warren Hastings.

After it assumed the *diwani* in 1765, the East India Company acted in an ambiguous fashion in Bengal, in part as a mercantile corporation and in part as regional prince. Warren Hastings' appointment as Governor of Bengal in 1772, and then Governor-General over all British India in 1774 saw the Company unambiguously asserting its right to rule in the subcontinent although it retained its commercial functions as a means to transfer revenue from India to Europe nonetheless. More than being the head of a corporate organisation, Hastings saw himself as the personal agent of British sovereignty, believing that some day the British state would assume direct political control over its Indian territories directly.

In his recent work on Britain's late-eighteenth-century empire, P.J. Marshall suggests that this more assertive attitude was partially driven from London. British politicians forced officials in India to be much clearer about 'how they were furthering Britain's national interests through the creation of a new empire based on the Company's uncontested exercise of sovereign authority'.[19] The new imperial sensibility was underpinned by the British desire to develop a far more stable fiscal relationship with their colonial possessions than had existed previously, perhaps to subjugate British possessions in India to a colonial financial relationship. As Marshall argues, the decision to impose the Stamp Act in America was one attempt to create a more stable financial relationship between the imperial metropolis and its colonial peripheries, an act with disastrous consequences. The increasing regulation of the East India Company's affairs in the 1770s and 1780s, in exchange for the periodic loans the state made to the Company was another. Well after the American defeat, many believed that Britain's empire could be best sustained through pacific commercial relations with the newly independent American territories. Nonetheless, Britain's imperial proconsuls began to place greater emphasis on the importance of sustaining an imperial role elsewhere, especially in South Asia.[20] The Court of Directors' constant insistence that officials in Bengal cut costs and regularise income show that in London's discussion of the relationship between Britain and India, finance was key.

Britain's connections with India were seen as increasingly important in the late eighteenth century. The customs revenue Company ships paid were a significant source of income for the British exchequer; Indian connections may have played a role stabilising Britain's balance of payments at wartime.[21] As importantly Bengal was seen as an increasingly significant source of prosperity for the looser networks of the British polity, as a site of investment for Britain's gentry, for example. Propertied Britons looked to the Company as an invariable source of income and were increasingly willing to lobby the Court of Directors and Parliament to ensure their income was secure.[22] These connections meant that in London empire was seen as a potentially stable financial relationship between the metropolis and a dependent colony, rather than as the more accommodating process of give and take involved with the exercise of political dominance over territory. Philip Stern shows that in the late seventeenth century the Company was a global polity that had a set of interests, and sometimes even foreign policy at variance with the British state.[23] But as Huw Bowen notes, by the mid-1780s contemporaries described the link between Britain and the Company's territories in South Asia as a 'union of interest' in a single imperial financial system.[24] These relationships also ensured that the Company's possessions continued to be ruled with the rigid and bureaucratic structures of corporate accountability more usual in an organisation owned by stockholders. In theory at least, the Company was governed in Calcutta and London through the endless board meetings and minutes that Ghulam Hussein Khan complained about, instead of the more flexible and accommodating political idioms of statecraft.

Warren Hastings was frequently criticised for abandoning these norms in India, acting in a secretive fashion and relying too much on his own personal authority. Yet Hastings himself defended this personal style of rule as the natural corollary of British state sovereignty in the subcontinent; for Hastings and other officials, the structures of accountability that London felt were necessary to ensure the regular flow of resources from colony to capital inhibited the exercise of sovereign power in India. As Robert Travers notes, Hastings' project was to assert the existence of the East India Company's absolute sovereign rights in Bengal. Hastings posited the existence of a single absolute point of sovereign power in Bengal, suggesting that the Governor-General had inherited the power of the Emperor in the Company's domains. In his vision of the colonial polity, there were no inalienable intermediaries standing between sovereign and subject; his judicial and revenue reforms were an attempt at '[c]lawing back the state's prerogatives from overmighty subjects'.[25] But there would also be no subjection to the rigid checks and balances London insisted his regime be accountable to.

As part of his effort to escape British supervision, Hastings argued that Britons were accountable to Indian institutions and obliged to govern according to India's 'ancient Mughal constitution'.[26] As Travers notes, the language of ancient constitutionalism provided a common intellectual landscape upon which British officials fractiously debated their governance of India until the mid-1780s. In seventeenth- and eighteenth-century Britain the idea of an ancient constitution was invoked to suggest that England had not been conquered in 1066, but had a free, undespotic constitution that had endured since before the Norman invasion.[27] But in colonial India ancient constitutionalism involved a far shorter timescale than its British (or English) variant, as administrators used it to justify forms of political practice that had survived through centuries, but had been jeopardised by a moment of tumult scarcely a generation away. In some accounts the 'revolutions' of the 1740s threatened to undermine the continuities of Bengal's Mughal constitution; in other versions it was Britain's political intrusion after the battle of Plassey in 1757 that did the damage. Nonetheless, in each case the invocation of an ancient constitution was used to deny the completely rupturing force of conquest, articulating instead a sense of legitimacy based on institutions' endurance through the transmission of experience that connected the past with the present.

Hastings did not have a monopoly on this kind of constitutional vocabulary: it was a language also used by the men who were sent from London to provide a check on Hastings' power. From 1773 until 1780, a group of Supreme Council members sent by parliament, centred around Philip Francis, engaged in verbal and occasionally physical combat with the faction surrounding Hastings. Conflicts which occurred between Indian nobles in the politics of Bengal's post-Mughal *Nizamat* regime intersected with these very British struggles, as Indian officers such as Mir Qasim, Ganga Govind Singh and Mohammed Reza Khan were used by British political actors to achieve their own ends and *vice versa*. Francis presented an alternative vision of governance based upon the delegation of authority to local Indian magnates and the role of landed property as a block on the encroaching power of the sovereign.[28] But he spoke with equal force about the Company's need to revert to 'the ancient customs and usages of the country' or 'ancient

rights' in its governance of Bengal even though he had a different interpretation about what those were from Hastings' party.[29] Francis has been treated
by some historians, notably Ranajit Guha, as the progenitor of the later
emphasis on *zamindari* property rights found within Cornwallis' permanent
settlement and after.[30] But Francis was primarily interested in the political
role of landholders within a diffuse, decentralised constitution, not their
economic function, as later officials were. And like Hastings' idiom, Francis
articulated his form of ancient constitutionalism in the language of experiential continuity discussed in the previous chapter, J.G.A. Pocock's 'mode
of continuous time'. Unlike later commentators, for the British officials who
invoked it in the 1770s and 1780s, India's putative 'ancient constitution' was
not an abstract structure. It was regarded as a living political reality, understood through personal interaction with the Asian officials who had lived
recently within it.

In contrast with the arguments expressed by Francis or his friends in
London, Warren Hastings regarded India's 'ancient constitution' as an historically sanctioned style of personal authority. The Governor-General thought
India's polity was a structure capacious enough to allow the tactical necessity
of responding to unpredictable events in order to stave off the decline of the
polity. 'The state of a kingdom', Hastings noted, 'is liable to dissolution from
causes as mortal as those which intercept the course of the human frame'.[31]
To maintain the 'state' required the sovereign's attention to public opinion,
the accumulation of practical experience and the exercise of virtuous action.
In the 'Memoirs' he wrote on the voyage back to Britain, Hastings argued
that the experience his Indian subjects had of his 'character' allowed him to
govern effectively. Experience had contributed to a 'degree of superstitious
belief in the minds of almost all other men' in the success of any measures
he might put in place in the future, as Indian subjects had developed an
affective relationship with his character.[32] Echoing a common eighteenth-
century British argument about the importance of sentimental attachment
in politics, Hastings suggested that his 'government subsists more by influence of public opinion than by its real power or resources'.[33] But 'public
opinion' did not consist of an abstract general will; it occurred through a
myriad of historically rooted social connections and linkages, which needed
to be continually managed and manipulated. Hastings justified the publication of English translations of works of Indian philosophy and law not
as tools for government, but as texts which would bridge the emotional
gap which separated British administrators from the Indians they ruled. As
he suggested in the preface to Charles Wilkins' translation of the *Bhagavad
Gita*, 'social communication with people over whom we exercise a dominion
founded on the right of conquest, is useful to the state' because it 'attracts
and conciliates distant affections'. Like the *Code of Gentoo Law*, translated by
Nathaniel Brassey Halhed, the aim of such a publication was to 'impress us
with a more generous sense of feeling for [Indians'] natural rights, and teach

us to estimate them by the measure of our own'.[34] The idea of a permanently binding textual law was anathema to this political discourse. When the regime suggested in 1772 that 'the Laws of the Koran with respect to Mahometans, and those of the Shaster with respect to Gentoos [Hindus] shall invariably be adhered to' in disputes regarding 'Inheritance, Marriage, Caste and all other religious Usages or Institutions', the point was to enshrine the centrality of Muslim and Hindu judges within the 'ancient' polity, not place textual law above the historical institutions which interpreted it.[35] Rather than being reliant on texts that codified abstract rules, the ancient constitution was associated instead with the institutions and offices through which sovereignty had customarily been exercised.

These views meant it was difficult for Hastings to make pronouncements about the general rights of social groups abstractly conceived. On his voyage back to England in 1785, Hastings criticised '[t]he high ideas of the right of the Zemindars in Hindostan', which 'the public in England have of late adopted'.[36] He did not deny that landholders possessed rights of some kind, nor suggest that the sovereign had the power to dispose of landed incomes in an entirely arbitrary fashion. Instead, his challenge to the emerging language of *zamindari* rights was an epistemological one. For Hastings, an abstract notion of *zamindari* right would have projected a theory about the province's propertied relations onto the distant future and so create too wide a gap between theory and practice. Government was an empirical process of 'trial and error'; every initiative depended on its exposure to practical experience and the 'minute scrutiny' of contingent, changeable 'facts' in the short term. In a world in which politics occurred through the continual action of men working to stave off the effects of contingent time on the polity, it was difficult to talk about the need for a permanent resolution to the Company's problems. In his attack on Hastings in the House of Lords, Edmund Burke was right to suggest that the Governor-General's conduct had been based on the belief that it was possible to know 'the constitution of Asia only from its practices'. Perhaps though, Hastings' experiential political epistemology was closer to Burke's own way of thinking than his fiercest critic thought.[37]

In many ways Hastings' regime continued the kind of complex negotiated political relationships the pre-colonial regime relied on. The system Hastings put in place to collect land revenue involved short-term alliances with agrarian entrepreneurs, a policy based on the precedent of appointing *ijaradars* (revenue-farmers) for a period of time to manage the collection of revenue in a district. These figures were sometimes local chiefs, otherwise officials and merchants with little knowledge of a district. Where such a system operated before British rule it relied on the *ijaradar*'s ability to negotiate with local forces, taking upon themselves the risks of local agricultural production. But a contradiction existed between the logic that underpinned this flexible form of absolutism, reliant as it was on the maintenance of these local political networks, and the demand for stable forms of revenue that emerged ever more strongly from the networks of British imperial finance. The *ijaradar* system was unable to bear the pressure of India-wide war, or the demand from London for a stable supply of Asian imports paid for by Bengal's revenue. In the past, Bengal's *Nawabs* had demanded extra resources in times of defensive war, to combat the Maratha incursions of the 1740s in the west of Bengal, for example. Landholders had contributed either from a sense of self-interested obligation or fear. It was far harder for the British to convince *zamindars* that they should increase their contributions when they were being used to fund the defence of Bombay or Madras or pay the Company's investment. The Company tried to increase Bengal's revenue by 9.8% increase in 1781, setting the *jama* (tax demand) at Rs 2.8 *crore* (£2.8 million) to pay the costs of war, the highest demand for any single year during the eighteenth century. But landholders refused to pay the tax hike without any reciprocal advantage; and British victory in a war hundreds of miles away in Madras was not considered of sufficient benefit. Unable to negotiate due to the growing costs of war, the consequence was a short-term increase in arrears and the outbreak of violent unrest in the Bengali countryside. Insurrection occurred throughout Birbhum district; more famously, the countryside of Rangpur was set ablaze by the *dhing* of 1783, as the effects of the Company's fiscal crisis spread deep into the Bengali countryside. Each were only suppressed after expensive detachments of troops were sent.[38] Alongside the Company's disastrous financial situation itself, the near collapse of British authority in a number of regions was a force instilling a desire for reform amongst the East India Company's service.

III

But fiscal crises were not unusual in the eighteenth-century history of the British relationship with Bengal. Indeed, they seem to have resulted from forces hard-wired into the structure of the Company's relationship with Indian politics; the kind of political relationship necessary to maintain Britain's sovereign authority prevented the sort of stable financial relationship the Company in Britain required. The Company's finances had been stretched by famine, war and the breakdown of relations with landholders in the late 1760s and early 1770s, resulting in Lord North's Regulating Act and Warren Hastings' efforts to directly assert British sovereignty in Bengal in line with his perception of the province's old Mughal constitution. But the financial and political collapse of 1783 and 1784 seems to have had more longer-lasting effects: it brought the demise of the 'ancient constitution' as a motif in the British discussion of Bengal's polity. It also undermined attempts to involve Indian intermediaries and govern Bengal with knowledge acquired through direct experience of Indian political practice. Military-fiscal crisis is a necessary but not sufficient condition to explain the dramatic reshaping of British rule that occurred under Lord Cornwallis' rule; nor can the influence of British ideas explain the transformation alone. Alongside structural tensions occurring within the East India Company's financial and political relationship with Bengal, two conjunctural forces need to be added to the analysis, which this chapter examines in turn. First of all, it considers the dynamics of British politics, particularly the increasing significance of 'property' as a rallying cry in political life. Secondly, it examines the changing structure of the East India Company's service and the attitude British officers had towards life in India, an attitude many expressed through the changing use of a second term – despotism – to describe their experience in Bengal.

First of all, property and London politics: paradoxically it was an effort at constitutional restoration emerging from the political manoeuvres of London that led to the creation of a new regime in Bengal and produced a self-conscious rupture between Indian history and the colonial regime. After the period of unstable jockeying that followed George III's coronation in 1760, Frederick North became Prime Minister in 1770. In the late 1770s and especially in 1780, 'property in danger' became a rallying cry for the vociferous opponents of Lord North's government, the group of 'whigs' who surrounded the first Marquis of Rockingham and, after his death, Charles James Fox. The Rockinghamites had been critical of Hastings since his apparent support for the imprisonment of their ally, Lord Pigot, the Governor of Madras, in 1775.[39] But in 1781, a political alliance was struck between Lawrence Sullivan, Warren Hastings' main ally on the Court of Directors, and the North ministry. The alliance meant the Rockingham whigs increased the vehemence of their opposition to the Governor-General and turned the language they used to attack North upon Hastings.[40]

In both Britain and India, this whig opposition challenged the North regime's supposedly arbitrary and despotic attempt to undermine the independence of landed proprietors. Property was seen as an essential element of the English constitution that North's centralising administration was supposed to have undermined. In Britain, increases in the national debt, large state pensions and the possibility of a further augmentation of land tax were seen as causing a rapid 'decline in the trade, manufactures and land rents of the kingdom'. What Burke called '[t]he excessive and dangerous power of the Crown' had undermined the existence of English gentlemen in their propertied, local life-worlds. The same accusations were levelled against both the Company and Warren Hastings' supposedly tyrannical regime in Bengal. Burke and his colleagues feared the emergence of an authoritarian, 'despotic' and thoroughly unconstitutional regime in Bengal as well.[41]

The opposition won political power in the Fox-North coalition of 1783. During their short-lived administration, a conception of the independent, ancient and hereditary property rights of Bengal's landholders that Burke propagated became a crucial element of the ministry's India policy, forming the core of Charles James Fox's second India bill, for example. It was the debate surrounding Fox's first bill that brought the fall of the Fox-North coalition in the House of Lords and inaugurated William Pitt's regime.[42] The lesser-known second bill, '[f]or the better Government of the Territorial Possessions and Dependencies in India' consisted of a series of regulations for the conduct of British officials in the province. Most significantly, it instructed officers in India to uphold the property rights of Bengal's inhabitants, in particular to restore its 'ancient families' to the lands that Warren Hastings' supposed nefarious regime had appropriated. Restoring the rights of India's proprietors was supposed to resolve, once and for all, the crisis in the British governance of Bengal and return property to its central role in India's ancient constitution.

Once the coalition collapsed in 1784, William Pitt's new government achieved support by appropriating elements of a whig language attacking corruption and defending private property.[43] As part of its usage of a Foxite rhetoric of 'oeconomical reform', an emphasis on the restoration of the prescriptive rights of Bengal's landholders was taken up by Pitt's government, and incorporated into his own second India Bill, passed as legislation in 1784. The act contained a clause intended to establish the security of landed property in India. Noting that

> complaints have prevailed, that divers Rajahs, Zemindars, Polygars, Talookdars and other native landholders within the British territories in India, have been unjustly deprived of, or compelled to abandon and relinquish their respective lands, jurisdictions, rights and privileges,

the Act mandated the Court of Directors to inquire and redress 'all injuries and wrongs' according to 'the laws and customs of the country', and to establish 'according to the laws and constitution of India' permanent rules for the collection of revenue'.[44] Arriving in Calcutta soon after Hastings left in 1785, this piece of legislation played a crucial role in directing the concerns of officials such as Cornwallis and his main advisors John Shore and George Barlow in Bengal.

The notion of property that arrived in Bengal was an idea firmly rooted in the British conception of political action examined in the previous chapter, in which politics was seen as a series of contingent connections and interests. In formulating his approach to property in Bengal, Burke picked up the emphasis on the property rights of *zamindars* and other supposed proprietors that had been articulated by Philip Francis in the mid-1770s converting his colonial version of 'country' rhetoric into a more conservative idiom. In both Britain and Bengal, Burke thought property rested on nothing but the continuity of propertied experience: property rights existed simply because they had endured through time. Prescriptive connections were supposed to sustain the connections and interests which the political community relied upon, because they could not ground political action on anything more than the sense of trust and obligation which fellow subjects owed one another in a hierarchial but participatory polity. Property generated familiar forms of affection: for Burke and others, property was a word that was used to think about what it meant to be at home in or familiar with a particular society. In India, Burke argued, British rule had broken the affective connections that bound ruler and ruled; the point of Fox's India Bill was to restore those links.[45] Hastings' 'despotism' threatened the polity because it subjected everyone to the will of a single sovereign who had no affective relationship with his subjects. Just as, later on, he criticised the French revolution for undoing the bonds of civil society, so Burke thought Hastings' regime had undone the complex bonds and connections that linked the members of the polity to each other. It would be the duty of a reformed Company regime to restore these connections by reverting to the propertied constitution of the Indian polity.

IV

The India Act, with its insistence on the restoration of private property in India, arrived in Calcutta on the *Lizard* on 25 February 1785, three weeks after Warren Hastings sailed for London. A hundred copies were immediately printed in English, larger numbers of Bengali and Persian translations were copied throughout Bengal in the following weeks. It was this moment, not the promulgation of the permanent settlement in 1793, which constituted the high point for private property rights in late-eighteenth-century Bengal. As we have already seen, Hastings critically noted the 'high ideas' of Bengali property held in London before he knew the India Act had been passed.[46] As early as April 1785 Charles Stuart at the Council of Revenue began to develop plans to implement the 'intentions' of the British legislature 'in favour of the Native hereditary Zemindars and Landholders'.[47] By 1789, John Shore, an official generally in favour of the property rights of *zamindars,* could complain that '[t]he avowal of their hereditary rights, and the great regard paid to them by the British Government, has inspired the zemindars with an idea that these rights are indefeasible'. Shore was concerned that the propagation of this 'opinion' had allowed landholders to acquire 'a permanent influence over all their tenants' which had not proved beneficial. The British 'avowal' Shore spoke of occurred after Warren Hastings departed but before Cornwallis' ten-year settlement of 1791.[48]

Even if Burke had been a crucial figure in transmitting a British discourse on property to Bengal, when it moved from the debating halls of Westminster to the more anxious councils of Calcutta the emphasis on restoring existing property had profoundly unBurkean effects. Officials from Cornwallis onwards were willing to acknowledge the property rights of 'native landholders' only so far as they were consistent with the East India Company's ability to administer and collect revenue. The inability to coerce landowners to pay land tax was one factor driving the expansion both of indirect taxation and the national debt in eighteenth-century England.[49] By contrast, within Cornwallis' dispensation the land of *zamindars* could be sold for tax arrears, for example. The exigencies of sovereignty and the rights of property began to separate in the official mind. Rather than being a category rooted in Britons' affective experience, property became an abstract 'principle' that was distant from the affective attachments of Indian life. The mood of British politicians cannot explain the peculiar way in which Westminster's rhetoric of property penetrated the official mind in Calcutta.

Charles, Earl Cornwallis had been discussed as a possible successor to Warren Hastings since he returned, defeated, from fighting in the American War of Independence in January 1782 where he had commanded troops at the battle of Yorktown. Cornwallis had begun his political career as a Rockinghamite whig, voting against the Stamp Act, for example, but stayed 'in royal favour' throughout the tumultuous first 20 years of George III's reign. Throughout his career he managed to combine a reputation for whiggish politics with attachment to the King's party.[50] Cornwallis had been consulted on Fox's India Bills. Otherwise he retained his distance from Britain's Asian empire. But 'the proposal of going to India' had been 'pressed ... so strongly' in February 1786 that he felt 'obliged to say yes and to exchange a life of ease and content, to encounter all the plagues and miseries of command and public station', as he put it. In addition, the large salary was a considerable inducement.[51]

Cornwallis' arrival saw the emergence of a new attitude to British sovereignty in India. Arriving in Calcutta in September 1786, the new Commander-in-Chief's first concern was to disentangle the Company from alliances and financial obligations negotiated by officers stationed throughout India that threatened to bring the uneasy peace Hastings negotiated to an end.[52] These efforts failed to prevent war; Cornwallis spent much of his time in India directing war with Tipu Sultan's Mysore, defeating Tipu famously at Seringapatam in 1792. While Hastings' practice had involved constant movement within a complex system of dependent networks, Cornwallis saw sovereignty as something that needed to be exercised in compact and self-sufficient states, based on military force and explicit written treaties between absolute sovereignties. But this new approach cannot be attributed to the Governor-General's introduction of a stable set of ideas from Britain: in Europe after all, Cornwallis had participated in a diplomacy based on tacit agreements and fluctuating alliances, as when he was sent to negotiate with Frederick in Prussia, nine months before his departure for Bengal.[53]

The arrival and influence of Cornwallis itself does not explain the particular style of rule his regime produced in Bengal. The demand for permanent statements of principle that would fix land revenue and remove Indians from positions of responsibility occurred from Cornwallis' engagement with British East India Company officials. These were men who spoke Indian languages and had spent decades in the subcontinent, but nonetheless had begun to articulate a more estranged relationship with Indian society than some of their predecessors. That relationship was rooted in the changing practices of colonial life in India. But it was expressed in part through the use of a second key term in the lexicon of colonial governance: despotism.

Cornwallis relied in particular on two senior officers, John Shore and George Hilario Barlow. Shore first arrived in Bengal in 1769 at the age of 18, and soon developed knowledge about and responsibility for large swathes of revenue policy. He acted as the sole and lonely revenue collector for the province of Murshidabad whilst other officials stationed in that town were engaging in the fractious politics of court. In the early years of his career Shore seemed closer to the Francis faction in Calcutta. But having been promoted as a member of the Board of Revenue he came to be on 'exceeding good terms with the Governor', an event met by surprise with his circle of friends in Bengal.[54] Shore returned to Britain on the same ship as Warren Hastings in 1785. The offer of a large salary persuaded him to return with Cornwallis the following year, to provide a Governor-General with no knowledge of India with the benefit of his experience of collecting revenue. Shore drafted the documents that formed the basis of Cornwallis' revenue settlement. At the end of 1789 he left India again, though not for the last time. Seen as a solid administrator who would maintain peace and implement the 'new constitution' to the letter, he succeeded Cornwallis as Governor-General, ruling as Baron Teignmouth between 1793 and 1798.

Twelve years younger than Shore, Barlow was appointed acting Governor-General between 1805 and 1807; by then the position of Governor-General was the preserve of known British political figures, rather than unknown Company administrators, so Barlow ended his career as Governor of Madras rather than in Calcutta. Like Shore, Barlow was a man known both for his austerity and his command of Indian languages. Arriving in India in 1778, Barlow, aged 15, was first appointed as assistant to the Collector of Gaya in Bihar. There, Barlow imbibed a hands-on understanding of revenue collection from the Collector, Thomas Law, a man who figures in the discussion of the British governance of agrarian relations in Chapter 5.[55] From Law he also inherited a strong belief in the possibility of 'improvement' in the management of rural India, a background that made him a stronger supporter of innovation than Shore.[56] Barlow was appointed to the secretariat of the Supreme Council at the age of 25 in 1788, in which role he probably wrote many of the Governor-General's minutes, and certainly drafted the regulations that Cornwallis enacted in 1793. Barlow was manager of the Bengal government's business for the next 13 years, until being appointed a member of the Supreme Council himself in 1801. Writing to Cornwallis in 1796, he noted that his position as Secretary had allowed him to 'superintend and see that nothing goes wrong' in the implementation of the new 'Bengal system of internal Government' throughout India.[57]

Barlow's father described John Shore as George's 'most intimate friend' in 1786; his older colleague was said to have 'the highest opinion of [his] integrity and ability', remaining 'on the best of terms' throughout their time together in Bengal.[58] Despite mutual friendship and respect, the two articulated different perspectives on the governance of property in Bengal, representing two poles between which official opinion circulated and some-times very politely clashed. Neither doubted the need for the Company to introduce a new system of law courts and revenue collectorships; nor did they disagree over the importance of collecting revenue from *zamindars*, declared 'proprietors of the soil'. The biggest difference was that Shore wanted to fix the amount of revenue collected from each landholder for a decade, whilst Barlow, along with Cornwallis, argued that the revenue should be settled permanently. Once Cornwallis had departed, Shore was more circumspect about unrolling the 'Bengal system' across the rest of the subcontinent. To begin with at least, Barlow had his way in both cases: Cornwallis declared the ten-year settlement fixed for ever once he had received permission to do so from the ministry in London in May 1793. The 'new constitution' framed in Bengal was introduced to Benares and territory around Madras, although by 1800 its extension across British-ruled India had stopped in the face of opposition from Britons in London and other parts of India.

The difference between the two men concerned the different way each responded to what they saw as the impossibility of procuring useful knowl-edge about rural social relations in Bengal. Here, Shore was more reluctant to frame permanent measures on uncertain grounds. Two detailed minutes by him, the first written in April 1788 and the second in June 1789, provided the intellectual basis for Cornwallis' 'new constitution', in particular the decision to treat Bengal's revenue-payers or *zamindars* as 'proprietors of the soil' and establish a series of judicial institutions which would uphold their property rights. Both were marked by a tone of anxiety and doubt, whilst also articu-lating a sense of the urgent need for decisiveness. The second minute began with a complaint about the absence of useful knowledge amongst British officers, despite the accumulation of experience and information. The mem-bers composing 'the British government of India' fluctuated so rapidly that experience could not be 'reduced to practice' he argued. Shore suggested that opinions altered rapidly as 'the information of one year has been rendered dubious by the experience of another': but 'in all cases decision is neces-sary'. Officers had no time for reflection; Shore went on, 'true information is also procured with difficulty, because it is too often derived from mere practice, instead of being deduced from fixed principles'. The problem that Shore identified was not an absence of information, but the impossibility of usefully interpreting it. Confronted with documents they did not have the experience to understand, officials had begun to face information overload. The impossibility of developing useful meaning from a mass of seemingly unreliable data meant Shore found it difficult to know which way to proceed.

'The multiplication of records, which ought to be a great advantage', he said, 'is in fact an inconvenience of extensive magnitude'.

A different perspective was articulated in Barlow's correspondence with Lord Cornwallis after the Marquis had returned to London. Barlow believed the insufficiency of colonial information called for decisive and sweeping moves rather than administrative diffidence. This case was made in a number of letters he wrote to Cornwallis between 1794 and 1798 asking the former Governor-General to lobby the Court of Directors to ensure the 'Bengal system' was introduced throughout the rest of Company-administered India. Barlow suggested that the chaotic, crisis-ridden character of British rule before had prevented experience and 'local knowledge' from playing any role in framing Cornwallis' regime. The 'improved state of the country' that had emerged since 1793 depended not on experience, but 'the introduction of new principles' which seemingly had no foundation in the Company's direct experience of Bengali rural life: most importantly the principle of private property rights.

Barlow was clear that the permanent settlement had not introduced a novel rule of property. The British, he noted, 'do not make the Laws, which remain in all essential points the same, but only nominate the judges and officers of the courts to administer them'. It was, Barlow noted, 'a great blessing to the public to have their laws properly administered, although they may not correspond with our ideas, and altho' we may not think ourselves authorized to alter them'.[59] Property rights already existed, but it was pointless to try to exactly gauge their place in pre-colonial India's constitution; and property was always subjugated to the interests of the East India Company in Bengal. Barlow's arguments here relied on an abandonment of the kind of experience that Hastings and, to a certain extent Shore believed was necessary to govern with. Instead, they involved a dramatic transformation in the basis of sovereignty in Bengal, and a severance of relations with large classes of Indian intermediaries who had previously been essential 'native informants'. Alongside the 'principle' of private property the 'principle' of Britain's authority was paramount. 'The whole', Barlow wrote, 'hinges upon the absolute sovereign power, as lodged partially here [in Calcutta] partially at home'. Absolute power meant not merely the construction of a single unitary state, as Hastings imagined, but the exclusion of Indians from positions of responsibility. '[T]he worst consequences might in a short time ensue', Barlow argued, 'were the smallest latitude to be given to the people to enter into any discussions respective the propriety of any Regulation'. 'Altho' it is essential to the improvement of the country', he said 'that the Laws . . . should be as strictly and impartially enforced as under the most free constitution' an Indians' plea for 'justice' must appear as a discretionary favour.[60]

Although it consisted of the protection of supposed *existing* property rights, Barlow described the 1793 reforms as a dramatic innovation in both Indian history and the Company's practice. The 'new constitution' would, he arrogantly argued, 'confer upon the people a greater degree of happiness than they have yet enjoyed, or probably would experience under their own wretched systems, and at the same time preserve our dominions over them for a very long time'; it would do all this by severing Britons from any close political relationship with the Indians they ruled.[61]

Shore had suggested that it was possible to defer the point at which experience could provide a stable basis for the British governance of India to some distant point in the future, a point at which experiential 'practice' and general 'principles' would coincide. By contrast, both Barlow and Cornwallis wanted to abandon reference to experience altogether; both doubted whether more information would lead to more useful knowledge at any point in the future. In the minute where he made his final arguments in favour of the permanent settlement, probably written by Barlow, Cornwallis noted that district Collectors had already submitted detailed reports on local conditions. He went on: 'at what point, and from whom', Cornwallis asked, 'are we to procure more perfect materials'? '[N]o further lights are to be expected from' the Company's Collectors on the details of local affairs. Cornwallis suggested that Shore himself 'had furnished the most satisfactory arguments, to prove the incompetency of government officers to enter into this detail'. Rather than 'leave the revenue affairs of this country, in the singular state of confusion in which they are represented to be by Mr. Shore', it was better to act decisively, and create a permanent rupture in the constitutional politics of British India based on the limited knowledge they had now.[62]

Cornwallis and Barlow had their way. To begin with, Shore's June 1789 minute formed the basis of the 'decennial settlement' of December 1789. Throughout 1788 and 1789 district officers had been asked to furnish details of local land revenue arrangements. These details formed the basis of the figure that the Board of Revenue used to fix the *jama* (revenue demand) for a period of ten years. In 1790, soon after his exchange with Cornwallis about making the decennial permanent, Shore left Bengal. Between his departure and March 1793, the government in Bengal waited for approval from the Court of Directors in London to declare the settlement permanent. On 22 March a proclamation was issued which stated that '[t]he Marquis Cornwallis, Knight of the most noble order of the Garter, Governor-General in Council' had been empowered by the Company in London 'to declare that the jumma' which had been fixed in 1790 was 'fixed for ever'. This proclamation became Regulation I of 1793. It was issued on 1 May alongside the 48 other regulations that were drafted by George Barlow which put Cornwallis' new constitution in place.[63]

The innovative, rupturing force of the new order emerged in Bengal not London. Nowhere in the 1784 India Act or his instructions to Cornwallis did Pitt ask the Governor-General to introduce a new political order to the province. Pitt assumed that the security of British rule required the establishment of a regime that would maintain some form of constitutional connection with India's past. But by the time Cornwallis returned to Britain, the East India Company's lawyers in London had been forced to admit that the Governor-General's reforms in Bengal had no precedent in either British or Indian law.[64] The subsequent decision to retrospectively legitimate Cornwallis' regulations with the command of statute was an imperial parliament's attempt to legalise the anomaly of an unprecedented 'new constitution' being created within the empire of a deeply historicist state. Barlow believed this move was necessary 'to prevent any bad or uninformed administration attempting to subvert its fundamental principles'.[65] As Barlow made clear, civil servants in India did not believe they were introducing a dramatically new 'rule of property' to Bengal, creating institutions to govern existing land law instead. But unlike contemporaries in Britain, they did think they needed to sever the lines of continuity that connected present-day government to the Indian and British past in order to maintain Indian property and British rule in the subcontinent.

What Shore and Barlow both had in common was their use of the category of despotism to explain why the British needed to abandon reference to the continuities of Indian constitutional history in framing a new regime. In his June 1789 revenue minute, Shore used the term to explain why stable norms for the governance of property were so hard to find. As he put it,

> [a] property in the soil, must not be understood to convey the same rights in India, as in Britain; the difference is as great as between a free constitution and arbitrary power. Nor are we to expect under a despotic government fixed principles, or clear definitions of the rights of the subject; but the general practice of such a government, when in favour of its subjects, should be admitted as an acknowledgement of their rights.[66]

The 'practice of despotism' made information about stable 'principles of right' impossible to come by; it was only reference to the reality of 'practice' divorced from broader constitutional principles or arguments which allowed the Company to do what parliament had asked it to find and secure property in Bengal. For Shore then, the idea that India had been administered under a despotic regime provided justification for the difficulty of finding stable sources of information about rural society.

Barlow was far more emphatic, using the idea of India's habitual despotism to justify the creation of a system of government in which the power of Government to 'do what acts it may think proper, must be held up to the people as absolute and sacred'. 'This system of Government would certainly not be very agreeable to Englishmen', Barlow noted. But the exigencies of Britons' 'political existence as Sovereigns', and the nature of Bengal's previous government prevented any sustained engagement or communication with Indian opinion or arguments being possible.[67]

Throughout Europe despotism had been the most important category used by travellers to and commentators about South Asia since the beginning of the seventeenth century, signifying the existence of absolute power wielded in an arbitrary fashion. Particularly, a despotism was a regime where all property was the possession of the sovereign; any wealth which was possessed by private citizens could arbitrarily be taken from them. Historians debate whether 'Asiatic despotism' was an abstract and 'orientalist' stereotype produced as part of Europe's efforts to wield power over Asia, a concept rooted primarily within insular European political arguments or a more complex and 'compelling tool for interpreting information gathered about the Orient'.[68] Sanjay Subrahmanymam suggests that 'the framework was one in which Mughal rule itself was politically anathema, so constitutionally corrupt and despotic that it could only be compared with that of the Ottomans', the classic early modern European dystopic state.[69] A more complex view emerged briefly in the late 1760s, as critics of British rule such as William Bolts and Alexander Dow began to argue that some despotisms were worse than others; the Mughal regime was seen as relatively mild and tempered, to be contrasted with the tyranny introduced by Robert Clive and his successors to Bengal. Indian despotism was not 'so terrible in its nature as men born in free countries are apt to imagine', Dow argued.[70] These arguments prevailed in the late 1760s and early 1770s; they continued to play an important role in the discussion of India in London until the mid-1790s, where they were central to the theoretical defence of *zamindari* property in the British press, for example.[71] In Calcutta though the meliorating effect of writers like Bolts and Dow emasculated the critical force of the category within British thought; in the arguments over policy which occurred in Calcutta, if Mughal India's regime had upheld a regular and benign rule of law, there was no reason why it needed to be called 'despotism' at all. Whilst, as Robert Travers notes, the notion of despotism was 'a powerful weapon in the linguistic armoury of British officials' between 1757 and 1772, it was not central to the 'historic constitutionalism' of the decade afterwards.[72] The word despotism rarely occurred in the minutes Warren Hastings wrote as Governor-General; for example, it was entirely absent from the memoirs he wrote on the boat home to London.[73]

But despotism returned as a category of serious political analysis from the early 1780s, around the same time as the fiscal crisis described in the first part of this chapter. Its focus had shifted though, to become a way of thinking about the personality of Indians who interacted with the Company's absolutist regime, rather than a description of a functioning political constitution. For example, in a 1782 minute on the administration of justice in which John Shore focussed on the 'national character' of the 'Hindoos' suggesting that '[t]heir manners partake of the nature of the Government under which they have ever lived. As this has been arbitrary or despotic, the natives are timid and servile'; in a vicious panegyric Shore continued: they 'have little sense of Honour'; 'the Natives are wholly devoid of public virtue', liable to engage in 'low vicious arts', he said. At a moment of financial difficulty, Shore's arguments were articulated whilst he proposed unifying the collection of revenue with the administration of justice, a scheme he believed would save money and introduce greater efficiency. In words that were later echoed by Barlow and many other officials, Shore suggested that such a project would be 'repulsive' to Englishmen, used to the separation between judicial and executive power, Shore said. But '[p]eople long accustomed to a despotic authority should only look to one master', he argued.[74]

Here, as in the 1789 revenue minute, the term 'despotism' offered a conceptual tool with which British officials could explain their failure to develop a stable and comprehensive relationship with the population they governed. In contrast to the way Bolts, Dow and Boughton-Rouse used the term, in this context a despotic regime was not seen properly as a 'state' at all. Here, the general and unrigorous way in which the word was used in British political inventive had seeped into colonial life. When Britons debated places other than India, the term referred to a state ruled as merely a collection of isolated individuals incapable of acting in any collective fashion at all, a place where the bonds of political and social connection had completely come undone. Absolute rule did not consolidate the authority of the sovereign; it led to 'the death of states', as the radical John Cartwright put it, in words which a more conservative figure Edmund Burke would have concurred with. It '[wa]s not a form of government, but a subversion of all government'.[75] For most Britons, just as for Shore, Barlow and others in 1780s Bengal, the word 'despotism' simply conjured up an image of a society so disorganised it was almost impossible to think about how it was able to exist at all.

Here, 'despotism' was a term used to articulate the distance officials felt between their governance and South Asian society. The term marked Britons' aloof orientation to the Indian population they governed, expressing a set of private moods and anxieties as well as public arguments; there is a very personal tone of unease and intellectual insecurity in Shore's later revenue writings, which reflected early opinions he developed about Indian society. Writing to his mother from Murshidabad in 1772, Shore noted 'the arbitrary authority of their own country Government', finding it strange that Indians 'have not that opinion that every Englishman glories in, and encourages such enthusiasm, of the essentiality of liberty to happiness'.[76] A lack of sympathy with the people he lived amongst (including the small number of other British officials he worked with) made his situation 'irksome', he said. In his first years in Bengal Shore spent most of his free time secluded away with his Indian language teacher and translator (*munshi*) learning Persian and Bengali. Lonely, textual 'Oriental studies' occupied him instead of interaction with the local population more generally.

V

For Shore and others, the category of despotism overlapped with the changing ways in which officials practically experienced their careers and everyday lives. From the early 1770s, the East India Company's British servants began to take greater interest in the detail of revenue collection and law. As a result, very young officials began to spend more time outside Calcutta in settlements where they were accompanied by a small number of Europeans, often before they had good command of Indian languages; in these contexts they began to encounter Indians primarily as criminals, litigants or revenue payers – not as political actors and statesmen. In 1770, the 19-year-old John Shore was solely responsible for adjudicating property disputes and managing the fiscal jurisdiction of the district of Murshidabad. A decade later, George Barlow began his administrative career at the age of 16 stationed in the small district capital of Gaya in Bihar, accompanied by no Englishman other than Thomas Law. The dispersal of young Company officials and the changing nature of their official role made their lives seem lonely and isolated, in need of categories such as despotism to explain their anxious relationship with the world outside. These officials went on to provide the core of Lord Cornwallis' regime in the late 1780s and early 1790s.

A mood of anxious detachment dominated the way officials privately discussed their lives. Writing to his mother again, Shore described his 'despair' at life in Murshidabad '[T]hought succeeds to thought', he noted in a letter written during the 1770s as his mind searched in vain for concrete objects of attachment. Shore only found solace in the idea of an abstract God who could provide a stable point of reference and affection in an uncertain world; certainly, conversations with Indians provided no basis for stable thought. On its own terms, the Indian world he inhabited made no sense, but '[u]pon this system, all is consistent and reconcilable, even to our imperfect understandings'. The abandonment of attempts to 'experience' Indian society often resulted in such a turn inwards, towards abstract forms of reflection. Abstract thought involved a leap of faith, sometimes towards an abstract God, as officials tried to create a more enduring, self-sufficient intellectual world based on something other than their practical encounter with the world. Shore and his contemporary Charles Grant were fervent evangelicals, both men becoming more devout as a result of long periods stationed in lonely district capitals. Guha's description of officials feeling anxious about 'the immensity of things in a world whose limits are not known' accurately describes the mood which Shore and his colleagues felt.[77]

The type of anxiety that Shore expressed was consistently articulated by officials in India from the 1780s until well into the nineteenth century and in many ways much further beyond. In his *Observations of the State of Society Amongst the Asiatic Subjects of Great British* Grant was a vociferous critic of the way 'Mahomedan despotism' was supposed to have created a people who were 'void of public spirit, and honour, attachment; and in their society base dishonest, and faithless'; similarly the 'ancient Hindoo government which preceded it was seen as replete with 'practices of oppression, corruption' and 'immorality' which made the people 'base and miserable'.[78] This description of Indian despotism can be linked to the way Grant described himself living in 'a world full of disorder [where] our passions deceive us by expecting too much' in the 1780s. His panegyric against Indian society was a response again to the highly anxious relationship he had with his Indian environment.[79]

Twenty years later, Edward Strachey wrote about his own inability to discipline his mind onto stable objects of understanding in India. Once stable 'thoughts flag', he said, 'we feel our real state, vacancy comes and miserable tedium and disgust'. In this enervated state of mind, Strachey's sense of anxious detachment reflected his inability to engross himself in the complexity of everyday life.[80] He found it difficult to distinguish between the different cases that came before his court, for example. '[T]here are few extraordinary occurrences. One day is very like another', he wrote in a melancholy tone. In 1818, Courtney Smith expressed a similar sentiment when he described himself as 'a melancholy individual . . . [a] man who seems to have lost any capacity he may have once possessed. I have sunk into a complete apathy with regard to everything'. As Chapter 5 will show, Smith was one of the few officials who defended the role of 'local experience' instead of abstract thought in his official life. Even so, his positive discussion of Indian social practice in court occurred alongside a private attitude in which Smith found it difficult to find stable objects of affection and understanding whilst contemplating his life as a whole in the subcontinent.[81]

This anxious mood seems to have been the product of a range of contingent forces that are hard to disentangle from one another. The changing dynamics of the Company governance, financial instability, the availability of concepts such as despotism to denigrate South Asian society: all operated to produce the aloof orientation to South Asian life discussed in this chapter. In analysing this process it is impossible to distinguish cause from effect with much rigour. But as well as those already listed, one force seems to have had a constant distancing effect: the place of 'home' in the Company officers' cultural imagination. Increasingly throughout the 1760s and 1770s, experience of India offered a way for high status but relatively low income members of the gentry to earn enough money to return home to live a life of rural leisure and local civic involvement in the English countryside. By the 1780s the pattern of official life had been well established. Officers rarely went to India with a sense of adventure or opportunity, more likely resigning themselves to a tedious and uncomfortable 20 years in the Indian countryside, earning money and doing their duty before retirement, in their forties, back home. The Calcutta judge William Jones was one of the few men stationed in India who saw their stay in vocational terms, in his case to develop his knowledge of 'Asiatic' learning. But in his letters home, even Jones discussed his plans to retire to rural England. Jones' desire to attain such a lifestyle was one of his reasons for being in India.[82]

The country estate in particular had a significant place in the thoughts of Britons in Bengal. Robert Clive had his Claremont; Richard Barwell had Stanstead. Warren Hastings spent the last years of his life ensconced in bucolic retirement on his Daylesford estate.[83] Macaulay suggested that '[w]hen, under a tropical sun, he ruled fifty millions of Asiatics, his hopes, amidst all the cares of war, finance, and legislation, still pointed to Daylesford'.[84] Most officials brought back less money than Clive, Barwell or Hastings. Few were as successful at turning their 'homely' rural fantasies into reality. But returning to Britain was the end point around which the Company servant's career was organised, more so when the length of the stay in India was lengthened by the Company's financial crisis, and more years were needed to accumulate an 'independence'. Home was conceived as something that lay in the future and a long way away. Sometimes life in the Indian countryside was arranged to make it seem closer to hand, as neo-classical villas were constructed and then depicted in paintings sent home.

Figure 3.1   The Judge's House at Dinajpur, watercolour, *c.*1790–1800, BL Add.Or. 3199. Reproduced with kind permission of the British Library.

Indian figures were usually entirely removed from such scenes. In this frame of mind it was very difficult for British officials to settle emotionally amongst the population of Bengal. The sense of estrangement from Indian society may have been further exacerbated by the circulation of familiar, British goods and correspondence which oriented officials to times and places outside their immediate Indian situation. George Barlow's time in Gaya was made more comfortable by the supply of 'necessaries' sent by his father which diminished when he moved to Calcutta.[85]

Of course, officials conversed with Indian 'informants' about a variety of subjects, in many cases developing forms of familiarity and friendship which seem similar to the forms of obligation and connection that dominated eighteenth-century British life. Officials described the way they were tied to their Indian informants with the familiar eighteenth-century British language of patronage and duty. Out of duty to his Persian teacher, John Shore became heavily involved with a series of disputes between children of his *munshi* when the latter died. Shore corresponded with a number of British officials, including the Calcutta Supreme Court judge William Jones about their obligation towards a number of Indian judicial officers.[86] For many officials, Anglo-Indian networks of patronage and dependence included sexual relationships, and spanned the distance that seemed to separate Britain from Bengal. Shore's friend and correspondent George Ducarel married an Indian noblewoman and returned home with her and their children. After he returned home, the friends he left behind in Bengal felt themselves obliged to support her brothers in Bengal. James Collie, a friend of Shore and Ducarel's stationed in Burdwan during the late 1780s, became heavily involved in an attempt to settle a dispute between Ducarel's brothers-in-law and the Company's commercial agents.[87]

In the letter in which he discussed the fate of Ducarel's Indian in-laws in Burdwan, Collie also articulated his sense of disconnection from the country he inhabited. Since his children had returned to England, he felt 'gloomy', finding few forms of stable affection other than in his relationship with a distant God, he said. Whilst Collie solipsistically contemplated his situation in India, the eighteenth-century forms of sentimental connection that linked him to Ducarel's wife's family in Burdwan didn't make him feel at home, it seems. Moments of intimacy didn't allow officials in Bengal in the 1780s and 1790s to believe they could trust their engagement with Indian informants and intermediaries in their political administration of the province. Where they occurred, these familiar forms of connection existed alongside a far more distant, aloof orientation to Indian society, a frame of mind often articulated with a mood of loneliness and anxiety in which Indian practice could easily be objectified.

VI

The measures that created Lord Cornwallis' new 'Bengal system of government' in 1793 emerged as an attempt to stabilise the fortunes of the East India Company's province of Bengal shortly after a series of financial and military crises. They did so by attempting to re-establish a rule of property which politicians in London and officials in Bengal believed had been disturbed by the revolutions of Indian politics and actions of the Company's state. Officials' were concerned with the relationship between the two terms this chapter has focussed on: how to make the existence of 'property' compatible with the India's supposed 'despotic' regime. Commentators and polemicists writing at a distance from the everyday governance of Bengal reconciled these seemingly incompatible terms by suggesting that Mughal despotism was peculiar in allowing regular laws and customs to emerge, as William Bolts and Alexander Dow had done. Once he returned to Britain Charles Boughton-Rouse suggested in 1791, 'the despotism of India has always been mild in its exercise under the princes of the race of Timur'. 'The usages', he went on, 'have been preserved continually by hereditary expounders called Canoongoes, who were not liable to removal, and had their offices and deputies in every part of the country'.[88] In this account, the existence of absolute sovereignty in theory was compatible with the creation of a regular regime that placed limits on potentially arbitrary power in practice. But the anxious and estranged relationship British officials stationed in Bengal had with Indian society during the 1780s and early 1790s seemed to make it far harder to disentangle the influence of 'property' and 'despotism' from each other in their understanding of India's past. Unable to translate any communication they had with Indians into official discourse, despotism seemed to offer a term that explained why no stable source of information about property was available. Parliament had insisted that the British uphold property rights: but governance only seemed possible if a decision was made to uphold private property rights without any reference to historical precedent at all. This rejection of historical experience created a very strange relationship between the East India Company's administration of Bengal and the way its agents experienced the passage of time.

The language used to frame the 1793 constitution signified a break in the style of Britain's political engagement with Bengal. Most immediately it marked the removal of senior Indian officers from the Company's administrative hierarchy, as officials were increasingly uncomfortable about engaging with Indian forms of political conduct. Indian officials had provided important elements of information, historical legitimacy and tactical support within the political battles that occurred in the Company's councils during the 1770s and early 1780s. But the reforms of the 1790s replaced this everyday sense of tactical engagement with its own more abstract logic, breaking the link between British officials and their senior Indian accomplices in the process. In the late 1780s, senior Indian officials who were crucial to Hastings' administration were removed from office. Men such as Hastings' chief revenue official Ganga Govinda Sinha vainly petitioned the Company for continued employment. But like Hastings himself they were forced to retire to their country estates.[89] One particularly significant post, the *qanungu* (or Canoongoe, as officials spelt it) was abolished in 1791, the same year Boughton-Rouse published a work celebrating that Mughal officer's role.

In high Mughal political theory the *qanungu* (in Persian, literally the 'speaker of regulations') was the central government's representative in local land revenue administration. The central *qanungu* and his district deputies had been both record-keepers and an important source of authority in revenue disputes.[90] This official was seen as vital component in the Mughal 'ancient constitution' which Warren Hastings attempted to uphold in the 1770s. But after a debate in the Governor-General's Council, the post was abolished. By the early 1790s officials had begun to doubt how effective the *qanungu* was as a source of information about rural social relations.[91]

The abolition of the *qanungu* shows how Cornwallis' 'new constitution' attempted to break the link with Bengal's real institutional history and the complex social networks of each locality. In doing so it marked the strange, anxious yet resolute relationship the regime created with local society. The minutes that British officers wrote on the subject were riven with an important contradiction. On the one hand, *qanungus* were seen as incapable of gathering effective information because they had become 'corrupt' and 'degenerate', and thus were a threat to the stability of the Company's information order. Britons observed the very real processes of political commodification and decentralisation that occurred since at least the 1730s in Bengal, as cash became more important and landholders tried to bring more aspects of the local 'state' under their control. But the way they encountered these changes were rooted in British anxieties about their ability to engage with Indian sources of information in any context, in particular those whose existence was embedded in the historical continuities of local society. The British feared the *qanungu* had recently become the voice of local interests and connections. According to this view, if these officers hadn't been pulled into the corrupt network of forces that Company officers identified with the province's apparent decline, they might have performed a useful role. Yet they made a second argument: Cornwallis suggested that the role of local information-gatherer was unnecessary in theory as well as practice, because agrarian relations were to be governed either by 'engagements' which 'had been reduced to writing', or by the 'customs and usages' which could be gathered by talking with local inhabitants. 'Suits between individuals' would 'be decided by the Engagements subsisting between the parties', Cornwallis suggested, not by Indian officials who claimed to have 'experience' of local agrarian relations. 'If a local custom is to be ascertained, better evidence regarding it will always be obtainable from inhabitants of the District of a respectable character, than could be procured from the Mofussil Canoongoes'.[92]

To argue that the office of *qanungu* was superfluous, the Governor-General projected an abstract fantasy of the way rural social relations were supposed to work onto the practice of agrarian society. Above all, that fantasy concerned the extent to which it was possible to separate propertied practice from the process of government, and place the agency of Indians firmly in the former, purely social or economic sphere. In both eighteenth-century Britain and pre-colonial Bengal property was inseparable from the workings of the polity. The subjective 'influence' of property over the actions of government made it impossible for politicians in each case to think they were ruling an objective sphere of 'economic' conduct, or distinguish between what Hegel called civil society and the realm of governance. In both countries an administrative office could be held as a form of heritable property right; until the early nineteenth-century 'economics' and 'politics' were essentially intertwined.[93]

But in Bengal from the mid-1780s, British officials argued that the principles which underpinned the actions of property-holders were very different from those that ruled politics or governance. Avarice was no bad thing in social life. Cornwallis's 1793 judicial minute noted that '[a] spirit of industry has been implanted in man, that in seeking his own good he may contribute to the public prosperity'.[94] The government's role was to ensure that the landholders had an incentive for their industry and investment, by securing their property rights. If property was secured by a regime that acted for the public good rather than the self-interest of its members, the freedom of landholders to augment their prosperity would benefit both the country and, ultimately, the Company. Nonetheless, this selfish spirit needed to be excised from the domain of political conduct.

Behind this simple, abstract train of thought, historians sometimes recognise the 'influence' of Scottish enlightenment philosophy, especially the political economy of Adam Smith. In a similar sounding passage, Smith famously noted that

> the natural effort of every individual to better his condition, when suffered to exert itself with freedom and security, is so powerful a principle, that it alone, and without any assistance, is not only capable of carrying on the society to wealth and prosperity, but of surmounting a hundred impertinent obstructions with which the folly of human laws too often incumbers its operations.[95]

Like officials in Bengal, Smith believed that the security of property was capable of unleashing the benevolent consequences of the natural human passion to accumulate. Occasional instances of biographical coincidence seem to confirm the connection. Alexander Ross, Cornwallis' private secretary, was a friend of Smith's, even though John Shore and then G.H. Barlow had a far more significant role in drafting minutes and regulations.[96]

But in fact, the contrast between the writings of the Scottish philosopher and the literature produced by officials in Bengal nicely illustrates the differences between metropolitan British and colonial thought. Although they used similar words, the point being made in each case was very different. In the anxious, detached mood they used to discuss policy, Cornwallis and his colleagues believed that experience or intellectual engagement with Indians could not be used to frame British rule. Reason alone was a sufficient guide to frame new institutions, although out in the countryside reason needed to be supplemented by real evidence of actual property rights. By contrast, Adam Smith was no believer in the superior powers of rational cognition.[97] Smith's language was circumspect and reticent, possessed with what Eric Stokes called a sense of 'the warmth of common life' instead of the cold, dessicated rhetoric of colonial thought.[98] Officials in Bengal usually used words like 'system' in a positive or neutral sense when referring to their administrative reforms, describing them with phrases such as 'the Bengal system of internal government'.[99] Smith bitterly condemned all 'systematical' forms of abstract projection, noting how easy it was for the 'the man of system...to be very wise in his own conceit' at one point in his *Theory of Moral Sentiments*.[100] Comments of this kind might easily have been levelled at the kind of innovatory thought that underpinned Cornwallis' reforms; after all both Cornwallis and Barlow believed the 'Bengal system' could be imposed on Benares and Madras with no allowance for different experience or local circumstances.

The important contrast in the style between Enlightenment philosophers of experience such as Smith and colonial officers in India consisted in part in a different set of attitudes to the relationship between political action and time. The previous chapter showed how Smith and his friend David Hume believed it was the contingent flow of sensory experience in the past that created the political actors' sense of who they were and how they could act in the future.[101] But in the subcontinent, from the 1780s at least, officials felt they were severed from the possibility of having this kind of historical experience of Indian society. As a result, they produced a very different way of perceiving the relationship between political and action and time, creating a set of expectations rooted not in an experience of historical continuity, but upon a detached, abstract frame of thought. This strange style of thought emerged as an attempt to resolve the imperial crises of the 1780s; but it prevented British officials from developing the kind of familiar relationship with India that might have produced a less abstract and more viable relationship between the Company's state and local society. As Reinhart Koselleck suggests '[i]t is in the nature of crises that problems crying out for solutions go unresolved'.[102]

Cornwallis' 'new constitution' certainly did not resolve the crisis from a financial point of view. Long after the permanent settlement was promulgated, the collection of revenue remained uncertain, and deficits from landholders continued to accumulate. Nonetheless, from the late 1780s, the Company had begun to tap into new forms of borrowing that allowed it to ride out short-term fluctuations in its income in a way it had not been able to before. In the immediate aftermath of Cornwallis' reforms the Company and its merchants borrowed too much, anticipating an immediate improvement of Bengal's property. But as they became 'more rational in their speculations', as John Shore put it, mercantile credit underpinned the Company's financial survival, linking the Company's expanding trade with China with British agency-houses in Calcutta and Indian sources of capital.[103] For at least the first 20 years after 1793, the security of Britain's empire in Bengal depended on the East India Company's ability to defer its losses through the expansion of these global credit Networks. Yet this was an uncertain basis to sustain a regime. Jeremiads continually feared the financial collapse of the Company, which nearly occurred with the financial crisis that began with the Anglo-Burmese War of 1824–1826 and subsequent collapse of the agency house system, events which contributed to a second set of arguments about both retrenchment and reform under Governor-General Bentinck (1828–1835).[104] Cornwallis' constitution created an image of security that allowed the Company to survive by being more closely linked into British and Anglo-Asian commercial and financial networks. But to contemporaries, threats to the contingent reality of British rule in the subcontinent seemed merely to have been precariously deferred.

Officials stationed in rural Bengal found it difficult to connect the emphatic, abstract language emanating from the courts and council of Calcutta with the contingent world of Indian practice they met in district revenue offices and courts. Colonial expectations occurred at an enormous distance from the everyday experience of governance. Officers inhabited two different worlds, with different and discordant temporalities, one based on the sense of duty they had to the conceptions and instructions transmitted from Calcutta, the other based around the everyday routine of the *kachchari* or court, with its complex and anxious encounter with Indian interlocutors. The practice of colonial rule began to be rooted in the gap between what Reinhardt Koselleck calls 'the space of experience' and 'the horizon of expectation'.[105]

The chasm that separated the abstractly expectant language of policy-making and the life of colonial experience in the districts made Bengal almost ungovernable after 1793, or so it seemed to many British officials stationed in rural Bengal. The next two chapters examine that chasm in practice. They show how officials attempted to construct practical mechanisms to connect expectation and experience by excising the vicissitudes of political contingency and creating new objective categories for governing Indian life.

4
Colonial Indecision and the Origins of the Hindu Joint Family

Writing to a friend in London in 1773, the young John Shore articulated his confident ability to decide property disputes in Bengal. 'Though you will judge this more properly the province of an able lawyer', the 22 year-old suggested,

> a tolerable knowledge of the language, and the being somewhat conversant with the religious and judicial customs of the natives (which are never infringed in our decisions) are sufficient qualifications for exercising the business.[1]

At the time British officials had produced no written texts about Indian law, nor had the Company's regulations been transcribed in an orderly form. As the last chapter showed, even in the early 1770s Shore articulated his anxious and unhomely relationship with India in letters home. But these sentiments don't seem to have affected his attitude towards his public responsibilities. The imperial crises of the early 1780s made the tone of Shore's later discussion of his official duties anxious as well. But in 1773 he wasn't concerned about administering justice without a body of textual rules.

For lawyers and litigants throughout the eighteenth-century Anglophone world, the law was a set of historical institutions and subjectively learnt practices not a series of rules. It was this essentially practical conception of law that Shore articulated in his reference to 'religious and judicial customs' in the passage above. For him, just like English lawyers, practicing law was not a question of applying codified laws or doctrines to a particular situation. Instead, 'going to court' involved the litigant's submission to a flexible process of adjudication. In Britain and North America a complex web of legal institutions incorporated experience and learnt habit into a 'procedural system for dispute resolution' that could not be defined in abstract terms.[2] This emphasis on the practical, unwritten character of law was not without its critics. Jeremy Bentham advocated the codification of law from the 1770s, arguing that where there were no written rules, there was no law. Bentham's follower James Mill criticised the 'deplorable condition' of law in both England and British-ruled India, where he thought that 'courts were originally set up without law'.[3] But in Britain these were marginal arguments, taken seriously by no more than a narrow sect of 'utilitarians'. Until the middle of the nineteenth century, few in Britain saw the absence of codified rules as a cause for anxiety.

In Bengal from the 1790s a different attitude to law began to prevail. In the 20 years or so that followed the permanent settlement of 1793, British officials perceived the task of governing rural Bengal as an uncertain enterprise. Their anxious, estranged orientation to Indian social practice rendered them incapable of connecting the facts they were presented with to the norms they needed to produce in order to adjudicate a dispute. Judges and revenue officers found it impossible to translate the stories that Indians told them into categories that allowed them to make decisions and rule. The almost instinctive approach to law Shore articulated in the 1770s treated the 'religious and judicial customs of the natives' as 'ready-to-hand' categories that could be wielded in court without analysis or abstract thought. Such an approach didn't last long, as John Shore's successors became anxious about the absence of stable legal doctrines and rules in the subcontinent.

In the making of Cornwallis' new constitution in the early 1790s, vague and abstract terms such as property and custom had been used in an effort to frame a new, stable relationship between the East India Company and Indian society. Up to a point, these words made sense in the councils of Calcutta. But a few days ride by boat or *palaki* from the colonial capital, in the district headquarters of rural Bengal or countryside itself, these terms could not be mapped onto the Indian practices that local officials observed from their offices. The language enunciated from Calcutta in the early 1790s was not able to determine who should inherit property, or control the labour that tilled the soil. As a result, in the early nineteenth century this vague vocabulary began to be replaced by an attempt to trace the activity of Indian subjects onto fixed written rules in a far more technical way. Colonial governance objectified spheres of activity such as property, domesticity and religion as areas of practice that were supposed to have their own autonomous, knowable regularities. Indian practice was treated as if it belonged to a sphere of social activity whose rules and norms were autonomous from the state, and not vulnerable to the fluctuating political contingencies of the present day. In some cases they were invented by the colonial regime. Others were supposed to have existed before the British presence in some cases being traced back to India's purported ancient past. The paradox, of course, was that these new forms of ancient indigenous law relied on the agency of colonial institutions for their authenticity and authority.

This chapter considers this process of rule-making, codification and political objectification with respect to the property law of Hindus, examining in particular the law which ruled the inheritance of Hindu individuals and families from one generation to the next. Compared to other legal subjects Hindu property law provided the basis for the most significant anxieties and arguments about colonial jurisprudence between 1780 and 1835; the first Indian Law Commission appointed in 1834 had as its first object the codification of Hindu property. The governance of property was central to colonial rule. And even though the majority of the population of Bengal were Muslim, the Muslim population were severely marginalised in the process of governance and Hindus regarded as the 'natives' who owned most of the land, a view echoed in Calcutta's burgeoning Hindu-Indian press. So, examining the British governance of Hindu property law allows one to trace both the changing forms of knowledge officials used in the course of administration alongside the changing way they defined and governed communities in Bengal.

Before British rule, India had a complex range of different juridical traditions, including both a number of strands of moral and legal thought articulated at predominantly Hindu centres of learning in Sanskrit, and a series of Persian- and Arabic-based schools of Muslim law. None of these were predominantly interested in the law and ethics of family life. They also concerned themselves with the law and ethics of commercial disputes and landholding, as British officers initially recognised. These latter spheres became the subject of increasingly general forms of regulation and legislation by the Company throughout the nineteenth century. The realm which Hindu and Muslim law was supposed to govern became ever more circumscribed. The process of governance allowed a sphere of family-oriented religious 'personal law' to emerge, as British officers began to presume that it was only with respect to family-oriented transactions (marriage, adoption and inheritance) that religious law applied.[4] Normatively at least, that law reflected a textual tradition of jurisprudence that continued unaltered since it had been promulgated by ancient legislators. For much of the colonial period many (but not all) British officials assumed that Hindu and Muslim jurisprudence were separate and unitary bodies of positive, textual law that applied uniformly to the domestic lives and property of Hindus and Muslims.

This chapter illustrates the way one instance of colonial India's legal positivism, the new rules which governed Hindu families, emerged within a complex interactive process. It begins by looking at British ideas about adjudicating property disputes in the 1790s. At that point in time, officials tried to govern with the heterogeneities of local custom and practice; they would have seen an attempt to construct Bengal-wide general rules or norms as a strange and unwarranted enterprise. But over two or three decades, the vicissitudes of colonial legal practice produced a new conception of law as a series of abstract, general statements, rooted in ancient Indian jurisprudence or colonial legislation. In particular, these theories of jurisprudence emerged as part of the effort to remove the uncertainties that officials experienced whilst administering other ways of viewing Indian law.

The estranged relationship officials had with Indian social existence prevented them from engaging effectively with the plural circumstances of South Asian propertied life, and allowed a judicial culture to emerge in which general principles mattered more than specific instances of practice instead. From the wreckage of earlier British ways of understanding the relationship between law, society and the state, a conservative, positivist and 'neo-traditional' form of Hindu law emerged. One consequence was the increasingly pervasive role of new doctrines and rules supposed to define the essential characteristics of the Hindu family in all times throughout the whole of Bengal. In particular, these began to define the Hindu family as a stable corporate body headed by a male family member, but which possessed and transmitted family from generation to generation collectively. As a legal entity, the 'Hindu joint family' came into existence as a consequence of colonial indecision, and the British attempt to develop stable categories for understanding and governing property in Bengal.

I

From the first moment its officials attempted to adjudicate property disputes in the province, the East India Company's regime articulated a set of statements about the need to decide with existing, indigenous 'laws' or 'customs and usages'. In 1772, when British officers began to actually decide cases rather than merely supervise the Indian administration of Indian law, Warren Hastings issued a regulation that insisted that

> in all suits regarding inheritance, marriage and caste, other religious usages and institutions, the laws of the Koran with respect to the *Mahomedans*, and those of the Shasters with respect to the *Gentoos* [Hindus], shall be inviolably adhered to.[5]

The judicial regulation that Hastings issued on 11 April 1780 repeated this statement, insisting that Indian judicial officers – Hindu *pandits* and Muslim *qazis* – needed to be consulted on those listed subjects. The word 'succession' was added to the list of subjects to be determined in this way in 1781. The regulations that underpinned Cornwallis' 'new constitution' repeated the same statement. On the face of it, words of this kind seem to insist that courts referred to a canon of textual religious jurisprudence. In fact though, the situation was far more complex. When Hastings referred to 'Mahomedan' and 'Gentoo' law, he was discussing the procedures that courts should adopt in adjudicating a dispute not defining a particular textual canon of law. The *Code of Gentoo Law* that Nathaniel Brassey Halhed edited and Hastings published in 1776 was intended to prove that the Indian polity possessed a civilised set of judicial procedures resting on its own sophisticated political theology, and did not need the introduction of English law or English religion. After all, in eighteenth-century British political rhetoric, national attachment, juridical identity and religious denomination were often inseparable. Neither Hastings nor the officials surrounding him were attempting to define the substantive source of Indian law.[6]

Hastings' regulation was perfectly compatible with John Shore's relaxed view about the need to uphold native 'religious and judicial customs'. But by the late 1780s and early 1790s, vague statements about the need to uphold existing practices began to be replaced by a different concern about the status of Indian law. Officials began to be more darkly concerned with the potential for unwarranted legal 'innovation' in Bengal, and attempted to create more precise legal mechanisms for such innovation to be prevented. This concern developed in part as a result of the moral critique of the Company's rule which Burke and others articulated in London from the mid-1780s. Building on the arguments that Hastings and others had made about the need to ensure the continued existence of Indian forms of law, commentators in London and India nonetheless saw both British officials and Indian elites as a potential source of disruption to established patterns of property and law in the subcontinent. The Welsh lawyer, Oriental scholar and radical whig Sir William Jones arrived in September 1783 as judge of the Calcutta Supreme Court, and was instrumental in articulating this new vocabulary. Without representative institutions, Jones believed law courts in Bengal were the only bulwark against the arbitrary act of either British officers or Bengali elites.

Jones argued that if the existing laws of Indians were

> superseded by a new system of which they could have no knowledge, and which they must have considered as imposed on them by a spirit of rigor and intolerance

it would be 'a violation of which they would have thought the most grievous oppression'. Writing in 1788, Jones suggested that Bengal's population needed to be governed by

> those laws, which the parties themselves had ever considered as the rules of their conduct and engagements in civil life.[7]

Jones believed that those rules existed in the practice of particular places in Bengal, not in a definitive body of textual doctrine that might easily be translated and used by British judicial officials. The problem, however, was to discern what those rules were. Without knowledge or experience, British judges needed to rely on information from the Indian judicial officers they employed in court. But British officials had no faith in their ability to determine whether the opinion which a Hindu *pandit* or Muslim *qazi* articulated was valid or not. 'If we give judgment only from the opinions of the native lawyers and scholars, we can never be sure that we have not been deceived by them', Jones had suggested, especially 'in any cause in which they could have the remotest interest in deceiving the court'.[8]

Jones' scepticism about trusting Indian informants led him to commission a Sanskrit compilation of Hindu law on questions concerning inheritance and contract. After Jones died in 1794 the text was translated by Henry Colebrooke, a man known for his 'pursuit of severe and abstract studies'.[9] It was eventually printed as the *Digest of Hindu Law* in Calcutta in 1798 and then published in London three years later.[10] Unlike Halhed's *Code of Gentoo Law*, the *Digest* was intended as a work that would be of practical use in deciding disputes. To begin with, Jones had wanted to be explicit within the *Digest* about the difference between eastern India's two main juridical traditions, the *Gaudiya* school centred around the Bengali town of Nabadwip, and the *Mithila* tradition focussed on Tirhut in Northern Bihar. His intention had been to work with two *pandits*, one from each region, in compiling the *Digest*

[s]ince two provinces are immediately under this government, in each of which are many *customary* laws, it would be proper to employ one Pundit from Bengal and one from Behar.

Later colonial jurists argued that the difference between the laws of Bengal and Bihar occurred because each had different texts, the *Dayabhaga* and the *Mitaksara*, as the source of law. By contrast, Jones believed it was the customary practice of the population, not medieval texts, which provided the source of legal diversity.

These plans were abandoned when Jones realised that the prominent Indian jurist Jagannatha Tarkapancanana would be willing to work with him. Jagannatha was the brightest luminary on the Bengali juridical firmament, far too important a figure not to be involved in the project. However, the distinguished Bengali jurist's purposes were very different from Jones's. Whilst Jones wanted to emphasise the difference in customs that occurred in different places, Jagannatha intended to assimilate and unite two different Indian strands of ethico-juridical intepretation, perhaps wanting to end his long career by producing a final synthesis of hitherto separate strands of *dharmasastra* literature. Jagannatha's *Vivadabhangarnava*, the text that was translated as the *Digest*, reproduced excerpts from a range of Hindu *dharmasastra* texts, which the author then commented on. Jagannatha employed the practice of Bengali *nyaya* logic, with its complex style of analogous reasoning, to make the different opinions and injunctions contained in these various sources form a consistent guide to a just and ethical life. The logic that structures the text is Jagannatha's, not Jones'.[11]

The attitude that underpinned his commissioning of the *Digest* was partially indebted to Jones' approach to English jurisprudence though. Like other English lawyers, Jones believed it was dangerous to treat abstract texts as the source of all law. English jurisprudence (and in a different sense also Scottish law) was regarded as 'unwritten law' – *leges non scriptae*. Jones saw the English common law as a complex network of practices and remedies, maxims and principles that made sense in the detail of everyday judicial practice but could not be abstractly codified as a systematic set of rules. For Jones this emphasis on the importance of juridical procedure was rooted in a conception of law as the consensual practice of the inhabitants of a particular place, which were then articulated within judicial institutions that had had long experience of the society they ruled. From this point of view, any systematic attempt to define the rules of law in a textual form would rely on the whim of the legislator, not the practices which individuals 'had ever considered as the rules of their conduct and engagements in civil life', as Jones put it in his discussion of the *Digest*. Jones was critical of commentators who emphasised the absolute legislative power of the state. For example, he challenged William Blackstone's attempt to offer a systematic account of English law as an enterprise based on the *Commentaries*' emphasis on the power of the sovereign in making law. In a letter to his student, Lord Althorp, Jones noted with concern that Blackstone defines Law as: 'a rule prescribed by a superior power'. I define it, 'The Will of the whole community as far as it can be collected with convenience.'[12]

Here, the 'will of the whole community' did not consist in parliamentary statute. It consisted in the practices that subjects were supposed to share amongst themselves in their everyday propertied lives, and which were then reflected and defined in judicial process.

Texts, of course, had a role within this juridical philosophy. As Henry Maine later suggested 'there is no such thing as unwritten law in the world'.[13] Jones noted that

> although this inestimable law be called unwritten, ... the only evidence of it is in writing, preserved in the public records, judicial, official and parliamentary, and explained in works of acknowledged authority.[14]

For Jones and his colleagues, medieval and early modern English commentaries like Glanville, Bracton and Coke played a key role in eighteenth-century legal practice because they offered descriptions of the customs and maxims which had become law by 'long and immemorial usage' of the English people. They, together with the practice of the court, were better guides to the consensual will of the people than the often arbitrary wishes of parliament. Amongst the unpublished notes which survived his death, Jones left an outline of a projected 'Plan of Compilation of Ancient Treatises on the Laws of England' which would have begun with Glanville and ended, seven volumes later, with Fortescue's fifteenth-century *Laudibus Legum Anglie*.[15]

Some of the practices referred to in these texts had been abrogated by legislation, others were being whittled away by changing social habits, but many more were still in force, so it was useful to transcribe and reproduce them as resources for use in court. It was up to the flexible logic of the court to decide which was relevant in each particular case.

Thus although writing was important for legal practice, the texts Jones celebrated and produced were very different from the kinds of code that James Mill admired, or which later colonial officials produced. For Jones, like his successor and mentee H.T. Colebrooke, the law was not an abstract, aloof set of doctrines or principles that had been handed down over the generations, or articulated by the command of a legislator. Instead it was something that subjects (British or Indian), in the present day, were supposed to make and participate within themselves. Like works such as Bracton and Glanville, the *Digest of Hindu Law* was therefore supposed to offer a useful source of evidence for particular kinds of practice, but it was not a source or body of law itself.

This is clear if we look at some of the few places where a tension between Jones and Colebrooke's approach and Jagannatha's own text occurred. Wanting to produce a great ethico-legal synthesis, Jagannatha himself did not distinguish between the 'law' which governed different regions of Eastern India within the work. But Jones and Colebrooke (it is impossible to tell who inserted which note) added a series of footnotes that attempted to divide and separate what Jagannatha had tried to bring together. In the main body of the text, Jagannatha had argued that adoption should be ruled by a single set of categories and practices across the whole of Eastern India. In doing so, he tried to assimilate the *krtrima* practice that predominated in the scholastic tradition centred on Tirhut in Bihar with the *dattaka* form of adoption emphasised at Nabadwip in Bengal into a single order. Colebrooke added a footnote to the chapter on 'the son made by adoption' which emphasised the difference between the 'practice of adopting sons' in the two provinces of Bihar and Bengal, further distinguishing the mode of adoption in the province of Orissa and the 'practice' with which *Goswamis* and other celibate Hindu devotees created their adopted progeny.[16] Jagannatha's assimilative sensibilities were mapped by Colebrooke onto differences of customary practice in a series of scattered annotations elsewhere in the text.

Within the eighteenth-century British juridical sensibility which the *Digest* reflected, the 'law' consisted of a process which determined the form of conduct that the litigants were supposed to practice amongst themselves. In Britain, the best example of this was Lord Mansfield's use of special juries in complex commercial cases. Mansfield believed that new commercial techniques had emerged which the law needed to take account of. As a result, he asked juries of merchants who had knowledge of them to decide each case, rather than insisting that the parliament create abstract and clumsy legislation.[17] Colebrooke's discussion of the adoption practices of *Goswami* devotees, and Hindus in Orissa reflected a similar emphasis on the existence of customary differences in legal practice amongst different social groups. As will be discussed later, the Company's courts frequently tried to discern local customary differences even where they had not been noticed by Colebrooke or Jones.

However, the paradox was that a British emphasis on the importance of custom and the complex particularity of Indian practice occurred at precisely the point at which Company officials began to become more and more anxious about their own practical relationship with Indian society. In part of course, the *Digest* was produced as a consequence of this anxiety. The text was a way of diminishing Indian participation within the judicial process, even though it was supposed to represent law that had been created by the active participation of Indian subjects in a sphere of customary activity outside the court. Jones and his colleagues may in part have been driven by practical English assumptions about the nature of law. But the logic of British judicial practice was translated into a colonial context in which officials saw themselves as strangers from the society they ruled. As a result, they increasingly separated 'custom' from the institutions and practices that were supposed to enshrine and articulate it in a juridical form.

In practice, very few officials were able to make sense of a work such as Jagannatha, Jones and Colebrooke's *Digest*. Its complexity meant that the only way anyone could have used the text in court was if they already understood the practice of Indian *dharmasastra* reasoning to begin with. But if an official was able to trust the logic of Bengali jurisprudence well enough to make sense of the text, he would have no need for the work in the first place. As Colebrooke suggested in the introduction to a later work, the *Digest* ended up having 'little utility to persons conversant with the law, and of still less service to those who are not conversant with Indian jurisprudence'.[18] The fate of the *Digest* was caught between a desire to govern with indigenous practice on the one hand, and an anxiety about engaging with the Indian interlocutors who would assist them in determining what that practice was on the other. Unsurprisingly, it was not used by British judges adjudicating inheritance cases in Bengal. In the 1790s and early 1800s there is no record that it was taken off the shelf in the Company's courts at all.

II

Judicial officials stationed in Calcutta such as William Jones and H.T. Colebrooke did not think their task was to discover and impose a pre-constituted set of textual rules on Indian practice. Instead they believed they needed to govern with the experiential continuities of customary practice itself. But if even the men who produced late-eighteenth-century Bengal's colonial 'codes' thought texts could not define the essence of the law, and if the texts they produced were so badly suited to the practice of colonial adjudication, what actually happened in court? How were judicial disputes resolved in the Company's local courts and offices scattered throughout the *mofussil* (interior) itself. The records of the *Sadr Diwani Adalat*, the highest Company appeal court in Calcutta, exist for the period between 1793 and 1801 and contain transcripts that also allow one to trace the logic that ruled both British practice and Indian engagement with the court. These records can be used to analyse how early colonial ideas, instincts and orientations operated in their encounter with Indian forms of agrarian practice.

British attitudes developed in relation to Indian practice: before examining the practice of colonial jurisprudence one must consider the logic that governed the actions of those whom British officials encountered in court, Indian litigants. In eighteenth-century Bengal, disputants could appeal to a sovereign or council of some sort to arbitrate a dispute that threatened to destabilise the contingent local political order. Where they referred to the *dharmasastra*, the tradition that the British later referred to as 'Hindu law', it was to what Richard W. Lariviere describes as

a highly flexible and ingenious science in which the standards of orthodoxy and righteousness of a given locale or group could continually be adapted to the needs and desires of its subjects and at the same time continue to be strictly enforced.

Thus the *dharmasatra* was endlessly reinterpreted to meet the needs of particular local contexts. But to resolve many disputes, Hindu litigants did not expect to appeal to Sanskrit *sastrik* texts, relying instead on other judicial traditions and resources (including Muslim law) and less rarified forms of adjudicative practice. Most litigants appearing before British district courts did not quote *dharmasastra* texts or concepts: one must be sceptical about Lariviere's claim that the *dharmasastra* 'was the standard by which Hindus conducted their affairs'.[19] Here there are parallels with the way in which eighteenth-century English litigants treated the common law courts in Britain. In both contexts, going to law was regarded as a way of using a particular juridical logic to settle a dispute rather applying a codified set of law. India's various traditions of juridical decision-making and the English common law were all systems of reasoning that offered procedures for resolving disputes, not bodies of abstract rules, and they each incorporated a number of different styles of reasoning, moral and theological as well as 'legal' norms. There were, though, important differences that exacerbated the British sense of unfamiliarity with what was going on in colonial courts. In Britain, adjudication involved the subject's submission before a disembodied realm that was more clearly distinguished as a sphere defined as 'law'. Although the court's conduct was ruled by uncodified habitual practices and ethical norms rather than textualised rules, the court was a space where the influence of 'politics' was supposed to be kept to a minimum. In Bengal, on the other hand, dispute resolution often occurred as an appeal to the personal qualities of the ruler. The close connection between the private virtues of the prince and the public duties of the magistrate make it difficult to distinguish quite so neatly between law and politics in the early modern South Asian context as in Britain.

The concept of *vyavahara* (the word had a range of meanings including comportment and practice as well as dispute resolution) was used in both Sanskrit and Bengali to describe what happened in court. The term described the sovereign's arrangement of matters in a specific situation to ensure the endurance of a local political hierarchy in the short term. Within this logic of dispute resolution, the nature of the court's decision depended on the specific political and ethical character of the local situation. Evidence of custom or 'whatever a person practices' (*achara*) had a role to play in the process of resolution, but was explicitly interwoven with a normative conception of proper ethical practice.[20] Colebrooke translated a passage from Jagannatha's text to suggest that where 'no express law is found [to govern a particular type of conduct], one should be established on approved usage'. But the 'usage' that was relevant to the adjudicative process consisted of 'what has been practiced by good men and virtuous *Brahmanas*', not the practice of a group of individuals who inhabited a particular space.[21] Indian jurisprudence offered a way of telling stories about the way an individual should act virtuously in a particular situation.

In Bengal, the local ethical politics of juridical decision-making was closely connected to the practices of landholding discussed in Chapter 2. Most important was the pervasive perception of each political society as an unstable entity whose continued existence depended on the affective connections between rulers and subjects. In eighteenth-century Bengal, the 'law' of family inheritance (*dayabhaga*, or the 'division of heritage'), the subject concentrated on in this chapter, was determined by this situational ethical politics of local interaction.

One of the most important questions in the Indian literature on the subject was how an ancestral estate was to be transmitted to and divided amongst the next generation on the death of a father and mother, an issue that resulted in an extraordinary degree of debate and litigation. Later, British and Indian nineteenth-century legal commentators emphasised the existence of a rigid set of rules supposed to govern the practices of domestic life, arguing that the 'Hindu joint family' was an enduring, stable and rule-bound institution that lay at the core of Indian civil society.[22] As Sripathi Chandrasekhar suggested in 1943, 'it is this institution of the joint family around which the whole of the Indian community is built up'.[23] The terms of this late-nineteenth- and twentieth-century debate would have made no sense to Bengali landholders a century earlier. In the eighteenth century, the joint family was not a substantialised, objective entity that existed separately from its engagement in the particular world of local landholding, with the particular relations between specific individuals. Nor was it regarded as an enduring characteristic that somehow defined the essence of Indian society.

In the late eighteenth century, the decision whether or not to divide an estate on the death of one's parents was not determined by a set of rules or legal doctrines legitimated by an authority that existed outside the locality. Instead, a loose set of ethical maxims were interpreted in the context of a particular situation determined whether and how the partition of an estate was to occur. According to Jagannatha Tarkapancanana, brothers could divide the patrimony into shares on the death of their father. A number of commentators suggested that 'partition among brothers is ordained' and was the most virtuous thing to do. Separation of heirs was 'morally right'; but so was a situation of cohabitation and joint proprietorship, and – as we shall see – in practice there were many points in between. 'Let the eldest son... undertake his father's charge, and support all his brethren, and let them thus live together; or let them live apart', Jagannatha said. Commentators argued that the division itself 'should be made in mutual kindness', for example. Those distinguished 'by science and good conduct' and siblings who had added to the wealth of the estate by '[their] own sole labour' were supposed to be entitled to receive more, but there were many local circumstances in which *pandits* suggested that such a maxim should not apply.[24]

The ethical content of this early modern Indian juridical logic meant that when Bengali litigants brought claims to property relating to family property, they didn't come armed with a copy of the particular legal doctrine they believed should determine the case. Instead, they told their story and expressed their claim as a call to the conscience of the prince or judge. To see this let us look at a dispute. When Bimala Dasaya, the widow of a distant cousin of the Rangpuri *zamindars* Gokul Nath and Naba Kisor Ray presented her claim to a share of the Idrakpur estate in Rangpur district, she ended her initial petition in the following, rather stereotyped, words:

> I have no person but you to look up to in this situation of distress, and am without any particular friend or Patron to assist me, I therefore pray that you will take my representation into consideration, and in consequence look into the justness of my claim.

Bimala appealed to the conscience of the judge on behalf of her minor son. She argued that for eight generations, the Idrakpur polity had descended jointly to all the sons. As the estate had never been divided, her son was entitled to a share of the property, she said. Her opponents, Gokul Nath Roy and Naba Kisor Roy, argued instead that as the sole surviving descendents of the eldest male line of the family they possessed the estate exclusively and that Bimala's lineage had no right at all.[25]

The point at issue here was whether the estate was owned jointly by all the male heirs of the original *zamindar*, or whether it descended to the eldest male heir by primogeniture. The problem for the British judge was that neither side in the dispute was able to tell a story which determined which of these two states of affairs was the case. We saw in Chapter 1 how effective Gokul Nath had been at playing the local politics of trust in order to maintain control of the estate. He was able to dominate the agrarian relations of Idrakpur because he conformed to the normative model of the good prince and appeared to his local public as a virtuous man, interested in patronising the poor and local religious establishments amongst other things. Engaged in these pursuits, Gokul Nath and his cousin had been more concerned with the politics of local patronage than whether they were 'legally' the proprietors according to the East India Company's courts.

From the British point of view, Gokul Nath and Naba Kisor's position in Idrakpur during the 1780s was ambiguous in two senses. First of all, while Rani Padmabati, the widow of the former male landholder, was still alive, their position was half way between that of land agent and proprietor. When Padmabati's husband Raja Gaur Nath died, Gokul Nath and Naba Kisor had brought a suit for exclusive possession of the estate. The two men had dropped this suit when Padmabati agreed to appoint them as managers of the estate. Padmabati was still formally the *zamindar*, but well before her death in 1793 they had an unassailable control of the Idrakpur estate and were seen by the British Collector as *de facto* proprietors. When the 25-year-old widow of Raja Gaur Nath died, the two cousins reasserted their dormant claim to Idrakpur as their 'hereditary zemindarry'. More concerned to ensure the predictable payment of revenue than the intricacies of Indian law, the Collector of Rangpur acceded to the request and wrote Gokul Nath and Naba Kisor's names as proprietors in his account book.

When Bimala sued for a portion of the estate, a second ambiguity emerged. It had, it seems, never been clear in the family itself whether the estate had been formally declared the property of the family's male heirs or was the joint possession of the entire lineage. The family had not resolved what would later become the most important question in Hindu personal law, whether land was the property of the joint family or of individuals. Each side in the dispute agreed that the oldest son had always actually managed the estate; but they also agreed that younger siblings were treated like 'princes' and paid an annual stipend to live in an opulent fashion. Bimala argued that this proved that the family was bound together by a legal bond which entitled every relative to an equal share. By contrast, Gokul Nath and Naba Kisor asserted that the payment of allowances was not the sign of the younger brothers' proprietary right but merely an expression of the *patria familias'* duty to maintain the family as a whole, a duty that did not entail the younger brother possessing a property right. For the British judge, neither set of claims on its own was sufficient to determine which claim was more just.

The suit began in March 1793 when M. Leslie, the district judge, asked the litigants to present texts or 'vouchers' that they hoped would prove their claims. Along with their long petitions, both the plaintiff and defendant submitted genealogical tables, which showed the familial connection between Bimala's son and the *raja*s of the estate. The tables each side submitted were identical. No one disagreed about who was related to whom. Quickly seeing that this initial set of paperwork was unable to resolve the verdict, the judge began to enquire into local 'custom'. For example, he interviewed the Idrakpur family's employees and neighbours to determine what the 'custom of the family' had been.[26] But again, Leslie was unable to interpret these stories about what actually happened in Rangpur in a way that allowed rule of decision to occur. The British judge in Bengal had no confidence in his ability to engage in the ethical vocabulary of Indian jurisprudence, nor was he a trained English lawyer. Without the practical ability to translate facts into norms, the court was wracked by uncertainty and indecision. More and more documents were submitted to the court, but the judge was unable to decide. The case dragged on. It was only in December 1794, after Leslie had considered the issue at 14 separate sessions that a decision was finally made.

The district court eventually resolved the case by appealing to an external authority – the court's *pandit*. The judge seems to have referred the case to the *pandit* in an act of desperation. He didn't seem to have had any idea of what point of law he was asking the *pandit* to form an opinion on. Instead, Leslie transcribed a brief summary of the case, asked the *pandit* to 'consider these matters' and simply waited for an opinion. The *pandit* decided that the estate had never been divided, and that the plaintiff was entitled to a half share of the estate. The judge did not understand the logic that underpinned this verdict, but issued it in his own name nonetheless.[27]

The dispute did not stop there. Gokul Nath and Naba Kisor won their appeal at the provincial court in Murshidabad, where judges Keating and Bathurst gave them back possession of the estate. Bimala then turned to the *Sadr Diwani Adalat*, the highest appeal court in Bengal, which upheld the provincial court's decision and continued to affirm the two cousin's claim to the whole estate. Both courts based their decision on their belief that a 'family custom' existed, which determined that inheritance was determined by primogeniture. But the two appeal courts gave different decisions to the district tribunal simply because the *pandits* took a different view of the local situation in each case.

The historian can only view the dispute through the documentary techniques of colonial judges whose understanding of the ethical practices of Hindu 'jurisprudence' was minimal. As a result, it is impossible to assess precisely what logic the court's Indian judicial officers deployed to understand the case. But we can detect a tension between the logic of everyday landholding and the practices that colonial officials used in court. That tension did not consist of a clash between British and Indian ways of understanding law. Although there were differences, the practice of English law courts was not dramatically different from the techniques used by Indian jurists.

Nor was it the result simply of British ignorance of Indian jurisprudence. Officials who were comfortable making decisions in court without codes of law, such as John Shore in 1770s or Courtney Smith in the 1820s, don't seem to have any better abstract knowledge of Indian jurisprudence than those who did not.[28] What officials lacked was not knowledge or cultural empathy, but skill in connecting the factual circumstances of the case to a normative ethical or legal vocabulary necessary to decide what was right or wrong and issue a decree. Officials were clear about the need to govern with indigenous 'custom'. Yet the anxious, detached way in which they oriented themselves to Indian society isolated them from any context which may have given them stable foundations for translating the stories they were told in court into rules of decision and converting facts into norms. As the rest of this chapter shows, the result was the slow adoption of an implicit form of legal positivism. Officers desperately appealed to an external authority instead of deciding cases with an interpretative logic grounded in their own practice for themselves.

In the case discussed above, the external authority consisted of the opinion of the court's *pandits*. But the judgement of *pandits* was an uncertain foundation for juridical authority because British officials were unable to understand the logic at work in the Indian jurist's reasoning. In most cases British judges preferred using other sources of authority, in particular their own interpretation of local 'practice' or 'custom'. As we saw, judicial officials tried, and failed, to resolve the Idrakpur dispute in this way. Other judges met with more success using this technique. J. Willis, the judge of Sylhet, tried to resolve a case about a woman's right to partition the estate of her deceased husband between herself and his relatives. In the case, the widow of one *zamindar* called Joy Narayan (we are never told the woman's name by the court's records) was attempting to prevent her husband's brothers from taking over the estate by gaining exclusive control of a proportion of the estate. Intriguingly, it was the widow – not the *pandits* or British judge – who first introduced Hindu legal 'texts' into the court, using them to claim that they authorised her right to partition the estate. Willis called on Ratikantha and Maheshnia, the court's *pandits*, for advice, but found the logic of their *vyavastha* (opinion) impossible to understand. Circumventing the authority of 'canonical' Hindu jurisprudence, Willis relied on evidence of local 'custom'. In the mountain of paperwork which had deluged the court, the plaintiff's *vakil* (pleader) had submitted a list of widows who had in fact 'divided and distinctly shared their inheritance' in the district in order to prove that a partition of this kind was sanctioned by local practice. The judge seized on this as potential evidence, asking the *pandits* to investigate its authenticity and produce a text that represented the state of local customary law. The next day they returned, suggesting that the list submitted by the plaintiff was entirely fraudulent. According to Ratikantha and Maheshnia, none of the women mentioned in the list had in fact partitioned an estate on the death of their husband. Accordingly, they said, there was no local custom allowing widows to partition an estate without their husband's consent. Willis decreed in favour of the defendant, directing 'that both parties jointly hold and manage the inheritance' and his verdict was eventually upheld on appeal.[29]

A third way officials tried to decide cases by appealing to an external authority occurred when they asked for guidance from their superiors in Calcutta, from the Company's Judicial Department or the *Sadr Diwani Adalat*. David Vanderheyden and John Champlain, two successive judges of 24 Parganas, tried to find a rule in this way to adjudicate a dispute about the possession of the image held by Hindu ascetics in the town of Khardah in this way. The descendents of the Nitanandi devotee Bir Chandra formed a corporation of *goswamis* in the town, and claimed they had an equal right to partition the income from worship of the Syam-Sundera *thakur* (referred to by the British as an 'idol') during the Rath Jatra festival that occurred each year in the town. The Rath Jatra possession was key part of the public life of the settlement. The town's corporation of *goswamis* argued that they had been deprived of legitimate participation as one of their number, Krsna Chandra *goswami*, treated the income from the site as his exclusive hereditary property. Again, one can see rival interpretations of the ethical practices of inheritance at work in Indian attitudes to the dispute. The litigants all told the same story about the origins of the *thakur*, but disagreed about the ethical or normative implications of that narrative. The British officer appealed to Calcutta to translate narrative into norms.

In the Khardah case, the British judge tried to avoid referring the dispute to the court's *pandit*. When the Hindu official, Kali Sankar Bhattacarya argued that all the members of the corporation should share in the income of the *thakur*, Vanderheyden rejected this view. His successor John Champlain upheld his decision. Their preferred solution was arbitration: British judicial officers wanted the disputing parties to appoint their own *pandits* or arbitrators, meet in public and hammer out an agreement that would result in 'lasting peace', but the litigants refused. If they were willing to compromise they wouldn't continue court proceedings.[30] Faced with such a fractious public dispute, Vanderheyden and Champlain wrote to the *Sadr Diwani Adalat* asking for a clear rule of decision in the case, a rule that would have relieved them from the responsibility of making a seemingly arbitrary choice in a matter that had excited an enormous amount of local public involvement. The superior court continually refused, avoiding responsibility for taking the decision itself, arguing that there must be a stable basis for a decision in local custom. Neither Vanderheyden or Champlain had access to the interpretative practices which would have allowed them to translate the stories they had been told into a publicly acceptable normative rule. The case drifted on without a resolution. In his final letter to the *Sadr Diwani Adalat*, Champlain noted that he 'ha[d] no rule in which to guide me', a telling testament to British anxiety about the absence of stable sources of judicial certainty in early colonial Bengal.[31]

III

The early years of the nineteenth century saw British officials respond to the anxious, uncertain juridical practices this chapter has described with the complaint that Indian law, especially the law of Hindus, was unknown and uncertain. Officials answering a questionnaire circulated in 1802 criticised the poor state of indigenous knowledge about the law. Most, like Henry Strachey, suggested that an understanding of legal texts such as 'the Koran and Shaster are of little service in the cutcherry' or court, but that it was difficult to find a stable rule of decision nonetheless. At that time though, officials rarely articulated an alternative conception of the sources of law very clearly. In 1815, one of Vanderheyden's successors as judge of 24 Parganas argued that Indian law was 'jus vaguum et incognito', vague and unknown law, in a book he wrote as a guide for young judicial officers.[32] A few years later, Mountstuart Elphinstone noted the 'looseness' and 'contradictions' inherent in both textual and customary Indian jurisprudence. Writing to Henry Strachey's brother Edward in 1820, Elphinstone noted that it was 'the custom of the country which regulates most things' in the countryside. But, he continued, 'the difficulty of ascertaining it is so great, that you may doubtless recollect civil suits in which you have spent days examining the evidence, to find out what is the custom on some issue, and yet have been diffident in your own decision after all'. For Elphinstone, all that really existed were some 'loose traditionary notions' that didn't really represent a coherent system of 'law' at all.[32]

These sentiments reflected a range of different responses to the anxieties of judicial interpretation. To understand these hermeneutic difficulties, officials conjured up a range of subjects and objects to attribute blame to. Concern about the vagueness of Indian law intersected with the emergence of a language that moved beyond the critique of India's politics and political culture noted in previous chapters. Rather than using a vocabulary of 'habitual despotism' to describe their disconnection from Indian politics, officers developed a critique of Indian society as a way to explain their uneasy relationship with propertied social practice. In the process, an apolitical domain of 'society' that seemed to exist separately from politics became the object of discussion and critique. In the essays and disquisitions published between 1800 and 1820 by official observers and Company officers who had retired or were on furlough, a contradictory range of actions were proposed to cure the subcontinent of what was increasingly seen as an instance of Indian 'depravity'. Some argued that the European role in Bengal should be reduced, others advocated mass conversion to Christianity and the migration of Europeans 'of character' to remedy the crisis of juridical uncertainty; still others, most famously James Mill, began to advocate the codification of law. These intellectual responses are considered in Chapter 6 below.

Such intellectual reactions to the crisis of judicial interpretation emerged alongside a series of less reflexive or explicitly theoretical responses that nonetheless produced very different way of doing things. Officials like Elphinstone began to lament the absence of something that had never been present in British law: a comprehensive, textual 'body of law' that provided a clear set of rules which were supposed to determine judicial practice in each case. As far as the law of inheritance was concerned, the search for these forms of positive authority congealed around the emergence of colonial practices that aimed to textualise or codify Indian law in a new form. Such practices were underwritten by the formation of a new juridical epistemology in which texts were not merely seen as evidence of legal practice, but themselves had the force of law.

From the 1810s, but especially the 1820s, printers such as William Carey's Baptist Mission Press in Serampore or H.H. Wilson's Hindoostanee press in Calcutta produced a spate of texts that had a very different content and function from earlier works such as Jones and Colebrooke's *Digest*. In 1810, H.T. Colebrooke published his *Two Treatises on Inheritance*. By then Colebrooke had begun to participate in institutions intended to discipline and educate a more coherent sense of shared practice amongst British officials in Bengal. He was appointed an honorary Professor of Hindu law and Sanskrit at Fort William College, the institution at which young Company servants were to be trained, in 1801.[33] His *Two Treatises* were part of this broader pedagogic project, intending to replace the *Digest of Hindu Law* with translations of what he believed were more certain and more ancient sources of Hindu law. The *Two Treatises* reproduced the two most important texts in *gaudiya* and *mithila* traditions of judicial interpretation, Jimutavahana's *Dayabhaga* and Vijnanesvara's *Mitaksara*. Trying to get to the root of Indian jurisprudence by going backwards in time, he argued that these works had been 'the standard authorities of the Hindu law of inheritance' in eighteenth-century Bengal. They were supposed to offer an easier guide to the state of the law than Jagannatha's 'general compilation' in which the doctrines of many schools and authors had been 'greatly multiplied' and combined.[34]

Some years ago, the anthropologist Bernard Cohn argued that the texts which Colebrooke and other officials produced reflected the belief that 'there was *a* Hindu law (*dharmasastra*), a fixed code, a known and stateable body of rules, which, as they thought, by the late eighteenth century had become overgrown by later commentaries'.[35] Cohn suggested that this view defined British attitudes to Indian jurisprudence throughout the colonial period, from the 1780s onwards. Like many scholars since, Cohn's suggestion contrasted this colonial belief in the existence of a rigid form of Indian codified law with the flexible way in which Indians actually resolved disputes. Cohn correctly noted that officials like Colebrooke saw India as an ancient society whose institutions had degenerated in recent times. Colebrooke believed the colonial state could return to the original, pristine source of Hindu law by printing what Cohn called 'an Ur-text'. The intention was that translations of works such as Jimutavahana's *Dayabhaga* or Vijnanesvara's *Mitaksara* would take the law out of the hands of its present-day Indian interpreters.

However, there are two problems with Cohn's account. First of all, he missed the fact that Colebrooke's belief in the need to turn to ancient texts in the early 1800s involved a dramatic revision of the assumptions the official had held before the publication of the *Digest of Hindu Law* in 1798. The fact that William Jones and H.T. Colebrooke had originally translated Jagannatha Tarkapancanana's contemporary commentary demonstrates that a very different conception of law was in play 20 years before; their aim was to check the *pandit*'s reference to contemporary textual evidence of custom, not return to a pristine, unchanged ancient law. Colebrooke's change of approach occurred as he, like other officials, found the *Digest* useless in court. For the practice of judicial administration to work, 'the perpetual conflict of discordant opinions and jarring deductions' in the recent past needed to be reduced. It was only after the turn of the nineteenth century that officials such as Colebrooke began to fantasise about the existence of a form of jurisprudence that offered coherent, pithy rules from the ancient past. But in doing so the 'orientalist' Colebrooke who wrote from the 1810s articulated a very different methodology from that which governed the common lawyer William Jones and judicial practice more generally 20 years earlier.

The attempt by Colebrooke, along with a small number of British and Indian officers, to project stable forms of meaning onto the distant past introduced a new temporal sensibility to the discussion of Hindu jurisprudence in the early 1800s. During the 1790s, men like Colebrooke and Jones did not believe the oldest texts provided the most useful form of textual law: they felt that contemporary commentators like Jagannatha could successfully interpret Hindu legal texts for the present day. But, without the ability to understand how Jagannatha related current social practice to the *sastras*, officials began to invoke the existence of a simple set of rules that had not changed over time. For men like Colebrooke, just like Indian interlocutors such as Radhakanta Deb writing in the 1820s and 1830s, 'time was perceived to have stood still in India', as Michael S. Dodson puts it.[36] As a result, the temporal frame which British administrators used was stretched. Whilst in the 1780s, Britons and Bengalis used the word 'ancient' to refer to a period less than a 100 years before, talking about an 'ancient constitution' dating back to the late 1600s, for example. By the 1820s 'ancient' was a word used to discuss texts that were believed to be over a thousand years old. With their attempt to use archaic texts in order to construct stable juridical norms, officials like Colebrooke produced a new conception of Hindu Indian society as a stable set of practices that had continued unchanged for centuries.

Colebrooke's *Two Treatises* were used far more frequently in court than the *Digest of Hindu Law* had been. But Colebrooke himself saw the project of transcription as a failure. In practice, his translations of the *Dayabhaga* and *Mitaksara* faced the same difficulty as any other work of *dharmasastrik* literature: it simply did not provide British officials what they wanted in court. However far back into India's past one delved to find a stable form of textual law, medieval Indian texts still needed to be interpreted by someone. The analogous reasoning that underpinned medieval works such as Jimu-tavahana's *Dayabhaga* or Vivnanesvara's *Mitaksara* simply did not produce the abstract, general statements law officials desired. Translations of Indian texts were one external source of authority for judicial decision-making, but they were not sufficient on their own to determine what happened in court.

It was left to others with a less abstract and scholastic frame of mind than Colebrooke to distil the alleged vagaries of Hindu law into a form that could be used in court. The second problem with Cohn's interpretation is that he failed to note the quite conscious process of reconstruction which most officials engaged in whilst codifying Hindu law. By the 1820s, most officials did not believe 'the Hindu law' was a coherent 'known and stateable body of rules' that could be recovered after overgrowing commentaries had been pruned back. Instead, they thought they needed to actively reinvent Indian law; most officials working in the 1820s and 1830s believed the construction of a coherent canon of Hindu property law required the active intervention of the colonial state.

Amongst British officers in Bengal, 'orientalists' like Colebrooke or his close friend Henry Hayman Wilson were exceptions in believing Indian texts might be able to provide the basis of legal practice on their own. Their view was slightly better received in London; in Calcutta it was spurned by the official establishment. The authors of more usable forms of codification were clearer than Colebrooke about the need for British officials to take an active role in making, not just recovering, Hindu law. In Bombay, for example, Governor Mountstuart Elphinstone drew from his experience in Eastern India and his communication with friends in Bengal to suggest that his staff needed to reconfigure the structure of Indian jurisprudence to produce a new form of Hindu law; it was Elphinstone who first seriously proposed the codification of law in India. Elphinstone's purpose was to rationalise Hindu law into a consistent set of rules that could be used in court. To prevent judicial uncertainty from completely undermining British rule, Elphinstone intended to

> compile a complete and consistent code from the mass of written law and the fragments of tradition, determining on general principles of jurisprudence those points where the Hindoo books and traditions present only conflicting authorities, and perhaps supplying on similar principles any glaring deficiencies that may remain when the matter for compilation has been exhausted.[37]

Instead of returning Indian law to its pristine ancient sources, the Governor of Bombay aimed at consciously inventing a new tradition. He wanted to actively construct a coherent, textual canon of Hindu law, in a form that, for the first time he believed, would provide stable source of legal authority in court.[38] Here, the relationship between sources of law unearthed from the distant past and the forward-looking action of the colonial state was far more ambivalent and complex than most scholars recognise.

A similar concern underpinned codificatory efforts emerging in Bengal a few years later. The Supreme Court judge Sir Francis MacNaghten and his son, *Sadr Diwani Adalat* register William Hay MacNaghten both published significant works. Sir Francis' *Considerations on the Hindoo Law as it is Current in Bengal* was printed in 1824. Often seen as articulating a similar set of arguments about Hindu law as both Jones and Colebrooke, their perspective was different from each. Sir Francis began by repeating the stock argument that 'the Right of Hindoos to have their contests decided by their own laws, has been established by the legislature of Great Britain'. In practice though, he suggested that '[t]here is hardly any question arising out of *Hindoo* law, that may be either affirmed or denied, under the sanction of texts, which are held to be equal in point of authority'. Articulating a lack of trust in what was going on in court, MacNaghten argued that cases were decided by Indian law officers and lawyers acting from entirely venal motives. In practice 'all claims may be countenanced, all decrees may be sanctioned by authority'. Bengal's *pandits* and *vakils* were 'men whose importance and profits depend upon the obscurity of the laws', MacNaghten argued. MacNaghten's discussion of the way Indian lawyers were supposed to use intricate arguments and legal ambiguity to fill their own pockets was similar in tone to Jeremy Bentham's critique of English lawyer's venality.[39] His solution was the same as Bentham's: to produce a text that rationalised the uncertainties of juridical practice into a code of concise, pithy rules. McNaghten's project reflected a judge's practical concern to fix law that would otherwise be uncertain by providing an external, textual authority for judicial decision-making that could replace other sources of law. MacNaghten was fully aware of the fact that he was constructing a novel code as much as a compiling of existing law. His point was to 'establish . . . a fixed system of Civil Jurisprudence for the two great classes of the Population of this Country'. For him the process of 'selection' required a substantial British reconstruction of the 'foundations' of Hindu law.[40]

Sir Francis's son William Hay MacNaghten became more famous as a political agent in Afghanistan, where he died in the first Afghan War. Perhaps more significantly though, he was the Register of the *Sadr Diwani Adalat* until 1830. On being appointed in 1822 MacNaghten undertook a similar project as that which his father had begun. MacNaghten junior argued that 'no fixed principles [we]re to be extracted either from the original authorities [of Hindu law] or their translation'. Like Colebrooke, Elphinstone and his father, William

MacNaghten argued that the vague multiplicity of the law supplemented by the venality of lawyers and law experts meant that 'law' in any coherent, certain sense did not exist in present-day Bengal. The logical conclusion was to compile a textual digest of coherent judicial opinions that would 'be servicable as precedents'. MacNaghten's purpose was to 'fix' the many points 'where a contrariety of opinion has hitherto prevailed'. Producing a text would allow 'questions of the highest importance' to be 'finally determined one way or the other'. It didn't matter which way doubtful points were decided, as long as a consistent text was produced. 'The mode is nothing: – the determination is everything', as MacNaghten put it.[41] By proceeding in this way, 'Hindoo and Mahommedan Laws would at no distant period be reduced to some degree of consistency', he argued.[42] MacNaghten's *Principles and Precedents and Mahommedan Law* and *Principles and Precedents of Hindoo Law* printed in 1825 and 1827, respectively, were published with the sanction of both the Governor-General and the judges of the *Sadr Diwani Adalat*.

Precedent was an important conception in this colonial discussion of Indian law. H.T. Prinsep, the judicial secretary at the time, noted that printed collections of precedents were 'the most safe and practicable method of establishing a fixed system of Civil Jurisprudence for the two great classes of the Population of this Country'.[43] The textual projects of the 1820s were accompanied by printed summaries of cases that would offer precedents for future decisions. But precedent was not a principle that could govern Hindu law on its own. It needed the active, systematising mind of officials outside the court to reduce the law to a clear and pithy form that could provide a rule in court. In the introduction to his *Principles and Precedents*, MacNaghten himself acknowledged that the majority of cases that went unreported offered little guidance to officials in search of a coherent source of law.[44] In practice it was the selection and publication of disputes that made a particular rule good law.[45]

MacNaghten's *Principles and Precedents* was not an attempt at 'moulding India's vast body of customary and textual law to fit the English notion of precedent'.[46] The doctrine of precedent began to be formalised in English in the early nineteenth century, and was only consolidated as a fixed principle of English law in the twentieth century. There were important differences between legal practice in Britain and colonial Bengal.[47] Case records published in England did not contain the kind of pithy summaries of the substantive 'principle' which was discerned from a particular dispute. In England it was up to the judge to decide how a previous precedent was to be used to draw principles from practice in other words.[48] But in Bengal, Company officials did not trust the practical experience of the court to make decisions and draw generalisations on its own accord. So in the colonial environment, compilations of previous cases always gave a brief summary of the case with an explicit statement of the substantive rule of law that it was supposed to authorise, printed in the margin. The substantive points of 'law' determined in each case were indexed at the back of the volume for the judge's easy reference; again something which did not happen in England.

Of course, in practice the uncertain events of the court sometimes worked against this codificatory design. Unsurprisingly, MacNaghten found it impossible to summarise a clear rule from the complexity of the Idrakpur case we discussed earlier, offering instead a brief account of the dispute in the margin.[49] But in most cases, MacNaghten and his colleagues codified the legal principle which could be drawn from the case as a pithy rule: 'Among the holders of separate shares of an hereditary zemindarry each, according to the Hindoo law, may sell his share to whom he pleases' was one. 'By the Hindoo law, a son not born in wedlock may inherit, if such be the custom of the province, but not otherwise', and 'An adopted son taking the estate of his adoptive father is excluded from inheritances in his own family' were others.[50] This style of discourse was alien to the colonial juridical mind of the 1790s; but by the 1820s, such a generalising, rule-making idiom had become second nature. By then, a compilation or code was seen as a text that itself systematically defined the law. In reality it was the text produced by MacNaghten, not the institutional practice of previous judicial decision-making that defined the source of law. As Thomas Macaulay noted in this discussion of precedent in the sphere of criminal law, precedent worked very differently in colonial Bengal. Macaulay suggested, 'the power of construing law in cases in which there is any real reason to doubt what the law is amounts to the power of making the law'. Adopting a similar logic as that which underpinned MacNaghten's *Precendents*, Macaulay's Penal Code concluded with a series of cases which would have binding legislative authority.[51]

The desire to construct a 'fixed system of jurisprudence' in textual form was a response to officials' failure to develop stable hermeneutic practices in court. Unease about the uncertainty of judicial proceedings led to the articulation of a new theory of law in Bengal, a theory that fed back to influence the practice of the court. Rather than being something that existed in the customary practice of either Indian society or the court itself, this theory asserted that the 'law' consisted of a coherent, comprehensive body of positive, textual rules. Those rules were supposed to determine the conduct of a particular group of people who inhabited an extensive territory. Those rules were supposed to have endured over a considerable period of time. The function of the court was not to engage in the complex process of contextual reasoning that underpinned the practice of both pre-colonial Indian *vyava-hara* or the English common law. Instead, it had a purpose that no British court in England or elsewhere across the British empire had had before: to apply authoritative rules that were framed and codified by an authority that existed outside the court. Nonetheless, colonial officials remained ambivalent about what that authority was.

Before considering the ambivalence of colonial legal theory in more detail, this chapter returns to the scene of the colonial court one last time to examine the way this changing attitude towards texts worked itself out in the practice of the court. One particularly long-running dispute illustrates the transformation in judicial practice and juridical theory. The case concerned the fate of a boy called Bhola Dhami. In 1780, the boy was adopted by Nawazu, the widow of his birth uncle, in the town of Gaya in Bihar. As Nawazu's adopted son, Bhola Dhami acquired the right to inherit the house in Mirzapur in which they both lived and income from the temple in Gaya at which his mother's husband had officiated. But as he grew up, Nawazu and her adopted son argued vehemently, until eventually the widow ejected Bhola Dhami – then in his mid-twenties – from their house. As a consequence of these arguments, Nawazu tried to disinherit her adopted son and take her daughter's child Musan Dhami as a new son and heir.

When Nawazu tried to disinherit him, Bhola Dhami sued his adoptive mother to reclaim the property he believed he was entitled to. Nawazu was widowed before she adopted Bhola Dhami. The first question at stake was whether a son could be adopted by a woman without the consent of her husband. The second issue was whether an adopted son could be disinherited. When the case initially came before the court in 1800, the judge tried to adjudicate the case using local 'usage' instead. The opinion of Bhara Bhatta, the *pandit*, was sought, but it was criticised for its 'inexplicitness'. Instead, a report from the court's *amins* (local investigators) was commissioned about the practice of adoption in the local area. The text that these Indian officers submitted seemed to prove the existence of a local custom that allowed women to adopt without the consent of their husband's, and also to disinherit their adopted children. The judge used evidence of this 'custom' to dismiss Bhola Dhami's claims to the estate.

The argument between Nawazu and Bhola Dhami simmered on through the 1800s and early 1810s. It appeared again when it came before the appeal court in Patna in 1821. Instead of referring to local 'usage', the Patna court engaged in a far more detailed discussion of textual Hindu law. The three judges who sat in the court, Courtney Smith, John Bardoe Eliot and William Fleming, referred the case back to the new *pandit* of Gaya district. Operating within the ethical logic of Indian jurisprudence, the *pandit* Lila Dhar reinterpreted older texts to suggest that the husband's consent was inferred automatically in the adoption. A son adopted after a husband's death could be treated as a legitimate heir and such a son could be disinherited, the *pandit* said. The judges found this answer inexplicable. Instead of appealing to the authority of custom, they articulated their own newfound confidence in their ability to interpret texts by arguing with the *pandit*'s view. The colonial regime's new form of instinctive legal positivism led them to suggest that a clear, textually sanctioned 'principle' existed throughout Bengal and Bihar which prevented a widow from adopting a son without the consent of their deceased husband, a view they developed from reading publications such as Colebrooke's *Two Treatises*. Officials responded to the threat of judicial indeterminacy by trying to base their judgement on a clear set of textual rules, attempting to produce a form of law not subject to the vagaries of practice in the court but dependent on a set of straightforward rules in texts they could control. The three judges rejected the *pandit's* decision and used their own interpretation of textual Hindu law to overturn the original decision and give Bhola Dhami his property back.[52]

The case was appealed a second time, when Laksmi Narayan Dhami, Bhola Dhami's son, challenged the provincial court's verdict in the *Sadr Diwani Adalat*. The case was heard in 1830. The court's judges, Cudbert Seally, Robert Rattray and, once again, Courtney Smith, who had been appointed from the court in Patna to Calcutta's supreme court, sat to decide the case for a final time. The first two, Seally and Rattray, again based their judgement on a textual interpretation of Hindu law, upholding the Patna court's view. The third judge, Smith, articulated a now archaic judicial sensibility and suggested that custom be used to uphold the district court's original decree. Smith lost the argument. The court finally agreed with the verdict of the court's *pandits* Vaidya Nath Misra and Ram Tanu Serma, who articulated what had by then congealed into an orthodox interpretation of Hindu jurisprudence. Instead of using the logic of *dharmasastra* reasoning to interpret the practice of inheritance in a particular local ethical context, they noted bluntly that 'there was no text', in any book current in either Bengal or Bihar 'which allowed a woman to affiliate a son given without the leave of her husband'. Whilst the *pandits* in the Patna appeal court had been able to reconstruct the precepts of Hindu law to find a new ethical environment, those attached to the *Sadr Diwani Adalat* in 1830 could not.[53] The textualist epistemology of colonial law had become to influence the way the colonial state's Indian informants thought and spoke about the nature of the law.

IV

By the 1830s, a general discourse about the rules that were supposed to determine Hindu family life had begun to emerge, a discourse that did not exist 30 or 40 years before. That discourse's increasing stability depended on a new set of institutions, in particular the Company's law courts and the circulation of printed texts that purported to describe the pithy principles that were supposed to govern Hindu inheritance law. Those texts, not the practice of the court, had become the law. When MacNaghten's digest of *Sadr Diwani Adalat* cases was reprinted in 1871, a footnote was added to the report of the Bhola Dhami case. The editor noted that '[t]he necessity of the husband's permission to legalise the widow's adoption in Bengal, is established by many printed cases'.[54] In practice, the authority of a point of law was based on its reference to other texts. This self-referential process of textual circulation meant that, from the 1830s onwards, judges confronted most inheritance dispute knew how they were supposed to decide. They were not, however, sure about the authority upon which the rules they used relied.

The problem was that officials were never certain whether the texts they produced merely represented existing indigenous law, or if they were a new form of jurisprudence that needed to be validated by the authority of the colonial legislature to become law. This ambivalence ran through the debates that surrounded the publication of William Hay MacNaghten's *Principles and Precedents* of Indian – Hindu and Muslim – law. MacNaghten's work began as an official text, supported and financed by the Governor-General in Council. The Governor-General Lord Hastings and his successors John Adams and Lord Amherst originally wanted the text to be given the official authority of the *Sadr Diwani Adalat*. Because he thought Indian law was so vague and indeterminate, Hastings believed that officials needed to have a stable set of rules to determine their conduct in court. The work involved the 'determination' of doubtful points of law in an arbitrary fashion. Because of this necessary arbitrariness, the text could not claim to be an authoritative and accurate representation of canonical Hindu law; the text needed to be given authority from somewhere else. It needed to be stamped with the authority of a branch of the state.[55]

The attempt to give the text official status was opposed by a majority of the judges of the *Sadr Diwani Adalat*, who were unwilling to give MacNaghten's work their formal stamp of approval. The judges argued that the text should replace the diverse set of authorities and precedents used previously to decide property disputes. 'Hereafter', the judge H.T. Prinsep wrote, it would 'become a manual of establish[ed] precedents of equal authority with the books [of Hindu law] themselves and of much more practical utility', in practice becoming the source of textual law. But for the court to declare the work an official text would violate the separation of powers between the judiciary and the legislature, and also undermine the Company's claim to rely only on indigenous law in deciding property disputes. The court believed the text to be authoritative, but that it should 'have only such authority as its intrinsic merits', whatever those might have been.[56] Hastings was asking for the court to actively promulgate and make the law – something the court could advise on, but only the legislature could do.

MacNaghten's *Principles and Precedents* was printed at the expense of government. Copies were distributed to district officials throughout the province in 1823, and used extensively thereafter.[57] In practice, it had 'official' status, circulating in the self-referential world of colonial judicial practice as an authoritative text, playing a critical role in the crystallisation of the kind of 'neo-traditional' interpretation of Hindu family law David Washbrook and other scholars discusses,[58] in which the inheritance of women and the division of property between members of the 'Hindu joint family' is forbidden. MacNaghten's work was invoked in Calcutta in the famous dispute concerning Prasanna Kumar Tagore's estate that occurred between 1869 and 1872.

The text was used to uphold the view that a father could not dispose of his estate without consulting his sons, in this case to bequeath some of his estate to found the Tagore Law Professorship at Calcutta University.[59] But within colonial legal theory, the status of the text remained ambivalent. It was always more than merely a representation of the diffuse canons of Hindu jurisprudence. But always less than a formal code backed up by the legislative authority of the state.

Over the next few decades, others did argue that a code of law needed to be formally enacted by the sovereign authority of the colonial state. A decade after MacNaghten's text was published, the former *Sadr Diwani Adalat* chief justice, William Butterworth Bayley, suggested that a code of Hindu law should be compiled 'on rational lines' and 'promulgated' by the legislative authority of the colonial state. Bayley is usually seen as a conservative, 'orientalist' figured who wished to preserve rather than transform Indian forms of law. But, speaking before the House of Commons' Indian Select Committee in 1833, Bayley sounded like a Benthamite, arguing that Hindu law needed to be actively rationalised by the colonial state. Bayley acknowledged that MacNaghten and others had systematised Hindu law to some degree. But the project of 'codification' (Bayley used Bentham's neologism) was still incomplete. Not only were there areas of law that were still governed by a disorderly collection of what James Mill had called 'loose, vague, stupid or unintelligible quotations and maxims', but Hindu law had no formal authority. Bayley argued that his activist, codificatory project would be a collaborative one. Expressing a commonly articulated colonial view about the weakness of the Indian mind, he believed that it wouldn't be difficult to enlist Indian support because '[t]he law of the natives, and the minds of its interpreters, are equally pliant'. Indian *pandits* were so eager to 'raise themselves in the eyes of their masters' that '[i]t would require little management to obtain the cordial co-operation of the doctors' to a reconstruction of Hindu law on rational, systematic lines. Bayley wanted a code to reform existing law, suggesting that the rules which allowed the minute subdivision of property could be 'restrained', for example. The 'promulgation of a code so concocted ... would not shock the prejudices of the natives', he suggested, although it would dramatically reform of both the structure, content and authority of Indian law.[60] The object of codifying Hindu law was taken up by the Select Committee and made one of the initial purposes of the first Indian Law Commission appointing in 1834.

But the commission never did codify Hindu law. Arguments in favour of 'rationalising' the complexity of Hindu jurisprudence by giving a code of Hindu law the sanction of the legislature waited over a century to be put into practice. In 1956, the legislature of the newly independent Indian state enacted the Hindu Code Bill. The bill summarised Hindu inheritance law in a series of pithy rules. It also undid some of the colonial process of traditionalisation, reforming practices which modernising Indian nationalists saw as irrational such as polygamy, limitations on female inheritance and the impartibility of the joint estate. The bill articulated a new, nationalist conception of the 'will of the whole community' as something enshrined in the legislative power of a nationalist, democratic state. Strikingly, the state was confident about its ability to represent and intervene in the lives of its Hindus subjects, whilst it doubted its power to represent India's Muslims. In India, Muslim family law remains uncodified.

These twentieth-century debates involved new conceptions of nation-hood, representation and legislative authority whose genealogy we are not concerned with here. Before independence though, proponents of a leg-islatively enacted Hindu code bill lost the argument fairly quickly, in part because officials began to doubt whether Indian society was so malleable, in part because textualised 'Hindu law' began to function as a stable body of jurisprudence without it. Although the status of the texts officials used in court remained ambivalent, a stable set of general norms emerged which gave judicial officials the confidence to decide disputes. Disagreements occurred, but they tended to reflect the opposition of clearly articulated doctrines, rather than a more diffuse sense of the absence of stable sources of law.[61] The emergence of stable forms of institutional practice in court meant that the spate of texts on Hindu law published in the 1820s and 1830s abated until the 1870s. In the second half of the nineteenth century, British trea-tises on Hindu law rarely mentioned canonical Hindu texts as a source of law. Where they did, they often cited them merely to criticise the assump-tion that the actual practice of Indians was determined by a limited number of 'Brahmanical' injunctions.[62] From the 1880s onwards, a generation of nationalist Indian lawyers began to examine the *dharmasastras* once again to suggest they provided the basis of an ancient, civilised indigenous law that could rival the jurisprudence of Europe. But most legal practitioners remained content to draw on the circular logic of previous case law to actu-ally argue and decide cases.[63] Other spheres of law were formally codified by the imperial legislature, but Hindu family law was not. Until the 1950s, indeed in many cases well beyond, the existence of stable norms in this sphere of law allowed judges, lawyers and civil servants to remain ambiva-lent about whether 'Hindu personal law' reflected Hindu India's 'ancient' legal traditions or was a recent artifice constructed by the colonial state.[64]

In the meantime though the colonial search for stable forms of meaning led officials, and some of their Indian interlocutors, to produce new conceptions of Indian social life. By the 1830s both sought to find stable, enduring and often supposedly 'ancient' rules to determine the kind of conduct that should have occurred. Within this process, Hindu and also Muslim families were constructed as supposedly stable realms of activity governed by a general set of textual rules that determined practice across the whole of Bengal and Bihar. A few key principles had been established to govern the realm of Hindu domesticity: widows could not adopt a son without the prior consent of their deceased husbands; they could not inherit property; property was inherited by sons collectively unless the estate was partitioned and so on. That sphere had become the object of Indian and British scrutiny, action and intervention for the first time, resulting eventually in the intervention of the post-colonial state. As Chapter 6 will show, when men such as the (so-called) Indian reformer Rammohan Roy argued with these new orthodoxies they didn't dispute the fact that rules existed which governed domestic social life across the whole of Bengal, or that such rules needed to be founded on a stable textual authority of some sort. Where they did argue with colonial officials, it was to suggest that Indian law didn't need the active efforts of the colonial state to make sense.

The new subjects of 'Hindu law' and the Hindu joint family emerged as British officials sought semantic coherence in a world they found difficult to comprehend. To overcome incoherence, officials such as H.T. Colebrooke looked to India's ancient past. As MacNaghten put it, 'the Hindu law, in its pure and original state, does not furnish many instances of uncertainty and confusion'.[65] Yet for MacNaghten at least, this notion of a 'pure and original' ancient Hindu law was a fantasy, created to provide British juridical practice with a credible source of legal authority. 'Ancient' authority was incapable of providing a stable foundation for this British search for the textual rules that were supposed to govern Indian civil society in the present. Removed from the fluid hermeneutic contexts that gave it meaning, the British couldn't make sense of the texts they believed provided the 'original' source of Hindu family law. The authority of the colonial state also needed to be called on. Whilst officials invoked what is sometimes problematically referred to as Indian 'tradition', tradition only made sense if it was produced by the actions of a self-consciously reforming colonial state. Far from being antagonistic terms, Indian tradition and colonial reform were both elements in a single process. Fundamentally, they were both rooted in the colonial search for stable categories with which to govern Bengal. The complex relationship between these two terms and the political theory of the colonial state will be discussed in Chapter 6. Before doing that, this book moves to another sphere in which the anxious and indecisive practices of colonial administration produced new social objects and new concepts of rule: the governance of Bengal's landholders.

5
Governing the Power of Proprietors

A year after the permanent settlement was promulgated, Thomas Brooke, judge of the district of Birbhum in north-western Bengal, wrote to his superiors in Calcutta. Brooke was perplexed. He wanted an answer to a 'general question' about how he should govern disputes between landholders and their tenants. From 1793, the British regime insisted that all Bengal's cultivators accept documents, called *pattas*, that stated the amount and price of the land cultivated. Once *pattas* were issued, did landholders have the right to force their tenants to continue cultivating the same piece of soil year after year? Or were peasants entitled to pick up their implements, take their cattle by the leash and find new fields to plough once they had harvested their crop?

Brooke had no way to decide whether Birbhum's landholders or its peasants were right. In the process of trying to decide he found himself caught between two competing conceptions of his purpose in governing rural Bengal. On the one hand, he believed that he should adjudicate according to 'the general custom of the country', which would have led him to support the *zamindars*. Brooke was susceptible to the arguments of Birbhum's proprietors. They were the men and women he had most contact with. As a member of the English landholding class, it was easiest for him to understand their point of view. Preventing tenants from fleeing their land seemed consistent with 'the Right which the very term Proprietor of the Soil seems legally and naturally to invest them with', he argued. But, this supposed 'custom' contradicted another 'general principle'. 'The grand leading principle of the new system' which Governor-General Lord Cornwallis had introduced to Bengal, Brooke argued, was to give 'the right of Free Agency to all', including the peasant the right to move at will.[1]

The question of whether the rights of landholders and tenants were determined by 'custom' or freedom of contract was central to Victorian debates about the British relationship with agrarian India. Many colonial officials had begun to use the idea of 'ancient', customary rights to defend peasant livelihoods well before Henry Maine emphasised the role of custom in his 1861 *Ancient Law*. For Maine, and for historians since, agrarian society in both Britain and British-ruled India was a battleground in the clash between the destructive forces of capitalist government and the historical, customary rights of the poor.[2] Yet in Birbhum in 1794, 'custom' was used to uphold the privileges of Birbhum's rural elites, not the rights of the rural poor. Nor was there anything 'ancient' about the type of custom Brooke talked about. Brooke's exchange with the Board of Revenue illustrates how inappropriate it is to use the language of nineteenth- and twentieth-century social science to describe what was going in early colonial Bengal.

Instead, this chapter places the British governance of rural Bengal, especially the administration of the relation between landholders and peasants, in a different frame. In Bengal as in other provinces, the emergence of a colonial political culture was not rooted in the British desire to transform Indian society, but in the colonial administration's anxious search for semantic coherence in a world they did not understand. Rather than describing British attitudes towards rural Bengal as a battle between grand ideas about capitalism and modernity, it suggests that practices of governance were underpinned by the colonial search for stable categories of rule.

Brooke's confused response to what he encountered occurred because the colonial regime had not settled the question of how to govern relations between landholders and their tenants in the countryside. The abstract strategies and concepts enunciated by Cornwallis and his colleagues had not created a legible conception of the subjectivity of *zamindars* or *raiyats*; not one, at least, which made sense in the everyday process of governance. Like judges faced with the seeming uncertainty of Hindu law discussed in the previous chapter, Brooke attempted to overcome his anxiety by appealing to an external authority. Unable to understand the practical logic that underpinned the world of landholding to fit his own tactical purposes, he asked his employers in Calcutta for instructions. Brooke's first letter began an exchange of correspondence between himself and the *Sadr Diwani Adalat*, the appeal court in Calcutta. The court didn't offer a rule to guide him, noting that each dispute was to be decided with reference to existing engagements between landholders and tenants or 'the Custom of the district' and forwarding a copy of the regulations without further comment. Not surprisingly, the judge still felt himself 'at a loss how to decide'.

Brooke appealed for the colonial regime to issue and implement a single general set of rules for the governance of agrarian society. He was unsuccessful because, in the 1790s, the courts and councils of Calcutta did not regard themselves as the final authority in the process of establishing stable forms of meaning in the countryside, believing instead that the rules for adjudicating property disputes emerged from local society itself. Later, however, officials were more successful in their appeal for external authorities to resolve these local anxieties. This chapter shows how officials such as Brooke began to rely on a new state-authored definition of the 'rights' of Bengal's landholders. This new conception perceived the agency or power of landholders as an object of governance in a new way. In Brooke's time, the relationship between custom and contract was not clear. By the late 1820s, officials were sure that Bengal's proprietors possessed the freedom or agency to contract. By the 1860s, and the time of Sir Henry Maine, the battleground of agrarian politics was clearly presented as an opposition between 'ancient' custom and 'modern' contract.

One way of perceiving this shift is to describe it as the rise of the doctrine of *laissez-faire* in colonial India. In the period under discussion in this chapter, the view emerged that Bengal's landholders should be allowed to get on with managing their affairs without being hindered by the colonial regime. *Zamindars* were allowed increasing autonomy to manage the relationship with their tenants without interference. As agrarian conditions began to move in favour of the possessors of land not labour in the nineteenth century, this meant the standard of living of peasants and landed intermediaries suffered. But this colonial conception of *laissez-faire* also involved a new conception of colonial authority. It depended on the colonial regime's definition of the powers which landholders were supposed to 'freely' exercise in an ever more technical fashion, a process which made them the target of colonial governance in a new, more systematic way.[3] It involved a conception of agrarian civil society as a field of activity occupied by subjects whose rights and powers could be defined by the state and transcribed in writing. In short, the emergence of colonial *laissez faire* required the colonial state to define its own powers to act upon Bengali landholders in a way it had not done before, to 'make use of the power of individuals', as one official wrote, for the first time.[4]

I

Historians from Ranajit Guha onwards have argued that the permanent settlement was driven by a set of coherent intellectual forces that were then 'implemented' or 'imposed' upon rural society. French physiocracy, Scottish enlightenment political economy or Lockean liberalism are some of the ideological candidates which have been considered as dominating the intellectual environment of Cornwallis' regime.[5] Yet, arguments about the dominant role of one 'doctrine' or another on British rule presume that colonial ambitions possessed a degree of coherence they did not have. In fact, the regulations enacted by Cornwallis' administration did not offer a coherent understanding of the amount of power landholders were supposed to have, or of the relationship between landholders and their tenants. The abstract principle of 'property' was central to British ideas about governing Bengal from the mid-1780s; but other forces were more significant in shaping what actually went on in the district revenue office.

One of the reasons why historians fail to recognise the hesitant and inconclusive character of the debates that took place during Lord Cornwallis' regime is because they confuse the forceful and strident language of political debate in London with the vocabulary used in Calcutta. In Britain, the governance of Bengal was discussed in the London press with a different set of arguments, and in a different style of thought than Calcutta. For example, Ranajit Guha suggests that the 'radical' official Thomas Law was 'the brain behind the permanent settlement', arguing that Law put in place a radical system of *laissez-faire* in Bengal.[6] Yet the evidence Guha presents for Law's significant role comes from his role in defending a settlement with Bengali *zamindars* in London. Between his return to Britain in 1792 and migration to the United States in 1794, Law successfully portrayed himself as the author of Cornwallis' permanent settlement.

After a successful period as Collector of Bihar, Law had been briefly appointed to the Board of Revenue, where he briefly found favour with the Chairman, Thomas Graham. Later he had a direct contact with Cornwallis through his protégée, the secretary to government, George Barlow. But these connections didn't allow Law's arguments to dominate policy-making for the whole of Bengal as he later claimed. Law was the only official who argued in the 1780s that it was possible to sweep away existing customary arrangements and replace them with new forms of contract. The scheme which Law implemented in Gaya and wanted to be introduced to the rest of Bengal was referred to as the 'mocurrey' system after the Persian term *makararidar*, or holder of a form of land grant from the Mughal emperor. If Law had been the architect of the permanent settlement, this word would have recurred throughout British discussion; but the term 'mocurrey' entirely disappeared from the archive after 1793. Law's views went against the grain of the far more historicist position most officials held in the late 1780s. Early in 1789 his position was criticised by one Council member for being 'subversive of the principle of the ancient Mogul Government and contrary to the sense and spirit of the late act of Parliament'.[7] But, on his return to London, Law was briefly successful at convincing the British public that Lord Cornwallis had put his scheme in place, that the permanent settlement had created a new form of property right and left the management of relations between landholders and their tenants to the principle of *laissez-faire*.[8]

Of course, officials in Calcutta had made no such decision. As the *Sadr Diwani Adalat* had insisted to Brooke, district courts were supposed to uphold peasants' rights on the basis of local 'usage' or custom. The governance of relations between landholders and their tenants was left to be determined 'according to local manners, customs, or particular agreements' by district courts.[9] When copies of the 1793 regulations actually arrived in London in 1794, those critical of Law's arguments in the metropolis happily reflected on this fact. One former official, John Prinsep

> observe[d], with infinite satisfaction, that the Government of Bengal, convinced by the hardship and injustice which the Ryots are deemed to suffer under [Law's] Mocurrey system, have already adopted some of the measures for their relief, which it was the object of these letters to suggest.[10]

H.T. Colebrooke, who had been in Bengal in 1793, made a similar point when he wrote that Cornwallis' regulations had not annihilated the *raiyat*'s 'title of occupancy to the soil they so cultivated' in the way he had expected it to. 'In recognising a proprietary right belonging to zemindars', he went on,

> no more can have been intended than to disclaim all pretension on the part of the sovereign to a property in the soil, not to abridge or annul the rights and privileges of other classes.[11]

Samuel Davies, a member of the Court of Directors who had been in Burdwan in 1793, made a similar point. Davies was right to note that it had never 'entered the mind of Lord Cornwallis...to confer on the Zemindars, any new privileges calculated to abridge or destroy in any way the privileges of others'.[12] Cornwallis' government did not offer a blueprint for transforming Bengal's agrarian society. It made a set of anxious but decisive moves in order to create stable structures of administration, and made a vague commitment to uphold local custom; the rate of rent paid by a tenant on a new lease was limited by custom, for example.[13] But the relationship between officials stationed in the Bengali countryside and the rural population was governed by other forces.

The central figure in the process of district revenue extraction was the East India Company's Collector. In 1793, the task of collecting revenue was separated from the function of administering justice. From then onwards, separate judges and collectors were sent to each district in Bengal. For the most part, the British Collector's encounter with Bengali landholding practice occurred in their revenue office or *kachchari*, a building which usually lay in a fairly small official compound in the midst of the district capital, close to other Company buildings such as the court and treasury. The Collector's government of agrarian relations in the revenue office occurred through his manipulation of the flow of written words and numbers in the *kachchari*. During the 1790s, most of the Collector's time was spent reading and writing letters and compiling various kinds of accounts. Correspondence from British officers in Calcutta, from the district judge and officers in neighbouring districts and from subordinate Indian officials and landholders were read and answered.

At the centre of this process of textual exchange, the Collector was surrounded by the Indian officers whom he relied on to perform business. Each Collector had a staff of between 20 and 50 officers, a figure which increased incrementally in the early nineteenth century as the Collector's office was given more routine bureaucratic tasks. These men performed a variety of functions: revenue officials (*amins* and *sezawuls*), record-keepers (*qanungus* and *sarishtadars*), guards, peons and so on.[14] The flow of written work was constantly interrupted by the arrival of landholders and suppliants coming into the 'presence' of the district official. The *kachchari* was often 'full' of people dealing with a variety of business. In Dhaka William Massie noted how difficult it was to 'command silence in [his] kutchery'.[15] Collectors described the task of maintaining order as a difficult one.

As Ghulam Hussein Khan noted, Bengal's new British princes did not 'live among their people'. Hidden away in their offices, collectors rarely physically encountered rural social relations. District tours became commonplace by the middle of the nineteenth century. In the 1790s, officers only left their station because of sickness or leave. District officials conducted business from their *kachchari*, understanding their office as the repository of ordered, textual information about the social and economic relations of the countryside. By contrast the countryside was often perceived as a scene of chaos and tumult, interpreted through the often-perplexing correspondence of Indian subordinate officials who had been sent into the *mofussil* to investigate local matters. Much of the time, the complex tactical negotiations that determined the pattern of rural social relations were seen by European officials as nothing but a tumultuous riot, a contagious form of disorder that continually threatened to engulf the physical space of the office and the texts it relied on. Officials sometimes developed a close relationship, perhaps even friendship, with the small number of prominent landholders who they got to know well. For the most part though, they lacked these affective connections and were wary about the chaos of the countryside infecting the records they used to try to govern it. Indian record-keepers frequently 'appeared suspicious' to British Collectors. Their removal as a consequence was not rare.[16]

The colonial description of disorder was an articulation of the crisis of meaning that bedevilled the eighteenth-century official, an expression of the gap between the abstract categories that were available to them and the practices that they encountered. Nonetheless, forms of knowledge needed to be developed within the *kachchari* which seemed at least to correspond in some fashion to the 'real state of things' in the tumultuous countryside. In particular, knowledge was needed about local agrarian society to decide who should pay how much land revenue to the East India Company. The permanent settlement had fixed the amount of revenue to be collected forever, but it left the task of assigning a revenue demand to each *zamindari* estate in the district's accounts to the Collector.

Even in areas dominated by a small number of landholders, British officials found this a complex enterprise. In the district of Burdwan, an area dominated by a single estate, it involved an understanding of the relations within the *Raja's* family, and an assessment of the relationship between the Burdwan estate and its various dependencies and satellites, a question we shall consider in more detail in the pages below.[17] In Rangpur, the job required the disentanglement of complex political and kinship relations between the 20 or so estates which populated the district; many estates were held jointly by numerous different family members. In areas like Dhaka or Bakarganj the complexity seemed even perplexing. There, as the Collector of Dhaka put it in 1810, 'property is very much divided'.[18] The district of Bakarganj alone had 2659 small estates paying revenue directly to the Company. In these districts, calculating an 'equitable' quantity of revenue was an impossible task. Landholders paid anywhere between half an *anna* to 12 *annas* (0.025 to 0.6 of Rupee) per acre of land in Bakarganj.[19]

The most important texts in the Collector's office during the late eighteenth century listed the names of estates, proprietors and revenue demand.[20] These documents were referred to as the *jama wasil baki*, or settlement accounts. After 1798, they existed alongside the Quinquennial Register, a more complete record of local tenurial arrangements supposed to be written every five years. Officials often found the latter impossible to complete.[21]

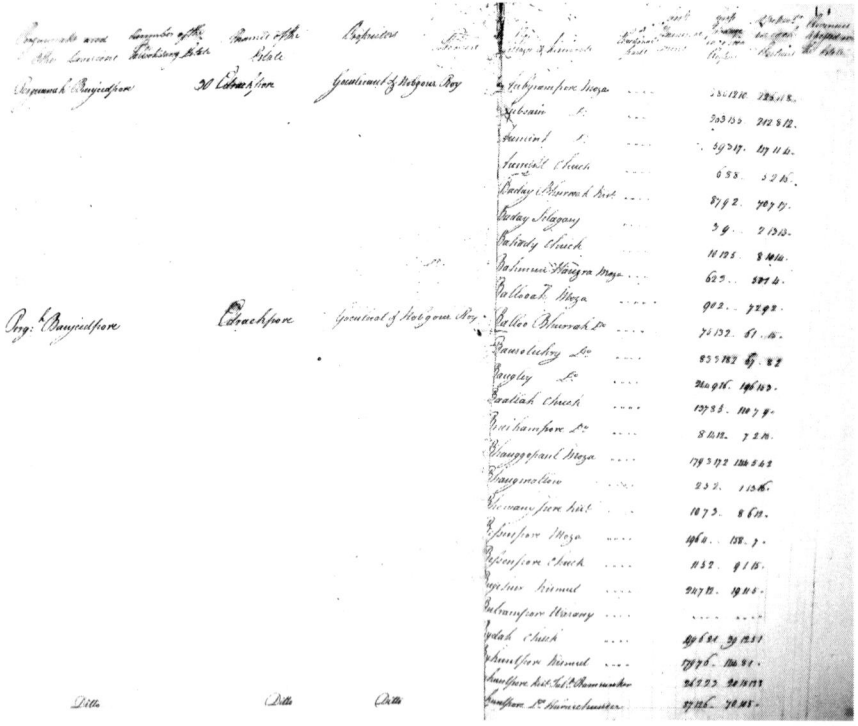

Figure 5.1   Page from Quinquennial Register, 1799, Rangpur District Record Room.

Nonetheless, if they did ever exist in a completed form, these documents would have offered a snapshot of agrarian relations at a single moment, freezing them in time. During the 1790s and early 1800s, officials understood the relationship between landholders and their tenants as little more than a series of stable, cash transactions between different layers of the rural social order. Each tier from peasant to landholder was supposed to pay a non-negotiable sum to the strata above until a fixed amount was received by the Company.

Whilst thinking about custom or usage in the practice of administration, officials instinctively drew from a habitual British repertoire about the inter-dependent hierarchies that structured agrarian landed society in England and lowland Scotland. Normatively, British landed estates were divided between landowners, farmers and labourers: between people who owned, leased and laboured on the land. More important than the details of this threefold divi-sion though was the premise that underpinned it. Propertied social relations and political society was governed by what Scottish philosophers called the 'distinction of ranks', in which each social strata knew their place but had rights, duties and affection towards their superiors and inferiors. Gilbert Stu-art suggested that the idea of the 'distinction of ranks' was 'the first of any value formed by men'. In practice in Britain it was custom, opinion and sen-timent, not the determining power of abstract rules that determined these relationships. They were instinctive responses embedded in the habitual practice of rule, not rigid concepts, so were able to account for the con-tingent ebb and flow of political society. For eighteenth-century English and Scottish commentators, it was this constant connection between different social strata that were supposed to hold political society together.[22]

In Britain this way of perceiving the social order was inseparable from an understanding of the fluid and contingent forms of interaction that con-stituted the polity. The forms of interaction that existed in a particular locality consisted of political relationships of domination and incorpora-tion, based on intuition and habitual forms of interpersonal understanding instead of abstract right. Some of these habitual forms of understanding were transported to India, to influence Thomas Brooke's attitude to *zamindars* in Birbhum, for example. But they had very different effects in a colonial context. In pre-colonial Bengal, connections between *zamindar*, *taluqdar* and *raiyat* had had a political dimension based as they were on short-term fluctuations in the terms that bound each to one other. But in Bengal the Company's officers used an idea of the distinction of ranks to describe a set of relationships that were not supposed to have this dynamic participatory character. Without an understanding of the contingencies of local politics, British officials attempted to enforce a stable financial hierar-chy between landholder and tenant in which these tactical manoeuvres and political negotiations played no part.

Of course though, agrarian relations in Bengal did not remain static for long. The textual technologies used to implement the permanent settle-ment produced a gap between the static, synchronic, texts produced in the *kachchari* and the constantly changing practice of landholding in the 'tumul-tuous' countryside outside. In particular, what they did not provide was a set of rules to determine whether the actions of particular subjects, *zamindars* or *raiyats*, were legitimate or not.[23] Without categories able to comprehend these tactical and contingent political relationships, instances of negotiation and resistance were seen as signs of 'ignorance and incapacity' or 'arbitrariness'. Normal alterations in the rate of rent or movement of cultivators from one estate to another were treated as evidence of the lamentable, pathological state of governance before the British arrival. John Shore considered 'the arbitrary impositions of the zemindars' (in other words the way they varied rent according to changing local conditions) as an 'abuse' which undermined the prosperity of Bengal. The mobility of peasants and the 'continual breach of engagements with the ryots' were treated in a similar fashion. Shore was perceptive enough to note 'the ryots derive advantages even from abuses' on occasion, because it gave them opportunity for 'imposing on their landlords'. But like other officials, he believed that such fluctuations were 'oppressive' to Bengal's lower classes in general. Officials were concerned that the dynamism of Bengali landholding practice made 'dominion over a populous and extensive country vested in a few strangers differing in language, religion, habits and laws' ungovernable.[24]

The British attempt to govern a stable distinction of ranks in Bengal intersected with a second influence on the Company's practical government of landholding, the pre-colonial, Mughal forms of documentation and surveillance which had encrusted themselves into the practice of the district revenue office. The Company abolished many key Mughal posts. But some of the habits and techniques which eighteenth-century Mughal and post-Mughal regimes had used to govern agrarian society continued to exist informally within the *kachchari*, as British officers employed Indians who had been employed by the Mughal regime to compile records and accounts. The business of revenue collection was conducted in the Mughal language of government, Persian. Documents such as the *jama wasil baki*, the *tauji* accounts (which denoted which tenant should pay what) or the *bazi zamin daftar* (register of revenue free land) were written in Persian before being translated into English, having been compiled by Indian officials who retained some allegiance to the late Mughal regime's governing practice. What underpinned much of this documentation was the attempt to survey and define relations between landholders and their tenants.

These techniques were the lingering after-effects of an early-eighteenth-century Mughal attempt to tighten its control of agrarian relations. As Muzaffar Alam and Sanjay Subrahmanyam argue, Bengal's Mughal governors had attempted to introduce a much tighter form of provincial governance in the 1720s and 1730s, at precisely that point that the province's relations with Delhi were loosening.[25] However vain this attempt to assert a coherent Mughal conception of rural governance over the complexities of local society may have been, fragmented elements of Mughal practice survived and congealed around the district revenue office. Post-Mughal Indian officials such as the *qanungu, sarishtadar* and *amin* saw themselves as men whose role was to monitor the relationship between landholders and their tenants, as well as engage in the protracted negotiations that revenue collection actually relied on. Some of these had been abolished by Cornwallis' new constitution. Especially at a junior level, many remained essential to the everyday functioning of British administration.

II

Within the institution of the district revenue office, these two influences intersected to produce a series of practices by which the district Collector's office attempted to regulate the relationship between *zamindars* and *raiyats*. Fearing the effects of arbitrary imposts on peasants' livelihoods, Collectors tried to abolish the discretionary levies that landholders used to collect money to pay for short-term expenses such as weddings, funerals and particular religious rites. They occasionally scrutinised the accounts of *zamindars* to ensure that rent was reasonable, often insisting that rents should be charged at the putative *nirik* or customary rate, even where there was no evidence such a fixed rate had ever existed. In the rare instances when they were convinced of the existence of a stable local 'custom', judicial officials were willing to uphold the supposed rights of *raiyats* and leaseholders against their *zamindars*. And Collectors insisted that landholders issue *pattas* to their cultivators. Each of these practices was supposed to secure the place of each strata, *raiyats* as well as *zamindars*, in Bengal's stable distinction of ranks. Each also involved an attempt to ensure the dynamism of 'real life' outside the *kachchari* conformed to the static lines written on the district's accounts in documents held within the revenue office, a project which post-Mughal Indian officials, with their fantasy about the power of the local revenue office over local society, were often willing to be enlisted within. But, faced with the necessity of finding stable sources of revenue, the colonial regime's attempt to freeze the dynamism of landholder–tenant relations didn't last long.

An examination of the Company's *patta* policy shows this. *Pattas* were pieces of writing supposed to offer a representation of the stable, customary financial relationship that was between landholder and tenant. The *patta* regulation made it clear that the rules governing landholder–tenant relations were not created by the text. 'The rents to be paid by the ryots', it stated, 'by whatever rule of custom they may be regulated, shall be specifically stated in the pottah'. *Pattas* were supposed to be adaptable to the 'various descriptions of tenure by which Ryots generally cultivate', not introduce a new form of right.[26] *Pattas* were not meant to create new forms of tenure, but supposed to make existing arrangements legible to the colonial regime. Reducing the relationship between the landholder and tenant 'to writing' would stabilise local agrarian relations and prevent the 'arbitrary' and abusive exercise of local power.

British officers expected *zamindari* hostility to the measure, but were surprised to note that landholders enthusiastically distributed the new documents. But landholders didn't see the text as a representation of an existing set of relationships. They used it to try to reconstitute their vulnerable polities on a more secure basis with colonial support. By contrast, the British assumed peasants would eagerly seize on the documents as a way of having their rights secured at last; in fact the attempt to fix the terms and conditions of peasants was vigorously resisted by the rural poor. Mobility and landholder insecurity had been the weapon used by the weak to improve their living standards. Tenants preferred to engage in face-to-face, negotiated transactions rather than have their 'rights' fixed in a written form in advance.[27] As one cultivator in Bihar put it, 'the *maliks* [landholders] are wealthy and we are poor, so they should be bound and we should be free'.[28] Where Collectors did manage to circulate *pattas*, they only did so once they had assured the rural population that the terms of their cultivation could be altered after the document was issued. This condition in turn depended on the Collector's unauthorised assurance to landholders that the government's revenue demand could be deferred in difficult times as well.[29]

Without an effective understanding of the politics of local landholding, district officials viewed peasants' resistance as evidence of their irrrationality. John Lumisden, the Collector of Rangpur suggested that the introduction of *pattas* would occur gradually, 'after the mass of the people shall be convinced by the experience of the more Enlightened few', he noted.[30] This British view of peasant irrationality was rooted in the colonial fantasy that agrarian practices occurring outside the revenue office exactly mirrored the rigid relationships transcribed in documents inside the *kachchari*. Colonial rhetoric's critical description of peasant behaviour emerged from the impossible British attempt to apply the vague and abstract concepts that emerged in the disconnected world of colonial administration to the practice of landholding outside.

In the face of peasant resistance, the Company's insistence that *zamindars* issue their tenants with *pattas* was quietly dropped. By 1800, the *patta* had disappeared as a subject of attention for colonial officials. Fifteen years later, the *patta* policy had been almost entirely forgotten, many officials not even believing the relevant regulation had been implemented at all. So little trace of the policy survived into the nineteenth century that Samuel Davies, an official who returned to England in 1806 and took a seat on the Court of Directors, noted that it became a 'dead letter' before any effort was made to put it into practice in the countryside.[31]

The fate of the Company's *patta* policy is a good example of the conflict that occurred between the dynamic politics of rural Bengal and the methods officials used to govern them. But it connected to a broader process, in which British officials redefined the categories they used to govern rural Bengal in response both to peasant politics and their most pressing imperative, the need to find a stable source of revenue. The 1790s and early 1800s were far more difficult decades for the Company's revenue collection machine than most historians recognise.[32] Coupled with the growing cost of military activity in north India, the difficulty of collecting revenue allowed the Company's debt increased significantly. In 1793, the Company's debt in India was around £9 million. By 1810, it stood at around £32 million, with an additional £7 million owed to investors in Britain, as the costs of war grew and the collection of revenue remained a fraught enterprise.[33]

At a local level, landholders were frequently unable or unwilling to pay the amount of revenue specified in the Collector's accounts each year. Every month, a letter arrived in the district *kachchari* anxiously asking the Collector about the amount of arrears and reasons for their 'balances'. In the late 1790s and early 1800s, most districts and many estates were significantly in arrears. When landholders were unable to pay the rent specified in the permanent settlement, Company officials attempted to sell their estates.[34] The regulations of 1793 had contained the infamous 'sunset clause', which allowed the British government of Bengal to dispossess landholders of their land rights if they were unable to meet their obligations to pay revenue to the Company. Land had been sold for arrears well before 1793. What was novel, however, was the rigidity with which officials attempted to enforce the sale law. Previously, the sale of land was accompanied by a process of negotiation between the government and Bengali landholders. But in the new, post-1793 environment, officials were unable to trust their experience of local landholding enough to know whether the complaints of landholders who insisted they were unable to pay were legitimate or not. Even where a district Collector did try to be charitable, local views were invariably overruled by the Board of Revenue in Calcutta. Isolated from the tactical manoeuvres that underpinned the practice of landholding, officials treated the financial relationships codified in documents such as the *jama wasil baki* as absolute statements of what *should* occur in the countryside. Landholders who protested about their inability to pay were rarely able to circumvent the increasingly rigid logic of the Company's bureaucratic machine and prevent their land from being put up for sale. The result was that when a landholder went into arrears, the Board of Revenue ordered that a portion of their estate adequate to meet the deficit was rapidly put up for sale.

Whilst the Company followed the financial logic codified in its revenue accounts rigidly, landholders needed to bend and accommodate themselves to the demands of their tenants if they were to be able to retain control of their local polity and collect rent at all. *Zamindars* frequently complained about being caught between these contradictory pressures. In March 1798, a petition arrived in the Collector of Rangpur's office, signed by the vast majority of the district's 20 or so powerful landlords. The petitioners complained that the Company had not made any allowance 'in the event of any calamity of season'. The petitioners claimed that when peasants had been issued with *pattas* in 1792, the Board of Revenue had promised that it would 'make due consideration of our situation and our circumstances' each year and 'allow the necessary deduction, and in proportion to the amount remitted to us, a similar indulgence would necessarily be extended by us to our ryots'. In fact, this had not happened. A devastating flood had occurred in 1796. Early in 1798, the rice crop was diminished by a lack of rain.

> [D]eprived of the means of payment [the ryots] plead total inability when called upon for their rents. To use any coercive measures to secure payment would cause a desertion among [them], and be productive of infinite losses both account the demand of the previous and the ensuing year.

The East India Company had not granted the 'indulgence' it had promised. Hence, the *zamindars* complained that 'many of our estates have been subjected to sale, and we reduced to the distress of disposing of [our] effects and taking loans from bankers'. These measures, they argued, would further weaken their authority over their tenants and make it yet harder for the Company to collect revenue.[35]

The petition concluded with a request for a remission of revenue for two months, to be repaid over the following years. Alexander Wright, the district Collector, was sympathetic to the landholder's point of view. But from the aloof perspective of Calcutta, the Board of Revenue summarily dismissed the landholders' complaints, and continued to enforce the sale of estates for arrears each month. In the midst of the flood of 1798, land with a revenue value of Rs 49,000, roughly 8% of the district, had been put up for sale in one month alone. A Rs 8,800 portion of the Idrakpur estate was sold the following month; Rs 22,000 was put up for sale again in March 1799.[36]

In his pathbreaking examination of the 'permanent settlement in operation', Sirajul Islam shows that something like 45% of the total revenue value of Bengal changed hands between 1793 and 1802 through sales of this kind. Islam's analysis, along with the detailed study of Ratnalekha Ray, show that the main impact of the 'sale law' was to break-up the largest landed estates in Bengal and redistribute the possession of *zamindari* rights amongst a larger number of local gentry.[37] As Sugata Bose notes, '[t]he impotence of zamindars squeezed between a grasping state and recalcitrant raiyats was evident during the immediate aftermath of 1793'.[38] As they were caught between the rigidity of the Company's revenue demands and the insistence by peasants on flexibility, nine out of Bengal's twelve 'great *zamindaris*' were dismembered. Two of the large estates which have been discussed in this book vanished in the process. The estate of Idrakpur in Rangpur district, subject to a protracted battle over the interpretation of the law governing the Hindu joint family that we examined in the previous chapter, was sold to a number of different local portfolio capitalists in the late 1790s. The Chandradwip Raj in Bakarganj, once in the possession of the powerful local leader and *gosthipathi* Durga Kuar Narayan, was sold to a conglomerate of local financial interests including the Greek brothers Alexander and George Paniotty at the same point in time. The only large estate that survived was Burdwan, in west Bengal. It only survived because its ruler, Raja Tejchandra, changed the way local agrarian society was ruled.

The sale of estates had a significant impact on the Company's ability to collect a stable revenue stream because new purchasers were rarely able to gain control of the estates they had bought. The British administration presumed that the inscription of a new name in the district account book would quickly correspond to a new proprietor exercising the role of local *zamindar*. This rarely occurred, as evicted landholders used a range of tactics to retain their sentimental connection to local rural society. As Chapter 2 argued, local rulers and their subjects were temporarily bound together by a dense network of institutions and practices, which included support for the poor, religious institutions and other sites of local cultural authority. Where the previous landholder had played the local game of patronage well, it was difficult for the new purchasers to collect rent. New purchasers could only sever the affective connections that linked landholders with their 'subjects' if they quickly established their own image of authority by offering financial support to tenants, patronising local civic establishments and spending lavishly on festivals and food.[39] Where the new purchaser was less adept, and the previous ruler effectively fulfilled all these local roles, as the Raja of Chandradwip and landholders of Idrakpur had been, it was difficult for the new purchaser to establish a local power base.

The difficulty the Company faced collecting revenue occurred because officials did not make sense of Bengali landholding practice. The Company's cash crisis was underpinned by a colonial crisis of meaning. Officials remained uncertain how they should adjudicate disputes between landholders and tenants, or between new purchasers and old *zamindars*. Frequently one official took one side, and another the other. In particular, district judges and collectors frequently disagreed.[40] The authority of the two main British officials were often set against each other. As rival groups of local forces attempted to mobilise the power of each, pitched battles occurred between the servants of the Judge and Collector. When the revenue official Fakhir Mohammed Chaprasi was sent into the countryside to put the Paniotty brothers in possession of the land they had bought from Durga Kuar Narayan, he found himself confronted by officers employed by the judge. As well as using his considerable local cultural authority to retain control of the estate, Durga Kuar initiated proceedings with the judge of Bakarganj against the Paniotty brothers, which allowed him to bring the judge's servants and *thanadari* (police) officers into the fray on his own side. At one point, Fakhir Mohammed found

Deepak Gopal, the *raja's* agent, assembled with hundreds of men wielding *lathis*. Deepak Gopal called out that he was acting on the authority of Mirza Ibrahim, the *diwan* of the judge. Fakhir Mohammed

> answered that Mirza Sahib might be Master of the Adawalut [judicial court], but this was a Revenue affair, and that [he] had come from the Collector to put the purchasers at the sale in possession. They took the Perwanna [*parwana*] from me, tore it up, and pushed me, saying they had nothing to do with my Collector

and so would ignore his orders.[41] The *raja's* men imprisoned the Collector's *gumashta* and *peons* and imprisoned them in the police office. They were only freed when the judge received an irate letter from the Collector demanding their liberty.[42] In cases such as this, landholders' use of the Company's institutions prevented the Company's own revenue from being paid.

The absence of stable criteria to decide disputes meant that officers were also dragged into conflict between various levels of the revenue-collecting hierarchy. Tensions between *zamindars* and *raiyats* occurred as officials had no criteria to decide whether a landholder trying to bind the tenant to the soil or the tenant who wished to flee was right. But disputes between *zamindars* and more prosperous sub-renters were more common, having a more serious impact on revenue collection. In Rangpur, a protracted argument between Mirza Ali Naki, a wealthy local portfolio capitalist whose family had farmed much of the region before Warren Hastings, and the *zamindar* of Kankina, Ram Rudr Chaudhuri, simmered on for years. Formally, Mirza Ali leased land from Ram Rudr Chaudhuri. But British officials were unable to decide what the 'customary' relationship between the two was. Ram Rudr complained that Mirza Ali had consolidated his own local power against the Company's best interests. 'From a refractory spirit', he 'drove away the sezawul [Company's agent appointed to divide the estate], and by inveigling away the Ryots and Putwarries, appropriates to his own use and thus embezzles the public revenue'. With the support of the district Collector, in 1796 Ram Rudr brought a case to sell the property of Mirza Ali. But, Mirza Ali successfully manipulated the judge's vague sense of 'the custom of the country' – and Ram Rudr lost.[43] The chaotic state of local decision-making is illustrated by the fact that four years later James Wordsworth, the same judge, decided an almost identical case involving the same landlord, Ram Rudr Chaudhuri in the plaintiff's favour.[44] Seeing themselves as strangers to Indian society, without a local hermeneutic framework to make sense of local agrarian society, the colonial state's local administrators were unable to decide who was right in each case, and found it difficult to secure a regular supply of revenue from the countryside. Indecision meant that disputes ricocheted around the different levels of judicial and revenue authority for years, obstructing the flow of revenue in the process.

III

The tensions and contradictions this chapter has discussed altered the way Company officials governed rural society. One sign of that shift was a change in the way in which officials spoke about the 'distinction of ranks' in Bengal. During the late 1780s and early 1790s, officials assumed that the conduct of landholders in varying the rate of rent was the greatest obstacle to the existence of a hierarchical 'distinction of ranks' in Bengal. Landholders' arbitrary power was seen as the greatest threat to social order. A decade later, one begins to see this language of the 'distinction of ranks' being used to make exactly the opposite argument. Writing in 1802, Henry Strachey, the Collector of Midnapore echoed a familiar concern with the distinction of ranks when he suggested that '[t]here exists not between the common people and the rulers, a middle order, who feel a common interest in the prosperity of the state'. But Strachey inverted the usual emphasis on the absence of intermediaries in pre-colonial India's 'despotic' society with the argument that it was under British rule that the proper 'distinction of ranks' had been disturbed. In Mughal times, he suggested, *zamindars* had 'possess[ed] a considerable degree of military, fiscal and civil power' which allowed them 'to keep their dependents in a state of union' and thus 'protect them and maintain themselves'. Under British rule landholders had been 'reduced to the same condition, and placed at an equal distance from us, as their lowest ryots'. Bengal had become ungovernable as a result. Without a clear conception of the power of Bengal's *zamindars*, 'government is unable to direct', Strachey argued, 'or in any way make use of the power of individuals' for its own ends.[45] By failing to form an adequate conception of the kind of power landholders were able to wield, British policy had caused the almost 'universal destruction of zemindars' in a way which countered the best interests of the British regime. Landholders would only be able to pay the Company revenue if they were able to 'maintain themselves'. That could only occur if a clear conception of the power that landholders had over their estates was enshrined in the Company's governing practices.

In one sense, it was Bengal's landholders themselves who put their 'power' over local agrarian society on the Company's conceptual map. In the late eighteenth century, *zamindars* had frequently complained about their own inability to collect revenue. But, these complaints usually consisted of an attempt to enlist the coercive authority of the British regime on their side to put them 'in possession' of land. George Paniotty, one of the purchasers of the Chandrawip estate, had complained about the Company's inability or unwillingness to institute 'vigorous measures' to put him in charge of the estate. The Rajas of Burdwan constantly bemoaned their powerlessness against 'refractory' tenants and initially tried to appropriate the authority of the British regime to bolster their local power.[46] In each case, landholders proposed a flexible, collaborate partnership between *zamindari* and British authority, not a clear set of rules that defined what actions a landholder was allowed to commit.

When the British began to be concerned about the 'power' of landholders they did something rather different. British officials did not want to assist *zamindars* whenever they needed British support; doing so would have led to an enormous drain on the Company's time and resources. Instead, they were interested in defining the authority which landholders were supposed to exercise autonomously, without continual Company assistance.

This process began with the infamous *panjam* and *haftam* regulations, the 'Law of Distraint' and 'Law of Eviction' passed in 1799 and 1812.[47] These regulations enshrined and consolidated the *zamindars'* ability to dispossess the property of tenants who did not pay them rent according to existing engagements, and then to make whatever terms with their tenants as they wished. Up to 1799 landholders trying to enforce the payment of rent had been subject to the fluctuation in British attitudes about 'customary' rents and tenurial terms, uncertainties which subordinate leaseholders were able to use to obstruct the flow of cash from their plots to the landholder to the Company's treasury. But as Regulation VII of 1799 put it '[t]he powers which the landholders and farmers of land paying revenue to Government are allowed to exercise, for enforcing payment of the rents due to them from under-tenants, ha[d] in some cases been found...insufficient'.[48] By passing Regulation VII, the Company cut through the semantic web of the colonial court and *kachchari*, and 'enabled' the landholder to distrain without engaging in the complex process of litigation.

Regulation V of 1812, the infamous *panjam* (fifth) regulation, was the first measure to define the rights and powers *zamindars* were allowed to exercise in a series of pithy, textual rules. In doing so, it marked the final end of the Company's belief in the role of local 'custom' as the standard of rent; at least until the 1860s.[51] As Samuel Davies noted in 1816, it also marked the final demise of the 'dead letter' of the *patta* regulation. A further regulation, VIII of 1816 was passed to make it easier to sell a *patni* tenure once it had been reclaimed by the *zamindar* by voiding all the subordinate leases. Both of these enactments seemed to enshrine the landholder's ability to determine the terms and conditions that tenants were subject to on their estates at will. But in defining the landholder's power in this way, it also involved a new conception of the Company's own ability to issue rules which determined the conduct of subjects across the Bengali countryside.

In part, these regulations were passed to legitimise the Burdwan Raja's increasingly bureaucratic approach to managing his estate. Beginning at the turn of the nineteenth century, *Raja* Tejchandra of Burdwan (1770–1832) developed a form of tenure that mirrored the permanent settlement on a more local scale. The Raja began to divide Burdwan into plots, and sell the right to collect revenue for a fee followed by a fixed, annual sum of rent. If these terms were not met, the leaseholders' land could be sold. These new tenures were called *patni*, its holders *patnidars*. Burdwan's new form of tenure reciprocated the relationship that Raja Tejchandra had with the East India Company. The *patnidar* system was Tejchandra's own permanent settlement of Burdwan. It was a way of redefining the agrarian relations that existed on the estate to fit with the logic that underpinned the Company's unrelenting insistence on a stable source of revenue. Before the turn of the nineteenth century, the connection between the *raja* or *rani* and his or her subjects had been forged in a complex process of negotiation in which terms and conditions were not fixed in writing. The *patni* system replaced this link with a fixed, non-negotiable relationship that was defined in a textual form.[49]

British officials had argued over the legality of Tejchandra's move. Without a clear way of delineating the 'custom of the country', district courts decided the issue in a variety of almost arbitrary ways. Even after the *haftam* and *panjam* regulations, officials still felt they had no clear guidance. At the Bankura *diwani adalat*, where many Burdwan disputes came up, the judges tended to side with Tejchandra or his son Pratapchandra's arguments, issuing decrees which upheld his absolute power to determine the shape of *patni* tenure. But in Burdwan itself before 1816 William Butterworth Bayley (the unlikely advocate of codification discussed in the previous chapter) attempted to uphold the rights of subordinate leaseholders. Bayley argued that the landholder should not cancel the rights of tenants at will.[50]

A complex range of intellectual resources were used to make the argument on each side of the *patni* question, some of which relied on an appeal to the past. Pratapchandra claimed it was his customary prerogative as *zamindar* to annul all leases subordinate to him; *patnidars* and *darpatnidars* themselves were acting in a fraudulent, arbitrary and illegal fashion by absconding from the estates. Officials built on these claims to argue that the Company's judicial regulations had introduced a restriction on the power of landholders that was unwarranted in Indian history. This historical argument had, we should remember, been made by Henry Strachey as well. In contrast, others argued that Pratapchandra's actions consisted of an attempt to overturn the historical rights of leaseholders, in order to 'plunder the undertenants of his Estate' in an unregulated, arbitrary fashion.[52] In each case, landholders and officials appealed to a static view of Bengal's agrarian past in order to provide justification for a regulation that would change things for the future.

The complex and seemingly marginal issue of leaseholding in Burdwan mattered because the estate was the largest single component of Bengal's land tax, constituting Rs 32.6 lakh (£326,000) to the Company's treasury in 1791.[53] If Burdwan descended into chaos and poverty, the Company's finances would be seriously undermined. However badly it fell into arrears, conflict between Tejchandra and the British in the years immediately after

1790 proved how difficult it would be to collect revenue by dispossessing its proprietor. But Burdwan was also taken more seriously because it was one of the few places where a close link existed between the Collectors and Raja in the district. There is evidence to suggest that Burdwan was one of the few places in Bengal where there was something of an Anglo-Indian social circle, in which Collectors and members of the ruling family socialised together.[54] Those connections, together with the scale of the financial odds at stake, meant the pleas of Burdwan's Raja could not be dismissed as easily as the plaintive voice of *zamindars* elsewhere. The Company's policy changed as a result of communication, perhaps even friendship, between a landholder and Collector concerned with the tactical immediacy of a set of local circumstances. Nonetheless, the only way the Company was able to make sense of the situation was to formulate a new set of general rules.

In one sense, this set of regulations tended to enshrine the principle of *laissez-faire* in the Bengal government's administration of landholder–tenant relations. Regulations VII of 1799, V of 1812 and VIII of 1816 left it up to landholders to determine the type of arrangements their tenants were subject to. They stopped the deluge of litigation from leaseholders trying to stop landholders from enhancing rent. By giving landholders the 'power' to determine the shape of local agrarian relations as they wished, these acts prevented the middle and lower strata of Bengal's rural society from appropriating the Company's institutions in order to achieve their own ends. In the process, they helped to enshrine the position of Bengal's new elite, the largely Hindu *bhadralok* who resided in Calcutta but earned an income from their increasingly absentee *zamindari* estates.

But this *laissez-faire* policy involved a new colonial conception of the relationship between government and landholders as well. Landholders had begun to be classified as men (and they were normatively perceived as men) whose actions were determined by a pithy set of rules that covered the whole of Bengal, not as individuals whose behaviour depended on local custom. This new relationship involved a shift in the British regime's conception of its own authority. By the late 1810s, the Company had begun to explicitly assert its power to define the rights of landlords and tenants in a way it had not done before. Regulations such as the *haftam* and *panjam* objectified the Bengali landholder as a being who possessed a form of agency defined in textual rules authorised by the state, instantiating the agency of both the 'landholder' and colonial 'state' in more concrete terms in the process.

This epistemological shift had a powerful influence on social relations in rural Bengal. Because the district court could no longer be used to interrupt the collection process, it was easier for landholders to collect rent. As a consequence, the spate of forced sales decreased. By 1820, the 'massive turnover' in property rights which had occurred since 1793 had ceased. Over time, 'landowners' became a new collective subject that began to express their identity and 'interests' with their own voice, articulated through organisations such as the Indian Landowners Association formed in 1838. Chapter 7 below shows how these new categories influenced a significant set of social and cultural changes that enabled a new intellectual environment in Calcutta and elsewhere to emerge. The transformation of Bengal's political society depended on the emergence of a new social subject, the Bengali *zamindar* or 'landed proprietor'.

In the 1790s, the category of the 'landed proprietor' only made sense in so far it denoted an individual with a financial relationship with the East India Company. Anyone who paid revenue directly into the Company's coffers was a 'proprietor' or 'landholder'. As Samuel Davies put it, 'the term proprietor serves only as an index whereby we refer to the terms and conditions of engagement' between the Company and themselves.[55] The actions of landholders outside the revenue office had not been objectified: the landed proprietor was a phantom figure who existed nowhere but in ledgers and accounts housed in the Company's revenue officers, in documents such as the Quinquennial register for example. For Bengal's rural elites themselves, *zamindars* were little kings and local political leaders, as words such as *zamindar*, *taluqdar*, *chaudhuri* (head man) and *raja* merged into one another. These titles, however, referred to conduct that had little to do with what was written in the Company's account books.

In the early nineteenth century, 'the Bengali landholder' or 'proprietor' appear as the dominant figure on the new epistemological terrain of Bengali 'society'. The 'landholder' began to appear as a social actor whose behaviour outside the Company's revenue office was mapped onto codified forms of written knowledge, most importantly within forms of textualised law such as regulations or Company orders. But this subject had a life of its own. Rather than merely describing themselves with the old Mughal administrative category of *zamindar*, this increasingly Hindu group drew from Sanskrit to occasionally use the Bengali neologism *bhumyadhikari*, literally 'land-right-holder', implying that they were attached to the territory of Bengal (*bhumi*) with rights and powers (*adhikar*) defined by ancient law.[56] Proprietors regarded themselves as individuals whose conduct was determined by a set of pithy textualised rules that extended far beyond the Company's regulations: it had ancient foundations which needed to be rearticulated by the colonial state. Here, their role began to be the object of both celebration and critique. They had become the object of stable forms of British and Indian discourse, and thus, in the process, could be acted upon by the Company's regime for the first time.

IV

The *zamindar* was a peculiarly Bengali character who, in his colonial form, emerged from the vicissitudes of government in one province. Officials in other regions of India emphasised the centrality of other figures to agrarian society instead: the 'cultivator' of the soil himself, the proprietary peasant, the village headman, for example. The appearance of these figures shared with the Bengal debate a common set of epistemological presuppositions about the relationship between agrarian society, governance and time that did not exist in the 1790s.

Traces of a new interest in the rights of peasants rather than landholders can be found in the debates between Thomas Law and his critics in London mentioned above.[57] But one has to look to British-ruled South India to see where serious concern about defining the rights and powers of India's cultivating population first emerged. The key figure here was Thomas Munro. First of all as Collector of districts ceded from the Nizam of Hyderabad, then Judicial Commissioner and later Governor of Madras, Thomas Munro was significant in placing the rights of *raiyats* on the colonial regime's mind.

In 1798, at the provocation of George Barlow in particular, the Governor-General and Board of Control insisted that Cornwallis' 'Bengal system' should be introduced to the East India Company's growing territory in Madras presidency. Munro was a staunch opponent of the extension of the *zamindari* system elsewhere.[58] Munro believed that India's cultivators, its *raiyats*, had a greater claim to be 'landed proprietors' than its *zamindars*. His response was to develop his own rival form of *raiyatwar* settlement, in which revenue was levied directly from peasants rather than through landed proprietors.

In part Munro's arguments were rooted in the different political history of the southern provinces where Munro gained most of his experience. Before British rule, the South's 'poligars' (the word is a transliteration of the Telugu *palegadu* or Tamil *palaiyakkar*) had been little chieftains, kings whose authority was far more closely connected to the use of violence than *zamindars* in Bengal. In Bengal the Company only engaged in sustained military conflict with the descendents of the former Mughal governor, but in the south they engaged in a protracted set of military engagements to 'subdue' these chieftains. The threat of military opposition seemed far greater in the South. It was, as David Washbrook notes,

not until 1799 that 'the menace' of Tipu [Sultan] was finally extirpated. Nor until 1804 that the Maratha threat to overrun the South was curtailed. And, even afterwards, British military power long loved in fear of challenge by 'contumacious' rajas, 'rapacious' Pindaris, 'fanatical' Mapillas, 'barbarous' tribesmen, the extensive kin-group of Tipu and even its own soliders – as manifested in the Vellore mutiny of 1806.[59]

Whilst in Bengal peasant rebellion was a more serious source of local violence, in Madras the greatest threat to 'peace' seemed to come from armed local chieftains. Munro began his career as a military officer involved in the process of 'pacifying' the South's armed elites. For him, collecting revenue directly from cultivators was a mechanism for removing the military and political capabilities of a class of men considered dangerous to the Company's authority.

Yet Munro's thought was guided by more than southern particularism. It was also intended as an attack on the 'system' implemented by Lord Cornwallis in 1793, a system he believed was as inapplicable to Bengal itself as it was to Madras. As Burton Stein argues in his detailed account of Munro's life and thought, *raiyatwar* offered an alternative approach to the governance of agrarian society that was supposed to apply to the whole of India.[60] Munro's thought about agrarian government was developed at precisely the point at which the crisis of revenue collection which we have traced in this chapter was at its most severe, between 1800 and 1805 or so. His writings on agrarian Madras confront the same concerns which dominated the British discussion of rural Bengal: first of all, the security of the Company's revenue collection; secondly, the ability of British officials to develop stable forms of knowledge which allowed agrarian India to be governable.

The problem with Cornwallis' 'Bengal system', Munro argued, was that it had not defined the rights and powers of the rural population clearly enough. Discussing Cornwallis' insistence that *raiyats* be issued with *pattas*, he noted that

[t]he language of both the Bengal and Madras regulation appears to me extremely vague and indefinite. In both it states that the proprietor shall enter into engagements with the Rayats, but in neither does it specify whether the proprietor may or may not fix the rent at what rate he pleases.[61]

Officials refused to define the actual terms on which peasants cultivated. They remained locked away in their *kachcharis* talking to no-one but a narrow strata of the district's landed elites. Munro argued that Bengal's Collectors knew nothing about what was really going on in Bengal. In practice, 'the assessment' of land revenue in Bengal was 'perfectly arbitrary'. In contrast, a direct settlement with *raiyats* would enable 'government at all times to know at all times the actual resources of the country, and to judge what can be drawn from it in the event of a war or other emergency'. The *raiyatwar* settlement would diminish the gap between ruler and ruled. 'By bringing Government into immediate contact with the people it enables it to know their situation', Munro suggested. His scheme 'keeps open a constant intercourse between [*raiyats*] and the Collector'.[62]

Munro was particularly concerned about the effect which the Company's separation of judicial and revenue powers had in exacerbating local chaos and uncertainty. Cornwallis left most questions concerning the relationship between landholders and their tenants to the discretion of local courts. Separated from the Company's revenue collecting machinery, the district courts were initially supposed to adjudicate land disputes according to local 'custom'. Without a context or set of practices able to convert facts into norms though, British officials were unable to determine stable forms of customary right. Munro noted that questions such as the amount of rent to be collected from a peasant, or the terms on which they rented their land were left 'as open to litigation as ever'; and litigation prevented the prompt receipt of revenue. A decade before James Mill made a similar argument, Munro proposed uniting judicial and revenue powers, and giving Collectors the discretion to adjudicate disputes as well as determine both local rights and the rates of revenue that *raiyats* paid.

Munro argued that across pre-colonial India the sovereign had been the ultimate proprietor of the land. Peasants had possessed stable rights to the soil they tilled. So unlike Mill, Munro claimed that his *raiyatwar* settlement was rooted in the 'ancient law' or 'ancient custom' of India. Compared to the arguments of the 1790s, Munro, however, transformed the epistemological basis on which this use of historical precedent occurred. Cornwallis and Shore suggested that pre-colonial history offered an uncertain, unstable source of authority for the general practice of British government but they claimed that the actual rights of peasants and landlords in each district needed to be adjudicated according to the historical precedent of local customary practice. Munro reversed the argument. History provided a general set of principles to shape the government's attitude towards agrarian society, but local rights were to be determined by the Collector's exercise of his discretionary authority.

Munro's scheme offers an interesting counter-point to discussion in Bengal. With its emphasis on the discretionary role of the experienced local British official rather than the determining power of abstract rules, it did represent an alternative 'vision of empire', as Burton Stein argues. But it was a vision which did not last long even in the South. But Munro's scheme was concerned to achieve a similar set of purposes as those that developed in the changing agrarian practice of Bengal, and was defended using a similar set of epistemological arguments. Like officials in Bengal, Munro experienced a gap between the abstract but unpractical formulations contained within Cornwallis' 'new constitution' and the tactical facts of district government; like their's, his scheme was aimed at closing that gap. As in Bengal, he did so by defining and objectifying the powers and rights of a particular strata of Indian civil society; in Munro's case, the *raiyats* of the South rather than the *zamindars* of Bengal. Munro believed that local 'experience' offered the key to maintaining 'the domination of strangers'. But, Munro's *raiyatwar* settlement was also rooted in an attempt to produce an abstract and textual definition of Indian 'society' which found it difficult to cope with the vicissitudes of everyday Indian agrarian life. In practice, the *raiyatwari* settlement developed its own set of documentary practices, producing texts that delineated the powers, boundaries and characteristics of landholding from the aloof posture of the colonial regime. Like the officials in Bengal who tried to define the power of proprietors across Bengal, the texts that Munro's system produced attempted to apply a set of consistent, general rules across the whole of Madras' agrarian society which offered little room for the vicissitudes of time and movement, or local diversity. And just as was the case in Bengal, those rules relied upon two different sets of authorities that pointed in two directions at once. On the one hand, they were supposed to be rooted in the 'ancient law' or 'ancient customs of Indian landholding practice'. But at the same time, they invoked a new conception of the power of the colonial state's functionaries to define and objectify the relations of India's rural civil society.

Through a complex process of transmission, Munro's arguments inflected the discussion of agrarian relations in Bengal itself. In London, they were taken up by a group of politicians and functionaries interested in Indian affairs. They were articulated in the 1812 *Fifth Report of the House of Committee on East Indian Affairs* that presented the most fervent vigorous critique of the 'Bengal system'.[63] The *Fifth Report* was written by the Board of Control clerk James Cumming and Director of the Company Samuel Davies, two men who worked closely with Munro when he was on furlough in England between 1808 and 1814.[64] By the 1810s, most officials had begun to see the permanent settlement as a measure which enshrined the absolute power of landholders to determine the conditions of agrarian life on their estates. Reinterpreted in this way, the *Fifth Report* was fervently critical of the measure. Such criticisms were articulated throughout the Company's hierarchy becoming, by the 1820s, an orthodox point of view. Lord Hastings, Governor-General between 1812 and 1823, noted that although there was never 'a measure conceived in purer spirit of generous humanity and disinterested justice than the plan for the permanent settlement', Cornwallis' system had 'subjected almost the whole of the Lower Classes throughout these provinces to most grievous oppression; an oppression too, so guaranteed by our pledge, that we unable to relieve the sufferers'.[65] Hastings' argument was authoritatively printed by the 1830 Calcutta Finance committee and then 1832 House of Commons select committee report, the former claiming that the permanent settlement meant that 'nothing is settled and little is known' in the countryside.[66]

Others had less pessimistic views about the Company's ability to reconstitute Bengal's system of governance. Influenced by Munro's work, in 1827 the revenue officer J.H. Harington proposed a regulation that aimed to 'secure the rights ... of resident ryots'. Harington did not suggest collecting revenue directly from peasants, or undoing the permanent settlement. But his regulation would have defined the general rights of peasants who were, he believed, 'by prescription entitled to a permanent hereditable right of occupancy, subject to the payment of a specific rent'.[67] Landholders would no longer have the power to specify the terms of local agrarian relations. Like Munro, Harington referred to the 'the ancient law and custom of the country' as the source of authority for this attempt to define the power of *raiyats* but did not believe it should be left up to local courts to determine 'custom'. The voice of India's enduring 'ancient law' needed to be articulated by the newfound legislative power of the colonial state.

A commitment to the principle of landholder power was too deeply embedded within the practices of the Company's Bengal establishment for Harington's regulation to be enacted. Senior officials argued that the regulation would 'generate extravagent pretensions which would never be realized [and] would confuse and perplex every existing notion of the relative rights of the landholder and his tenants', as one judge put it.[68] But the regulation's opponents appealed to precisely the same sources of authority to oppose Harington's measure that he had used to defend it: Harington and his critics shared the same epistemological field, arguing that ancient law was the basis of Bengali rights, but needed to be continually reasserted by Company sovereignty. For example, Alexander Ross, a man who described himself as a disciple of Bentham whilst defending the powers of *zamindars*, noted that such a regulation 'could not...be established with reference to either the ancient law or the ancient custom of the country. It would be difficult to show when the law referred to was in force'. Ross went on to suggest that:

> As to the custom of the country, it has always been opposed to such a privilege, it being notorious that the zemindars and other superior landholders have at all times been in the practice of exacting from their ryots as much as the latter can afford to pay.

For Ross, the landholder's freedom to determine their 'terms of contract' with their tenants was a principle enshrined in the enduring practices of Indian society. Ross concluded his minute by suggesting that the colonisation of Bengal by 'European capital and intelligence' was the only way to improve the prosperity of all social classes in Bengal. If the courts were strong enough, Ross argued, European colonisation need not undermine the ancient rights of Indian proprietors.[69]

Harington lost his battle to defend the rights of Bengal's *raiyats*. Laws were enacted in 1859 and then 1885 to fix the rents of peasants and limit the powers of landholders. But by the late nineteenth century, the vicissitudes of Bengal's rural economy had begun to diminish the *zamindar's* practical power to determine the shape of agrarian society. Other social groups, such as the 'rich peasant' or *jotdar* had been better able to dominate rural society in many areas.[70] Yet the battle illustrates the emergence of the assumption that it was possible to use general, social scientific categories which were supposed to have meaning across the whole of the province to define the conduct of each strata within Bengal's civil society. In the practice of district administration during the 1820s and 1830s and beyond, this tendency was clearly evident in the increasingly formulaic approach to district administration. By the second quarter of the nineteenth century, instead of writing detailed investigations into local customs in prose, officials were asked to fill in forms. In doing so they were forced to classify the inhabitants of the districts they governed according to a limited number of general categories, such as the *zamindar* and the *raiyat*. Some officials resisted, articulating an earlier mentality which emphasised the diversity of local custom; the Collector of Dhaka complained that the categories imposed from Calcutta 'are not applicable to the usages of the district' on a number of occasions. But such resistance didn't make a difference, as rigid, centrally produced categories were imposed across the province.[71] Bengal's population and 'society' were not only being classified in written rules, but also in forms, tables and maps as well. The first revenue surveys began to be produced in 1845. These surveys exactly drew the boundary between different estates. In doing so they flattened out distinctions of tenure and presumed that the relationship between state, landholder, territory and population was exactly the same in different places. Increasingly explicit anxiety about the distance between what actually happened and what the Company official knew was reduced by texts that projected a new, graphic form of knowledge about rural Bengal. Perhaps, though, anxiety was sublimated into other, more institutionalised moods of uncertainty.

This chapter has shown that the colonial search for stable forms of meaning with which to govern rural Bengal led to the articulation of a new set of general categories supposed to define the conduct of the various inhabitants of Bengal's nascent civil society. Whichever side they were on, arguments about the relative rights of each assumed that landholders and peasants were subjects who had 'rights' which could be transcribed in written texts that had a general application across the whole of the province. Yet when they discussed the source of those rights, colonial officials spoke with forked tongues, articulating an ambivalent understanding of the relationship between colonial governance and time. On the one hand, they articulated a new conception of the Indian past. In the 1790s, the Company had attempted to root the particularities of property relations within the diversity of local 'custom', a term they used to refer to the immediate past. But by the 1820s, India's British rulers also argued that a more distant (one might say abstract) past provided them with a set of general propositions that could be used to govern the conduct of agrarian civil society as a whole. The colonial regime in Bengal articulated this conception of 'ancient law' long before the publication of Maine's book with that title. Ancient law was

130

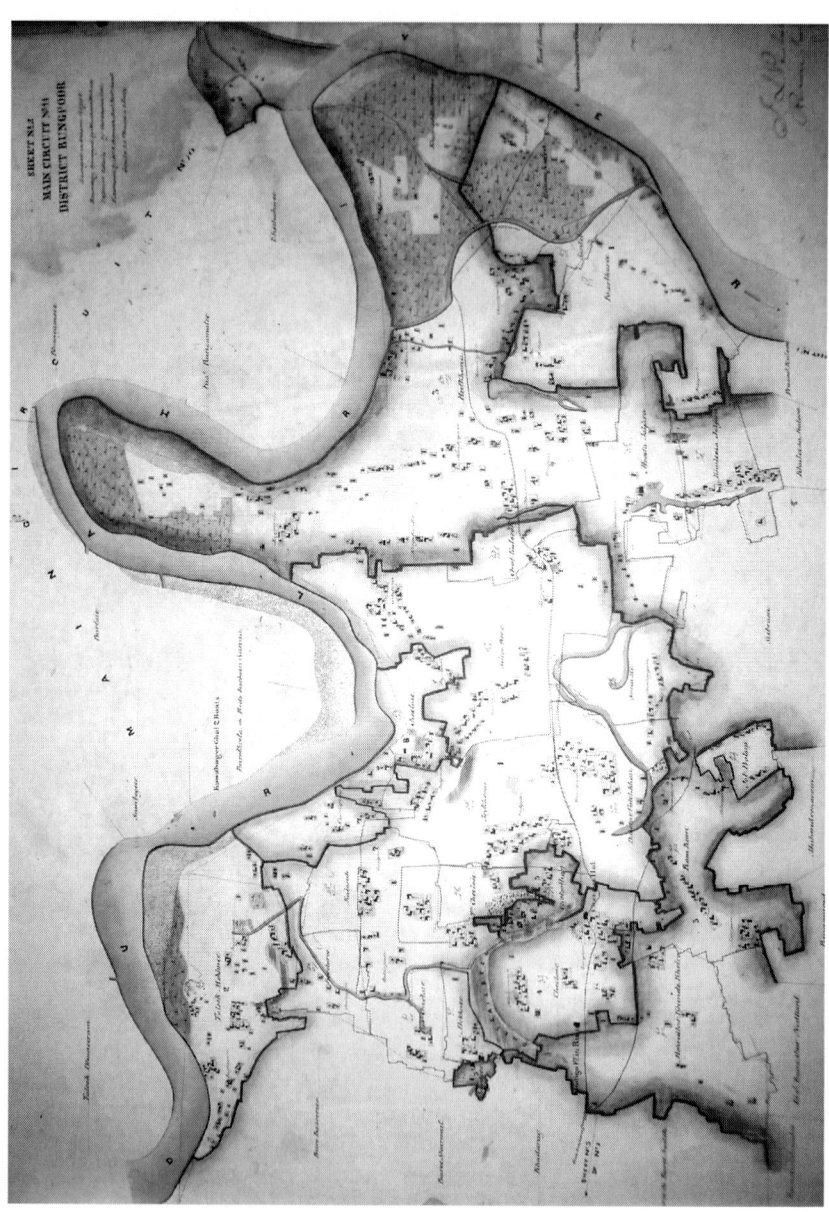

Figure 5.2   Revenue Survey Map, 1858–1859, sheet 2, circuit 11, Rangpur District Record Room.

invoked so that officials could overcome their inability to understand the diversity of local Indian practice through experience, as the long-forgotten past seemed to offer a source of meaning governed by stable, enduring regularities that were not vulnerable to the vicissitudes of the present day. But this position had a strange circular logic: present-day practice was the only source of authority available for ancient rights, and officials were incapable of definitively tracing ordered forms of past action into a present they experienced as disordered. As Alexander Ross' comments made it clear, any appeal to the supposedly enduring power of India's 'ancient law' was easy to disprove by reference to the realities of rural society.

Reference to the authority of 'ancient law' offered a useful tactical argument in the courts and councils of Calcutta. As we shall see in Chapter 7, it was taken up by Indian critics of British interference in Indian social life. But as a tool for deciding property disputes, it needed to be supplemented by other sources of meaning. In particular, the authority of India's enduring past was continually supplemented by the legislative action of the colonial regime. Ever ambivalent about their ability to find stable regularities within South Asian 'society' itself whether in the present or past, 'ancient law' needed to be inscribed definitively upon the fabric of India by the power of the colonial state. The regulations and laws that constituted the positive commands of the state were a last refuge for officials looking for stable, ordered forms of meaning. However, many officials wished to ascribe the norms they used to govern India to indigenous sources, 'the state [became] the terminal point of ascription, the point at which the ascription, which constitutes juristic consideration can stop'.[72] This new conception of the role of the state will be examined in the next chapter.

Nonetheless, the debate about the powers of landholders and the rights of peasants that have been traced in this chapter continued throughout the nineteenth century. What began as a tactical discussion rooted in the Company's search for stable sources of revenue became a set of arguments concerning the relationship between India and Europe in a far more general sense. Colonial Indian debates connected with other strands of thought to influence the work of men such as Henry Maine, interested in examining the particular kinds of law that existed in different societies. In his *Ancient Law*, published in 1861, Maine contrasted the rule of custom in the past with what he saw as the rule of legislation, contract and *laissez-faire* in the European present day. Maine was, of course, heavily influenced by the new turn of German historical thought, in particular the work of Freidrich Karl von Savigny. But he also read widely about British governance in India. Maine's arguments are unimaginable without the colonial discussion examined in this chapter.

As this chapter has suggested, colonial governance produced an ambivalent discourse about the colonial regime's relationship with Indian society. Officials were never certain whether their task was to preserve what existed already or to introduce new forms of rule. When Henry Maine arrived as law member on the Governor-General's council in 1868, that ambivalence had encrusted into a dilemma about the force of Indian 'tradition' on the one hand and the potentially modernising effects of the colonial state on the other. By then, the colonial regime's ambivalence had been mapped onto a linear, progressive notion of time. Maine was explicit about that dilemma. 'Custom' and the ancient Indian village community, he argued, provided the basis of Indian civilisation. For the colonial regime to rip both up would annihilate the bonds that bound Indians together and make the country ungovernable. Yet Maine was a liberal moderniser, someone who wanted colonialism to lead India out of a traditional past of status and custom into a world of contract and individualistic free trade. The agency of the colonial state was meant to stand between the unchanging regularities of India's past society and a very different, 'modern' future ruled by 'free agency' and competition. For men like Maine, it needed to look both ways at once, and seemed forever uncertain which way to turn. Such an uneasy, ambivalent position was characteristic of nineteenth-century British colonial thought. It developed out of the colonial regime's contingent search for semantic coherence in a world it experienced as strange and uncertain.

6
The State as Machine and the Ambivalent Origins of Colonial Utilitarianism

I

Writing from Calcutta in July 1830, Holt Mackenzie criticised the uncertain and 'vacillating' nature of British government in Bengal. Mackenzie was at the centre of the colonial regime in Calcutta. As secretary to the government for the 14 years before he returned to London in 1831, he was the pivotal figure around which the concepts and correspondence of British rule revolved.[1] Governor-General Lord William Bentinck (1828–1835) suggested that he 'probably has more knowledge of Indian affairs with all their minutest details than any other man in the east'.[2] A Scot 'of retired and studious habits', Mackenzie has been seen as the classic example of a new kind of utilitarian official, willing to implement the abstract ideas of philosophers such as Jeremy Bentham in India. More conservative colleagues noted his 'spirit of speculation' with extreme alarm.[3] But in July 1830, Mackenzie believed that theoretical speculation and the production of abstract rules were necessary for very practical reasons.

Mackenzie was concerned with the constant disputes occurring amongst Europeans within the East India Company's administration in Bengal. The new constitution created in 1793 had enshrined a division of powers between officers who collected revenue and others who administered the law. It also retained the separation between the King's Courts, with their jurisdiction over the city of Calcutta, and the Company's courts that ruled the rest of Bengal. Over the next 40 years, those divisions allowed disorder to engulf the institutions of British rule, enabling the seemingly fractious social relations of the countryside to find their way into the colonial regime's corridors of power. British officers were set against other British officers. The future was radically uncertain: no one could plan or predict. Mackenzie noted that officials were 'thrown into a position of hostility and counter-action, toiling to effect what to-morrow will be destroyed', 'deprived . . . of all means they ought to possess, of anticipating or directing the consequences of their acts'. He went on:

> [T]o disjoin the several parts of government, in a country which is not self-governed, is like placing the different members of the body in the charge of different physicians, severally acting with their respective limbs according to individual theory, without reference to the treatment of other parts, and each holding in his hand the power of destroying life, but helpless to save, from the blunders of his brethren. It is to animate the lifeless frame with a plurality of souls.

In this account, the failures of the British government in India could be traced to its disunity of purpose and 'the want of any strong connecting link between the several departments' of the Company's state. Mackenzie wanted the British state in India to be a single bureaucratic apparatus that made law and applied it to Indian society in a systematic and effective way. His use of the metaphor of physician and patient is significant. It shows how, by 1830, an estranged, distant relationship between British officials and Indian practice had been codified into a discourse about the surgical action of the British state on the distant, static and objectified field of Indian civil society.[4]

Mackenzie's concerns shed light on the active process of state-formation occurring in British-ruled Bengal. The first third of the nineteenth century saw the emergence of a new form of liberal authoritarianism in colonial India, a form of governance very different from the style of rule that occurred back home. The first aspect of that new form of rule was the belief that India needed to be governed with abstract principles and general rules. The previous two chapters traced the convoluted process in which general categories such as the Hindu widow, the Bengali landholder or the hereditary peasant replaced earlier emphases on the heterogeneity of local custom. Around the same time these categories were joined by other ways of objectifying social activity in Bengal: at different points in time terms such as Brahmin, Muslim, criminal tribe or 'suttee' began to be used to describe individuals within general population groups that had a legal existence, whose conduct could be governed by general rules. Each emerged from the practical attempt to govern the conduct of individuals and groups who were supposed to have purely private and particular ends, rather than lives that were connected to the political life of the community as a whole as they had before. It was the construction of those categories that created a conception of what Hegel called *bürgerliche Gesellschaft* (civil society) in Bengal for the first time.

This new emphasis on abstract rules emerged alongside the process examined in this chapter. New rules led to the emergence of a new set of ideas about the state, the body that was to give them power and authority. Instead of being regarded as a network of social and political forces balanced by the authority of the sovereign, the state was described as a unitary, bureaucratic machine that stood apart from civil society, and which produced and practically enforced the general rules that governed social life. It was this kind of state that Holt Mackenzie described in the passage above. His particular use of an organic metaphor was significant, with its implication that the state needed to act like a body governed by a single will. More commonly though, this new sense was articulated by comparing the state to a machine. Whether biological or mechanistic, these metaphors were normative rather than descriptive; they described the state as officials wanted it to be, not the 'failed state' of their own present time.

This chapter has three parts. Its second and third sections describe the emergence of legislation and English education as devices to make the colonial regime act in a coherent, unified fashion. These two parts suggest that the colonial desire to enact codified law or introduce new forms of pedagogy were concerned with the governance of the colonial state; they were not primarily targeted at the Indian subjects of British rule. Even in this so-called 'age of reform', officials did not begin with coherent ideas of the Indian objects of their rule objects or the kinds of political and social change they wanted to introduce. Most importantly, reform was a by-product of the attempt to rule a colonial state that, from the official British point of view, had to be governed with a different political logic from that which ruled politics back home.

With this theme in mind the chapter begins by engaging with the relationship between colonial governance and utilitarian political thought. Ever since Eric Stokes' famous *English Utilitarianism and India* was published in 1959, scholars have been concerned with this question. Since Stokes' time, the rationalist character of the colonial state in India has been identified as a consequence of its connection with utilitarian political thought, and seen as something that was caused by the export of British ideas. The propagation of utilitarian political philosophy and the emergence of an idea of the machine-like, law-making colonial state occurred at the same time – both happened between 1800 and 1830. Some colonial officials had certainly read Jeremy Bentham or James Mill. But the utilitarianism articulated by men such as Holt Mackenzie and his fellow East India Company officials was not a coherent doctrine adopted through a mysterious network of transmission connecting Westminster with Bengal. It was a more diffuse set of instincts and theoretical orientations that emerged from the practices of colonial governance, which influenced, as much as they were influenced by ideas published in London. Far from being the culmination of a European intellectual heritage, colonial India's utilitarian theory of the state was used by officials to understand their sense of rupture with the continuities of British political life. This was certainly the case within the production and reception of the most important text in the history of colonial utilitarianism, James Mill's *History of British India*.

II

Published in 'three fat volumes' in 1818, Mill's *History of British India* led
to its author being appointed the examiner of correspondence at the East
India Company a year later. By the 1820s Mill's work had started to be read
by trainee officials at the East India Company's college at Haileybury. H.H.
Wilson, who became Professor of Sanskrit at Oxford University after teaching
at Fort William College, suggested that Mill had a great influence on British
officers. Writing in his edited edition of the *History* published first in 1840,
H.H. Wilson noted that 'a harsh and illiberal spirit has of late years prevailed
in the conduct and councils of the rising service in India, which owes its
origin to impressions imbibed in youth from the History of Mr. Mill'. Wilson
noted disapprovingly that Mill's purpose was to set forth the 'theoretical
views' on law and government of Jeremy Bentham as 'standards by which to
try the conduct of the East India Company'.[5]

Mill's most important propositions were indeed unflinchingly Benthamite.
He wanted to create a unitary state guided by a single 'theory' or legislative
will. The most important function of that bureaucratic state was to frame
and administer a single code of law, written on universal rational principles
but based loosely on existing laws and customs. These proposals were consistent with the emphasis throughout Bentham's work on the need for a single
legislative authority to govern the state, and his advocacy of a code of laws,
even if both men believed a code should reflect the peculiarities of time and
place.[6] But Mill began work on the *History* 18 months before he met Jeremy
Bentham. His purpose, at least as expressed in the preface to the *History*,
was to fill a gap in the market for a book that summarised and rationalised
'scattered' and 'heterogeneous' accounts that already existed of the increasingly important topic of the British in India, not to articulate a coherent
utilitarian creed. Mill's argument about the need for a more actively assertive
law-making state was not simply the logical result of applying Benthamite
principles *a priori*. It emerged as Mill worked through the 'dispersed and
confused' writings of those who had written about India already.

The text began with an account of the inadequate state of British knowledge about the subcontinent. Mill famously argued that he was able to
understand India better from reading the second-hand reports of officials
and administrators than if he had experienced India himself. Direct experience allowed the observer to be seduced by sensational 'impulses' and 'partial
impressions'. Someone with experience of India tended merely to 'trea-
sure . . . up the facts that are presented to his senses'. The existing literature
on India was an 'assemblage of heterogenous things', he suggested, a random
'body of statements, given indiscriminately as matters of fact, ascertained by
the senses' with no order or rational principle. Echoing a similar phrase written by Cornwallis 30 years before, Mill suggested that '[w]hatever is worth
seeing or hearing in India can be expressed in writing'. For Mill (perhaps also

Cornwallis) the calm distance occurring between author and reader allowed the mind to construct knowledge on a rational basis. It enabled the reader to form a critical account of what the British needed to do to the Indian sub-continent, something impossible for those faced with the over-abundance of sensory impulse and impression occurring in India itself.[7]

But of course Mill's text depended on the 'partial impressions' of British observers for its analysis: his argument about the inadequacy of direct experience was itself drawn from reading colonial texts written by officials with experience of the subcontinent. Mill quoted John Shore's comment that 'true information is often procured with difficulty, because it is too often derived from mere practice, instead of being deduced from fixed principles'.[8] Along-side Shore, he relied on a short-lived genre of texts critical of British rule published by British officials and other colonial observers in the first decade and a half of the nineteenth century. Mill cited Henry Strachey's discussion of the 'imperfect connexion' between Indians and Britons in a number of published minutes. He heavily relied on Alexander Fraser Tytler's *Political State of India*, a book based on its author's long experience as judge of 24 Parganas district in the late 1800s. Mill's other main sources were clergyman William Tennant's *Indian Recreations*, the missionary William Ward and the medic and topographer Francis Buchanan's writings. These texts quoted each other, forming what Edward Said described as a 'system of knowledge' that consisted of a 'set references, a congeries of characteristics, that seem[ed] to have its origin in a quotation, or a fragment of a text, or a citation from someone's work on the Orient'.[9] Although they actually presented their argument through this process of citation and reference, each text nonetheless invoked their author's direct experience of the subcontinent to claim that the real India was difficult to know and govern.[10] The absence of anecdote or descriptions of personal experience is striking, but it was the officials' existence within the estranged, alienating culture of early colonial rule that 'proved' that such knowledge was so unreliable.

Throughout the *History of British India*, Mill echoed the arguments articulated in this citationary web of texts published between 1801 and 1815. Most of these observers made the contradictory claim that India was governed by an oppressive, unchanging set of rules that determined every aspect of Indian practice on the one hand, but was also a land of chaos, disorder and anarchy, a society wholly without rule or rules on the other. The juxtaposition of these two opposing ways of describing India was an instance of cognitive dissonance that provided the staple of nineteenth-century colonial and 'orientalist' analysis. The first part reflected the long-standing discussion of 'Asiatic despotism' which, as William Tennant argued, could sometimes provide security to 'the body of the people' but was 'powerful only in chaining it down in a state of torpor and depression, wholly incompatible with all the high advances on the grand scale of human improvement'. Unlike Jones, Colebrooke or many others commenting in the 1790s, Tennant,

Tytler and their contemporaries believed that India's 'despotism' prevented it from rising 'to the character of a commercial people'.[11] This account of despotic rule linked to a newly emerging colonial rhetoric which saw Hindu caste as a rigid social hierarchy kept in place by the powerful 'priestcraft' of Hindu élites.[12] Mill echoed these sentiments by suggesting that Indians were governed by a 'system of priestcraft, built upon the most enormous and tormenting superstition that ever harassed and degraded any portion of mankind, their minds were enchained more intolerably than their bodies'.[13] At the same time though, Tennant attributed India's disorder to the loss of 'virtue and spirit' on the part of India's governors. Chaos subsisted because of a 'relaxation of discipline' and the 'want of an efficient control' that allowed 'corrupt and illiterate' Indian officers to proliferate. Like Tytler, Tennant viewed Indian law as vague and unknown.[14] Mill's account of the chaotic vagueness of India was the main thrust of his venomous critique of South Asian society.

Despite the similar account of Indian politics and society they presented, these works offered a different prescription from Mill's. The books referenced in *The History of British India*'s footnotes were critical both of the pre-colonial Indian past and British rule. But most saw the solution as the creation of virtuous, patriarchal despotisms that invoked a return to some kind of pre-colonial past. Many felt that the 'vigour' and 'manliness' of Mughal governance needed to be restored. British officials could act as good local despots, administering justice in an authoritarian yet benevolent fashion without a rigid code of laws.[15] This kind of discretionary despotism was the antithesis of colonial utilitarianism's emphasis on the need to define every action of ruler and subject in written rules. Instead of renewing past modes of rule, Mill believed the absence of *any* kind of ordered governmental norms in the subcontinent meant the colonial state had no choice but to produce new forms of knowledge to govern with. Codification and the definition of governing practices in written rules, rather than expansion in the scope for official discretion, were Mill's response to the failure of colonial knowledge in India. Rather than continuing pre-existing modes of rule, such an approach would ensure India's future would be radically different from its past.

Early in the first volume of his *History*, in the chapter on 'The Form of Government', Mill contrasted 'the monarchies of Asia' with 'the more skilful governments of Europe'. In the latter 'officers are appointed for the discharge of particular duties in the different provinces of the empire', one to administer justice, another to collect taxes, control violence and so forth. Because they were all part of a single bureaucratic apparatus acting out rules communicated from a single sovereign power, in the more 'civilized' parts of Europe,

the powers of all center immediately in the head of government, and all together act as connected and subordinate wheels in one complicated and artful machine.

By contrast with the best European polities Mill suggested that emperors in Asia appointed vice-regents with uncontrolled power over a particular locality and left them to their own devices, allowing governance to occur in an arbitrary and fragmented fashion. Instead of being coordinated in a single machine, authority was divided between local kings and Brahmin 'priests', each of which seemed in fact to share legislative and executive power.[16] Hindu ideas were 'so extremely loose, vague and uncertain', Mill argued, that any textual law that did exist was liable to many different practical interpretations at the same time.[17] The use of a mechanistic metaphor to castigate Indian rule is striking.

Mill's *History* is famous for its suggestion that India was not 'advanced' or 'civilised', but was in fact a 'barbarous' society. The idea of 'barbarism' was central to eighteenth-century political thought. Philosophical historians, including David Hume, William Robertson, Adam Smith and, for the most part, Edward Gibbon, mapped barbarism onto a stadial theory of social development based on changing modes of subsistence. Hume and Smith equated barbarism with poor, pastoral forms of agriculture. Gibbon added an argument about the role of hyper-rationalist forms of religious belief in allowing barbarism to triumph in the middle ages over the civilised scepticism of ancient Rome.[18] None of these historical philosophers spoke of what Thomas Macaulay later called 'the pacific triumphs of reason over barbarism'.[19] In fact, in each case barbarism was associated with a surfeit rather than a deficit of abstract thought.

Mill's definition was different though. Associating progress with the march of reason instead of production, barbarism was defined in terms of ignorance and irrationality instead of poverty. Mill might have adopted this emphasis on the progress of mental capacities from his Edinburgh teachers, in particular John Millar and Dugald Stewart.[20] But he modified the concepts he inherited, characterising barbarism by the disordered or fragmented character of its interpersonal relations and the absence of general rules or norms for the governance of society. Barbarism was associated in particular with the exercise of power uncontrolled by written law. Barbarians were people who were 'guided by caprice' and motivated by 'passion' instead of rational norms or rules. A society was in a 'barbarous state' when 'there was so little of any thing fixed or certain' where the law was left in an 'unwritten', 'traditionary' condition, and 'a wide field was commonly assigned to the arbitrary will of the judge'. For Mill, as for the jurist and imperial official Sir Henry Maine 40 years later, human progress was marked by the definition of rights by written laws, and the judge, magistrate or sovereign's discretionary powers being limited by rational legislation. Throughout the *History*, Mill castigated the 'vague and indefinite' nature of law in the subcontinent, associating it with India's barbarism, sometimes contrasting it with the state of Europe, but often also seeing barbarous elements within Europe itself.[21]

Unlike Scottish conjectural historians and later advocates of rational progress like Macaulay and Maine though, Mill did not see human social and political development as an incremental process that could be gauged on a finely graded scale of civilisation. Jennifer Pitts suggests his was a 'dichotomous' view that divided human societies between 'civilised' Europe and the rest of the world, although Britain's place in the scheme of global society is sometimes hard to place. Mill believed change needed to be dramatic even in Britain. There, 'moderate exertions' – codification and parliamentary reform – would 'produce great results'.[22] In the words of Donald Winch, Mill believed that 'history, given a little shake, will usher in the millennium'.[23] The more dramatic move from barbarity to civilisation was seen as a sudden rupture, something that could be created by the action of a single human mind. It would occur as the rational utilitarian lawmaker imposed his will on the caprice and chaos of uncivilised society.[24]

In India Mill believed the colonial state needed to produce such a rupture, creating rational intellectual order from the disorder and uncertainty that he associated with pre-colonial Indian society. But instead, since it had exercised sovereignty in Bengal, the East India Company governed with the chaos of existing forms. Unable to trust the intuition of British or Indian officials, Mill castigated the Company for failing to construct a machine-like bureaucratic state. It had created a government with no consistency of action, and no system of what Mill elsewhere called 'general control'.[25] Rather than exercising the powers of their mind to create rational forms of law, men such as Sir William Jones translated and published the writings of 'the unenlightened and perverted intellects of a few Indian pundits'. Jones and Colebrooke's *Digest of Hindu Law* was 'a disorderly compilation of loose, vague, stupid, or unintelligible quotations and maxims ... attended with a commentary, which only adds to the mass of absurdity and darkness'.[26] By contrast, Mill argued that the mind of the colonial state needed to handle the chaotic form of Indian society in precisely the same way he himself, the 'judging historian', treated the 'fragments of information' gathered about the history of India. If not exactly a *tabula rasa*, Mill believed those fragments were malleable enough to be remoulded into a single, logical form of historical consciousness and law. In writing the *History*, Mill plotted his own role as author onto a narrative about India's transition from barbarous incomprehension and ambiguity to civilised, rule-bound, machine-like order.

Although its author claimed his texts marked a radical break with the forms of governance and political thought that preceded it, Mill's *History* had a close link to the practice of colonial state formation. The work was circulated and read alongside a new set of colonial texts which criticised the absence of certain knowledge about Indian society, then purported to define, rather than just merely describe, the social relations of Bengal in precisely the way Mill advocated. If officials in the 1800s tended to advocate a return to discretionary despotism, by the time Mill's *History* was printed an emphasis on the production of texts that contained written rules had begun to emerge. Unable to trust the discretion of district officers, the Company began to issue regulations which hesitantly voiced the state's authority to define new forms of property right in the face of uncertainty and local indecision. As the previous two chapters showed, new codes and digests of law, revenue manuals and accounts, maps, circular orders, regulations and legislative enactments were produced to counter exactly the colonial sense of vagueness and disorder that Mill projected onto Indian society. Francis and William MacNaghten began to work on their rational reconstructions of Hindu law in the second half of the 1810s, long before Mill's *History* reached India, for example. But each started with a similar premise: that Indian jurisprudence needed to be reconstructed and codified by British minds if it was to allow stable forms of governance to emerge in the subcontinent.

By the time Mill's *History* was published, officials in Bengal had begun to think that the logical response to Tytler's critique of 'vague and unknown law' was to construct a centralised machinery of government with the authority to create and apply clear rules instead of placing trust in custom or paternalistic intuitions. The practical proposals Mill made were supported by men who did not accept the rest of Mill's argument. Officers who were far less critical about Indian civilisation than Mill drew from their own experience of colonial governance to make similar suggestions about what the British should do. For example, H. H. Wilson defended the virtue and integrity of 'the Hindoo character' against Mill's aspersions; but even he echoed Mill in suggesting that the fragmented and discordant nature of Indian society prevented improvement. Wilson argued, like Mill, that the solution lay in India's governance by a reforming state that engaged in a programme of education and textualisation that would create a more unified, cohesive and governable society.[27] Henry Strachey's brother Edward celebrated the arts and sciences of ancient India. In a work published in 1813, he argued that 'the Hindus had an original fund of Science not borrowed from foreign sources' before the twelfth century.[28] But Strachey shared Mill's scepticism about the observer's ability to know India and advocated the construction of new law as a consequence. Despite spending 22 years as a judge in Bengal, Strachey doubted how far the 'traveller or resident in a foreign land' could ever understand the strangers they observed. In a set of notes made after reading Mill's *History* in 1818, Strachey suggested that the observer could only ever be

> ignorant of their manners, their cause and connexion of thought, and their peculiarities of expression. He sees men's actions through a mist, and does not know the thing signified. He ascribes to one set of motives what may proceed from another.

Strachey seems to have been equally critical of the praise men such as Wilson bestowed on Indian morals as of Mill's castigation of Indian character.

'Thousands of such testimonials should not weigh one further on the scale of truth' than Mill's critical account, he suggested.[29] Articulating colonial India's sceptical epistemology, Strachey thought that experience could not be used as a guide to governance. He believed it was impossible to truly understand the conduct, motives, customs or laws of his Indian subjects through intuition and local knowledge. As a result, he argued for the creation of a novel code of law and new judicial machinery to administer it. Once he returned to London, Strachey was appointed an examiner of correspondence along with Mill, where he was responsible for drafting judicial despatches. Strachey died in 1831 but in the papers found on his death were a set of notes made for the House of Commons Select Committee, which included a scheme for judicial reform. India was 'almost without a law', Strachey argued. In reality local collectors and judges decided cases using their discretion, he thought. In place of the morass of existing practices and institutions, Strachey wanted the Company to produce a clear text that defined 'wrongs' on the one hand, and a single set of courts that provided 'remedies' on the other in a thoroughly utililtarian way.[30] There is, however, no evidence that he rejected his high views of Indian science.

III

The History of British India's argument developed in part from Mill's engagement with the estranged culture of colonial rule in the subcontinent. But Mill's work emerged from the intersection of colonial and metropolitan ideas and arguments. Unlike the officials who read his work in Bengal, Mill's critique of the role of experience and intuition in governance, and his advocacy of a rationalist, codifying state were also dependent on a set of domestic British contexts and references which had nothing to do with colonial administrative life. As Javeed Majeed argues, Mill's *History* offered a radical critique of British institutions alongside its challenge to India and British rule there. Yet this criticism of British institutions was not taken up by Mill's colonial readers, who were more likely to use Mill's critique of the vagueness of Indian jurisprudence to argue for the superiority of English courts and English law. Mill's *History of British India* and with it the broader utilitarian critique of India thus had two lives. One offered a consistent challenge to the absence of codified law across the globe, and was critical of institutions in both England and India, although (in Mill's case at least) reserved its greatest venom for the latter. The second used the utilitarian challenge to any form of governance reliant on experience and intuition to attack Indian practice, but found such a critique either irrelevant or unnecessary in the case of Britain. To explore the peculiarities of colonial political thought, it would be helpful to examine the British context to *The History of British India* for a moment.

As Majeed argues, the *History* was dependent on a set of radical arguments about the relationship between language and politics that were not widely received in Britain. Both Mill and Bentham believed that language needed to be a precise instrument that had to be made to correspond to the real world. Each developed arguments made by the radical politician and philosopher Horne Tooke to make that point. As William Hazlitt noted, Tooke's 'literal, matter-of-fact, unimaginative nature of his understanding' came into conflict with the 'web of old associations wound round language' which members of Britain's elite accepted as crucially important for political or legal conduct.[31] Like Tooke, Mill and Bentham attacked the complex associations and 'fictions' present in the language of the law.[32] The root of the problem was that Britons thought the law was contained in the vocabulary encrusted upon particular institutions and processes, not in a clearly defined textual body of rules that had a life outside the court. 'The irrational notion', Mill suggested in the *History*,

> appears to have established itself in the minds of most Englishmen, that courts, or tribunals, are also law; and that when you have established tribunals, you have not merely provided an instrument for the administration of law, if any law exists; but you have provided the law itself.

Without an understanding of the need to define general, textual rules, the 'rights of Englishmen' depended on 'any thing that the judges choose to call law'. 'Englishmen in general', he argued, 'have no conception of the extent to which they lie under a despotic power in the hands of the judges'. The state of law in England was 'absurd' and 'deplorable'. It was this condition, the condition of English as well as Indian law, that Mill described as a 'barbarous state'.[33]

In Britain itself, opponents of views such as these were far more numerous than their supporters. Critics of the utilitarian approach believed language was part of the historical flow of social existence, not a mere tool for instrumentally manipulating an objective world. Words were, as Samuel Taylor Coleridge put it, 'living things', which represented local and national cultures. To codify its law in the desiccated language of utilitarianism was to treat society as a lifeless body; it would interrupt the complex forces that worked their way through the history of institutions, and prevent experience from modifying the practice of the law. For men such as Coleridge and the King's College London jurist John James Park, the law, like the polity as a whole, was an organic entity that depended on the historical interrelation of each part. For Park, to codify was to 'dissect away the whole mass of historical and dialectic matter by means of which it coheres together, and reduce it to one million of insulated propositions'.[34]

Most famously perhaps, the utilitarian approach to language, politics and law was criticised for its overly abstract, rationalist line of analysis by the young Thomas Macaulay. In 1829, Macaulay attacked Mill's 'Essay on Government' for using language to draw elaborate conclusions from questionable abstract premises. Macaulay associated Mill's mechanical style with medieval scholasticism, contrasting it with the less abstract and more refined empirical tone of his own more civilised present-day. In his critique, Macaulay argued that Mill was 'an Aristotelian of the fifteenth century born out of season'. Like other critics, Macaulay suggested that Mill was willing to forsake experience of the world for a systematic form of *a priori* logic that contradicted common sense and the intuitive practice of everyday life.[35]

Coleridge, Park and, later, James Mill's own son John Stuart Mill explicitly drew upon post-Kantian German historicist philosophy in order to critique the rigid a-temporal abstraction of utilitarianism. But as John Burrow suggests, a similar challenge could have been made by drawing from the eighteenth-century scepticism, sometimes also pessimism of Edward Gibbon, Adam Smith and David Hume, with its emphasis on the role of sentiment and the beneficial unintended effects of often irrational acts for society as a whole.[36] In Britain, it was Macaulay, Coleridge and the younger Mill not the first generation of utilitarians who were the heirs of Scottish enlightenment history. It was Macaulay's brand of empiricist whiggism, rather than Mill's rationalism that predominated in British political discourse. But in colonial India even Macaulay became a philosophical radical.

Thomas Macaulay sailed for India three years after writing his stinging critique of Mill's abstract approach to politics and law. Immediately before doing so, in a debate about the government of India in the House of Commons he suggested that the *History of British India* was 'the greatest historical work that has appeared in our language since that of Gibbon'.[37] As Law member of the Legislative Council in Calcutta from 1834, Macaulay was given the task of codifying Indian law. When thinking about India in parliament before his departure or in the Calcutta council, Macaulay abandoned the experiential and historicist attitude he took to British politics. As Macaulay's fluctuating attitude makes clear, Mill's call for a rational mind to impose a coherent taxonomy upon a fragmented society and a failed polity had a different fate depending on the context it was directed towards. For whigs like Macaulay, Strachey, Bayley and even Holt Mackenzie, such a rationalist approach was redundant in Britain. But governing India required a different attitude to government, indeed a different style of thought. Returning to examine the writings of Holt Mackenzie once again allows us to develop this contrast between colonial and domestic British languages of state.

IV

Mackenzie's October 1830 minute on the administration of justice had an important footnote. The minute argued that the colonial regime needed to be reformed so it acted as a single bureaucratic machine ruled by one legislative authority. The state's unitary will needed to have its commands transmitted by 'a strong connecting link' to all departments, including the

East India Company's local courts. But Mackenzie added a caveat: such a theory of the state only applied to 'a country which is not self-governed'. In the footnote he suggested that '[t]his condition must always be kept in mind, because the government of the people will introduce entirely new principles of action'. Mackenzie assured his reader that he maintained what 'may seem rather arbitrary doctrines' because in British India 'all public functions are arbitrarily appointed by the Government'. Arbitrary rule was necessary in India, but was not a principle more generally applicable.[38]

Mackenzie's understanding of the difference between 'Britain' and 'British India' was more clearly articulated in a document he wrote the year before. Again, Mackenzie was discussing conflicts between different branches of the state in Bengal. This time though, he was concerned with a series of disputes which had occurred between the Supreme Courts, the King's Courts in Calcutta, Bombay and Madras, which applied English law, and the East India Company's revenue machinery and own *mofussil* courts. In England, he suggested the government should leave litigants to fight it out in different courts. 'Justice' could 'blindly...hold the scales, in the confidence that each party will throw onto them everything in his favour', and a system of competing jurisdictions and laws would produce a fair result in the end. In England such a principle was 'safe and wise' only

> because there we have freedom and knowledge, community of language, publicity of proceedings, the fellowship of man with man, the thousand social ties that link a population accustomed to self-government, and knit together by the institutions through which the work of government is done.

In lowland Britain during his own present day, public opinion and what he elsewhere called a sense of 'friendship and neighbourhood' allowed a more diffuse and de-centred form of government to exist. Mackenzie contrasted this situation with colonial Bengal, but also with the relationship between 'Saxon serfs' and 'Norman conquerors' who spoke 'barbarous French' in England's past; and to imperial situations closer to the metropolis in Ireland and the Scottish highlands, where supposedly uncivilised people were ruled by people with a different language and culture. In times and places where the governors were strangers to those they ruled, judges needed to 'have all their eyes about them'. In a colonial environment governance could only function if a superior power established clearly defined and publicly-known rules.[39]

For Mackenzie self-rule did not involve elected control of a bureaucratic state. Self-governance was a complex process of participation, involving many dispersed sites of authority, each of which were based on local forms of affection and trust. After returning to Britain, Mackenzie appealed to the sentiments of one such dispersed site, the 'independent electors of the burghs of Elgin, Cullen, Banff, Inverbury, Kintore and Peterhead', when he stood for parliament in 1832. The former official presented himself as someone who would strengthen 'ties of friendship and neighbourhood' by standing above factions and parties that, he argued, prevented local interests from being heard.[40] Mackenzie wrote as if in Britain the state was woven from the forms of sociability which Hegel had disparagingly spoken of as 'family connexions, political conversations and speeches at dinners'. The ease with which this most abstract and utilitarian of officials could slip back into the familiar registers of British politics is striking. His almost Burkean description of the polity as a de-centred web here sharply contrasted with his colonial utilitarianism in India, in particular his sense of the need for an administrative machine capable of effectively articulating a single general will for Bengal.

The particular occasion that led Mackenzie to draw these contrasts was a dispute concerning a 'joint Hindu family' in Bengal that spread across the jurisdiction of two courts, and which became something of a *cause celebre* throughout British India. An estate that consisted of lands in the districts of Nadia, Jessore and 24 Parganas had, it seems, been jointly possessed by two brothers, Ratanchandra Pal Chaudhuri and Premchandra Chaudhuri, who lived on Clive Street in Calcutta. Premchandra's heir tried to seize control of the whole estate. Because they were residents in Calcutta, his cousin, Wames Chandra Pal Chaudhuri sued in the Calcutta Supreme Court for his half share. In a quick trial before Sir Edward Grey and Sir Edward Ryan, Wames Chandra won the case for his share without any legal complications. Calcutta's common law court appointed a receiver to go into the countryside to collect revenue from the estate until it was partitioned.

The case occurred in 1828, at a time when the metropolitan courts of Calcutta and Bombay, with their English, common law judges and rules of procedure, had begun to assert their power with renewed vigour once again. Calcutta's Supreme Court had been established by parliament in 1773 in order to provide a balance to the potentially corrupt and arbitrary acts of East India Company officers. Its first moment of self-assertion occurred in the 1780s when, in a brief struggle between the court and Warren Hastings, the court's judges claimed they, and not the Company, had jurisdiction over the whole of Bengal. The court's powers were limited to cover Europeans stationed throughout Bengal, and 'native inhabitants' who lived within the Maratha ditch which encircled Calcutta.[41]

Over time though, the changing practices of Company governance, some of which were identified in the previous chapter, made it easier for landholders to be absent from their estates and live in the colonial metropolis while owning and managing land in rural Bengal. In the 1780s, Calcutta's wealthy Indian population had mostly been merchants. By the 1820s, a *bhadralok* class had emerged whose social and cultural world was urban, but whose prosperity was dependent on the management of resources in the countryside. Their straddling of the divide between country and city brought with it a clash of jurisdictions, as men who lived in Calcutta but owned, inherited, bequeathed and partitioned property that was normally subject to rule by the *mofussil diwani adalat* courts, began to litigate in the King's Courts as if they were Calcutta inhabitants.

In Bombay, clashes between the city's Supreme Court and the Company's hierarchy developed in a similar way. There, though, they often developed from the growth of urban financial interests with connections to the royal courts of Bombay's hinterland, rather than changing patterns of agrarian relations. In two notorious cases, members of Bombay's city elite used the Supreme Court to free a boy taken to the court of the former Peshwa in Poona by his grandfather, and an official guilty of embezzlement from the Company's gaol in Tannah. Heard in 1828, the two cases led to a violent battle for jurisdiction between the Court and John Malcolm, the East India Company's Governor of Bombay. The disputes were only resolved when the British Privy Council declared in favour of the Company.[42]

Growing co-operation between increasingly wealthy residents of cities like Bombay and Calcutta and English lawyers and judges in the presidency towns meant that the Supreme Courts of Bombay, Calcutta and Madras were 'gradually extending their jurisdiction' in a fashion that, for Holt Mackenzie and many of his colleagues, threatened to undermine the basis of British authority in India. Charles Metcalfe, former resident of Delhi and member at the Governor-General's council, worried that there was 'no ward in British India whose affairs are not able to be brought within [the] jurisdiction' of the Bombay or Calcutta Supreme Courts. 'According to the present practice of the King's Courts', he said, 'a native of the snowy mountains of Himala, not amenable to the Court's jurisdiction...may be dragged a distance of 800 miles or more, to the swamps and jungles and stifling heat of Bengal, merely to show that he is not amenable to its jurisdiction'. Connecting these fears to an emerging colonial stereotype of Bengali cunning, Mackenzie wondered if 'the process of the Supreme Court may, through the chicanery of the Bengalese, be rendered a source of intolerable oppression'.[43]

In Calcutta the Wames Chandra case was concerned with the law that governed property possessed within Hindu families that was discussed in Chapter 4. As the next chapter shows, the rules that governed Hindu property law once again became a controversial matter for Indian landholders and journalists soon after the Wames Chandra case was decided, when Rammohan Roy and other commentators debated the implications of the dispute within Calcutta's public sphere. But for the British officials concerned with the dispute, the rules themselves governing Hindu property did not matter, as long as they were certain and applied in a uniform fashion. Discussing the case, the Supreme Court's judges could nonchalantly state that the 'ordinary state of a Hindu family in respect of property is that of co-parcenary between all the males, but any one member may claim a partition' as if this doctrine was uncontestable.[44] By 1830, the vast majority of British judicial officers assumed that this judicial conception of the Hindu joint family was established law: the next chapter will show how Rammohan vehemently challenged this point. For European officials though, the problem was not the nature of the law itself, but who should enforce it: in particular, did a British officer of the Supreme Court have the authority to seize property outside the court's jurisdiction in Calcutta, or did they become an ordinary subject, governable by the East India Company's court system once they crossed the Maratha ditch which separated the city from the *mofussil*? As long as there was no danger of a violent Indian reaction, British officers were not particularly interested in the extent to which a particular judgement conformed exactly to pre-colonial practice or not. For most officers, indecision, dissension and intra-British strife were far more dangerous than judicial innovation. Mackenzie suggested it was 'dangerous' for officials from different British institutions or departments to disagree in public, as they had done in the Wames Chandra case. The Calcutta Council member Charles Metcalf supposed that British power 'depends on that respect and awe entertained of us by the native population', which itself relied on a 'belief in our perfect union amongst ourselves'. 'Nothing', he argued, 'can more certainly tend to shake them than the appearance of discord between our highest authorities'.[45] The response to such sentiments was a continuous effort at 'reform' that would ensure the colonial state in India acted in an entirely predictable and rule-bound way.

Discussion of the colonial state was marked by the increasing tendency to describe the apparatus of governance as a machine. In Britain itself, a mechanistic political language did not emerge for another generation at least. Equating the polity to a machine only occurred when states were contemplated at a distance, not where observers were wrapped up in the immediacy of political practice. Of the 44 references to the 'machine' or 'machinery' of 'government' or 'state' occurring in the House of Commons' official papers between 1830 and 1850, only one referred to the domestic British state, the remainder concerned India, the Caribbean, Canada, Australia and, more rarely, foreign states like Greece and France.[46] Mechanistic language crept into the discussion of British India from the very beginning of the nineteenth century, when Lord Wellesley referred to the type of administrator he wanted the Company's schools and colleges to produce in 1801 – something this chapter will consider later – and when James Mill discussed the nature of 'civilised' government in 1818. Both usages suggest that automatic action was required in political contexts where reflection led to unease and indecision.

The immediate response to the dissensions and controversies between the East India Company's executive and the Supreme Court, including the Wames Chandra case, was the construction of a new supreme authority, 'a single paramount council armed with legislative power' as Thomas Macaulay put it in his speech before the House of Commons in July 1833. Initially, officials suggested the new body consist of the Supreme Court's judges along with the existing members of the Governor-General's Council, in order to ensure both acted single-mindedly. As Charles Metcalf put it, the new council would wield power 'for the benefit of the State over all parts of the governing machine'. But the involvement of judges was quickly seen as an unnecessary blurring of executive and judicial power. The proposal sent to London merely added a fourth law member to the existing members of the Governor-General's Council. But the new body was to make laws that applied to the Supreme Courts as well as Company territory for the first time. After 1793 it had been an uneasy British ministry that insisted Parliament act to retrospectively legitimate Cornwallis' constitution. By contrast, in 1832 it was the Company in India that demanded it be given the right to actively make new law by the 'Imperial Parliament'. The Legislative Council would be India's utilitarian sovereign, actively making law which applied 'to all parts of our Indian empire, and which all descriptions of people are bound to obey' for the first time.[47]

After lobbying from Company officials in India and London, the Legislative Council was created by the act that renewed the East India Company's charter, passed in August 1833.[48] The act is usually noted for its abolition of the Company's commercial functions, finally terminating the Company's slow transition from trader to sovereign. As importantly though it marked a second dramatic shift in the culture of British governance, what Henry Tucker called 'the new constitution for India'.[49] The act unambiguously defined the Westminster parliament as the sole source of sovereign legality in British India, over-riding the Company's lingering historical relationship with its Mughal and regional predecessors as a source of authority. It then gave a Legislative Council stationed in India absolute power to make law, subject only to revision by the Imperial Parliament 8,000 miles away. In doing so it removed any doubt that the British had the right to abolish or modify existing Indian forms of customary and religious jurisprudence if it chose; if it did not choose to reform them it was merely acting out of 'wise restraint'.[50] The act formally defined South Asian society as a terrain for consistent British intervention, 'that great scene of British action' as James Mill put it, upon which officials used the instruments of law to intervene.[51]

As well as preventing conflict between the Company and the Supreme Court, the Legislative Council's purpose was to create a comprehensive and consistent code of law. Thomas Macaulay, appointed assistant commissioner of the Board of Control in June 1832, and the main architect of the Charter bill, noted that hitherto British 'regulations in civil matters do not define rights, but merely establish remedies'. The Company's enactments were mere by-laws.[52] As previous chapters have shown, from 1793, the Company's regulations had provided little more than a set of rules for the management of the institutions of government, although they had begun to define new forms of right (unnoticed by Macaulay) from the late 1810s. But until the Charter Act of 1833 the potential sources of legal rules were many, and there was no stable hierarchy to determine whether one source took precedence over another.

Judges spoke of the equal importance of custom, 'tradition', medieval or more recent religio-juridical texts and British parliamentary statute. In principle (if not always in fact), the 1833 Act broke with the complex range of historical authorities colonial law relied on, to posit the command of the British colonial state in India as the final source of legal authority.

Macaulay was aided most of all in framing the bill which created the Legislative Council by Holt Mackenzie. After failing to be elected as an M.P. in 1832, Mackenzie became Secretary of the Board of Control. Described by Bentinck as the 'interpreter of Indian hieroglyphics' Mackenzie was a conduit for the technical views of officials in Calcutta to be transmitted into British parliamentary life. It isn't surprising that one of Company servants' main demands, the codification of Indian law, found itself in the charter bill.[53] Whilst the bill was passing through parliament Macaulay argued that the Legislative Council's first task would be to codify Hindu and Muslim law in India, to replace the 'confusion' that governed Indian law with British-created order.[54] Once the bill was passed it was Macaulay who was appointed as law member of the Legislative Council and chair of the first Indian Law Commission, and given the task of codifying Indian law. In fact of course, the commission's codificatory aspirations were first realised in the Penal Code it produced in 1838. Hindu law was seen as too complex a subject to codify in a short number of years. The sense of failure that accompanied this decision was elided by the total absence of any reference to the original objectives of the Law Commission in its first publication.[55]

V

Like the debates about law and legislation which one can trace from James Mill's arguments to the creation of the Legislative Council in 1833, British discussion of education was driven by anxious sensibilities about the colonial state's seemingly chaotic and discordant action. This chapter concludes by broadening the frame of horizon to consider the role of governance and statecraft in what has been labelled 'the great education debate', and seen by some scholars as a clash between diametrically opposed ideologies of colonial rule. On one side lay the so-called Anglicist position. Men such as Thomas Macaulay, Holt Mackenzie and Charles Trevelyan wanted to transform Indian society in a small space of time through the introduction of European science, English education, utilitarian law and Christianity as well. This Anglicist project of reform was based on a thorough denigration of Indian arts, culture and society. It was defined most of all by Macaulay's infamous 'Minute on Education', with its remarkable statement that 'a single shelf of a good European library was worth the whole native literature of India and Arabic'.[56] On the other side figures like W.B. Bayley, W.H. MacNaghten, H.T. Prinsep and H.H. Wilson defended the teaching of classical languages such as Sanskrit and Arabic and advocated a closer partnership between European and Indian scholars. These so-called Orientalists argued that Asian institutions needed to be conserved, and that any change should be gradual and occur within indigenous media. For the historian Thomas Metcalf and others, the Anglicist position was founded on confidence 'in the supremacy of British power, culture and religion'; the latter rooted in a more sceptical sense of the virtues of British domination.[57]

The debate about the education of Indians in Bengal that occurred in 1835 was the final culmination of a much longer series of arguments about the relationship between the British imperial state in Bengal and the education of its colonial functionaries. That debate was intricately connected to the process of colonial state formation. Just as in the colonial discussion of legislation, it was a debate in which the superiority of practical experience over abstract, codified rules was questioned, and the importance of ensuring that colonial officers, whether Indian or British, acted as cogs within the 'complicated and artful machine' James Mill wrote about. In the early nineteenth century these arguments were made about the education of *British* Company servants. A later focus on Indian education only occurred because the colonial regime began to rely on cheaper Asian officers from the late 1810s, and became concerned to ensure they acted as part of a unitary governing mechanism.

In 1800 Lord Wellesley, the Governor-General, could still believe that 'the system of confiding the immediate exercise of every branch and department of the government to Europeans, educated in its own service, and subject to its direct control, should be diffused as widely as possible'.[58] As a result there was little interest in Indian schools. In 1800, senior officers were concerned that practice and the experience of governance were not sufficient to train British civil servants, some of whom had had only a 'commercial education' in academies in London and Edinburgh; similar points were made later on about the inadequacies of the practical education of Indian officials. From this, Wellesley drew the conclusion that a series of colleges needed to be founded to educate young British officers in the arts of state. The result was the creation of Fort William College in Calcutta in 1800, followed by Haileybury College in Hertfordshire in 1806. The arguments that Wellesley made contain one of the first explicit attempts to think about the Company's institutions in India as a machine-like state.

Wellesley noted that the British empire in India had been created by war and conquest, a process that had 'always furnished men equal to the exigency of the occasion'. Extraordinary combinations of human affairs, wars, revolutions and all those unusual events which form the marked features and prominent characters of the history of mankind, naturally bring to light talents and exertions adapted to such emergencies'. Governance and the stability of an empire created by heroic violence needed something different. If warfare required the instinctive ability to respond to contingency, imperial rule needed precisely the reverse. Empire was secured by 'the durable principles of internal order; by a pure, upright, and uniform administration of justice; by a prudent and temperate system of revenue' and so on. It needed 'a succession of able magistrates, wise and honest judges, and skilful statesmen, properly qualified to conduct the ordinary movements of the great machine of empire'. The 'arts of peace' and the colonial diffusion of 'affluence and happiness' in India required rule-bound order and efficiency to be taught by Company institutions. To inculcate these, officials needed to be educated by the Company and sent to the subcontinent from a fairly early age. Wellesley was clear that elite life in Britain involved a different set of habits and skills from governance in India, not least the greater independence and room for discretion and intuition which continued residence in the metropolis allowed. He wanted to prevent his officials from developing strong 'habits and connexions at home', that would make them 'untractable instruments in the hands of the government of India'. Company servants should, he argued, leave for India at the age of 15 or 16. But departure at such an early age would also allow them to return to Britain whilst relatively young, and ensure they stayed strangers to Indian society. Wellesley was as concerned that British officials might develop long-lasting local links to India. 'Evil consequences' would ensue if individual Britons were to 'establish themselves permanently in India'.

When he spoke of implanting 'sound and correct principles of government and religion' in the minds of British officers, Wellesley did not link this to any form of culture or civilisation other than the form of personal cultivation which good, regular authoritarian governance required. The purpose of institutions such as Fort William College was not primarily to instil the value or virtues of Britishness, nor heighten the sense of difference between European and Indian ways of doing things in young British officers. The only relevant contrast was between 'unsettled' ideas propagated by Britons who supported the French revolution and the colonial habits he wished to inculcate. Official education was intended to detach Company servants from political opinions and 'habits and connexions' formed outside the Company's official hierarchy, forcing them to become strangers to their homeland as much as India, making them instead 'tractable instruments' of the colonial machinery of state.[59]

The years after the foundation of Fort Willliam College saw a gradual expansion in the number of Indian officers employed by the East India Company as the cost of administration was increased by the addition of more territory to rule without a corresponding increase in revenue. Ensuring that elite Indians were similarly tractable agents of British rule became the major educational concern. As a consequence, the General Committee of Public Instruction was founded in 1823 to consider provision for 'native' education. To begin with, different members of the committee shared a common point of view. It supported colleges such as the Calcutta *madrasa* and Benares college, and established Calcutta's Sanskrit college in 1823. These institutions taught law and literature in classical Indian languages as well as vernacular tongues. The committee was keen to introduce 'western literature or science', but noted that 'the prejudices of the natives against European interference with their education in any shape' prevented the teaching of European learning in English. Holt Mackenzie's original advocacy of English-language education occurred in the minute that established the committee. In 1823, Mackenzie noted the 'difficulties' in introducing English education, and did not suggest that a move could be made in the short term. Showing the close link between concerns about education and the adminstration of law, Mackenzie argued that the committee needed to be administered by the Company's judicial department, as 'nothing can be more nearly connected with the good administration of justice and the prevention of crime, than the public instruction of the people'.[60]

Despite this rhetorical concern with the education of the public at large, attention to the practice of the Committee shows it was interested in training a fairly narrow section of the Indian population: young Asian officers who would be appointed as *qazis, pandits, amins* and in other positions within the Company's machinery of state. Education, whether in English or classical Indian languages, was used as an instrument for ensuring British and Indian officers acted as functionaries within a disciplined colonial machine. It was to be used to instil rational forms of mental order rather than allowing what officials saw as the natural chaos of Indian society to reign supreme, acting as an instrument that could be used to remove the role of intuition and discretion from the Company's administration. Just as Wellesley had done, the committee criticised too much reliance on local 'experience' as a guide to official governmental action. One of its earliest acts was to ensure 'as far as is practicable' that Indian law officers were graduates of the Madrasa or Sanskrit college, rather than merely local inhabitants 'of good character' – the sole qualification for official office beforehand. The committee felt that most *vakils, qazis, pandits* and *munsiffs* were 'generally quite unworthy from want of education'. Attending one of the government colleges would provide candidates for office with 'their means of viewing the world'; the British wanted Indian officers who shared their world view and had some grounding in 'the language and theory of the law'. Unless Indian officials shared common administrative knowledge with their colonial employers, 'there is no hope of having such administration of civil justice as is at all worthy of our country' as Mackenzie put it.[61]

By 1825, these arguments came up against the lingering remains of an older point of view, which emphasised the role of experience and informal exposure to local practice instead of formal training and rule-learning as the best way to train Indian law officers. A brief skirmish occurred when Courtney Smith, the most prominent exponent of local experience, was appointed acting Chief Judge of the *Sadr Diwani Adalat* for a brief period of time. As a judge, Smith continued trying to decide property disputes with reference to

custom and local usage long after most judges had begun to rely on canonical texts of Hindu and Muslim law. It was Smith who wrote the minority
opinion in the Bhola Dhami case reliant on 'usage', examined in Chapter
4, countering the other two judges' attempt to resolve the dispute with the
textual norms of Hindu law with reference to the particular customs of Gaya
district. In his critique of the General Committee of Public Instruction's proposals for training law officers, Smith suggested that 'decent moral conduct,
plain sense, an acquaintance with the local usages, and a moderate profi-
ciency in the language is all that is required' to act as a local Indian court
officer. When it came to appointing lawyers, Smith went further, suggesting
that 'it should be an indispensable condition' that a pleader had no connection to one of the Company's colleges for at least ten years before his
appointment. 'In which time', Smith went on,

> he might have rubbed off some of the numbness of his erudition, travelled
> a little in the interior, mingled to some degree with the world and acquired
> some sort of insight into the multifaceted concerns and transactions of
> common life...without a knowledge of which he could not be of the
> smallest use to his clients.

Such intangible virtues as 'tact', intuition and a good sense of judgement
came from experience alone. By contrast, the Company's colleges produced
'crude pedants and unlicked bear-whelps' who were no practical use in the
everyday administration of justice.[62]

The education committee was unanimous in its opposition to Smith's argument. Men who would later occupy opposing sides on the English-language
question shared a common sense of the necessity of formal educational qual-
ifications for Indian law officers, and the need for students to be trained
with texts. Although it remained significant in other provinces, in Bengal
the last vestiges of this emphasis on the role of uncodified experience disappeared in the late 1820s as written rules and abstract knowledge became
more important. So, in 1825 the judicial officer Henry Shakespear wrote a
minute highly critical of the extent to which the Company's pleaders relied
on uncodified experience in court, which Mackenzie used heavily to make
his own arguments. Both men believed the only way they would act as a
smoothly functioning part of the judicial machine was if they were given an
education framed by Europeans to make them strangers both to the practices of their own (supposedly degenerate) society as well as to the ways of
British life.

A decade later Henry Shakespear and Holt Mackenzie made very different
arguments in the Anglicist/Orientalist debate. Shakespear was an articulate
defender of Sanskrit and Arabic, and fierce critic of Macaulay and Trevelyan's
arguments. By the early 1830s officials had clustered around rival, forceful personalities to make the labels 'Orientalist' and 'Anglicist' useful to a

degree; after all these terms were used by contemporaries when referring to the position officers took in the debate on education and language. But arguments about language did not correspond to positions taken in the discussion of law or other aspects of governance, nor in debate about the virtues or otherwise of Indian civilisation. Coming from a common concern with the practice of judicial governance, the positions officials occupied was far more complex. For example: Edward Strachey was an advocate of a rationalist form of codification and English-language instruction, but he also defended the value of ancient Indian civilisation; James Mill opposed English education but offered the most vehement attack on Indian culture articulated in the first three decades of the nineteenth century by anyone; William Butterworth Bayley was a keen codifier, but a supporter of Sanskrit and Arabic rather than English education; William MacNaghten supported the funding of education in Asian languages in Company-funded schools but called for the British state in India to officially sanction texts offering a dramatically new form of Muslim and, especially, Hindu law.[63]

The argument was described by Macaulay as a contest between reforming young men such as Charles Trevelyan and himself and 'half a dozen of the oldest and most powerful men in India'. In fact, with the exception of the 27-year-old Trevelyan, Company servants who debated English-language on either side in the late 1820s and early 1830s were in their mid-forties, belonging to the first generation educated at the East India Company's college at Haileybury after the turn of the nineteenth century. Both Orientalists and Anglicists were reformists. Participants on different sides in these debates shared a common belief in the need for the colonial state to actively produce new forms of knowledge to rule India, and doubted whether India could produce the rules for 'civilised' conduct of its own accord. H. H. Wilson was almost unique in suggesting that Indian knowledge needed little reform and in defending the 'high state of civilization' amongst Indians in the 1830s and 1840s. But Wilson was never subject to the estranged culture of colonial administration with its failed efforts to collect revenue or administer law.[64] He moved from the Company's medical service to educational institutions. Otherwise, amongst the whole spectrum of officials engaged in the project of colonial governance, Company servants believed British minds needed to reconfigure Indian knowledge in order to make India governable. In particular, each side was sceptical about the ability of the British to administer India unless they were guided by textual rules, many of which needed to be constructed by themselves.

Texts produced in the 1830s continued to be couched in terms of the importance of literature and language as matters relevant to the character of practical administration. Charles Trevelyan was Macaulay's brother-in-law; it was Trevelyan who initially enlisted Macaulay as a supporter of English language teaching in the 'furious contest' about education in Calcutta.[65] Trevelyan's notes on 'native education' were published as a short book,

On the Education of the People of India, immediately after he returned to London in 1838, but which circulated long beforehand. Trevelyan's text was primarily concerned with the role of education in the functioning of the colonial regime, especially judicial practice: a new approach to law required a new form of legal education. The introduction of new law and codification of India's 'uncertain, redundant and contradictory' laws was a 'cause of movement in native society', he argued. Trevelyan suggested that the early nineteenth century had seen the colonial regime shift from Cornwallis' principle of 'doing everything by European agency' to employing more Indian officials. As a result '[t]he Government wants well educated servants to fill the responsible situations opened up to the natives'. The language of legal texts would be English. To ensure the state acted in a consistent fashion, Trevelyan argued that Indian lawyers and judges should speak the same language as their European masters.

Like Trevelyan, Macaulay saw a close relationship between education and law. Parliament had 'commanded' British officials to digest Indian law; as a result, 'before the boys who are now entering the Madrassa and Sanscrit college have completed their studies', 'the Shaster and Hedaya will be useless to a Moonsiff or Sudder Amin', he argued. Macaulay famously advocated the creation of 'a class of persons, Indian in blood and colour, but English in taste, in opinions, in morals and in intellect' who would 'refine the vernacular dialects of the country' and 'enrich those dialects with terms of science borrowed from the Western nomenclature'. When discussing this class of intermediaries, Macaulay was referring to Indian judicial officials, needed because the British were unable to educate or govern the population alone.[66]

Trevelyan and Macaulay argued that stipends and scholarships to support Indian students studying Sanskrit, Arabic and Persian should be suspended, and the £20,000 which had been allocated to Indian education since 1813 spent entirely on English-language education. The orientalist response to this position rested on the suggestion that, in order to be of use in ruling India, Indian officials needed to be able to read texts written in these languages. The Sanskrit colleges of Calcutta and Benares had, they noted, 'been endowed and established for the express purpose of educating Pundits capable of expounding the Hindoo law', and the 'Mudrussa or Arabic College of Calcutta' established 'with the same express view' with respect to Muslim officials. Codification into English would not happen instantly, so rules needed to be distilled from texts in 'ancient' Indian languages. In general, the Company's 'conservatives' (men such as MacNaghten and Prinsep explicitly used this word) supported the process of codification, and were not opposed to the introduction of English education. 'None', they said, 'can be more impressed than ourselves with the superiority of British Literature, Arts and Sciences, and none can more ardently desire that they should be introduced to India'. But they were critics of rapid 'innovation' that would instantly replace a class of Indians who had an advanced education in Sanskrit, Arabic or Persian scholarship with another group of men with a bare 'smattering' of English. 'Any crude sweeping innovation' would be likely to produce a violent reaction from Indian elites, 'having a tendency to defeat rather than promote the object in view'. Advocates of teaching indigenous languages wanted to reconstruct Indian knowledge and literature to produce a new 'national literature', as Brian Hodgson, a supporter of vernacular education, put it.[67] In Calcutta, if not necessarily in London, the debate between the complex range of different positions on language and education articulated during the 1830s was not an argument between critics of defenders of the claims of Indian civilisation. Instead it was an argument about the best practical means by which British sovereignty and civilisation could be propagated in Bengal.[68]

The so-called great education debate came to a head in the early months of 1835. The Governor-General declared victory for those wanting to see education in English after a decision was made to fund English-language schools. But just as neither Hindu or Muslim law were codified, and the original purpose of the Legislative Council not achieved, the decision in favour of English schools was not fully implemented. Influenced by the stronger arguments being made for the virtues of Indian language and culture in London, metropolitan authorities allowed a more pluralistic approach to operate throughout British India, as Governors subsequently moved money to fund regional vernaculars like Bengali and Hindi rather than either the Indian classics or English. In practice, after 1835 English education was fuelled by demand from Indian students not official patronage.

VI

Like Wellesley's founding of Fort William College and the creation of a new Legislative Council, the reforms in the system of 'native education' proposed by the General Committee of Public Instruction in the 1830s were attempts to replace what was seen as the vacillating and disorganised operation of the colonial polity with machine-like regularity. As this chapter has shown, by the early 1830s, a utilitarian concept of the state as a single bureaucratic machinery separate from local habits and connections, responsible for authorising the rules that governed Indian social life, was present in British discussion of law and education in Bengal. It was that conception, with its strong sense of the difference between British and colonial political culture, which was articulated in the 1833 Government of India Act and the decision two years later to introduce English language education.

These moments defined a second new constitution for colonial India, to replace Cornwallis's 'new constitution' of 1793. Like France, British-administered Bengal had more than one constitutional moment in this 40-year long age of revolutions, while Britain had none. The creation of a legislative state in India, together with the attempt to introduce English-language education and codify law might be seen as part of a second global, imperial moment of constitutional reform that came to a head in the early 1830s. The 1833 Government of India act was preceded, the year before, by the first systematic reform of the British parliament, an act that as Miles Taylor suggests, had imperial consequences.[69] It was followed a few days later by the act that abolished slavery throughout most of the British empire and replaced it with an indenture system, followed by full emancipation in 1838.[70] Taken together, accompanied by the Act of Union in Canada, the Cameron-Colebrooke reforms in Sri Lanka, the beginning of state-funded education in England and reform of local corporations, these pieces of legislation consisted of a major reconfiguration of the British state at home and abroad during the 1830s. Most of them occurred in a few short months in 1832 and 1833.

Generations of historians saw these moments as the death-knell of an *ancien regime*, and the articulation of a new, confident attitude towards political change radiating from Britain.[71] More recent scholarship has suggested that parliamentary reform and the abolition of slavery, like the British government's own attempts to fund educational institutions, were not acts that confidently articulated a reforming ideology. Instead, they were anxious attempts by Britain's ruling elite to prevent catastrophic disaster occurring at moments of crisis. The late 1820s and early 1830s were a period of global economic depression. Parliamentary reform and the abolition of slavery were preceded by serious instances of political upheaval that threatened to fundamentally undermine the political and social order. Fuelled by growing poverty, nation-wide violence occurred in Britain before the passing of the Reform Act. The abolition of slavery quickly followed after the slave rebellion in Jamaica in December 1831.[72] The Canadian uprisings of 1837 led to the creation of a new constitution for British North America. Both Lord Durham's report and the earlier Parliamentary Inquiry into Canadian 'grievances' saw the problem as disunity within 'the body of the state'; the solution was similar to that proposed in India, the creation of a single, absolute legislative authority able to make general rules to improve the welfare of all.[73]

This chapter has shown how the description of the so-called age of reform in Britain as 'an age of uncertainty' (to use David Eastwood's phrase) can be applied to the colonial politics of British-ruled India, alongside other imperial locations as well. Reforming initiatives such as the creation of the 'new constitution' giving the government in India active law-making powers and the emphasis on English-language education were not confident instances of imperial consolidation. They occurred as a response to British anxieties about their ability to make sense of the world they governed, to frame and apply rules in a consistent and effective fashion. In some cases they were seen as an attempt by the British to ensure their survival as a ruling force.

But the anxieties charted in this chapter led to the construction of a very different kind of state in each place. In Britain reform was usually regarded as an attempt to continue existing patterns of development rooted deep into the past.[74] Metropolitan disorder after the end of the Napoleonic wars as well as anxiety about the effects of industrialisation were not severe enough to dent most elite Britons' confidence in the viability of the polity they believed had endured over centuries. Reform reflected a broad sense that politics was an essentially historical art; for some indeed, politics was nothing more than the art of practically reflecting on history, and history little more than past political practice. This emphasis on the role of political continuity and histor- ical experience became the central theme of Whig accounts of British history, articulated by 'philosophical Whigs' such as James Mackintosh in journals such as *Edinburgh Review* and in historical publications which culminated in Macaulay's *History of England*. For Mackintosh, instances of reform in Britain needed to be 'judicious and timely reformations' which were justified by instances of historical precedent and needed not only to be adapted 'to the peculiar interests of a people, but engrafted onto their previous usages, and brought into harmony with those natural dispositions on which the execution of laws depends'.[75]

Both Mackintosh and Macaulay were men with significant Indian 'experience' who shared a far more critical view of the uses of the Indian past. For them and others, reform in India involved a dramatic rupture with a past that was seen as both barbaric and unknowable at the same time. Britons believed that, by creating an authoritarian state in India with codified rules and a uniform bureaucracy, they were doing something unprecedented. Macaulay argued that India's difference from Britain meant that

we cannot introduce those institutions which all our habits, which all the reasonings of European philosophers, which all the history of our own part of the world would lead us to consider as the one great security for good government.

'Habits' here was a significant word, denoting the importance of historically rooted instincts in British political life. Habit had no place in India, because the construction of a bureaucratic despotism required Britons to think about politics in uncharacteristic ways. It also forced them to create a rupturing distance from existing habits, practices and forms of historical experience. For Macaulay, 'political science' required the study of history. Politics in the future would be a modified continuation of the politics of the past, so could use historical study as a guide to action. But the unprecedented character of colonial governance in India meant 'the lights of political science and of history are withdrawn: we are walking in darkness: we do not distinctly see whether we are going'.[76] Like Mill, Macaulay believed that the only use for history in India was to show how the colonial state needed to jettison the past and push India towards a radically different future. Colonial governance involved a radical critique of the present, and the projection of order and civilisation onto a future time after the state had acted as the agent of significant change. That project necessarily undermined any foundation it might have had in historical practice or experience as it went along. As a result, Macaulay's confident tone was always undercut by a considerable degree of anxiety.

The roots of that anxiety lay in the way colonial officials were always critical of the particular historical context they found themselves acting in at any particular moment in time. Its effect was to make failure a continual component within the rhetoric of colonial governance, and reform a continuous state. Without the confidence that came from practical experience or a sense of historical rights, the validity of every governmental act was assessed by balancing a calculation of the anticipated increase in the welfare of the population with a result with a sense of the dangers to the British regime in the short-term. The fragile basis of such calculations meant that, in most cases, 'expediency' and inaction won out, especially when faced with a growing concern about critical Indian 'sentiment'.

Though this sense of expediency usually led to a nominally conservative approach to existing institutions and social practices, Indian society was continually constituted as a *potential* field for intervention by the mechanisms of the colonial state. The end result of British deliberation was usually to do nothing. But the colonial regime's anxious freedom, the restless form of inaction which allowed its officers to move fitfully without any kind of sustained experiential connection to South Asian society allowed a permanent sense of the possibility of 'encroachment' into the practices of Indian social life to occur. The restlessness of colonial practice produced insecurity, fear and alarm. As the next chapter shows, it was that sense which aroused the criticism of Indian liberals in early nineteenth-century Bengal.

7
Indian Liberalism and Colonial Utilitarianism

In 1904, Rabindranath Tagore used a meeting about water scarcity in Calcutta to lecture his audience on the nature of the Indian body politic. What was distinctive about India, Tagore argued, was the absolute separation between *samaj* and *sarkar*, or between society and the state. In England, he believed, social organisation depended on the actions of the government. There he supposed, 'the state is mainly responsible for the welfare of the people'. If the state collapsed, society fell as well. In India, by contrast, 'the *Sarkar* has no relations with our social organisation'. For Tagore, the regeneration of India did not depend on 'a change of sovereignty'. It required recognition of society's autonomy from politics, and the separation of the forms of sociability that sustained social relations from the exercise of sovereign power. Compared to the important task of social work, of energetic leadership by 'bands of workers' going from village to village improving education, industry, religion and sanitation, state politics was an empty and mechanical exercise. 'Society waits for no help from outside; external irritation undermines its magnificence', he suggested.[1]

Tagore believed Indian social organisation was underpinned by familiar social relations, while the modern, Western state treated its subjects as strangers. 'To establish a personal relationship between man and man was always India's main endeavour', he noted. Making this argument, Tagore romantically celebrated the sociability of the countryside. For the most part familiarity and face-to-face forms of reciprocity and obligation governed life in India's rural hinterland. In days gone by, 'the pomp of the metropolis, or the glories of the imperial audience had never succeeded in drawing their hearts away from there'. But under the British, Bengal's rural leaders 'had been drawn away to the metropolis', had begun to speak English, wear suits instead of *dhotis* and 'carry watches on gold chains'.

Tagore's critique was levelled against the kind of state examined in the previous chapter, a mechanical entity governed by rigid rules and hierarchical chains of command. By supplicating themselves before the machinery of the colonial state, 'we [Indians] are now crystallized into rigidity by the

161

Englishman's law', Tagore complained. Assuming that the essence of being Indian was to be a Hindu, he went on: 'every departure is compelled to declare itself non-Hindu' as those ways of life which lay 'at the core of our *samaj*' were exposed to the 'aggression' of the state. At the beginning of Bengal's first nationalist campaign of civil disobedience, the *swadeshi* ('own-country', homeland) movement, Tagore's text called on his compatriots to refrain from engaging with the modern state in all its guises.[2] Instead they should retreat to the villages and regenerate their own society.

One can detect the complex interweaving of three different political languages in Tagore's comments. First of all, his argument was part of a broader challenge to industrial modernity that could be found in almost every country from the United States to Japan, from the mid-nineteenth century to the Second World War, in the work of writers ranging from Ralph Waldo Emerson and John Ruskin to Leo Tolstoy to T.S. Eliot, Martin Heidegger and of course, M.K. Gandhi and Tagore himself. In different ways these commentators celebrated the country above the city, agriculture and handicraft against mechanised industry, culture against political economy and, perhaps most importantly, the community, *samaj* or *gemeinschaft* above the modern bureaucratic state. Each was opposed to what they saw as the abstract, technological and overly rational way modern subjects behaved with each other and oriented themselves to the world.[3] The alienated process of capitalist production and consumption was just one example of that estranged sensibility. Indian versions of this critique articulated what Andrew Sartori calls 'a culturalist critique of the west'.[4] South Asian critics posited essential differences between East and West, often suggesting that the inner, intact civilisational core of Indian society had endured through the ages intact, but needed to be protected from too much European encroachment of the wrong kind.

Secondly, Tagore's text belongs to a longer tradition of Indian writing which from the late eighteenth century began to be levelled against the estranged institutions of the colonial state; it represented a late modern articulation of what C.A. Bayly calls an Indian language of ethical governance. Here, there are similarities between Tagore's interpretation of modern Indian politics and the critique of British rule made in the *Seir Mutaquerrin* which this book began with. Both essentially saw governance as the art of face-to-face interaction, a process of reciprocal give and take based on human relationship not codified rights or rules; as a form of inter-subjective ethical practice in other words.[5] Each criticised colonial rule and colonised Indians for adopting an overly mechanical way of perceiving the art of politics. Tagore, then, was making a late contribution to a centuries-old narrative of political decline. The story he told associated the deterioration of the polity with the demise of face-to-face skills of human interaction, and saw the arrival of the colonial state as a moment of *inquilab* (revolution) which overturned the affective basis of civilised order.[6]

But by the time he wrote, the language of ethical governance Tagore espoused had been dramatically reconfigured by more than a century of colonial politics. In particular, colonial politics allowed the emergence of a distinctly liberal language that asserted the autonomy of Indian society from the colonial state: it is with that transformation that this chapter is concerned. Instead of attempting to modify the relationships that constituted the polity, as Ghulam Hussein wanted to do, Tagore responded to colonial institutions by trying to draw a sharp boundary between *samaj* and *sarkar* (society and state), asking Indians to insulate themselves from the corrupting force of alien power politics. Rather than petition the British to provide a better supply of water, Tagore thought Indians needed to regenerate their 'broken-up *samaj*' and own civil society and solve such problems themselves.[7]

In a recent essay Sudipta Kaviraj argues that the use of terms such as 'civil society' to describe political practice in India involves the use of 'systematically misleading expressions'. The 'actual behaviour' of political actors in the colonial and post-colonial third world is 'quite substantially different from what we are led to expect by the long-standing meanings of these terms in Western political or social thought'.[8] At the core of the 'long-standing meaning' of the term civil society in political and social thought is the idea of a sphere of activity which exists outside, by necessity often in tension with, the coercive mechanisms of the state. This notion of civil society is central to one modern liberal vision of freedom. As many liberals have articulated it since the mid-nineteenth century, individuals are free when they have unrestrained autonomy to act upon their own interests and desires in a realm of free association. This realm of negative liberty or civil society necessarily has an ambivalent relationship with the state. On the one hand, it needs to be protected from the potential encroachment of the coercive powers of political power, which have the capacity to restrict an individual's autonomy. On the other hand, only state institutions are powerful enough to protect the autonomy of the self from encroachment by other forces. Liberals are constantly on guard to ensure that areas of life better governed by the consensual rules of social life do not become subject to the command of the state, continually anxious about the boundary between the two domains. From a liberal point of view, politics and governance are necessary evils. They are required sometimes to protect liberty, but should always be kept subordinate to non-political, economic, social or cultural practices that provide the basis of human interests, identities and ways of life.[9]

For Kaviraj and others who make a similar argument, this liberal conception of power, freedom and politics has a peculiarly Western provenance. Contrary to Kaviraj's claim, this chapter argues that the *samaj* or 'society' which Bengal's Hindu intellectual elite spoke about from the 1820s onwards was initially articulated within a colonial Indian tradition of liberalism that, although not derivative of European categories, was not dramatically different from the vocabulary of 'western' liberal thought. The category of Indian 'society' was articulated by Indian political thinkers to protect the autonomy of Bengali practice against the colonial state and other potentially malign, interfering forces. As this chapter will show, it was also based on a positive view of commercial civilisation and concerned with such classic liberal themes as the protection of property. Throughout the nineteenth century, élite Bengali intellectuals were concerned to carve out a space outside, often in tension with, but frequently also reliant on the juridical mechanisms of the state. In that sense, the way they talked about individual and collective social life occurred in a classically liberal style, privileging free association above the state's leadership or coercion. For writers articulating this liberal political rationality in the middle 50 years of the nineteenth century, the country's social institutions were supposed to offer a realm of rule-bound yet free sociability, ruled not by external force but by consent.[10]

This chapter pays particular attention to the arguments of Rammohan Roy, a man described recently as the first Indian liberal, by far the most prominent political character in Calcutta in the late 1810s and 1820s and a good friend of Rabindranath Tagore's grandfather.[11] Along with a number of his contemporaries, Rammohan articulated a liberal style of thought that was not derived from British intellectual influence, although it did develop from Bengal's relationships with Europeans. This chapter shows how Rammohan's liberal rhetoric emerged as a counter-point to the threat of 'intervention' from the increasingly rule-obsessed colonial state described in the last chapter. Colonial Indian liberalism emerged in part as a critique of colonial utilitarianism. As a predominant feature of political thought, it developed long before similar liberal arguments were commonplace in the United Kingdom.

Of course, Bengali liberalism had its distinctive characteristics, shaped by the particular context from which it emerged. To a large degree those characteristics concerned the relationship between social activity and time, and consisted of the claim that 'civilised' forms of liberal practices had existed continuously in India for centuries. When commentators from Rammohan to Tagore tried to emphasise the existence of a sharp boundary between the sphere of Indian social activity and the realm of the state, they did so by claiming that India's *samaj* was an autonomous entity that had endured for centuries unhindered by government action of different kinds. In doing so, they were specifically challenging the argument made by colonial critics such as James Mill, discussed in the last chapter. Bengali liberalism was a challenge to the colonial utilitarian claim that Indian social relations were chaotic and disordered, unknowable and ungovernable without the intrusion of the colonial state's classifying mind. Instead Rammohan defended the continuous historical reality of an Indian social formation, insisting 'that reality develops, goes its own way, and follows its own course according to the laws, principles and mechanisms of reality itself', the 'basic' and 'fundamental' move made within the game of liberal politics according to Michel Foucault.[12] These claims and desires challenged the language of temporal rupture and the call for dramatic legislative or codificatory action articulated by many British officials. Liberals from Rammohan onwards were always sceptical and often highly critical of the colonial state's intervention into the continuous fabric of Indian social existence in the name of reform. Like Tagore, they preferred to see India's *samaj* regenerate itself.

I

Since the late nineteenth century at least, the theologian, intellectual, journalist and government official Rammohan Roy has been described frequently as the 'maker' or 'father' of modern India. Born to a landholding family in Burdwan district in 1772, Rammohan developed a large and varied business portfolio that led to his employment by a succession of British officials as *munshi* (translator) and *diwan* (agent) in the early nineteenth century. Eventually, that portfolio allowed Rammohan to liberate himself from the patronage of Indian rulers and British officials; it also led to a series of fractious court cases that shall be examined later.

In a range of contexts, from the condition of Indian women to the state of Hindu law or the character of Hindu theology, Rammohan has been described by subsequent Indian generations as having had a reforming or modernising effect. But in an important work published a decade ago, Bruce Robertson shows that Rammohan did not regard himself as an innovator in the theological domain. Robertson suggests that Rammohan was no theological maverick, having been a pupil of the foremost *vedantic* scholars in Calcutta. Whether or not one accepts Robertson's claim that Rammohan was not actually doing anything new, the Bengali intellectual's initial rhetorical strategy was certainly to claim his thought didn't mark a dramatic break. Despite being charged by his enemies as an innovator, Rammohan did not describe himself as an *adhunikatva* or modernist, portraying himself instead as the successor to the ninth-century *vedantic* scholar Sankara who wanted to purify existing traditions rather than do anything dramatically new. Rammohan's distinctiveness lay not in a desire to see radical change in doctrine, but in the argument that anyone should be capable of exercising independent reason and attaining 'divine knowledge', even those who could only access the *vedant* in Rammohan's own Bengali translations.[13]

A similar argument can be made about Rammohan's discussion of society, politics and law. Rammohan emphasised the historical continuity of Bengali Hindu social practice, most importantly the condition of women and inheritance law. But this emphasis on the historic stability of Indian social practices intensified throughout the 1820s as Rammohan articulated a subtle but forceful critique of British writing about Indian society as well. Throughout the 1820s he became increasingly hostile to the language of the colonial state, more concerned to defend what he saw as Indian practices against encroachment and thus clearer about defining the indigenous autonomy of Bengali Hindu social life.

Rammohan's 1822 'Brief remarks regarding Modern Encroachments on the Ancient Rights of Females' was a powerful defence of Hindu widows' ability to inherit property under 'ancient' Hindu law and a component in Rammohan's broader attack on widow self-immolation or *sati*. Rammohan argued that if they could inherit property, Indian women would not choose to burn on their husband's funeral pyre (and Rammohan believed *sati* occurred because women did choose). The essay suggested that a continuous tradition existed from ancient times until the 'encroachments' of recent years in favour of widows' right to inherit landed property. Rammohan argued that this law initially emerged from the sentiments and practices of the population, and inhered within India's social organism, but had been expressed in unchanging textual rules. There were important parallels with the way William Jones thought about the source of law, although Rammohan's timescale was much longer, and he imputed far greater stability to particular rules. The essay started with a challenge to those like James Mill who doubted the high status of ancient Indian civilisation. Rammohan began,

> with a view to enable the public to form an idea of the state of civilization throughout the greater part of the empire of Hindostan in antient days, and of the subsequent gradual degradation introduced into its social and political constitution by arbitrary authorities, I am induced to give as an instance, the care and attention which our antient legislators took in the promotion of the comfort of the female part of the community.

Rammohan began by making an emphatic case for the existence of very clear, textual rules in ancient texts from the *Manusmriti* and *Yajnavalkya* to *Vyasa* allowing widows to inherit. Rammohan went on to argue that 'moderns', by which he meant commentators since the ninth century CE such as the authors of the *Mitaksara* and *Dyabhaga*, 'had limited the rights' noted by ancient commentators. But it was only under British government that jurists had 'still further reduced the right of mothers to almost nothing'. The author went on to attack other causes of *sati* by quoting rules from ancient texts against polygamy and the sale of girl brides.[14]

Rammohan Roy's opposition to the 'self-destruction of women' on their husband's funeral pyre was well known, the cause of celebration in Britain and both praise and criticism in Calcutta. His attack on *sati* employed three tactics, none of which championed legislative action by the colonial state. First of all, he made a strong case against forced immolation, arguing that the only form of *sati* validated by Hindu theological writings was the voluntary choice of the widow, an active act of suicide where the women walked on to the pyre by herself. Secondly, using a similar exegetical technique he argued that *sati* was not required of Hindu widows. After the death of their husbands they had a choice between 'suicide' or a life of asceticism. The latter was more highly regarded as it allowed a woman to spend time developing 'divine knowledge' with the prospect of 'eternal beatitude', rather than the merely sensual pleasures that occurred to the *sati* in the afterlife.[15] Finally, Rammohan worked to remove the incentives to suicide and obstacles to the middle-class Hindu widow living a fruitful life, their inability to inherit property, competition with other wives of her dead husband and the sale of girls by the receipt of a bride price. For Rammohan, property was an essential element in his critique of *sati*. By implication, *sati* only concerned Bengal's *bourgeois* proprietors.

The arguments Rammohan made against *sati* between 1818 and 1828 represented an alternative strategy to legislative abolition by the colonial power, reliant on the rational powers of the individuals who inhabited Indian civil society rather than interfering force of British law. Rammohan was a fervent opponent of widow self-immolation, but criticised the intrusion of colonial legislation, expressing doubt about the validity and polity of British intervention in the ancient rules which governed Bengal's religious and social life. Making a rare visit to Government House to discuss the matter with Lord Bentinck in 1828, Rammohan counselled against colonial legislation to ban *sati*. Before Bentinck passed the *sati* abolition regulation in 1829, Rammohan argued that 'any public enactment [against *sati*] would give rise to general apprehension'. In his discussion of their conversation, Bentinck drew a legitimate connection between Rammohan's point and the orientalist-reformist arguments of H.H. Wilson.[16] Here, Rammohan's arguments were targeted at Henry Derozio's explicitly pro-western Young Bengal nationalists, who supported legislative abolition, as much as against conservative critics such as Radhakanta Deb and his old teacher, Mritunjoy Vidyalankar who supported the continuation of the practice. As he suggested, *sati* would fade away if it became a voluntary act that women had no incentive to perform. That would only happen if the autonomous rules Rammohan suggested already existed within Indian civil society were allowed to prevail over illegitimate encroachments into that sphere; if, in other words, indigenous social 'reality' was subtly directed to ensure it autonomously ended the practice of its own accord.

Rammohan believed the law emerged from the rational social practice of the population, but was then codified by jurists in pithy, written rules. His views about the origins of Hindu Indian jurisprudence were articulated in a long historical footnote to his 'Brief Remarks'. Rammohan traced the emergence of the 'civilised' rules governing women's property by telling a story from the Hindu *puranas*.[17] The Brahman prince Parasuram's father had been murdered by a group of 'royalist' Rajput Kshatriyas, whom Parasuram 'put cruelly to death' in turn. In Rammohan's interpretation, Parasuram's fight had been a revolt against 'arbitrary and despotic practices'. The result was that Brahmans were prevented from holding power over 'the actual government of the state', but did possess 'legislative authority'.[18]

In his discussion of this passage, C.A. Bayly suggests that Rammohan articulated a conception of an Indian constitution with the separation of legislative from executive authority and a series of checks and balances to limit despotic authority.[19] Bayly is right to note that Rammohan was interested in asserting India's place within a global history of constitutional liberal polities here. But the text was also a liberal narrative in a different sense, directed against a more specific context: it presented a story about the origins of Indian laws and customs in a sphere of unfettered social conduct autonomous from the dangerous and corrupt realm of power politics. The aim of the story was to challenge over-zealous legislation by the colonial state. Rammohan's ancient Brahmans had 'no share in the actual government of the state, or in managing the revenue of the country under any pretence'. Instead they 'devoted their time to scientific pursuits and religious austerity, and lived in poverty'. Rammohan went on: '[f]reely associating with all the other tribes they were thus able to know their sentiments, and to appreciate the justness of their complaints, and to lay down such rules as were required'. Ancient Indian civilisation was founded on the existence of a realm of un-coerced sociability ruled by consensus, separate from the sphere of government.

Rammohan's understanding of contemporary India was rooted in his belief that over time, the malign force of political power had begun to creep into the un-coercive social institutions of ancient India. Some time around the second or third century CE, 1000 years before Muslims arrived to the subcontinent, Brahmans began to accept political office and 'institute new rules according to the dictates of their contemporary princes', allowing 'an absolute government to prevail'. Brahmanical autonomy succumbed to resurgent, Ksatriya royalist power and then Mughal domination. As a result, new rules were introduced which abrogated women's rights and absolutist polities began to 'encroach' on the ancient sphere of free sociability that gave women virtually the same right to property as men. Rammohan argued that this process of degeneration had accelerated in recent times, and the limited power women had to inherit done away with. Throughout his narrative, social and civilisational decline occurred because the malign force of self-interested political power was allowed to encroach upon the rational, rule-bound process of human association that occurred in an autonomous, fundamentally apolitical sphere of Indian sociability. Rammohan's discussion here, and in texts such as his *Brahmunical Magazine*, were a challenge to emerging British arguments about India's Brahman elite illegitimately usurping authority for self-interested political ends; an argument that justified the colonial state's assumption of strong legislative power, in particular its production of a reforming code. Rammohan suggested that, in contrast to colonial legislation, the rules of Indian social life were not upheld by the force of political power. Instead, in ancient times, Brahmans had been essentially anti-political beings, peacefully articulating the laws that emerged from the free exercise of reason in the social sphere but not engaging in the coercive practices political power entailed. It was this phenomena that had allowed India to develop what Rammohan described as a high 'state of civilization'.

As a youth Rammohan had been an opponent of British rule. Later in his career, he was reluctant to embroil himself in detailed arguments for or against the British presence, but retained some degree of hostility to colonial institutions. 'The succeeding generation', he laconically suggested in the 'Brief Remarks', would 'be more adequate to pronounce on the real advantages of this [colonial] government' than his own.[20] But despite his critical engagement with colonial attitudes to Indian history and law, Rammohan's argument about Hindu jurisprudence depended on its colonial context in one important respect. Like James Mill and British officials such as Holt Mackenzie and W.H. MacNaghten, Rammohan thought that the law consisted of a single set of written rules applicable to every member of the society. Rammohan shared the colonial utilitarian assumption that law needed to occur in written codes if there was to be a stable rule of law. The difference was that the Bengali intellectual believed ancient legislators had clearly articulated laws that were still in force. Rammohan confidently articulated the claim which marginal official figures such as H.T. Colebrooke and H.H. Wilson sometimes hesitantly made: that in the ancient and medieval texts of Manu, Vyasa and Yajnavalkya, India already had what Mill, the MacNaghtens, Bayley and Bentinck believed the colonial state needed to produce, a rational and complete set of written rules.

Rammohan's position was marked by a clear break from the sense of adjudicative practice that existed in the tradition of juristic commentary that preceded him in eighteenth-century Bengal. As British officials complained, jurists such as Jagannatha Tarkapancanana as well as *pandits* paid to advise the Company's court were unable to lay down clear rules that applied to the population in general. As Chapter 4 noted, the logic they used to adjudicate disputes was highly argumentative, rooted in a complex practical understanding of the specific context the dispute emerged from within. Although Rammohan claimed he was participating in this tradition of commentary, the form in which he intervened in Hindu jurisprudence was new. To articulate general rules without explaining how they related to the specifics of time and place, to be able to say that there was a general rule that Hindu widows could inherit the property of their deceased husband and leave it at that without caveat or qualification, for example, was to write about law in a novel way.

As Chapter 4 noted, dispute and public debate was a necessary part of pre-colonial Indian jurisprudence. Rammohan critically observed that when, for example, a question of female inheritance occurred Brahmans 'generally divide into two parties, one advocating the cause of those females and the other that of their adversaries'. His censorious comments about the publicly argumentative character of dispute resolution can be read as a critique of the way *pandits* gave their decisions based on a sense of the complex relationship between textual interpretation and local opinion; this was the voice of an Indian official habituated to colonial forms of law. As a result of their inability to formulate the kind of general rules he was looking for, Rammohan argued that Indians would 'place greater confidence in the honest judgement of European gentlemen than in that of their own countrymen', at least until '[t]he Natives receive the same advantages of education that Europeans generally enjoy'. He had 'met with many honest men' amongst Muslim law officials, but suggested that Hindu legal officials 'do not enjoy much of the confidence of the public'.[21]

Rammohan's views about law and 'native education' were similar to some of the British officials he criticised. Rammohan wanted education to provide Indian officers with the ability to articulate general rules and norms applicable to the whole of Indian society. As an early advocate of English-language education in Calcutta he opposed the teaching of Sanskrit to students destined for most official and commercial careers. Rammohan thought English could replace Persian as the language of the court, but suggested that if 'a code of civil law' was printed and distributed 'in the current languages of the people, they might render the rights of property secure'. Rammohan's difference from British officialdom lay in his belief that the law, however it was transcribed and translated, needed to be reflected in the consensual practice of India's inhabitants in an autonomous social sphere. Of course, 'the law of inheritance should remain [as it is] at present', he said, 'until by the diffusion of intelligence the whole community may be prepared to adopt one uniform system'. Legislation was not ruled out entirely. But a successful 'project of law' could only ever be countenanced if the proposal was widely circulated amongst landholders, merchants and Indian officials and was favourably received without causing the public alarm. Rammohan noted that this mode of paying attention to 'the feelings and interests' of 'the principal members of the community... would not confer upon them any political power', although it would 'give them an interest in the government, and inspire them with greater attachment to it'.[22]

II

One of the most important differences between Rammohan and British officers was that the vicissitudes of Hindu property law in Bengal touched Rammohan's own life directly. Some of Rammohan's evolving thoughts about indigenous society, or what he called in 1830 'the social institution of Hindu Bengal', were articulated in arguments to defend his own land. Rammohan was from a Brahman family who took up service with the Mughal and *nizamat* state in Bengal; his grandfather had been employed by *nawab* Alivardi Khan. As sovereignty passed to the British, Rammohan's father Ramakanta Roy accumulated landed property near Burdwan, in Hughli and elsewhere. Before he died in 1803, Ramakanta divided his land between his four sons, giving each absolute possession of a quarter of his estate. Rammohan's wealth grew from lending money and purchasing land whilst he grew more controversial within Calcutta's public life. As a result, his brothers and cousins attempted to undermine his public position through control of his property. They argued that their father's estate had been unjustly divided because Ramakanta did not consult his heirs when he partitioned it. Consequently, it continued to exist as a joint estate, with all relations equally joint proprietors having some say over property previously solely under Rammohan's control.

The dispute led to a long, protracted series of court cases, which culminated in 1830 around the same time the Wames Chandra case was decided. That dispute, examined in the previous chapter, concerned a similar issue, whether property was held individually or by the 'Hindu joint family'.[23] Perhaps because the issue had become a matter of broader public controversy, Rammohan's tactics in resolving the dispute did not merely involve the submission of a petition to the court about his own case; he also made an appeal to the Bengali public at large. Rather than directing his claim to the conscience of the prince about his property particular to a specific time and place, as many of his predecessors had done, Rammohan printed arguments in favour of a general rule, valid across the whole of Bengali society, giving a father the right to dispose of property as he chose. A father should be 'the sole and independent owner of the property in his possession', he argued.[24]

This defence of a father's ability to bequeath property freely was articulated in a pamphlet published in 1830, 'Essay on the rights of Hindoos over ancestral property according to the law of Bengal'. Like the essay on women's property rights, Rammohan couched his case for a class of person to possess 'sole and independent' property rights as a plea for non-interference in the consensual rules that governed Bengali Hindu society. But two things suggest a change in Rammohan's argumentative tactics since 1822. First of all, Rammohan emphasised the peculiarity, and superiority, of law in Bengal as opposed to the rest of India; in 1822 he had spoken of 'Hindostan' (including Bengal) as a whole. Secondly, the text emphasises the importance of continual social practice even more strongly than the first pamphlet; in fact, even where it contradicted the will of a particular commentator. Along with their dress and language, Rammohan suggested, the unrestrained sociability of Bengali Hindus had allowed them to develop their own distinctive forms of inheritance practice, in which a man could dispose of his property without consulting his family. This law had been articulated – codified – by the medieval jurist Jimutavahana in his text the *Dayabhaga* and 'the natives of the country have for ages afterwards adhered to the rules he has laid down'. But had Jimutavahana not upheld 'the doctrine of free disposal by a father', even though the doctine had 'been prevalent in Bengal for upwards of three centuries', it would still be 'most rash and injurious' for a change to be introduced by 'any administrator of Hindu law'. In this case, social practice alone was the source of the rules of inheritance law.[25]

Until recent times, Rammohan suggested that Bengal's British 'conquerors' had upheld these rules. Lately though, he argued that an 'arbitrary change' had been introduced by the Supreme Court in Calcutta: most likely, Rammohan was discussing the Wames Chandra case, which the last chapter examined. There, the court had decided that a father did not have the power to bequeath his property as he wished but could only dispose of it 'with the sanction of his sons and grandsons', a decision that seriously undermined Rammohan's own property. Rammohan articulated his anxiety by expressing concern about innovation in the rules that governed Bengal's social sphere.

> the people are now struck with a mingled feeling of surprise and alarm, on being given to understand that the Supreme Law Authority of this country...is resolved to introduce new maxims into the law of inheritance hitherto in force in the province of Bengal.

Using a striking phrase, Rammohan said that this 'innovation' was 'retrograding in the social institution of the Hindu community of Bengal'.[26]

Two material forces influenced Rammohan's ability to make this argument. First of all, Rammohan's attempt to 'unfetter property' depended on the emergence of a series of colonial practices which constituted the landholder as an autonomous subject who was seen as possessing the power to do what he chose with his property for the first time. As a result of changes to the governance of agrarian society which this book examined in Chapter 5, an earlier sense of the *zamindar* as a figure at the intersection of a number of reciprocal relationships, or as simply a line in a colonial revenue chart was replaced by a new understanding of the landholder's ability to freely act on the society around him. The power of the proprietor became an object of concern and governance in the early nineteenth century, as he (this new normative landholder was male) became subject to rules articulated by the colonial state that both enabled and proscribed what they could and could not do. In practice, the *zamindars'* subjection to such new rules strengthened their ability to extract resources from agrarian society. Tenants were prevented from suing landholders for violating 'ancient' rights that had not been codified in colonial legislation, for example. As a result, the 1810s and 1820s saw the consolidation of landholding power in Bengal. A few old *zamindars* such as the Raja of Burdwan, together with merchants who invested in land such as Rabindranath's grandfather Dwarkanath Tagore consolidated their estates and increased the profitability of their holdings by increasing rents. Sugata Bose suggests landholders used the legal tools the British had placed at their disposal in a 'rental offensive' which mirrored the colonial government's own attempt to squeeze more revenue from agrarian society.[27] Men such as Dwarkanath Tagore and Rammohan Roy did not see themselves as local princes or sovereigns, but instead as owners of property that was possessed purely for financial gain; in some parts of his estate Dwarkanath was notoriously unsympathetic to *raiyats*' complaints; as the historian Blair Kling notes, he 'had no intention of acting the part of a benevolent and paternalistic landlord'.[28] At a time of economic depression and population growth, therefore diminishing cultivating opportunities, landholders were able to appoint an estate manager and take the continuous stream of income from their rural holdings for granted, without having to engage in the messy game of patronage and protection required during the previous century to hold on to a landed estate. It was this new, rule-based form of governance, rather than economic changes which allowed the emergence of a new urban *bhadralok* (polished or polite people) class to emerge. This class of well-to-do men owned real estate in the countryside, often alongside loans and factories, but had a social existence that revolved around their residence in the *mahanagar* (great city) of Calcutta.

Changes to the way land was governed intersected with the economic dynamics of rural Bengal to make it easier for landholders to make money. But they also constituted the landholder as a moral agent in a new way. Colonial rules strengthened the distinction between acts proscribed by law and those that were immoral but where the law could not intervene; the payment of revenue was a legal duty but treating one's tenants or family well was not. In doing so, they created a sharp division between the landholder's accountability to the system of judicial administration for his obedience to law and to public and private opinion for his moral character in a way that had not been the case before. 'The alienator of an hereditary estate', as Rammohan put it, 'is only morally responsible for his acts, so far as they are unnecessary [in other words, not illegal] and tend to deprive his family of their means of support'. Arguments about the relative merits of income-maximising individualistic behaviour against duty to one's community occurred throughout early modern South Asia, where Indians were no more community-minded than Europeans at the same point in time.[29] Morality and law could always be separated in juristic discourse in pre-colonial Bengal. What was new was that law and morality were separated by governmental techniques that involved the printing of general rules. Before the early nineteenth century the relationship between regulations and moral sentiment needed to be discerned on a case-by-case basis, where they were often subject to a series of highly public adjudicative arena in which ethics and law were not clearly demarcated. The gap between law and morality began to be rigidly defined in textual form, with no room allowed, in the theory of colonial jurisprudence at least, for the specificities of time and place in discussion and decision-making.

Rammohan's argument about the 'social institution' of Bengal was dependent on a second material context: not merely the articulation of general rules by colonial judicial institutions, but their discussion in Calcutta's emerging print culture by a new Bengali reading population. Newspapers had circulated amongst Calcutta's English-reading public since the late eighteenth century. A Bengali-reading public emerged from the mid-1810s. Pamphlets on a range of subjects were printed in Bengali and English. And from 1817, when press restrictions were lifted, periodicals such as the Serampore missionaries' *Samachar Darpan*, Rammohan's English *Brahmunical Magazine* and Persian *Sambad Kaumudi* and the *Samachar Chandrika* edited by Bhabanicharan Bandopadhyay began to appear.[30] Each of these texts invoked new forms of collective being. The distribution of newspapers implied the existence of rules, or at least common regularities, that define the standard and general forms of conduct that the readership have in common. Most obviously, they necessarily imply a shared language and set of reading practices. But as Benedict Anderson noted some time ago, they also propagated a sense of shared forms of dress, opinions, conduct and consumption that create an imagined national community.

III

What Anderson's analysis does not consider though is the extent to which the press also expands the scope for 'public' disagreement about the rules that define the essence of each particular community.[31] Calcutta's early-nineteenth-century public sphere witnessed a series of deep-rooted arguments about the practices and rules that should govern Hindu Bengalis. Believing he was merely continuing a long-standing tradition of theological and political thought, Rammohan and the so-called 'reformists' who surrounded him were objects of fervent attack and satire nonetheless. Even though they disagreed about what the character of the rules that governed it should be, Rammohan's critics articulated a conception of the rule-bound autonomy of Hindu society that, in form if not content, was very similar to his own. Bhabanicharan Bandopadhyay had initially been an ally of Rammohan's, but after establishing his own newspaper, he quickly established himself as one of the foremost challengers to Rammohan's arguments about the *vedant* and Bengali social practice. By the 1830s, Bhabanicharan was secretary of the society established to defend 'orthodox' Hindu practice against both colonial and Bengali radical reform, the *Dharma Sabha*. Bhabanicharan's *Kalikata Kamalalay* ('Calcutta, abode of the lotus'), published in 1823, was structured as a dialogue between a resident of Calcutta and a country-dweller.[32] The text was intended to articulate a common sense of Bengali Hindu life that unified city and countryside against the supposedly innovative practices introduced by Rammohan and his friends. Produced in a world in which employment in the East India Company's institutions was a crucial source of income for Calcutta's bourgeois (the text described this group with the word *madyasreni*, literally middle class), the text suggested that engagement with the institutions of the British regime need not undermine the common practice that defined the community of Hindu Bengalis. But a clear separation between the realm of government and the sphere of social life needed to be maintained. Whilst Persian and English words and even foreign dress were acceptable in the former realm, *bhadra* (refined, polite) language and comportment needed to be maintained within the sphere of social interaction and religious life. As Brian Pennington notes in his study of early-nineteenth-century 'orthodox' Hindu discourse, Bengali readers wrote to publications such as Bhabanicharan's *Samachar Chandrika* seeking advice about the legitimacy of particular forms of ritual practice, how funeral rites were to be conducted or what kinds of ritual needed to be performed. In each case, textual rules were backed up with a sense of the continuous practices of the community or authority of past scripture, even though the author writing the advice had no scholarly training as a *pandit*. Even at its most 'orthodox', the journalistic enterprise in early-nineteenth-century Calcutta transformed the reciprocal relationships of previous political hierarchies, democratically giving the middle class as a whole access to a new sense of Bengali Hindu conduct. By articulating a uniform set of rules supposed to govern Hindu Bengali society, in theory without distinctions of class, region or, in some cases, caste, Bhabanicharan was engaging in a project, of society-formation of a new kind.[33]

Like Rammohan's texts, articles in Bhabanicharan's *Samachar Chandrika* as well as books such as *Kalikata Kamalalay* were concerned about the potential for British institutions to step beyond their legitimate boundaries and interfere with the practices that governed social and religious practice. Legislation abolishing *sati* was defined as one such moment of intervention. The attempt by missionaries to convert Hindus into Christians was another. Like Rammohan, Bhabanicharan was not concerned about the power of Christian missionaries to persuade with rational argument. If missionaries participated in India's social sphere on its own terms and engaged in an unconstrained exchange of views, Bhabanicharan believed that Hindu *dharma* could look after itself. But commentators like Bhabanicharan were wary about the close connection between Christian missions and a Christian ruling power though. Attempts to convert were only alarming if they were backed up by the real or imagined coercive force of colonial power, something that both Bhabanicharan and Rammohan thought happened far too often.[34]

Thinkers on the more radical wing of Bengal's intelligentsia used a similar logic to talk about the relationship between people and state in the ensuing decades. The intellectuals who clustered around the *Bengal Spectator* journal, 'the only paper identified with the party who may be styled Young Bengal' until its demise in 1843, were guided by politics 'of a liberal cast' as the missionary *Friend of India* put it. Unlike Rammohan, on many occasions they explicitly described themselves as reformers.[35] These were men who fused Rammohan's sympathetic approach to Hindu 'society' with the Eurasian teacher and poet Henry Derozio's more forceful articulation of a language of reform.[36] But, although keen to support 'the welfare and improvement of the country', the *Spectator's* editor Tara Chandra Chakrabarty did not support action by the machinery of state to achieve these aims. Tara Chandra clearly saw the state as an entity that existed outside, often in opposition to society. As Satyendranath Pal notes in his study of the rise of radicalism in Bengal, Tara Chand did not think it was the state's function to 'harmonise different interests in the society'. For generations, he argued, caste councils and *kachcharis* had been able to regulate conflict between different social interests, especially the interests of property itself. For Tara Chand, the state's purpose was purely to secure public stability, protect society from outside interference and administer but not make the law. The law itself emerged from the rational, consensual practice of the people in a sphere of free associative activity.

Like Rammohan, Tara Chand saw public 'education' and 'enlightenment' as ways of enabling the public to articulate their rational interests, allowing them to better check the potential arbitrary or despotic encroachment of the state or other malign forces into civil society. As it was for John Stuart Mill, education was an essential component of the mechanism established to check that the negative liberty of the people was not undermined. Political participation was not a necessary part of human personality or an end in itself; Tara Chand's ideal subject was first of all a social animal whose interests and identities come from property and religion not engagement in the *polis*. From this point of view, political participation was nothing but a device to ensure good government. In this respect, Satyendranath Pal is not wrong to suggest that 'Tarachand [wa]s the predecessor of John Stuart Mill'.[37]

Later controversies, from arguments for or against the Hindu widow remarriage bill onwards, had a similar structure. Debates of this sort did not concern the rituals appropriate to different sections of Bengal's social or religious hierarchy, or the kinds of conduct it was necessary to engage in to climb the social hierarchy. Nor were they about the kinds of belief, or doctrines, which good Hindus should subscribe to. As Pennington notes, conservatives such as Bhabanicharan, just like radicals like Tara Chand, were 'more concerned with promoting a set of norms of Hindu practice than particular items of belief'. But Bengal's intellectuals argued vehemently about what proper indigenous norms were. In his English-language writings, Bankimchandra Chattopadhyay spoke of the corroding effect that 'English example' had had on what he described as 'the external feature of Bengali Society'. In an essay written in 1872, Bankim did not fear the effects of English education anywhere near as much as the impact of 'six month's visit to England ... to Anglicise one's tastes'. Different forms of educational practice were supported by Bankim who like Bhabanicharan, Rammohan and Tara Chand saw schooling as a means of allowing these norms to be better understood, articulated and in some cases steadily transformed from inside. But, Bankim's 'Society' (with a capital 'S') was defined by rules that were exactly contrary to those which marked the specifically Bengali character of Rammohan's 'social institution'. Bankim argued that the 'joint-family system', where land was owned collectively by a father and his agnatic heirs, was 'the only bond of social union in a society which has yet to learn the very first lessons in the art of co-operation', the core of 'the Hindu code of personal and social ethics'.[38]

IV

Throughout the nineteenth century, debate about 'the social question' dominated elite Hindu political argument in the province of Bengal. Those debates were ruled primarily by the attempt to define the code of rules and norms governing the common practice (one might use the word culture here) of Bengali Hindu society, and to ensure they were protected from outside interference so they could develop of their own accord. The construction of a liberal subject that was autonomous and free involved an attempt to draw a rigid boundary which implicitly excludes others who do not obey the rules, whether Muslims or non-Bengalis, or people not deemed to be capable of exercising individual free will. If liberalism relies on an idea that human freedom is based on forms of collective social conduct governed by consensually determined common norms, it necessarily involves an exclusionary move.[39] Alongside marginalised social groups, however, colonial liberalism tried to expel the messiness of political practice from the sphere of social life. Culture, economics, apolitical forms of sociability and religion were all seen as more fundamental to the nineteenth-century middle-class liberal's existence than conduct in a political sphere.

As this chapter has suggested, early-nineteenth-century Bengali liberalism was intricately connected to the construction of knowledge about social action, often to an explicit effort to articulate and frame the rules that governed social life. From the mid-nineteenth century, a colonial sociology of India emerged in which both Britons and Indian intellectuals participated whose aim was to produce legal and statistical knowledge about the rules and regularities that governed Bengali social reality. Bengali commentators understood that social institution in a fundamentally historical sense, as an entity whose stable rules had endured with little change from a distant past.[40] It was that connection which provided the basis of the Bengali critique of utilitarianism, from Rammohan to Bankimchandra and Benoy Kumar Sarkar. British officers tended to speak of it with less certainty, emphasising its unstable character, connecting their discussion of Indian social practice with arguments about the process of colonial state formation. In each case though, society was described as an objective entity from an aloof perspective, perhaps often with the 'unhappy consciousness' of one unable to decide between the disordered particularity of personal beliefs, and the generalised abstraction of the stranger.[41]

However different they may have been, the political thought at work in each case can be contrasted with the dominant discourse of British politics. In Britain social action and political practice remained entangled. 'Civil society' remained synonymous with 'the state' far longer than in South Asia, and the kind of liberalism discussed here far less common than it was in Bengal. The lags and differences at work here are evident in the way one figure in mid-nineteenth-century British politics translated (or mistranslated) domestic political idioms in the subcontinent. George Thompson was an evangelical and abolitionist, a man active in the campaign against slavery in both British empire and, after emancipation in 1833 and the abolition of indentureship in 1838, the United States. Thompson was not someone who was very conscious of crossing the boundaries that demarcated legitimate concern from illegitimate interference. On a tour of southern states of the United States he was driven from town after town as he spoke against slavery, often being described as a 'foreign meddler' on his way out.[42] In the early 1840s, Thompson turned his mind to the 'improvement' and 'amelioration' of India, actions which British government officials and some Indian journalists saw as meddling, but which others saw as potentially beneficial.

Thompson made two visits to India, the first a decade after Rammohan died, in 1843; the second a few months before the north Indian insurrection of 1857. Thompson had befriended Dwarkanath Tagore when the Bengali entrepreneur was in London, and came to Calcutta the first time after being invited by Tagore and his colleagues Prasanna Kumar Tagore and Tara Chandra Chakrabarty, all of whom had been close to Raja Rammohan Roy at some point in time. On both occasions, Thompson spoke at public meetings, met with Bengali dignitaries, and gathered information to allow himself to publicise the plight of India to the British people on his return.

Thompson's politics were described as 'liberal' in London, but he was not a liberal in the sense this chapter has used the term. His primary concern was not to ensure the population was able to go about its everyday affairs, or develop freely, unhindered by the exercise of legitimate power. Instead Thompson was interested in advancing what he saw as the progress of both British and Indian civilisation, where civilisation involved moral and political development along a predetermined path. Causes such as the emancipation of slaves, the expansion of British free trade across the globe and the improvement of political consciousness in India were all part of that process of global teleological change. Sometimes the advance of civilisation occurred by allowing groups to develop autonomously; at other times, it required positive, political intervention of the most direct kind.

Rather than being influenced by anything recent political theorists would define as liberalism, Thompson's attitude to both British and Indian politics was driven by a radical whig outlook that did not perceive any separation between society and the state, or indeed separate society from any other agent of positive social change. Thompson mapped agency onto social networks and political associations. The main force driving political change was not the machinery of state but the 'political community', a network in which the force of people and political institutions were united. 'If you recommend change', he said, 'be prepared to say what change you would have, and how it might be effected, and how a competent agency might be found, to carry it into execution'. Thompson lamented what he described as Bengal's lack of a 'public, in the English sense of the word'. 'Beyond your immediate neighbourhood, all is tame acquiescence', he suggested. Without an active political community, he said, political amelioration would be impossible. The solution, he argued, was the establishment of political organisations such the Bengal British India Association that would educate the *populus* and provide the driving force behind both social and legislative change. Each participant in such an association would become 'a conspicuous and active member of the body politic'.[43] These comments reflect Thompson's inability to imagine that subjects could be united by something other than a political network of some kind; a peculiarly British form of short-sightedness. The idea that Bengal's middle-class public might be connected through a shared sense of social belonging and common cultural practice, or that instead of seeking membership to the colonial body politic they were more interested in asserting the autonomy of indigenous practices through a programme of social reform was unimaginable. Despite occasional instances of political campaigning, those latter concerns predominated amongst the active section of Bengal's *bhadralok* until the latter years of the nineteenth century. Even after 1905, many participants in the nationalist *swadeshi* campaign that initially involved Rabindranath Tagore saw it as a movement for the regeneration of Bengali society as much as a protest against the political partition of the province of Bengal.[44]

Thompson could not conceive of social institutions at 'an advanced state of civilization', to use Rammohan's phrase, existing separately from an enlightened political community or without a participatory form of government. For him participation was not encouraged merely to represent the interests of society, as it was for Indian liberals and later British commentators like John Stuart Mill. Political participation was the very essence of civilised human existence, and in that sense an end in itself. As a result of these views, Thompson seems to have been rather an odd figure in Calcutta. He lectured extensively, but the impact of his lectures was negligible. Thompson's style appears now (and no doubt appeared at the time to his Bengali audience) patrician and condescending, telling an audience, that 'you must sit as disciples in the form, before you can aspire to the rostrum', for example. If one compares his speeches with the literature and journalism produced from Calcutta during the 1830s and 1840s, the personal style of his discourse is striking, as is the total absence of the abstract terminology found elsewhere in Bengali writing. However much it needed to be infused with a clear sense of moral agency, Thompson believed politics was indeed about the personal connections and networks, dinner parties and speeches that Hegel complained about. Nowhere did Thompson try to imagine Indian 'society' using the kind of abstract political or social terms Hegel, or indeed Rammohan might have proposed. Where Rammohan spoke of government and 'the social institution' or Bhabanicharan of the British *sarkar* and Bengal's *samaj*, Thompson found it difficult to speak of the state and society, government and social institutions as objective entities at all. Mid-nineteenth-century Britons such as George Thompson understood their society by telling stories about the rise and fall of 'civilisation' in which personality and social dynamics intermingled, not by debating the proper relationship between objective spheres of social activity, nor constructing abstract ideas of what the population shared in terms of common social practice, culture or race.[45] As this book has argued, British officials more habituated to the intellectual environment of early-nineteenth-century Calcutta, like their Bengali counterparts, were far happier producing abstract, objective categories and concepts, as if they were strangers to Indian society.

The problem that Thompson's approach could not face was how to judge which forms of social practice or culture had emerged within a realm of free social autonomy, and which were the result of external 'encroachment'; to determine the question which all liberals need to decide, how the 'laws, principles and mechanisms' which govern authentic social reality were to be known. That question was answered in a number of different ways by different authors, and provided fuel for a large proportion of nineteenth-century Bengali political debate. Rammohan had relied in part on the judicial (but not legislative) authority of the colonial state, checked and supplemented by the criticism of the Calcutta press. Throughout the nineteenth century, many followed his sceptical approach towards the colonial regime's legislative 'interference' in Indian social practices whilst relying on colonial judges to adjudicate Indian law. Indeed, many of the writers who prominently debated the Indian social question were *pandits*, lawyers or officers in the colonial regime's courts.

Rabindranath Tagore's uncle, Prasanna Kumar Tagore followed in Rammohan's stead by sponsoring a series of lectures on Indian law at Calcutta University, which were in part responsible for the revival of the study of 'indigenous' Indian jurisprudence from the 1870s.[46] Rabindranath himself, however, was reluctant to allow the institutions of the colonial metropolis to police the boundaries between the state and Indian civil society, arguing that colonial law was too far estranged from Indian social reality. Neither Rammohan nor Bhabanicharan saw anything essentially foreign or corrosive about commercial exchange or urban life – *vishay karma* (self-interested activity) was a necessity for both.[47] But instead of carving out a space of supposedly authentic Indian social freedom in the metropolis as both Rammohan and Bhabanicharan had tried to do, Tagore celebrated a retreat from the capital into 'the shade of Bengal's villages' and convivial homesteads, where civic obligations were supposed to be exercised communally rather than by the mechanical arm of the colonial state. Tagore himself physically abandoned the metropolis to make a home for himself at Santiniketan in the Birbhum countryside, claiming the field and the forest were more authentically Indian spaces. One crucial but neglected element within the story of Bengali political argument in the late nineteenth century concerns the way in which the culture of colonial governance, with its written rules, utilitarian rationality and machine-like chains of command came to be associated with the 'civilisation' of the 'west' as a whole within elite Bengali thought; in other words, how both commercial modernity and modern, governmental rules were imagined as 'alien' in a way neither Rammohan nor Bhabanicharan could imagine, a perspective best illustrated by the central role Jeremy Bentham had within late-nineteenth-century Bengali representations of modern British thought. By the end of the nineteenth century the entity that Tagore spoke on behalf of Bengali society or *samaj* no longer stood opposed merely to the specific machinery of the colonial statehood; its identity was constructed through its opposition to apparently Western, urban modernity as a whole. In Tagore's condemnation of the petitioning urban intelligentsia, 'crystalized into rigidity by the Englishman's law', one can read a challenge of the way in which the Calcutta's mid-nineteenth-century liberals relied on colonial rules and laws to construct and regenerate the autonomous sphere of Bengali society.

In his political thought Rabindranath was no liberal; much of his writing consisted of a critique of the forms of liberal governmentality whose genealogy has been traced in this book. But Bengali attempts to define and produce a sphere of authentically indigenous activity began through the articulation of a liberal political vocabulary about the relationship between society and the state in the first half of the nineteenth century. Traces of that earlier intellectual world remained in the thought of later critics like Tagore. They were especially present in the emphasis on the primordiality of the social above political action, and the call for the separation of *samaj* from *sarkar*. For many from Rammohan and Bhabanicharan onwards, Bengal's 'social institution' rather than its polity was seen as the place where proper indigenous practice occurred. The way Indian intellectuals responded to the practice of colonial governance meant that politics was often seen as a foreign art.

8
Reflections

In the nineteenth-century Anglophone world, the phrase 'the domination of strangers' referred to rule by one people of another. The word stranger meant foreigner. The domination of strangers was associated with conquest, usurpation and interference. It was a phrase used to criticise subjects as varied as 'Popish' dominance and the inability of a municipal corporation to manage its own waterworks. The domination of strangers was an unnatural state, not something any people was supposed to be able to 'brook' or 'submit to' for long.[1] Describing colonial rule in India as 'the domination of strangers' was intended to suggest that abnormal measures were needed to retain British power in a country where the majority of the population were potentially hostile. Charles Metcalf justified the size of Britain's military force in India by noting that the 'domination of strangers, in every respect strangers, in country, in colour, in dress, in manners, in habits, in religion, must be odious' to the country's inhabitants. It was impossible to retain foreign rule by consent and 'opinion'.[2] Thomas Munro believed that the 'domination of strangers' meant that the regulation of the press was necessary to suppress the otherwise inevitable voice of dissent. These officers thought its domination of strangers prevented the colonial government from operating according to the flexible connections of opinion and sentiment supposed to bind people to the polity in Britain.[3]

When nineteenth-century Britons used this phrase, they were assuming it was usual for a community to be ruled by people who were familiar to them. Yet as the nineteenth century progressed in many parts of the world, the domination of strangers occurred in another sense. In both colonial and non-colonial environments, more and more people began to be subject to modern, bureaucratic regimes of power that used general categories and rules to classify and administer populations. In other words, ever greater numbers of people were treated by the governments which ruled them as strangers rather than familiar beings with whom dialogue was possible on an individual, face-to-face basis. 'The domination of strangers' is a phrase that can, therefore, refer to two different forms of rule. First of all, it describes government by foreigners. Secondly, it denotes governance by modern, impersonal bureaucratic regimes based on abstract categories and positive rules rather than familiar political relationships, the kind of regime that Max Weber analysed and Martin Heidegger and Michel Foucault so vehemently criticised.

This book has shown how a form of governance emerged in early-nineteenth-century colonial Bengal characterised by the way it treated its subjects as strangers in this second way. But that form of governance emerged in Bengal because East India Company officials were highly aware of dominating strangers in the first sense. Abstract rules that subordinated particular differences to general categories emerged as a response to the colonial situation of governing people whom British officials regarded as different and impossible to communicate with. The East India Company's utilitarian thought and its positivistic, legislative state developed from the same process. Colonial India's impersonal idiom of governance, its bureaucratic, machine-like state and attempt to enforce equality before the law's codified rules emerged from what most Britons saw as the aberrant and marginal exercise of colonial power in Bengal. The paradox, of course, is that forms of governance based on an estranged relationship between ruler and ruler are regarded by most historians and social scientists as characteristically modern and European. The governance of strangers in the second sense discussed here was characteristic of more than just colonial regimes. It was central to the practice of political power in modern 'self-governing' polities. It was also crucial to many forms of explicitly anti-foreign nationalist political campaigns in the colonial world; nationalism relies on common belonging to an impersonal community obedient to a single set of rules rather than interpersonal familiarity. These concluding remarks are concerned with the complex relationship between colonialism and the different forms the domination of strangers took beyond Bengal.

I

In an essay written in 1872, the Bengali nationalist writer Bankimchandra Chattopadhyay complained that 'the Hindu code of personal and social ethics has been well-nigh wholly repealed'.[4] Bankim's 'Confession of a Young Bengal' was written in English to explain the province's situation to European observers; but perhaps more importantly to warn the inhabitants of other Indian regions not to emulate Bengal. In an ironic tone, Bankim feared what he saw as the corrosive effect of English education and English 'example', taste and fashion on Bengali 'society'. Hindu Bengalis had adopted a variety of different *isms*: deism, theism, Brahmoism 'compt(sic)ism'. None, Bankim said, reflected anything but a 'strong desire to exempt ourselves from the obligations of Hinduism'. The obligations of Hinduism had not been replaced with any other 'bond of social union'. Bengal's Hindu middle classes had undermined their indigenous social and ethical system without replacing it with a 'new code of morality' or a 'new public opinion to enforce its rules'.[5]

Particularly significant was the juridical tone Bankimchandra used in his English writings, and the way that tone was used to present Bengali society as an entity that existed above and beyond political differences. Bankimchandra wrote of a Hindu 'code' of ethics being 'repealed', for example. In an essay written five months later, he suggested a strong resemblance existed between the way John Stuart Mill and 'the higher forms of Hindu thought' discussed causality. Both, he argued, agreed in their 'recognition of Law as the only agency in the government of the universe'. In each philosophical system, all forms of natural and social conduct were governed by fixed general rules with no room for contingency, 'divine interposition' or 'miracle[s]' at all.[6] In this 1873 article, Bankimchandra was suggesting that science, just like ethics and administration, consisted in nothing but the determination of the general rules that governed the movement of objects in the world.

This way of viewing the world rigidly subordinated the particular instances of physical, social or family life to general law-like categories of some kind. Every specific event or object of thought, whether a chemical reaction or a Hindu family, was the manifestation of an abstract rule, the particular instance of a general law. Or to put it another way: to understand a particular phenomenon, Bankimchandra suggested that one needed to begin by deciding what general class of things it belonged to, then discover which general set of rules, codified (or codifiable) in writing somewhere, determined how that entity moved. In the field of Indian social ethics, his concern was that one system of general rules had not been replaced by another. Individuals were left to exist in an undetermined, amoral, anomic void. There was no sense here of patriotism as a series of complex ethical responses reliant on uneven and contingent forms of human interaction. Bankim's language presumed that nationalist politics needed to treat the public as a series of strangers united by their obedience to a single set of rules.

Of course, Bankimchandra Chattopadhyay wrote in a number of different idioms and languages. As Partha Chatterjee and Sudipta Kaviraj point out, Bankim's Bengali-language fiction was concerned to undermine and satirise precisely the rigid categories of colonial governance and Indian social life that he seems to have upheld in these English texts.[7] As Kaviraj notes, Bankim's writing recognised what he described as a 'central conflict – between the inevitability of moral orders and the inevitability of their transgression'. But where his writing was programmatic rather than satirical, especially when it was written in the language of colonial governance, Bankim described the moral rules necessary for social existence in the most rigidly legalistic way. When it came to trying to articulate authoritative forms of social practice, Bankim's writing as a whole reflected an ambivalence that occurred throughout colonial as well as Indian writing in the nineteenth century, between the search for rule-bound regularity and the recognition of radical contingency. Perhaps this was the same ambivalence that produced the stoical and sceptical attitudes that comprised the two poles between which the 'unhappy consciousness' of Hegel's *Phenomenology of Spirit* oscillated.[8]

This book has explained why one of the most important characteristics of nineteenth-century Bengal's elite intellectual culture was the way both Britons and Bengalis found particular forms of life inexplicable and ungovernable unless they could be reduced to general categories, and seen as specific manifestations of more abstract principles and rules. Far from involving the straightforward adoption of European attitudes to law or science, that language emerged as a very specific response to colonial India's particular culture of governance. But the emphasis on the individual's place within abstractly conceived rule-bound generalities which extended over space and back for centuries in time was a characteristic of nineteenth-century political discourse far beyond Bengal. Commentators from Friedrich Nietzsche and Max Weber to Uday Singh Mehta note that an important feature of modern forms of political and social thought is the way they attempt to assimilate the particular to the general in this way. The primacy of general categories occurred within strands of European nineteenth-century political philosophy as well as in India. The individual was assimilated into the community at large in the later stages of Hegel's dialectic, long after the oscillation between stoic and sceptic mentioned above had been superseded, for example. An emphasis on the importance of abstract notions of state and society allowed Hegel and other continental philosophers to be highly critical of the localism of British politics, with its concern for 'particular rights and privileges'. If it wasn't commonplace in British political practice, the same manoeuvre occurred in the more conceptual realms of British utilitarian and liberal thought, as Mehta points out. For James and John Stuart Mill, the individual was free only in so far as he or she belonged to a class of 'individual' defined in general terms. The characteristics that defined the abstract individuality of the liberal subject were always determined by an outside agency, ultimately needing to be sanctioned by the state.

But as Hegel constantly reminds us, political philosophy is always dependent on events occurring in the history of political practice. The bureaucratic, positivistic idiom of governance that was so significant across many parts of the world in the nineteenth century was the product of specific events and processes. The last years of the eighteenth century and first half of the nineteenth century saw a dramatic rupture in the political culture of many different parts of the world. One crucial aspect of that rupture was the attempt by politicians and administrators to abandon local political and juridical traditions, and use the agency of the state to create stable regimes based on new principles of legitimacy. In the generation which witnessed American independence, the French Revolutions and Cornwallis' creation of a new constitution for Bengal, a number of different polities emerged that abandoned any claim to being practically legitimised by the continuities of past political practice or founded on local forms of custom and interest. Many of these polities evoked a mythologised ancient history, whether the Rome championed by Napoleon and American federalists or the *puranic* India celebrated by Rammohan Roy. Nonetheless, regimes from the United States and Latin America to France and British-ruled India developed constitutions and invented forms of jurisprudence based on the supremacy of general rules and the printed written word instead of historical practices of accommodation and dialogue. So, alongside the emergence of new forms of textual law in India, the period saw Napoleonic code-making and the production of nation-wide legal doctrines and norms in the United States. It also witnessed the crisis and consolidation of Prussian bureaucracy, and attempts by the khedive Mohammed Ali to consolidate state power and reduce the power of local notables in Egypt.[9] These efforts at active state-building were only partially successful of course; failure was always a component of the attempt to produce a social world governable in rational rules to some degree. But as this book has argued, it was the logic that underpinned the intention to create new forms of governance that mattered, not the extent to which their framers saw them as a success.

In place of the complex, uneven and composite political cultures that had existed in early modern Eurasia, these transformations saw the emergence of 'the state' and 'society' as entities that seemed to stand apart from one another, mutually dependent yet in many places also vying for supremacy in a battle neither could ever win. On the one hand, the modern state's claim to legitimacy was based on the idea that it governed the free conduct of citizens and subjects whose intentions and purposes were not initially forged in a political sphere. Many nineteenth-century politicians believed that politics should not be the primary shaper of human personality. Primordiality was attributed to social or religious practice, cultural or racial identity, or the individual subject's apolitical preferences. But on the other hand, this idea of freedom depended on the assumption that the conduct of individuals or social groups could be understood and governed by written rules: and rules depend on the existence of an ultimate political authority able to guarantee and enforce them. Paradoxically, the existence of an autonomous sphere of civil society required the existence of a potentially interfering state even if the corrosive effect of the state was deplored.

Chapter 6 noted that the attempt to do such characteristically modern things as codify law, define the behaviour of subjects in general written rules or debate the potentially interfering relationship between state and society occurred in many different colonial environments long before it occurred in the British metropole. As a result, the very meaning of imperial domination, and the binary opposition between metropole and colony signified different things in each place. British officials often imagined they had introduced British ideas about law when they suggested Indian law needed to be codified in a written form. Yet until the middle of the century at least, English lawyers in England saw codification as the antithesis of their own domestic style of jurisprudence. Bankimchandra Chattopadhyay thought Britain was the land of utilitarian rationalist political and economic thought. But throughout most of the nineteenth century most British intellectuals saw utilitarianism as a minority sect that had closer connections to traditions of continental European rationalist thinking than anything belonging to Britain itself. The particular 'English example' that Bankimchandra feared had such devastating consequences on Bengali social life is hard to map onto historic English practices. The 'England' that Bankim imagined existed in binary opposition to Bengal was produced by the colonial interaction between Britons and Indians in the subcontinent, not the history of the metropole alone. This book has shown how imperial relationships worked to maintain and exacerbate the difference between 'British' political cultures in different parts of the world, perhaps also sustaining the difference between the political culture of Britain and continental Europe in the process. Perhaps the British empire might be better imagined as a set of disconnections and miscommunications than as a global network of successful intellectual exchange.

The book has also argued that the colonial state in Bengal was founded in moments of political rupture in which historical precedent was consciously jettisoned, and a 'new constitution' produced. Not experiencing either revolution or invasion, Britain did not undergo quite the same dramatically self-conscious process of state-formation. The difference between metropolitan British and colonial political cultures can partly be explained in terms of the absence of dramatic constitutional ruptures in the former, and their centrality to political thought in the latter. Consequently, comparison with and connection to simultaneous developments in parts of continental Europe can shed light on the history of governance in colonial India. For example, in both regions the seeming foreignness of the modern state forced the subjects of such regimes to trace national forms of belonging outside the political sphere. Early-nineteenth-century Germany and Bengal saw the emergence of forms of national identity based on supposedly general forms of cultural or social practice as a counter-pose to increasingly bureaucratic states. In each case national belonging was rooted in the sense of a common language, literature, folklore and common forms of social behaviour rather than political participation. Many of these new forms of national identity emerged as the assertion of local and individual interests were rendered illegitimate. Lynn Hunt and other historians argue that the French Revolution was made possible by the growing illegitimacy of the attempt to articulate particular interests in French political discourse. In Britain on the other hand, notions of nationality remained indelibly connected to the country's continuous political history, and could be far more easily superseded by class and locality.[10] Recent historiography has tended to corroborate Hegel's sense of the continued importance of local interest and connection to British politics, amidst the importance of ideas about the general interest that subsume the particular into the general in France or the German states. Paul Langford suggests that the British parliament acted as little other than a court for balancing specific interests. In the 1790s and 1800s at least, claims for the better treatment of the subjects of British rule in India, or for abolishing the slave trade were more successful if made on behalf of some sectional interest or other.[11]

II

Far from seeing it as the result of a smooth, successful process of political consolidation, this book argues that the emergence of the colonial state in Bengal was part of what C.A. Bayly calls 'the crisis of the old order', a process of dramatic political transformation occurring across the globe between 1780 and 1820.[12] Events in Bengal were part of a process occurring throughout Eurasia in which the flexible yet hierarchical networks that structured eighteenth-century political societies broke down in a relatively short space of time. For much of the eighteenth century, institutions such as the landed estate, manorial court, mercantile corporation, caste council, guild or local assembly had played a key role in the management of social and political relations and the redistribution of resources even in the most 'absolutist' form of state. But, in the critical 40 years that straddled the turning of the nineteenth century, rulers and subjects lost trust in the role of these corporate institutions and local hierarchies to negotiate the relationship between the individual, the family and political society. Colonial state formation in Bengal and Napoleonic centralisation alike consisted in the attempt to undermine the role of what Burke called the 'little platoon' as a crucial power in constituting the polity. Underpinning Burke's critique of both French republicanism and British imperialism was his sense that all forms of political community needed to begin with the particular and local and build upwards and outwards from there. The political transformations of the last quarter of the eighteenth century consisted of a global crisis in the role of the local and particular in political life. In France, Bengal, north America and Germany alike, the primacy of particular interests was replaced instead by a homogenous state which attempted (again one must emphasise intention instead of success) to govern a society that could be understood with abstract categories and general concepts and terms. In a fairly short period of time, an earlier sense of politics as the art of maintaining and balancing the complex network of interests and authorities that existed within the patchwork of political society was destroyed. Britain was unusual in not witnessing a dramatic political and conceptual upheaval on this scale.

To explain this great transformation on a global scale, one needs to investigate the conditions that led to such a persuasive sense of mistrust in the role of local political networks and hierarchies in constituting political relation-ships. As C.A. Bayly notes in his discussion of the period in *The Birth of the Modern World*, fiscal crises and 'a growing imbalance between the perceived military needs of states and their financial capacity' played an important role.[13] Having spent too much money fighting wars in the second half of the eighteenth century, polities across Europe, Asia and the Americas stretched the relationship with revenue-farmers and local notables to break-ing point. The American revolution occurred as the Westminster parliament abandoned the earlier practice of raising revenue by seeking the consent of local assemblies, and asserted its unilateral right to make laws which taxed each colony's 'internal' economic activity instead. In France, the impossi-bility of raising enough money to fund a growing fiscal deficit by taxing and borrowing from local elites created the distrust of aristocratic and cler-ical 'interest' mentioned in the pages above. The Bengali variant of this process was described in Chapter 3. There, the breakdown of the East India Company's negotiations with local revenue-farmers underpinned Lord Corn-wallis' attempt to standardise the payment of land revenue from *zamindars* (landholders) and the conscious attempt to construct a 'new constitution' for the rule of the region, which in turn led to a much more aggressively stan-dardising state. Fiscal crises fuelled a new scepticism about the supposedly self-serving behaviour of local interests and led to attempts to transform the relationship between centre and locality in each case. As Peter Mandler has recently noted, Britain's public and politicians alike were unusual in main-taining an unusually high degree of trust in fiscal functions which relied on traditional local hierarchies; the role of empire in maintaining that fiscal position needs to be investigated. In part perhaps as a result of their imperial connections, Britons remained almost uniquely 'backward' (as Hegel put it) in seeing statecraft as the art of balancing local 'particular interests' rather than making general forms of new law or representing and intervening upon society as a whole.

But this book has noted that human engagement with 'objective' forces such as economics and fiscality were always mediated by states of mind such as hope, fear and anxiety. The emotional history of colonial politics is a subject that this work has only begun to investigate, but again, comparison with research in other fields is fruitful. William M. Reddy argues that one cannot comprehend the French Revolution without understanding how a small group of revolutionaries believed they had the capacity to senti-mentally empathise with and speak for the 'nation' as a whole, without the mediation of pre-existing interests and elites.[14] Similarly, as Chapter 3 showed, it is impossible to understand the emergence of colonial India's new polity unless one explains why British officials believed they could articulate the interests of Indian society without engaging in the process of often face-to-face dialogue and negotiation with local interests that sustained political relations beforehand. British imperialism and French centralisation were both driven by a new almost instinctive belief that it was dangerous for government to trust familiar forms of contact with potentially self-interested local interests. Each attempted to place executive responsibility in the hands of a bureaucratic elite driven by a supposedly trans-local sense of national 'duty' instead. They tried (although invariably failed) to suppress interest, familiarity and passion by constructing new, rationalist polities that attempted to bureaucratically reorder the world.

These new regimes were not the result of the triumphal march of enlightenment rationalism from the seventeenth to nineteenth centuries. Instead, they came into existence in moments of rupture when other, older ways of balancing and negotiating with the plethora of institutions and interests that constituted early modern political society broke down and were replaced by heightened forms of both fear and anxiety. Crises, disjunctures and insurrections were common features of the uneven politics of early modern Eurasia. But until the 1780s they survived as their occupants worked to manipulate the complex forms of inter-subjective practice that constituted early modern sovereignty in some form. But in different locations at different points in time during the late eighteenth and early nineteenth centuries, something happened which meant the gap between interest and duty, between locality and centre and between peasants, nobles and rulers became so wide it needed to be reconstituted in a new form of rule. These new states still had to incorporate and negotiate with a range of local social forces; some did this more than others. As many scholars note, the nineteenth-century state in its colonial or European form was far weaker than its architects intended it to be. But the important point to note is not the state's weakness, but the wide-ranging effects that the attempt to create a new kind of polity had. State failure and the anxieties and ambivalences it produced became an integral part of the dynamics of modern politics. The modern state existed (and still exits) in a constant state of anxious movement, engaged in the project of attempting to overcome the weaknesses and limits that confront it, constantly trying to produce a different future in which the real, present-day world of messy human life is reordered in a rational, predictable and rule-bound form. Its continual failure to do so is a crucial part of the narrative of modern political life.

III

Colonialism is a form of political dominance in which a group of people actively maintain their strangeness from the population whom they dominate. Ghulam Hussein Khan began his discussion of British rule by suggesting that India's pre-colonial Mughal rulers had started out as strangers to the country they conquered, but then worked to assimilate themselves with the indigenous population. By contrast the British remained aloof and distant, maintaining their separation by refusing to engage in proper conversation or treating Indians as anything other than static objects. But, modern regimes across Europe and the Americas treated the population they governed as strangers as well, subjecting their heterogeneities to general abstract categories and rules. So what was the difference between the British colonial regime in India and non-colonial regimes elsewhere?

One answer to this question emphasises the importance of European conceptions of racial difference. Race might offer the key to the 'logic of difference' that Partha Chatterjee suggests worked to exclude Indian subjects from participation in Britain's imperial polity.[15] Yet, it is by no means obvious that race operated consistently on the minds of colonial officials before their engagement with Indian society. Before the late-nineteenth-century emergence of scientific racism, 'race' denotes a complex cluster of categories, concepts and analytical frameworks used to classify and act upon the bodies, minds, polities and social practices of non-Europeans. The specific way it worked to categorise a population as inferior still needs to be explained. This book has bracketed the category of race in order to examine the difference between colonial and other forms of rule in terms of differences in governmental practice, not in the prior categories used to classify subject groups. Perhaps though, the abstract generalisations of 'race' might itself have been a product of the estranged style of thought that emerged in colonial life.

Here, then, we might suggest that the difference between the British colonial regime in India and non-colonial regimes elsewhere lay in the degree of consistency with which the logic of estrangement examined in this book was followed through in each place. As historians emphasise, early-nineteenth-century continental European attempts to centralise and rationalise had their limits. States projected an image of authority that far exceeded their capacity. As John A. Davis puts it, 'modernity' had 'many faces'.[16] Old networks of political society were not entirely eradicated by the abstract logic of bureaucratic rationalism, or the purported homogeneity of the unitary nation-state. A plethora of recent local studies have emphasised complex patterns of 'resistance' and 'collaboration' to new regimes, such as the Napoleonic empire or newly unified German nation-state. To govern, collect taxes and administer the law, regimes still had to 'rally' and 'incorporate' a range of different social forces, including notables, merchants, peasants and workers. These forms of negotiation were, and often still are, underpinned by forms of parochial patriotism and interest based on a sense of rootedness in place. Whilst they contradicted the rationalist, universal claims of the state, the functioning of the supposedly centralised state often relied on the survival of these forms of local particularism. To take one example: as Michael Rowe notes, Napoleonic rule in the Rhine depended on the political inclusion and negotiation with local elites, in part on the continuation of pre-Napoleonic institutions. The survival after 1815 of the supposedly universalistic forms of law and administration that Napoleon had imposed on the Rhineland depended on local elites' attempt to defend Rhenish particularism against Prussian authoritarianism with Napoleonic ideas.[17]

Britons in India found negotiation of this kind far more difficult. Attempts were made to incorporate local elites, but they occurred from behind a grid of abstract bureaucratic classifications, demonstrating a far more rigid conception of Indian social structure than rulers in Europe articulated about their own societies. Serious challenges to the state's authority were met with aggressive displays of military force and governmental power, rather than attempts at conciliation. Conciliation occurred after cathartically violent colonial reaction to large scale Indian rebellion; after 1783, 1857–1858 and 1919–1921, for example. Until such extreme moments of crisis, British civil servants were wary of stepping outside the bureaucratic confines of their regime, retreating instead into highly ordered European spaces in both their domestic and administrative lives.[18] Colonial political culture was rooted in the fantasy that it was unnecessary to engage with Indians on familiar terms. The British did, of course, need to engage with Indians to collect taxes and adjudicate disputes. There, in court, the revenue office and in the country-side, the colonial desire for rational order was continually defeated by the complexities of everyday political life. The result was the sense of continual failure which this book argues was characteristic of colonial thought; but failure was continually met with a heightened sense of anxiety and new efforts to justify and explain actions, rather than successful conciliation. This persistent sense of failure led to the consolidation of officials' belief in the need to perform their duty whatever the outcome. It also influenced the crystallisation of abstract models of economics or law used to make policy, irrespective of the extent to which they accurately predicted the behaviour of their Indian interlocutors.[19] For many officials, solace existed in virtual trans-continental family networks or in a redeeming Christian god. Most officials longed for their return to the familiar fantasy of life back home.

The British made sense of the disjuncture between the complexities of everyday social practice and the colonial attempt to classify Indian society from a distance by mapping it onto a new conception of temporality. Officials' anxiety consisted in part in their sense of estrangement from the present moment in time. The failure to make abstract categories fit the world of everyday practice was regarded as something that could be overcome in the future. In the present, the messiness of everyday life was often perceived as a sign of India's inadequacies, its 'delinquency' or 'degeneracy'. The colonial state's project of reform, its attempt to regularise and codify the heterogeneity of Indian life, was intended to produce a future that would leave the difficulties of governing India far behind. Many elite Indians responded to this project with a critique that presented an alternative conception of the viability of Indian society, which nonetheless reaffirmed a similar sense of the relationship between political action and time.

Alongside this attempt to create a dramatically different future, this book has also noticed the emergence in the early nineteenth century of a new, celebratory attitude to a supposedly pristine ancient Indian past, an attitude articulated by Indian writers from Rammohan Roy to Bankimchandra Chattopadhyay and beyond, as well as marginal British officers such as H.T. Colebrooke and H.H. Wilson. Despite its seemingly more conservative orientation, this orientalist approach emerged from exactly the same dynamic as radically transformative, reformist attitudes to Indian state and society. Just like the future-oriented rhetoric of colonial utilitarianism, the orientalist position arose from the demise of forms of juridical and ethical discourse comfortable with the heterogeneity and particularity of experience in the present. Like colonial utilitarianism, it consisted of an attempt to describe the complexity of everyday social practice with rigid, general juridical categories from the standpoint of the stranger. Again, the rupture between abstract general categories and the concrete particularity of life was projected onto the flow of time, and seen as a gap between a degenerate present and a state of affairs occurring at a different moment: in this case in the past.

Scholars often describe the intellectual life of colonial India as a clash between conservative 'orientalist' attitudes that constructed and celebrated supposedly unchanging Indian tradition and reformist projects that aimed to found a new society on the legislative authority of the colonial state. This book has argued that colonialism did not have its 'orientalist' or 'reformist' phases, nor can individual officials be picked out and labelled with either adjective. Instead, the logic of colonialism led to a continual and deep-rooted ambivalence between these two positions, as well as a pervasive anxiety about the possibility of founding stable forms of authority or social practice on either. There were, for example, important similarities in the way Anglo-Indian orientalist pasts or colonial utilitarian futures were thought about. In neither case were the past, present and future merely moments that succeeded one another in the linear flow of time. In each case, a past or future world was conjured in which moral roles were clearly defined, general rules followed and every aspect of social life and society properly organised in a way which was not the case in their present time. These pasts or futures were not thought about historically; nor were they described as part of a narrative that plotted out the incremental succession of events. Instead they operated as mythical moments invoked to criticise the present moment, then to mobilise human agency to create a dramatically different future or return to a long-forgotten past. In a variety of elite genres, a literally unbridgeable chasm separated the mythical, orientalist past or the utilitarian future from things as they were now.[20] That gap made the attempt to found present-day authority on the past or future a forever uncertain enterprise.

A recent discussion of British utopian writing suggests that utopias do not merely emerge from a sense that the present moment is degenerate and worthy of critique. They became a common genre in the late nineteenth-century when 'the lived moment' became literally indescribable as well, something that is impossible to describe in rational language.[21] There are parallels between the way both Britons and sometimes elite Indians

experienced life in early colonial Bengal, and the experience of sociological observers of *fin-de-siècle* European society. Many colonial officials felt
their senses had been assaulted by what Georg Simmel described as 'the
rapid crowding of changing images' or 'the unexpectedness of onrushing
impressions',[22] neither of which could be properly classified with existing
forms of discourse. The same was true for some Indian observers of colonial
society. In his *Kalikata Kamalalay*, Bhabanicharan used a longstanding Sanskrit trope to depict the 'great city' of Calcutta as a swirling sea in which
contradictory set of languages, customs and moral codes mingled in a way
that was difficult to understand.[23] Bhabanicharan's attempt to comprehend
this heterogeneity in his own present time could only occur in a dialogic
form, where more than one classificatory voice was able to speak; and it is
striking that neither character consistently adopts the position of stranger to
his own society in his dialogue. Others, from James Mill to Bankimchandra
Chattopadhyay, found their own present time entirely impossible to describe;
especially so where they adopted the position of the stranger. Simmel thought
this characteristically modern figure was produced by urban, industrial social
life; others have suggested that the 'crisis of representation' that ensued from
the process of alienation and estrangement was 'endemic to the capitalist
mode of production'.[24] This book has argued that a far more convoluted
genealogy needs to be traced to understand the centrality of the stranger in
colonial India, one that is far more complex than a straightforward description of the arrival of modern European forms of thought. But wherever it
occurred, the sense of strangeness felt by observers of Indian politics led to
the construction of alternate realities, seemingly more rational than present-
day really-existing society, which had the potential to exist at other moments
in time, whether in the future or past. The writings of Rammohan, Tagore and
Bankim, even also later Muslim Bengali nationalists such as Sheikh Mujibur
Rahman, as well as colonial utilitarians such as James Mill were characterised
by their utopian mode of thought.[25] This utopian way of thinking underpinned the attempt to construct intellectually stable worlds in the fields of
social action and codified law. But it was not necessarily the sign of an opti-
mistic sense that better things could come, or the projection of political ideas
and aspirations existing in the present onto the future. Instead, utopias projected onto the past or future offered a response to the semantic crisis that
this book has examined; they were the last recourse of anxious individuals
to a present they found, for whatever reason, impossible to understand. The
role of these other, non-present moments in the politics of South Asia is a
subject that deserves further enquiry.

Notes

Preface and Acknowledgements

1. Madhavi Kale, 'Subject to Question: Empire and Catherine Hall's *Civilising Subjects*', *Small Axe* 7, 2 (2003), p. 135.

1 Introduction

1. For example, two of the most widely read Persian political treatises in early modern India were the volumes on *Ethics* written by Nasir al-Tusi (1201–1274) and Jalal-al-din Dawani (1426–1502). See W.F. Thompson, *Practical Philosophy of the Muhammadan People, Being a Translation of the Akhlak-I-Jalaly, from the Persian of Fakir Jany Muhammad Asad* (London, 1839); Wilferd Madelung, 'Nasir Al-Din Tusi's Ethics between Philosophy, Shi'ism, and Sufism' in Richard G. Hovannisian (ed.), *Ethics in Islam* (Lancaster, CA, 1985); Muzaffar Alam, *The Languages of Political Islam: India, 1200–1800* (London, 2004).
2. Baldassarre Castiglione, *The Book of the Courtier* (Harmondsworth, 1967); Niccolo Machiavelli, *The Prince* (Cambridge, 1988), pp. 51–71; William Paley, *The Principles of Moral and Political Philosophy* (Indianapolis, IN, 2002), pp. 2–32, 133–67.
3. For a discussion of the relationship between Simmel's work and the modern state, see Zygmunt Bauman, *Modernity and Ambivalence* (Oxford, 1991), Chapter 2 *passim*; and Uday Singh Mehta, *Liberalism and Empire: A Study in Nineteenth-Century British Liberal Thought* (Chicago, IL, 1999), pp. 24–5.
4. Georg Simmel, *On Individuality and Social Forms* (Chicago, IL, 1971), pp. 143–9.
5. Ibid., p. 145.
6. Politicians in Britain engaged with some of their subjects as strangers, in debates over the poor law, for example. Felix Driver, *Power and Pauperism. The Workhouse System, 1834–1884* (Cambridge, 1993), also David Eastwood, *Governing Rural England. Tradition and Transformation in Local Government, 1780–1840* (Oxford, 1994), pp. 166–90.
7. For a classic account of 'the official mind', see John Gallagher *et al.*, *Africa and the Victorians: The Official Mind of Imperialism* (London, 1961); Gallagher and Robinson's official mind was firmly located in the metropolis however.
8. Bernard Williams, *Morality: An Introduction to Ethics* (Harmondsworth, 1973), p. 138; Amartya Sen and Bernard Williams, *Utilitarianism and Beyond* (Cambridge, 1982), p. 16; the phrase was initially used by Williams to castigate Henry Sedgewick's justification of colonial politics.
9. Max Weber, *Economy and Society* (Berkeley, CA, 1978), pp. 956–1003; Michel Foucault, 'Governmentality' in Graham Burchell, Colin Gordon and Peter Miller (eds), *The Foucault Effect* (Hemel Hempstead, 1991), pp. 87–104; Michel Foucault, *Security, Territory, Population. Lectures at the College de France, 1977–1978* (Basingstoke, 2007), pp. 29–119; Oliver Macdonagh, 'The Nineteenth-Century Revolution in Government: A Reappraisal', *Historical Journal* 1, 1 (1958), pp. 52–67; Eric Stokes, *The English Utilitarians and India* (Oxford, 1959); Boyd Hilton, *A Mad, Bad and Dangerous People? England 1783–1846* (Oxford, 2006).

10. Gulfishan Khan, *Indian Muslim Perceptions of the West During the Eighteenth Century* (Karachi, 1998), pp. 84–92; Kumkum Chatterjee, 'History as Self-Representation. The Recasting of a Political Tradition in Late Eighteenth-Century India', *MAS*, 34, 4 (1998), pp. 93–118.
11. Ghulam Hossein Khan Tabatabai, *The Seir Mutaquerin, or Review of Modern Times* (Delhi, 1926), III, pp. 161–2 and 159.
12. Ibid., III, pp. 25–9.
13. Ibid., III, p. 191.
14. For a defence of such a position, see Alasdair Macintyre, *After Virtue: A Study in Moral Theory* (London, 1981), pp. 181–255.
15. Edward W. Said, *Orientalism. Western Conceptions of the Orient* (Harmondsworth, 1978); Ronald B. Inden, *Imagining India* (Oxford, 1990); Amal Chatterjee, *Representations of India, 1740–1840: The Creation of India in the Colonial Imagination* (Basingstoke, 1998); Gyan Prakash, *Another Reason: Science and the Imagination of Modern India* (Princeton, NJ, 1999); Manu Goswami, *Producing India: From Colonial Economy to National Space* (Chicago, IL, 2004).
16. Ranajit Guha, *A Rule of Property for Bengal: An Essay on the Idea of Permanent Settlement* (Durham, NC, 1996 edition); Sudipta Sen, *Empire of Free Trade: The East India Company and Making of the Colonial Marketplace* (Philadelphia, PA, 1998), pp. 120–44.
17. Peter Mandler, 'The Problem with Cultural History', *Cultural and Social History* 1, 1 (2004), pp. 94–117.
18. Two important criticisms of the emphasis on colonial attitudes rather than practices and projects are Homi K. Bhabha, *The Location of Culture: Critical Theory and the Postcolonial Perspective* (London, 1991); David Scott, 'Colonial Governmentality', *Social Text* 43 (1995), pp. 191–220. Edward Said, nonetheless, initially emphasised the extent to which representations of the Orient were rooted in material practices, not merely reliant on forms of thought. Said, *Orientalism*, p. 2.
19. C.A. Bayly, 'Liberalism at Large. South Asian and Britain, *c.*1800–1947', Wiles lectures, Queens University Belfast, June 2007; C.A. Bayly, 'Rammohan Roy and the Advent of Constitutional Liberalism in India, 1800–1830', *Modern Intellectual History* 4, 1 (2007), pp. 25–41; Jennifer Pitts, *A Turn to Empire: The Rise of Imperial Liberalism in Britain and France* (Princeton, NJ, 2005); Andrew Sartori, 'Emancipation as Heteronomy: The Crisis of Liberalism in Later Nineteenth-Century Bengal', *Journal of Historical Sociology* 17, 1 (2004), pp. 56–86; Andrew Sartori, 'The British Empire and Its Liberal Mission', *Journal of Modern History* 78, (2006), pp. 623–42.
20. Mehta, *Liberalism and Empire*, pp. 51–76; Uday Singh Mehta, *The Anxiety of Freedom: Imagination and Individuality in Locke's Political Thought* (Ithaca, NY, 1992).
21. Mehta, *Liberalism and Empire*, p. 11.
22. Douglas M. Peers, *Between Mars and Mammon. Colonial Armies and the Garrison State in India 1819–1835* (London, 1995).
23. David Eastwood, 'The Age of Uncertainty. Britain in the Early-Nineteenth Century', *Transactions of the Royal Historical Society* 6th ser., 8 (1998), pp. 91–115; Hilton, *A Mad, Bad and Dangerous People?*
24. Sartori, 'The British Empire and Its Liberal Mission', p. 624.
25. This discussion of the un-homeliness of empire is inspired by, and seeks to develop, the argument of Ranajit Guha, 'Not at Home in Empire', *Critical Inquiry* 23, 3 (1997), pp. 482–93. A more detailed discussion of this essay occurs in Chapter 3 of this book.
26. Bhabha, *The Location of Culture*, pp. 129–31, for example.

27. Insufficient attention to the role of this non-cognitive, non-conceptual context political thought is the main weakness of Quentin Skinner's approach to intellectual history. See the essays and criticisms collected in James Tully and Quentin Skinner (eds), *Meaning and Context: Quentin Skinner and His Critics* (Cambridge, 1988); Quentin Skinner, *Visions of Politics*, vol. I, *Regarding Method* (Cambridge, 2002).
28. Gilles Deleuze, *Foucault* (London, 1988), p. viii; 'Letter on Humanism' in Martin Heidegger, *Basic Writings: Martin Heidegger* (London, 1993), p. 217.
29. Michel Foucault, *The Archaeology of Knowledge* (London, 1972), pp. 31–40.
30. For an account which emphasises the role of practical coping and know-how in Heidegger's work, see Hubert Dreyfus, *Being-in-the-World: A Commentary on Heidegger's Being and Time, Division I* (Cambridge, MA, 1991), pp. 40–87 in particular. The best introduction to Heidegger's early work as a whole is Stephen Mulhall, *Heidegger and Being and Time* (London, 1996). Perhaps Heidegger's use of the German verb *verstehen* here is closer to the non-cognitive implications behind the Bengali verb *bojha* than the English word 'understand'; in both contexts understanding involves instinctual affective responses as well as rational cognition.
31. Martin Heidegger, *Being and Time* (Oxford, 1962), p. 191.
32. Ibid., p. 105.
33. Ibid., §69 *passim*, pp. 409–10; Mulhall, *Heidegger and Being and Time*, pp. 156–7.
34. Martin Heidegger, *Off the Beaten Track* (NY, 2002), pp. 57–85.
35. See Dreyfus, *Being-in-the-World*, p. 8, for the relationship between Heidegger and Aristotle.
36. Such an approach ultimately depends on G.W.F. Hegel, *Phenomenology of Spirit* (Oxford, 1977), especially the dialectic of lord and bondsman, pp. 111–19. For important discussions of the open-endedness of Hegel's approach, see Judith Butler, *Subjects of Desire: Hegelian Reflections in Twentieth-Century France* (New York, NY, 1987); Alasdair Macintyre, 'Hegel on Faces and Skulls' in Alasdair Macintyre (ed.), *Hegel: A Collection of Critical Essays* (Garden City, NY, 1972), pp. 228–32.
37. Philip Abrams, 'Notes on the Difficulty of Studying the State', *Journal of Historical Sociology* 1, 1 (1988), pp. 58–89.
38. Gupta, 'Blurred Boundaries: The Discourse of Corruption, the Culture of Politics, and the Imagined State', *American Ethnologist* 22, 2 (1995), p. 392. See also the introductory chapter in Aradhana Sharma and Akhil Gupta, *The Anthropology of the State: A Reader* (Oxford, 2006), pp. 1–42; C.J. Fuller and Veronique Bénéï (eds), *The Everyday State and Society in Modern India* (New Delhi, 2001); Veena Das and Deborah Poole, *Anthropology in the Margins of the State* (Oxford, 2004) for this general approach.
39. Talal Asad, *Formations of the Secular: Christianity, Islam, Modernity* (Stanford, CA, 2003), p. 13.
40. Bauman, *Modernity and Ambivalence*, p. 10. I would like to thank Shruti Kapila to directing me to Bauman's work.
41. Louis O. Mink, 'History and Fiction as Modes of Comprehension', *New Literary History* 1, 3 (1970), p. 558. For an alterative view, see Macintyre, *After Virtue*, p. 212.
42. Paul Ricoeur, *Time and Narrative* (Chicago, 1984), I, p. 150.

2 Comparing the Eighteenth-century polities of Britain and Bengal

1. Benoy Kumar Sarkar, 'The Futurism of Young Asia', *International Journal of Ethics* 28, 4 (1918), pp. 534–5.
2. For details of Sarkar's career, see Roma Chatterji, 'The Nationalist Sociology of Benoy Kumar Sarkar' in Patricia Uberoi *et al.* (eds), *Anthropology in the East: Founders of Indian Sociology and Anthropology* (Kolkata, 2007).

3. Most famously Quentin Skinner, *The Foundations of Modern Political Thought* (Cambridge, 1978). See also Richard Tuck, *Natural Rights Theories: Their Origin and Development* (Cambridge, 1979); David Armitage, *The Ideological Origins of the British Empire* (Cambridge, 2000) for other instances of the attempt to historicise the emergence of a particular feature of modern political discourse to contingent early modern origins.

4. For very different approaches which both nonetheless stress the difference between European and Indian political traditions, see Louis Dumont, *Homo Hierarchicus: The Caste System and Its Implications* (London, 1970); Ronald B. Inden, *Imagining India* (Oxford, 1990).

5. For attempts at making comparisons between early modern Europe and Asia, Victor Lieberman, 'Transcending East-West Dichotomies: State and Culture Formation in Six Ostrensibly Disparate Areas', *MAS* 21, 3 (1997); a good account of south Indian political culture by a scholar who understands early modern Europe is Sanjay Subrahmanyam, *Penumbral Visions: Making Polities in Early Modern South India* (Ann Arbor, 2001).

6. Hilton, *A Mad, Bad and Dangerous People*. See also the essays collected in John Brewer and John A. Styles, *An Ungovernable People: The English and Their Law in the Seventeenth and Eighteenth Centuries* (New Brunswick, NJ, 1980).

7. For example, Warren Hastings, 'Answer to the Third Charge', April 1786, *HCSP*, vol. 59, p. 31; *Ninth Report of the Committee of Secrecy*, June 1773, *HCSP*, vol. 137, p. 729.

8. For a discussion of Indian travellers to eighteenth-century Europe, see Khan, *Indian Muslim Perceptions of the West*.

9. For Harishchandra as private moral exemplar see Gadadhar Kavyatirtha, *Harishchandra* (Calcutta, 1898); Raghuvan Iyer (ed.), *The Essential Writings of Mahatma Gandhi* (Delhi, 1990), pp. 223–7.

10. Jaganmohan Tarkalankara, *Harishchandra-charitra* (Calcutta, 1869); Dinesh Chandra Sen, *History of Bengali Language and Literature* (Calcutta, 1911), pp. 168–71; Dinesh Chandra Sen, *The Bengali Ramayanas* (Calcutta, 1920), p. 84; Edward C. Dimock, *The Thief of Love: Bengali Tales from Court and Village* (Chicago, 1963), pp. 140–68.

11. Dimock, *The Thief of Love*, pp. 167–8.

12. Alam, *Languages of Political Islam*.

13. Quoted in Sheldon Pollock, 'The Theory of Practice and the Practice of Theory in Indian Intellectual History', *Journal of the American Oriental Society* 105, 3 (1984), p. 499; Dimock, *Thief of Love*, pp. 137–8.

14. Benoy Kumar Sarkar, *The Positive Background of Hindu Sociology: Book I, Introduction to Hindu Positivism* (Allahabad, 1937), p. 447; Indrani Chatterjee, *Unfamiliar Relations: Family and History in South Asia* (New Brunswick, NJ, 2004), p. 76.

15. Rajat Kanta Ray, *The Felt Community: Commonalty and Mentality Before the Emergence of Indian Nationalism* (Delhi, 2003). See also C.A. Bayly, *Origins of Nationality in South Asia: Patriotism and Ethical Government in the Making of Modern India* (Delhi, 2001).

16. Alam, *Languages of Political Islam*.

17. Sajjad H. Rizvi, 'Mysticism and Philosophy: Ibn Arabi and Mulla Sadra' in Peter Adamson and Richard C. Taylor (eds), *The Cambridge Companion to Arabic Philosophy* (Cambridge, 2005), p. 228.

18. Thompson, *Practical Philosophy of the Muhammadan People*. For the role of Iranian political philosophy in early modern India, see Alam, *Languages of Political Islam*.

19. Dipesh Chakrabarty, *Provincialising Europe. Postcolonial Thought and Historical Difference* (Princeton, NJ, 2000), pp. 125–6.
20. C.A. Bayly, *Empire and Information. Intelligence Gathering and Social Communication in India, 1780–1870* (Cambridge, 1996); Michael H. Fisher, 'The Office of Akhbar Nawis: The Transition from Mughal to British Forms', *MAS* 27, 1 (1993), pp. 45–82.
21. Ratnalekha Ray, *Change in Agrarian Bengal*, p. 29.
22. John R. Mclane, *Land and Local Kingship in Eighteenth Century Bengal* (Cambridge, 1993); David L. Curley, ' "Voluntary" Relations and Royal Gifts of *Pan* in Mughal Bengal' in Stewart Gordon (ed.), *Robes of Honour: Khil'at in Pre-Colonial and Colonial Bengal* (Delhi, 2003), pp. 50–79, also Tillotama Mukherjee, 'The Co-ordinating State and the Economy: The *Nizamat* in Eighteenth-Century Bengal', *MAS* 42, 1 (2008), pp. 1–48.
23. For a discussion of *zamindari* gift-giving in Bengal, see Ronald B. Inden, *Marriage and Rank in Bengali Culture: A History of Caste and Clan in Middle Period Bengal* (Berkeley, CA, 1976), Mclane, *Land and Local Kingship*; for the *nizamat*, Mukherjee, 'The Co-ordinating State and the Economy'.
24. For an account of the importance of patronage in England, see Dustin Griffin, *Literary Patronage in England, 1650–1800* (Cambridge, 1996).
25. Rachel McDermott, *Mother of My Heart, Daughter of My Dreams: Kalai and Uma in the Devotional Poetry of Bengal* (Oxford, 2001); Samita Sinha, *Pandits in a Changing Environment: Centres of Sanskrit Learning in Nineteenth Century Bengal* (Calcutta, 1993), p. 222.
26. J.H. Harrington's Survey of Radhanagar Village, Proceedings of the Board of Revenue, 22 March 1790, IOR P/71/22. Also David Carmichael Smyth, *Original Bengalese Zumeendaree Accounts* (Calcutta, 1823); Somendra Chandra Nandy, *History of the Cossimbazar Raj in the Nineteenth-Century* (Calcutta, 1986).
27. The argument here rests on a survey of temples listed in George Michell (ed.), *Brick Temples of Bengal: From the Archives of David Mccutchion* (Princeton, 1983).
28. McDermott, *Mother of My Heart*, pp. 31, 181.
29. Between 5 and 10% of the income of English estates was spent on 'charity'. See G.E. Mingay, *English Landed Society in the Eighteenth Century* (London, 1964), p. 118; Paul Langford, *Public Life and the Propertied Englishman, 1688–1798* (Oxford, 1991), pp. 491–500.
30. James Graham, Collector of Rangpur, Proceedings on the petition presented by Gokhal Nath Roy and Naba Kisor Roy, 1 June 1793, NAB, Rangpur DR, vol. 292, p. 13; Mclane, *Land and Local Kingship*, p. 104.
31. *Raiyats* with plots smaller than seven *bighas* were able to ensure that they paid rent for an average of 52% of the soil they tilled; tenants with larger plots had 58% of their land recorded. Account *bandabast* of Rangpur in Bengal Year 1190, enclosed with Collector of Rangpur to Committee of Revenue, 23 July 1783, *Mss Eur* D506, 283f; 'Deductions allowed in 1189', enclosure no.15 with John D. Paterson to Committee of Revenue, 7 May 1785, *Mss Eur* D506, f.224; E.G. Glazier claimed that the deductions for 1782–1783 were even larger, almost Rs 400,000 which represented almost half of the total amount demanded. Walter K. Firminger, *Bengal District Records, Rungpore* (Calcutta, 1914), p. 19.
32. Gautam Bhadra, 'The Mentality of Subalternity. *Kantanama* or *Rajdharma'* in Ranajit Guha (ed.), *Subaltern Studies VI* (Delhi, 1989), p. 84.
33. F. Steingass, *A Comprehensive Persian-English Dictionary* (reprint, Madras, 1892), p. 795 translates *zamn* as 'Answering or being surety for; suretyship' and *zamn-dar* and *zimn-dar* as 'A sponsor, an ally'.

34. William Armstrong, Collector of Dhaka to Board of Revenue, 2 July 1794, NAB, Dhaka DR, vol. 129, p. 82.
35. Henry Beveridge, *The District of Bakarganj, Its History and Statistics* (London, 1876), p. 204.
36. Ratnalekha Ray, *Change in Bengal Agrarian Society, C1760–1850* (New Delhi, 1979), pp. 240–1; Beveridge, *Bakarganj*, pp. 203–7.
37. Lord Cornwallis, Minute, 18 September in Walter K. Firminger (ed.), *The Fifth Report on the Affairs of the East India Company* (Calcutta, 1917), II, p. 512.
38. Enclosure no.2 with Harrington's Survey of Radhanagar, IOR P/71/22.
39. Statistical Return of Circuit no.3, 1855–1856 Revenue Survey Maps and Returns, Rangpur Collectorate Record Room, Rangpur, Bangladesh.
40. C.A. Bayly, *Indian Society and the Making of the British Empire* (Cambridge, 1988), p. 146; Khondker Iftekhar Iqbal, 'Society and Ecology in Nineteenth and Early Twentieth Century Bengal Delta', PhD, University of Cambridge, 2005, pp. 24–79.
41. Jon E. Wilson, ' "A Thousand Countries to Go to": Peasants and Rulers in Late Eighteenth-Century Bengal', *Past and Present*, 189 (2005), p. 85.
42. William Armstrong, Collector of Dhaka to Board of Revenue, 9 February 1797; NAB, Dhaka DR, vol. 132, p. 22.
43. Collector of Nadia, to Governor-General in Council, 16 December 1791 quoted in Nag Chowdhury-Zilly, *The Vagrant Peasant: Agrarian Distress and Desertion in Bengal, 1770–1830* (Wiesbaden, 1982), p. 75; also William Massie, Collector, Dhaka to Board of Revenue, 18 March 1800, NAB, Dhaka DR, vol. 135, p. 208. Compare with David Washbrook, 'Land and Labour in Late Eighteenth-Century South India: The Golden Age of the Pariah', in Peter Robb (ed.), *Dalit Movements and the Meanings of Labour in India* (New Delhi, 1997), pp. 68–87 and Michael Adas, ' "Moral Economy" or "Contest State"?: Elite Demands and the Origins of Peasant Protest in Southeast Asia', *Journal of Social History*, 13, 4 (1980), pp. 521–46. Richard Eaton, *The Rise of Islam and the Bengal Frontier, 1204–1760* (Berkeley, 1993).
44. For example, petition of Durrup Deo, *zamindar* of Baikantpur, enclosed with Charles Purling to Governor-General in Council, 28 March 1778 in Firminger, *Bengal District Records. Rungpore*, I, 33–4.
45. J. Grose to Richard Becher, Resident at the Durbar, 23 June 1770, Firminger, *Bengal District Records. Rungpore*, I, 5; petitions enclosed with letters from Collector of Rangpur to Governor-General in Council, 28 March 1778, Firminger, *Bengal District Records. Rungpore*, II, pp. 33–4 and to William Harwood, Chief of Provincial Council of Revenue at Purnea, 20 March 1778, Firminger, *Bengal District Records. Rungpore*, II, 34–5.
46. Lal Behari Day, *Bengal Peasant Life* (London, 1878), p. 127.
47. Collector of Birbhum to Board of Revenue, 18 January 1788, Ranjan Kumar Gupta, *The Economic Life of a Bengal District, Birbhum, 1770–1857* (Burdwan, 1984), pp. 48–9.
48. Quoted in Sukumar Sen, *History of Bengali Literature* (New Delhi, 1960), p. 269. Sen's translation has been slightly modified.
49. Bhadra, 'The Mentality of Subalternity'.
50. Gupta, *The Economic Life of a Bengal District, Birbhum, 1770–1857* ; Atis K. Dasgupta, *The Fakir and Sannyasi Uprisings* (Calcutta, 1992).
51. Wilson, 'Thousand Countries'; A.M. Serajuddin, 'The Origin on the Rajas of the Chittagong Hill Tracts and their Relations with the Mughals and the East India Company in the Eighteenth Century', *Journal of the Pakistan Historical Society* 19, 1 (1971).

52. Iqbal, 'Society and Ecology'; Iqbal's thesis offers a perceptive discussion of the relationship between ecology and political action.
53. Nirmalendru Mukhopaddhyay (ed.), *Bharatcandrer Annadamangal* (Kalikata, 1978) translated as 'Vidya-Sundera' in Dimock, *Thief of Love*, pp. 32–4; Bhadra, 'The Mentality of Subalternity'.
54. Kumkum Chatterjee, 'History as Self-Representation. The Recasting of a Political Tradition in Late Eighteenth-Century India', *MAS* 34, 4 (1998), pp. 913–48; André Wink, *Land and Sovereignty in India: Agrarian Society and Politics under the Eighteenth-Century Maratha Svarajya* (Cambridge, 1986), pp. 21–51. Wink argues that the Mughals possessed a vocabulary of absolute authority but that the reality of Mughal power was achieved by a constant process of struggle and accommodation or *fitna*.
55. Sinha, *Pandits in a Changing Environment*.
56. C.A. Bayly, *Rulers, Townsmen and Bazaars: North Indian Society in the Age of British Expansion 1770–1870* (Cambridge, 1983), p. 353. For a discussion of this locally embedded sense of juridical decision-making at work amongst Muslims in India in the late-twentieth century, see Gregory C. Kozlowski, 'Loyalty, Locality and Authority in Several Opinions (Fatawa) Delivered by the Mufti of the Jami'ah Nizamiyyah Madrasah, Hyderabad, India', *MAS* 29, 4 (1995), 893–923.
57. Peter Robb, *Ancient Rights and Future Comfort: Bihar, the Bengal Tenancy Act of 1885, and British Rule in India* (Richmond, 1997), pp. 5–10.
58. Inden, *Marriage and Rank in Bengali Culture*; Nicholas B. Dirks, 'The Invention of Caste: Civil Society in Colonial India', *Social Analysis* 25 (1993), pp. 42–52.
59. Radhika Singha, *A Despotism of Law. Crime and Justice in Early Colonial India* (New Delhi, 1998); Sudipta Sen, *Empire of Free Trade: The East India Company and Making of the Colonial Marketplace* (Philadelphia, PA, 1998), pp. 91–120 and Sudipta Sen, *A Distant Sovereignty: National Imperialism and the Origins of British India* (New York, 2002), pp. 1–20.
60. 'The English Reform Bill' in T.M. Knox and Z.A. Pelcyzynski (eds), *Hegel's Political Writings* (Oxford, 1964), p. 300.
61. Not a word of Hegel's writings was available in English before 1855, when part of his *Logic* was translated as G.W.F. Hegel, *The Subjective Logic of Hegel* (London, 1855).
62. The best account of the complex art of eighteenth-century British politics is Langford, *Public Life and the Propertied Englishman*.
63. Thomas Gisborne, *An Enquiry into the Duties of Men in the Higher and Middle Classes of Society in Great Britain* (London, 1794), p. 510.
64. J.G.A. Pocock, 'The Classical Theory of Deference', *American Historical Review* 81, 3 (1976), pp. 1–8.
65. Gisborne, *Enquiry into the Duties of Men*, p. 590.
66. Quoted in Frank O'Gorman, *Voters, Patrons and Parties: The Unreformed Electorate in England, 1734–1832* (Oxford, 1989), p. 259.
67. Joanna Innes, 'Parliament and the Shaping of Eighteenth-Century English Social Policy', *Transactions of the Royal Historical Society* 5th ser., 40 (1990), pp. 63–92; Joanna Innes, 'Legislation and Public Participation 1760–1830' in D. Lemmings (ed.), *The British and Their Laws* (Woodbridge, 2005), pp. 102–32.
68. Langford, *Public Life and the Propertied Englishman*, both quotations, pp. 50–1.
69. Michael Lobban, personal communication.
70. For the range of juridical institutions, see Craig Muldrew, 'Rural Credit and Legal Institutions in the Countryside in England 1550–1700' in Christopher

Brooks *et al.* (eds), *Communities and Courts in Britain, 1450–1900* (London, 1997), pp. 155–78.

71. Michael Lobban, *The Common Law and English Jurisprudence, 1760–1850* (Oxford, 1991). See Chapter 4 below for a more detailed discussion of the practice of English law.

72. 'Thoughts on the Present Discontents' in Paul Langford *et al.* (eds), *The Writings and Speeches of Edmund Burke* (9 vols, Oxford, 1981–1991), II, p. 242; 'Reflections on the Revolution in France' ibid., III, p. 97; see also Richard Bourke, 'Liberty, Authority, and Trust in Burke's Idea of Empire', *Journal of the History of Ideas* 61, 3 (2000), p. 470.

73. Emma Rothschild, *Economic Sentiments: Adam Smith, Condorcet and the Enlightenment* (Harvard, 2001).

74. A.D. Megill, 'Theory and Experience in Adam Smith', *Journal of the History of Ideas* 36, 1 (1975), p. 80.

75. Catherine Packham, 'The Physiology of Political Economy: Vitalism and Adam Smith's *Wealth of Nations*', *Journal of the History of Ideas* 63, 3 (2002), pp. 465–81.

76. Partha Chatterjee, *The Nation and Its Fragments. Colonial and Postcolonial Histories* (Princeton, NJ, 1993), p. 225; Uday Singh Mehta, *Liberalism and Empire: A Study in Nineteenth-Century British Liberal Thought* (Chicago, IL, 1999), pp. 47–65.

77. William Paley, *The Principles of Moral and Political Philosophy* (Indianapolis, IN, 2002), pp. 291–303.

78. Ross Harrison, *Hobbes, Locke and Confusion's Masterpiece: An Examination of Seventeenth Century Philosophy* (Cambridge, 2002).

79. Frederick D. Weil, 'The Stranger, Prudence and Trust in Hobbes's Theory', *Theory and Society* 15, 5 (1986), pp. 759–88; also the essays collected in Quentin Skinner, *Visions of Politics.* Vol. III, *Hobbes and Civil Science* (Cambridge, 2002), especially pp. 177–208.

80. Peter Laslett (ed.), 'Introduction' to John Locke, *Two Treatises of Government* (Cambridge, 1988); also Richard Ashcraft, *Revolutionary Politics and Locke's Two Treatises of Government* (Princeton, NJ, 1986).

81. J.P. Kenyon, *Revolution Principles: The Politics of Party, 1689–1720* (Oxford, 1977), pp. 10–11.

82. For more positive responses to Hobbes in the seventeenth century though, see Jonathan Parkin, 'The Reception of Hobbes' *Leviathan*' in Patricia Springborg (ed.), *The Cambridge Companion to Hobbes's Leviathan* (Cambridge, 2007), pp. 441–59.

83. For two very different perspectives of two very different sets of events, see Michael Brock, *Great Reform Act* (London, 1973) and Gareth Stedman-Jones, *Languages of Class. Studies in English Working-Class History* (Cambridge, 1984).

84. Different versions of this argument are made in Manu Goswami, *Producing India: From Colonial Economy to National Space* (Chicago, IL, 2004), p. 162; Chatterjee, *The Nation and Its Fragments*, pp. 77–85. For criticisms of oversimplified attitudes to pre-colonial temporality, see Romila Thapar, *Time as a Metaphor of History: Early India* (Delhi, 1996) and Velcheru *et al.*, *Textures of Time: Writing History in South India, 1600–1800* (Delhi, 2001).

85. Walter Benjamin, 'Theses on the Philosophy of History' *Illuminations* (London, 1973), pp. 252–3; Talal Asad, *Formations of the Secular: Christianity, Islam, Modernity* (Stanford, CA, 2003), pp. 223–5. For a discussion of some of these themes which nonetheless tends to flatten out the differences a little itself, see Reinhart Koselleck, *Futures Past: On the Semantics of Historical Time* (Cambridge, MA, 1985).

86. Boyd Hilton, *The Age of Atonement: The Influence of Evangelicalism on Social and Economic Thought, 1795–1865* (Oxford, 1988).
87. For a discussion of these themes, see Chapter 6 below.
88. Goswami, *Producing India*.
89. J.G.A. Pocock, 'Modes of Political and Historical Time in Early Eighteenth-Century Britain' in *Virtue, Commerce and History* (Cambridge, 1985), p. 94. See also the J.G.A. Pocock, *The Machiavellian Moment: Florentine Political Thought and the Atlantic Republican Tradition* (Princeton, 1975), pp. 1–82, for a discussion of these themes.
90. David Lieberman, *The Province of Legislation Determined: Legal Theory in Eighteenth-Century Britain* (Cambridge, 1989), 463–546; James Oldham, *The Mansfield Manuscripts and the Growth of English Law in the Eighteenth Century* (Chapel Hill, NC, 1992); Paul Lucas, 'On Edmund Burke's Doctrine of Prescription; or, an Appeal from the New to the Old Lawyers', *Historical Journal* 11, 1 (1968), pp. 35–63.
91. Mehta, *Liberalism and Empire*, pp. 20–1, 201–12 in particular.
92. 'Reflections on the Revolution in France' in Langford *et al.* (eds), *Writings and Speeches of Edmund Burke*, vol. III.
93. Chatterjee, *Unfamiliar Relations*, pp. 58, 224–6, for example.
94. Indrani Chatterjee, *Gender, Slavery and Law in Colonial India* (New Delhi; New York, 1999); Mccutchion and Michell, *Brick Temples of Bengal: From the Archives of David Mccutchion*.
95. A.D. Campbell, 'Extracts from a Paper on the Land Revenue of India' (1833) in Burton Stein, *The Making of Agrarian Policy in British India, 1770–1900* (Delhi, 1992), p. 37.
96. For two different arguments about the role of custom in Hindu law, see J.D.M. Derrett, *Religion, Law and the State in India* (London, 1968) and Werner Menski, *Hindu Law. Beyond Tradition and Modernity* (New Delhi, 2003).
97. Pocock, *The Machiavellian Moment*.
98. Quoted in John Marriott, *The Other Empire: Metropolis, India and Progress in the Colonial Imagination* (Manchester, 2003), p. 19.
99. Eliga H. Gould, 'To Strengthen the King's Hands: Dynastic Legitimacy, Militia Reform and Ideas of National Unity in England 1745–1760', *Historical Journal* 34, 2 (1991), pp. 329–48; John Robertson, *The Scottish Enlightenment and the Militia Issue* (Edinburgh, 1985).
100. Wink, *Land and Sovereignty in India*.
101. For this response to 1745, see Bob Harris, ' "American Idols". Empire, War and the Middling Ranks in Eighteenth-Century England', *Past and Present* 150 (1996), p. 121.
102. Gangarama, *The Maharashta Purana: An Eighteenth-Century Bengali Historical Text* (Honolulu, HA, 1965), p. 3.
103. Ghulam Hossein Khan Tabatabai, *The Seir Mutaquerin, or Review of Modern Times* (Delhi, 1926), I, 405.
104. Ibid., I, 417, 424–5, 427.
105. *Arzi* of Rani of Chunderdeep, in W.W. Massie to Board of Revenue, 22 March 1800, NAB Dhaka DR, pp. 243–5.
106. *Dirkhast* of Alexander Paniotty, with Letter W.W. Massie to Board of Revenue, 4 April 1800, NAB Dhaka DR, 135, pp. 268–80.
107. Langford, *Public Life and the Propertied Englishman*.
108. Wintle to Judicial Board, 7 January 1802, quoted in Beveridge, *Bakarganj*, p. 424.

3 Crisis, anxiety and the making of a new order

1. Ranajit Guha, *A Rule of Property for Bengal: An Essay on the Idea of Permanent Settlement* (Durham, NC, 1996 edition), pp. xiii, 3.

2. William Pitt to Cornwallis, 8 February 1795, PRO, 30/11/270; John Shore to Mrs Shore, 9 January 1789, Charles John Shore Teignmouth, *Memoir of the Life and Correspondence of John, Lord Teignmouth* (London, 1843), I, p. 163.

3. C.A. Bayly, *Indian Society and the Making of the British Empire* (Cambridge, 1988), p. 65.

4. Sirajul Islam, *The Permanent Settlement in Bengal: A Study of Its Operation, 1790–1819* (Dacca, 1979); Khondker Iftekhar Iqbal, 'Society and Ecology', PhD, University of Cambridge, 2005, pp. 24–52.

5. Robert Travers, *Ideology and Empire in Eighteenth-Century India. The British in Bengal* (Cambridge, 2007).

6. Fifth Report of the House of Commons Select Committee on East India Affairs, *Parliamentary Papers (PP)*, 1812 (377) VII, p. 18.

7. Ranajit Guha, 'Not at Home in Empire', *Critical Inquiry* 23, 3 (1997), p. 488.

8. Martin Heidegger, *Being and Time* (Oxford, 1962), p. 231 quoted in Guha, 'Not at Home in Empire', p. 487.

9. C.A. Bayly, *Imperial Meridian: The British Empire and the World, 1780–1830* (London, 1989), p. 2.

10. Lord Stormont, 17 February 1783, quoted in P.J. Marshall, *The Making and Unmaking of Empires: Britain, India, and America, 1750–1783* (Oxford, 2005), p. 369.

11. A good survey of these conflicts is found in Pradeep Barua, *The State at War in South Asia* (Lincoln, NE, 2005), pp. 51–88, but there is no comprehensive recent study of warfare in the third quarter of the eighteenth century.

12. Marshall, *Making and Unmaking of Empires*, p. 367.

13. Warren Hastings, *Memoirs Relative to the State of India* (London, 1787), p. 22; Governor-General to CoD, 10 December 1784, *FWIH*, IX, pp. 503–7.

14. L. Archdekin to G.G. Ducarel, 22 November 1784, D2091/F14, no.9, Gloucestershire CRO.

15. Quoted in Alfred C. Lyall, *Warren Hastings* (London, 1889), p. 118. See also secret letter from Governor-General in Council to CoD, 25 March 1783 in *FWIH*, XV, pp. 380–2.

16. Samuel Johnson, *A Dictionary of the English Language* (London, 1756).

17. Richard Sir Sullivan, *An Analysis of the Political History of India* (London, 1784), p. 8.

18. Lucy Sutherland, *The East India Company in Eighteenth Century Politics* (Oxford, 1952), pp. 374–5.

19. Marshall, *Making and Unmaking of Empires*, p. 256.

20. Joseph Cawthorne, *The Crisis: Or, A Defence of Administration against the Imaginary Victory and Ill-Grounded Triumph of Opposition* (London, 1785); Marshall, *Making and Unmaking of Empires*, pp. 359–62.

21. For a discussion of these themes, see H.V. Bowen, *The Business of Empire: The East India Company and Imperial Britain, 1756–1833* (Cambridge, 2006), pp. 29–35; Javier Cuenca Esteban, 'The British Balance of Payments, 1772–1820: India Transfers and War Finance', *Economic History Review* 54 (2001), pp. 56–86. For the importance of customs duties, which accounted for between 20 and 30% of state income in the late eighteenth century, see Patrick K. O'Brien, 'The Political

Economy of British Taxation, 1660–1815', *Economic History Review* New ser., 41, 1 (1988), pp. 22–8.

22. For the financial functions of the Company and their relationship to governance, see Bowen, *The Business of Empire*, pp. 84–117.

23. Philip Stern, ' "One Body Corporate and Politick": The Growth of the East India Company-State in the Later Seventeenth Century', PhD, Columbia University, 2004.

24. Bowen, *The Business of Empire*, pp. 41–3. The phrase comes from comments by Governor Thomas Pownall.

25. Travers, *Ideology and Empire*, p. 139

26. Ibid., p. 109.

27. J.G.A. Pocock, *The Ancient Constitution and the Feudal Law: A Study of English Historical Thought in the Seventeenth Century* (Cambridge, 1957); for an important revision, see Glenn Burgess, *The Politics of the Ancient Constitution: An Introduction to English Political Thought, 1603–1642* (Basingstoke, 1992).

28. Travers, *Ideology and Empire*, pp. 141–80.

29. Quoted in Robert Travers, 'Ideology and British Expansion in Bengal', *Journal of Imperial and Commonwealth History* 33, 1 (2005), p. 154. References by others to India or Bengal's 'ancient constitution' can be found in William Bolts, *Considerations on India Affairs* (London, 1772), p. 64; Charles Caraccioli, *The Life of Robert Lord Clive, Baron Plassey* (London, 1775), IV, p. 267.

30. Guha, *A Rule of Property*.

31. Hastings, *Memoirs Relative to the State of India*, p. 161.

32. Ibid., p. 68.

33. Hastings to Shelburne, 13 December 1782, quoted in Marshall, *Making and Unmaking of Empires*, p. 263.

34. Charles Wilkins, *The Bhagvat-Geeta, or Dialogues of Kreeshna and Arjoon: In Eighteen Lectures* (London, 1785), p. 13.

35. Travers, *Ideology and Empire*, pp. 119–25.

36. Warren Hastings, *The Present State of the East Indies* (London, 1786), p. 76.

37. Burke's Speech on the Opening of the Impeachment, 16 February 1788 in Langford *et al.* (eds), *The Writings and Speeches of Edmund Burke*, VI, p. 350.

38. Robert Travers, ' "The Real Value of the Lands": The *Nawabs*, the British and the Land Tax in Eighteenth-Century Bengal', *MAS* 38, 3 (2004), p. 548; Wilson, 'A Thousand Countries', pp. 81–110.

39. Travers, *Ideology and Empire*, p. 179.

40. Sutherland, *East India Company*, pp. 310–16. The alliance between Hastings and North was arranged by James MacPherson, a close friend of the philosopher Adam Ferguson, the 'translator' of Ossian, and kinsman and close political ally of the future acting Governor-General, John MacPherson. James MacPherson to Warren Hastings, 19 April 1780, Hastings papers, BL *Add Mss* 29145, f.37. MacPherson noted that 'a revolution very favourable to your interest had just happened in the management of affairs at Leadenhall street . . . You may remain as long as you please'.

41. Edmund Burke, 'Speech on the Bengal Judicature Bill', 27 June 1781 in Langford *et al.* (eds),*Writings and Speeches of Edmund Burke* II, pp. 390–400; 'Articles of Impeachment', Langford *et al.* (eds), *Writings and Speeches of Edmund Burke* VI, pp. 188–90; Richard Smith, 'Speech in Debate on India Affairs', 10 April 1782, William Cobbett (ed.), *The Parliamentary History of England* (London, 1806), 21, col. 1290; Philip Francis, 'Introduction' to Philip Francis, *Original Minutes of the Governor-General and Council of Fort William* (London, 1782).

42. John Cannon, *The Fox-North Coalition: Crisis of the Constitution, 1782–4* (Cambridge, 1969), pp. 111–12, 119.
43. Philip Harling, *The Waning of 'Old Corruption': The Politics of Economical Reform in Britain, 1779–1846* (Oxford, 1996), pp. 45–61.
44. 24 Geo III, *c.* 25, s. 39.
45. Mehta, *Liberalism and Empire*, pp. 170–1.
46. Letter from Court, 20 August 1784 and Letter to Court, 28 February 1785, *FW-IH*, vol. IX, Public series 1782–1785, pp. 166, 550.
47. Charles Stuart, Minute and Plan for the Management of Revenue, 10 May 1785, BRC, IOR P/50/58, f.309.
48. John Shore, Minute, 18 June 1789, *PP* 1812 (377), Appendix, p. 187.
49. J.V. Beckett, 'Land Tax or Excise: The Levying of Taxation in Seventeenth- and Eighteenth-Century England', *English Historical Review* 100 (1985), pp. 285–308.
50. For example, William Barlow to G.H. Barlow, 9 April 1789, BL *Mss Eur* F176/1, f.5, with its assumption that George III's return to mental health would consolidate Cornwallis' position in Calcutta.
51. Cornwallis to Ross, 23 February 1786, Charles Cornwallis and Charles Ross, *Correspondence of Charles, First Marquis Cornwallis* (London, 1859), I, p. 208.
52. Cornwallis to Charles Malet, Resident at Pune, 24 September 1786, Ibid., I, p. 222; Minute, 2 October 1786, Cornwallis and Ross, *Cornwallis Correspondence*, I, p. 224.
53. 'Heads of What the King of Prussia said to Lord Cornwallis', 17 September 1785, Cornwallis and Ross, *Cornwallis Correspondence*, I, pp. 201–3.
54. John Shore to G.G. Ducarel, 5 December 1784 and D. Killican to G.G. Ducarel, 31 January 1785, D2091/F14, nos 12, 18, Gloucestershire CRO.
55. For the relationship between Law and the young Barlow, see William Barlow to G.H. Barlow, 14 August 1782, *Mss Eur* F176/1, f.17.
56. For a discussion of Thomas Law, see Guha, *A Rule of Property*, pp. 185–201.
57. Barlow to Cornwallis, 14 July 1796, PRO 30/11/136, f.13.
58. William Barlow to G.H. Barlow, 10 September 1786, *Mss Eur* F176/1, f.2.
59. Barlow to Cornwallis, 11 February 1795, PRO 30/11/136, f.1; Barlow to Cornwallis, 14 January 1794, IOR Pos 4211, n.p.
60. Barlow to Cornwallis, 14 July 1796, PRO 30/11/136, f.17.
61. Barlow to Cornwallis, 14 January 1794, IOR Pos 4211, n.p.
62. Lord Cornwallis, Minute, 3 February 1790, *PP*, 1812 (377), Appendix, p. 486.
63. Regulation I, 1793 printed in *PP*, 1812 (377), Appendix, p. 738.
64. J. Anstruther's Opinion on Lord Cornwallis' Judicial Regulations of 1793, IOR H/414, pp. 57–78. Also 'Plan for a Bill Declaratory of the King's Sovereignty over the British Territories and Possessions in India', IOR H/414, pp. 70–106.
65. Barlow to Cornwallis, 14 January 1794, IOR Pos 4211, n.p.
66. John Shore, Minute, 14 June 1789, *PP*, 1812 (377), Appendix, p. 205.
67. Barlow to Cornwallis, 14 January 1794, IOR Pos 4211.
68. For these two arguments, see Asli Çirakman, 'From Tyranny to Despotism: The Enlightenment's Unenlightened Image of the Turks', *International Journal of Middle Eastern Studies* 33 (2001), pp. 49–58; Joan Pau Rubiés, 'Oriental Despotism and European Orientalism: Botero to Montesquieu'. *The Journal of Early Modern History: Contacts, Comparisons, Contrasts* 9, 1–2 (2005), pp. 108–80.
69. Sanjay Subrahmanyam, 'Frank Submissions: The Company and the Mughals between Sir Thomas Roe and Sir William Norris' in H.V. Bowen *et al.* (eds), *The Worlds of the East India Company* (Woodbridge, 2006), p. 95.
70. Quoted in Travers, *Ideology and Empire*, p. 63.

71. Charles William Boughton Rouse, *Dissertation Concerning the Landed Property of Bengal* (Calcutta, 1791).

72. Travers, 'Ideology and British Expansion in Bengal', p. 18.

73. Hastings, *Memoirs Relative to the State of India.*

74. John Shore, 'Remarks on the Mode of Administering Justice to the Natives of Bengal', 18 May 1785, IOR P/50/58, 382, 387ff.

75. David Hume tried to domesticate despotism, or at least its less pejorative cousin 'absolutism' to describe aspects of government that occurred in legitimate, functioning state. Even Hume though was sceptical of the long-term moral consequences of absolute rule. See Duncan Forbes, *Hume's Philosophical Politics* (Cambridge, 1975).

76. John Shore to his mother, 26 April 1772, Teignmouth, *Life and Correspondence*, I, p. 38.

77. John Shore to Mrs. Shore, 28 May 1772, Ibid., I, p. 41.

78. Charles Grant, 'Observations on the State of Society amongst the Asiatic Subjects of Great Britain', (1792) printed in *PP* 1831–1832 (735-VI), p. 121.

79. Charles Grant to G.G. Ducarel, 7 March 1788, Ducarel Papers, Gloucestershire CRO, D2091/F14, no.31.

80. Edward Strachey, journal, *Mss Eur* F128/206, 18 May 1805, f.4.

81. Courtney Smith to Robert Smith, 1 August 1818, *Mss Eur* C247, f.42.

82. For an account of E.M. Forster's discussion of the impossibility of experiential knowledge about India, see Javed Majeed, 'Bathos, Architecture and Knowing India: E.M. Forster's *A Passage to India* and Nineteenth-Century British Ethnology and the Romance Quest', *Journal of Commonwealth Literature* 40, 1 (2005), pp. 21–36.

83. Percival Spear, *The Nabobs: A Study of the Social Life of the English in Eighteenth Century India* (London; New York, 1932); Michael Edwardes, *The Nabobs at Home* (London, 1991).

84. 'Warren Hastings', Thomas Babington Macaulay, *Critical and Historical Essays: Contributed to the Edinburgh Review* (London, 1860), III, p. 222.

85. Margot Finn, 'Colonial Gifts: Family Politics and the Exchange of Goods in British India, c.1780–1820', *MAS* 40, 1 (2006), pp. 220, 227; Correspondence between William and G.H. Barlow, 1782–1789, *Mss Eur* 176/1, and Finn, 'Colonial Gifts'.

86. Shore to Jones, 16 August 1787, Garland Cannon (ed.), *The Letters of William Jones* (Oxford, 1970), p. 762. For details of Radhakanta's career, see Rosane Rocher, 'The Career of Radhakanta Tarkavisaga, an Eighteenth-Century Pandit in British Employ', *Journal of the American Oriental Society* 109, 4 (1989), pp. 627–33.

87. James Collie to G.G. Ducarel, 12 February 1788, D2091/F14, no.29, Gloucestershire CRO.

88. Rouse, *Dissertation Concerning the Landed Property of Bengal*, p. 170.

89. P.J. Marshall, 'Indian Officials under the East India Company in Eighteenth-Century Bengal', *Bengal Past and Present* 84 (1965), pp. 115–16.

90. Abu Al-Fazl, *The A'in-I Akbari* (Calcutta, 1927), II, pp. 50–1. Abul Al-Fazl saw the officer working alongside another official termed *bitikchi* (accountant), but this function seems to have been swallowed into the *qanungu's* role in Bengal. Irfan Habib, *The Agrarian System of Mughal India* (New Delhi, 2000), pp. 272, 331–4.

91. Regulation XXI, 1793.

92. BJC, 11 February 1793, IOR P/52/55, f.194.

93. Keith Tribe, *Land, Labour and Economic Discourse* (London, 1978).

94. BJC, 11 February 1793, f.194. In his defence of Cornwallis' proposals, Charles Stuart used an almost identical phrase, arguing that the security of property

and permanent settlement would unleash 'the spirit of improvement which consideration of self-interest ought universally to excite', IOR H/384b/10., f.132.

95. Adam Smith, *An Inquiry into the Nature and Causes of the Wealth of Nations* (Oxford, 1976), part IV.v.b.43 (II, 540).
96. For example, Smith to Ross, 13 December 1786 and 13 June 1787, Adam Smith, *The Correspondence of Adam Smith* (Oxford, 1977), pp. 299, 303.
97. Adam Smith, *The Theory of Moral Sentiments* (Oxford, 1976), I, pp. iii, 2.
98. Stokes, *The English Utilitarians*, p. 58.
99. G.H. Barlow to Cornwallis, 10 July 1796, PRO/30/11/136, f.13; also Shore to Dundas, 10 January 1797, Holder Furber (ed.), *The Private Record of an Indian Governor-Generalship. The Correspondence of John Shore with Henry Dundas, 1793–1798* (Cambridge MA, 1933), p. 116. In 1820, John Malcolm suggested he was reluctant to stay in India unless charged with 'the introduction of [a] new system'. Burton Stein, *Thomas Munro. The Origins of the Colonial State and His Vision of Empire* (Delhi, 1989), p. 279.
100. Smith, *The Theory of Moral Sentiments*, VI, pp. ii, 2.
101. David Hume, *A Treatise of Human Nature* (Oxford, 1978), IV, p. vi.
102. Reinhart Koselleck, *Critique and Crisis: Enlightenment and the Pathogenesis of Modern Society* (Cambridge, MA, 1988), p. 127.
103. See John Shore's discussion of the Company's precarious finances in his letter to Henry Dundas, 10 January 1797, Furber (ed.), *Shore-Dundas Correspondence*, p. 113. Also J.R. Ward, 'The Industrial Revolution and British Imperialism, 1750–1850', *The Economic History Review* 47, 1 (1994), pp. 44–65; Anthony Webster, 'An Early Global Business in a Colonial Context: The Strategies, Management, and Failure of John Palmer and Company of Calcutta, 1780–1830', *Enterprise and Society* 6, 1 (2005), pp. 98–133.
104. Amales Tripathi, *Trade and Finance in the Bengal Presidency, 1793–1833* (Calcutta, 1979), pp. 4–7, 162–4; Douglas M. Peers, 'War and Public Finance in Early Nineteenth-Century British India: The First Burma War', *International History Review* 11 (1989), p. 645.
105. Reinhart Koselleck, *Futures Past: On the Semantics of Historical Time* (Cambridge, MA, 1985), pp. 259–63.

4 Colonial indecision and the origins of the Hindu Joint Family

1. John Shore to Bury Hutchinson, 20 October 1773, Charles John Shore Teignmouth, *Memoir of the Life and Correspondence of John, Lord Teignmouth* (London, 1843), I, p. 49.
2. Daniel J. Hulsebosch, 'Writs to Rights. "Navigability" and the Transformation of the Common Law in the Nineteenth Century', *Cardozo Law Review* 23, 3 (2002), p. 1053; also Michael Lobban, *The Common Law and English Jurisprudence, 1760–1850* (Oxford, 1991).
3. James Mill, *The History of British India* (London, 1826) V, p. 141. See Chapter 6 below for a more detailed discussion of this passage.
4. Richard W. Lariviere, 'Justices and Panditas: Some Ironies in Contemporary Readings of the Hindu Legal Past', *Journal of Asian Studies* 48, 4 (1989), p. 759.
5. 'Plan for the Administration of Justice' (1771), G.W. Forrest, *Selections from the State Papers of the Governors-General of India: Warren Hastings* (Oxford, 1910), II, p. 290; G.R. Gleig, *Memoirs of the Life of the Right Hon. Warren Hastings* (London, 1841), pp. 399–404.

6. For accounts of these debates, see J.D.M. Derrett, *Religion, Law and the State in India* (London, 1968); P.J. Marshall, *British Discovery of Hinduism in the Eighteenth Century* (Cambridge, 1970), pp. 9–11; Werner Menski, *Hindu Law. Beyond Tradition and Modernity* (New Delhi, 2003); Rosane Rocher, *Orientalism, Poetry, and the Millennium: The Checkered Life of Nathaniel Brassey Halhed, 1751–1830* (Delhi, 1983). For a discussion of the relationship between theology and nationality in Britain, see Colin Kidd, *British Identities Before Nationalism. Ethnicity and Nationhood in the Atlantic World, 1600–1800* (Cambridge University Press, 1999).
7. Jones to Cornwallis, 19 March 1788, Garland Cannon (ed.), *The Letters of William Jones* (Oxford, 1970) II, p. 795.
8. William Jones to Lord Cornwallis, 19 March 1788, Ibid., II, pp. 795–6.
9. T.E. Colebrooke (ed.), *Miscellaneous Essays [of H.T. Colebrooke], with Life of the Author* (London, 1873), p. 12.
10. H.T. Colebrooke (ed.), *A Digest of Hindu Law on Contracts and Successions, with a Commentary* (Calcutta, 1798).
11. Rosane Rocher, 'British Orientalism in the Eighteenth Century: The Dialectics of Knowledge and Government' in Carol Breckenbridge *et al.* (eds), *Orientalism and the Postcolonial Predicament* (Philadelphia, 1993); Rosane Rocher, 'Weaving Knowledge: William Jones and the *Pandits*' in Garland Cannon *et al.* (eds), *Objects of Inquiry: The Life, Contribution and Influence of Sir William Jones (1746–1794)* (New York, 1995), pp. 63–70; Ludo Rocher, *Jimutavahana's Dayabhaga. The Hindu Law of Inheritance in Bengal* (New York, NY, 2002).
12. Jones to Viscount Althorp, 21 November 1777, Cannon (ed.), *Letters of William Jones*, p. 333.
13. Henry Maine, *Ancient Law* (Tucson, AZ, 1986 reprint of 1864 edition), p. 12.
14. Jones to Thomas Yeates, 7 June 1782, Cannon (ed.), *Letters of William Jones*, II, p. 553.
15. William Jones, Memorandum, *Add Mss* 8889, ff. 2–5.
16. H.T. Colebrooke (ed.), *A Digest of Hindu Law on Contracts and Successions, with a Commentary* (London, 1801), III, p. 276. Colebrooke drew a similar distinction elsewhere – for example, in commenting on Jagannatha's discussion of the ceremonies performed after death, he notes the difference between *mithila* and *gaudiya* practice, where Jagannatha had identified none. Colebrooke (ed.), *A Digest of Hindu Law on Contracts and Successions, with a Commentary*, III, p. 460.
17. David Lieberman, *The Province of Legislation Determined: Legal Theory in Eighteenth-Century Britain* (Cambridge, 1989), pp. 113–15; James Oldham, *The Mansfield Manuscripts and the Growth of English Law in the Eighteenth Century* (Chapel Hill, NC, 1992), pp. I, 91–9, 242–9.
18. H.T. Colebrooke (ed.), *Two Treatises on the Hindu Law of Inheritance* (Calcutta, 1810), p. v.
19. Lariviere, 'Justices and Panditas', p. 760.
20. Pandurang Vaman Kane, *History of Dharmasastra: Ancient and Medieval Religious and Civil Law in India* (Poona, 1968), III, pp. 304–7.
21. Colebrooke (ed.), *Digest of Hindu Law* , I, p. 68, see also I, p. 381.
22. Krishna Kamal Bhattacharyya, *The Law Relating to the Joint Hindu Family* (Calcutta, 1885).
23. S. Chandrasekhar, 'The Hindu Joint Family', *Social Forces* 21, 3 (1943), p. 327.
24. Colebrooke (ed.), *A Digest of Hindu Law on Contracts and Successions, with a Commentary*, III, pp. 109–10.
25. Plaint filed, 27 March 1793, Bimala vs Gokul Nath Roy, SDA, 21 August 1799, no.2. IOR P/154/8.

26. Proceedings of the Rangpur court dated, 24 September 1793, SDA, 21 August 1799, no.2. IOR P/154/8.
27. Decree, 30 December 1794, SDA, 21 August 1799, no.2. IOR P/154/8.
28. For the first argument, see Nicholas B. Dirks, 'From Little King to Landlord. Property, Law and the Gift under the Madras Permanent Settlement', *CSSH* 28, 2 (1986); for the second, Lariviere, 'Justices and Panditas'.
29. 'Proceedings of the Cause', 9 November 1793, SDA 5 June 1794, IOR P/152/45.
30. D. Vanderheyden to SDA, n.d., SDA 5 June 1794, IOR P/152/45. For a successful instance of arbitration in Chandradwip, see 'Petition of Budder-ud-deen Khan *et al.*', SDA 24 July 1794, no.69, P/152/46.
31. John Champlain, Judge 24 Parganas to George Barlow, Register to Sudder Dewanny Adawlut, 6 March 1794, SDA, 10 April 1794, no.1, IOR P/152/44.
32. Alexander Fraser Tytler, *Considerations on the Present Political State of India* (London, 1815), II, p. 198. Elphinstone to Edward Strachey, 3 September 1820, *Mss Eur* F128/166; 'Minute of Governor of Bombay', July 1823 in Thomas Edward Colebrooke, *Life of the Honourable Mountstuart Elphinstone* (London, 1884), II, p. 115.
33. David Kopf, *British Orientalism and the Bengal Renaissance: The Dynamics of Indian Modernization 1773–1835* (Berkeley, 1969).
34. Colebrooke (ed.), *Two Treatises*, pp. iii–v.
35. Bernard S. Cohn, 'Anthropological Notes on Law and Disputes in India', *American Anthropologist* 67, 6 (1965), pp. 111–12; a similar statement can be found in Bernard S. Cohn, 'Law and the State in Colonial India' in *Colonialism and Its Forms of Knowledge* (Princeton, NJ, 1996), p. 69.
36. Michael S. Dodson, *Orientalism, Empire and National Culture. India, 1770–1880* (Basingstoke, 2007), p. 39.
37. Minute of Governor of Bombay, July 1823, Colebrooke, *Elphinstone*, p. 113.
38. Ibid., II, p. 115.
39. Ross Harrison, *Bentham* (London, 1983); Gerald J. Postema, *Bentham and the Common Law Tradition* (Oxford, 1986).
40. MacNaghten, *Considerations on the Hindoo Law*, pp. vi, xiv, xv.
41. William Hay MacNaghten, *Principles and Precedents of Hindu Law* (Calcutta, 1828), pp. i, v.
42. MacNaghten to W. Leycester, 1 August 1822, Board's Collections, IOR F/4/899, pp. 5–16.
43. H.T. Prinsep to W.H. MacNaghten, 27 August 1922, Board's Collections, ibid., p. 20.
44. MacNaghten, *Principles of Hindu Law*, I, pp. vi–vii.
45. William Hay MacNaghten, *Reports of Cases Determined in the Court of Sudder Dewanny Adawlut* (Calcutta, 1827), 'Advertisement'.
46. Katherine Prior, *MacNaghten, Sir William Hay, Baronet (1793–1841)*, http://www.oxforddnb.com/view/article/17705.
47. Rupert Cross and J.W. Harris, *Precedent in English Law* (Oxford, 1991), pp. 3–10.
48. Lobban, *Common Law*, pp. 258–9; John James Park, *A Contre-Projet to the Humphreysian Code* (London, 1828).
49. MacNaghten, *Principles of Hindu Law*.
50. 'Ramrutin Sing &ca. vs Chunder Naraen Rai', 29 September 1792, 'Mohun Sing vs Chumun Rai', 20 November 1799; 'Duttnaraen Sing vs Ajeet Sing &ca.', 14 February 1799; MacNaghten, *Reports of Cases in Sudder Dewanny Adawlut* all indexed at I, p. 376.
51. Thomas Macaulay to Lord Auckland, 14 October 1837, with Penal Code, 1837–1838 (673), pp. 7–9.

52. Jai Ram Dhami *et al.* vs Musan Dhami, MacNaghten, *Reports of Cases in Sudder Dewanny Adawlut* , V, pp. 3–10.
53. Ibid., V, p. 6.
54. Ibid.
55. John Adams, Acting Governor-General, Minute, 22 May 1823, Board's Collections, IOR F/109/27, no.2; also Extract from Judicial Letter to CoD from Bengal, 10 April 1823, Board's Collections, IOR F/4/899, no.2.
56. Judges of SDA to Lord Hastings, Governor-General in Council, 11 November 1822, Board's Collections, IOR F/4/899.
57. H.T. Prinsep to W.H. MacNaghten, 27 August 1822, Board's Collections, IOR F/4/899, p. 18.
58. D.A. Washbrook, 'Law State and Agrarian Society in colonial India', 15, 3 (1981), pp. 649–721.
59. John Cochrane, *A Defence of the Daya-Bhaga* (London, 1872), pp. 5–35.
60. William B. Bayley, Evidence Before Select Committee on the Affairs of the East India Company, *PP*, 1831–1832 (735–IV), p. 4011.
61. Perhaps the most significant debate occurred over the question of whether a father in Bengal could dispose of his property without consulting his male sons, an issue that came to a head in the famous Tagore will case. See Cochrane, *Defence of the Daya-Bhaga*. This question will be discussed in more detail in Chapter 7.
62. Herbert Cowell, *The Hindu Law, Being a Treatise on the Law Administered Exclusively to Hindus in the British Courts in India* (Calcutta, 1870–1871); John D. Mayne, *A Treatise on Hindu Law and Usage* (Madras, 1878); H.D. Cornish, *A Short Manual of Hindu Law* (London, 1937).
63. For the new Bengali interest in texts such as the *Dayabhaga* and *Mitaksara*, see Jogendra Nath Bhattacharya, *A Commentary on the Hindu Law of Inheritance* (Calcutta, 1885).
64. Debate about Hindu law by less reflexive commentators continued to be rooted in this ambivalence after 1956. See, for example, Derrett, *Religion, Law and the State in India*.
65. MacNaghten, *Principles of Hindu Law*, p. iv.

5   Governing the power of proprietors

1. Thomas Brooke to SDA, 2 May 1794, *Sudder Dewanny Adawlut Proceedings*, 5 June 1794, IOR P/152/45.
2. Henry Maine, *Ancient Law* (Tucson, AZ, 1864); E.P. Thompson, *Customs in Common* (London, 1993); Peter Robb, *Ancient Rights and Future Comfort: Bihar, the Bengal Tenancy Act of 1885, and British Rule in India* (Richmond, Surrey, 1997).
3. David Scott, 'Colonial Governmentality', *Social Text* 43 (1995), pp. 191–220.
4. Henry Strachey, 'Answers to Interrogatories Received by Judge and Magistrate of Midnapore', in W.K. Firminger (ed.), *The Fifth Report on the Affairs of the East India Company, 1812* (Calcutta: R. Cambray, 1917), II, p. 610.
5. For arguments about these various influences, see Guha, *A Rule of Property*; Jon E. Wilson, 'Governing Property, Making Law: Land, Local Society & Colonial Discourse in Agrarian Bengal, C.1785–1830' (University of Oxford, 2000); Sudipta Sen, *Empire of Free Trade: The East India Company and the Making of the Colonial Marketplace* (Philadelphia, PA, 1998); Sudipta Sen, *Distant Sovereignty: National Imperialism and the Origins of British India* (New York, 2002); Chittaranjan Sinha, 'Doctrinal Influences on the Judicial Policy of the East India Company's Administration in Bengal, 1772–1833', *Historical Journal* 12, 2 (1969).

6. Guha, *A Rule of Property*, p. 175.
7. John Mackenzie, Minute on Mr. Law's Settlement Plans, 25 February 1789, Bengal Revenue Consultations, (BRC) IOR P/51/32, f.812.
8. Thomas Law, *A Sketch of Some Late Arrangements, and a View of the Rising Resources, in Bengal* (London, 1792); George Francis Grand, *Summary Remarks on the Resources of the East Indies . . . Intended as a Contrast to the Pamphlet of Mr. Thomas Law, Entitled 'Rising Resources'* (London, 1792); Thomas Erskine, *Resolutions of the First Meeting of the Friends to the Liberty to the Press, to Which is Added a Letter by Thomas Law* (London, 1793), p. 22. Law continued to argue that he was the author of the permanent settlement after his migration to America in Thomas Law, *Remarks on the Ryotwaree and Mocurrey Systems* (London, 1820).
9. CoD to Governor-General in Council, April 1786.
10. John Prinsep, *Strictures and Observations on the Mocurrey System of Landed Property in Bengal* (London, 1794), p. vi.
11. H.T. Colebrooke, *Remarks on the Husbandry and Internal Commerce of Bengal* (Calcutta, 1804), p. 69.
12. Samuel Davies, 'Rights of Zemindars and Ryots', 4 March 1816, IOR H/530, p. 344.
13. Regulation XLIV, 1793; see Robb, *Ancient Rights and Future Comfort: Bihar, the Bengal Tenancy Act of 1885, and British Rule in India*, p. 124 for comments on the later colonial discussion of this text.
14. For the role of record-keeper in Dhaka collectorate office, see Massie to Board of Revenue, 23 February 1797 and 31 June 1797, NAB Dhaka DR, vol. 132, pp. 48, 140.
15. Massie to Board of Revenue, 28 July 1800, NAB, Dhaka DR, vol. 136, p. 79.
16. Alexander Wright, Collector of Rangpur to Board of Revenue, 11 August 1797, NAB, Rangpur DR, vol. 297, p. 87; Massie, Collector of Dhaka to Board of Revenue, 3 July 1798, NAB Dhaka DR, vol. 133, p. 238.
17. John R. Mclane, *Land and Local Kingship in 18th Century Bengal* (Cambridge, 1993), especially the narrative account of colonial relations with the estate pp. 251–87.
18. C. D'Oyly, Collector of Dhaka to Board of Revenue, 24 September 1810, NAB Dhaka DR, vol. 150, p. 270.
19. J.C. Jack, *Final Report of the Survey and Settlement Operations in the Bakarganj District* (Calcutta, 1915), p. 96. One *anna* was worth 1/20th of a Rupee.
20. Such accounts existed both for estates where the British had a significant interest, such as those managed by the court of wards, and for the district as a whole. See *Jama Wasil Baki* of Idrakpur and Ghoraghat, NAB Rangpur DR, vol. 290, pp. 124–36; 'Account of the Settlement Made with Zemindars for Ten Years', enclosed with Charles Purling, Collector of Rangpur to Board of Revenue, 11 July 1790, NAB Rangpur DR, vols 288, 93.
21. W. Massie, Collector of Dhaka to Board of Revenue, 30 April 1798, NAB Dhaka DR, vol. 133, p. 124.
22. Gilbert Stuart, *An Historical Dissertation Concerning the Antiquity of the English Constitution* (London, 1770), p. 127. John Millar, *Observations Concerning the Distinction of Ranks in Society* (London, 1771) offered historical accounts of the division of ranks. Works such as Thomas Gisborne, *An Enquiry into the Duties of Men in the Higher and Middle Classes of Society in Great Britain* (London, 1794) described the duties of each rank. Perspectives of late-eighteenth-century and nineteenth-century British ideas on rank and hierarchy are provided by Dror Wahrman, *Imagining the Middle Class: The Political Representation of Class in Britain, c.1780–1840* (Cambridge, 1995) and David Cannadine, *Class in Britain* (New Haven, CT, 1998).

23. For the absence of records relating to change of ownership and the difficulty of compiling the Quinquennial register, see E. Moore, Collector of Dhaka to Board of Revenue, 22 February 1799, NAB, Dhaka DR, vol. 134, p. 57. For uncertainty surrounding the shifting relationship between *zamindars* who paid revenue to the Company and local gentry (*taluqdars*) who did not, Moore to Board of Revenue, 22 July 1799, Ibid., pp. 341–3.
24. John Shore, 'Minute on the Rights of Zamindars and Talookdars', in Walter Kelly Firminger (ed.), *The Fifth Report from the Select Committee on the Affairs of the East India Company* (Calcutta: R. Cambray, 1917), II, p. 56.
25. Muzaffar Alam and Sanjay Subrahmanyam, *The Mughal State, 1526–1750* (Delhi, 1998).
26. Regulation VIII, 1793.
27. Letters from Collectors of Midnapore, Mymemsingh and Bihar, Board of Revenue, 12 June 1793, IOR P/72/17; Rajshahi, Ramghar and Rangpur, Board of Revenue, 27 March 1794, IOR P/128/10.
28. A. Seton, Collector Bihar to Board of Revenue, 6 January 1793, Board of Revenue, 12 June 1793, no.17, IOR P/72/17.
29. James Graham, Collector Rangpur to Board of Revenue, 30 March 1792; NAB Rangpur DR, vols 292, 76; Alexander Wright, 5 March 1798, with encl. Translation of a Petition delivered in by the Zemindars, Talookdars and other landholders of Rangopur *zila*, NAB Rangpur DR, vol. 298, p. 29; Ranajit Sen, 'A Note on Land-Resumption in Bengal in the Second Half of the 18 Century', *Quarterly Review of Historical Studies* (1986), pp. 25, 3, 4.
30. See, for example, James Graham, Collector Rangpur to Board of Revenue, 26 July 1794 with enclosed Translation of a *patta* granted to 'Chamaroo Mauljadd', 20 Bhadun 1174, Translation of a *patta* granted to Joypur Kasbi, NAB Rangpur DR, vols 294, 120–3; Petition from the *zamindars* of Kundi, Fakir Kundi &ca., enclosed with James Lumisden, 17 January 1792, NAB Rangpur DR, vol. 290, p. 66.
31. Samuel Davies, 'Rights of Zemindars and Ryots', p. 349.
32. Amiya Kumar Bagchi, *The Evolution of the State Bank of India: The Roots, 1806–1876* (Bombay, 1987); J.R. Ward, 'The Industrial Revolution and British Imperialism', pp. 44–65.
33. 'Exposition of East India Company's Finances at Home and Abroad', *PP*, 1810 (290), p. 6.
34. For a comprehensive discussion of sales, see Islam, *The Permanent Settlement in Bengal*.
35. Petition enclosed with Alexander Wright, Collector of Rangpur to Board of Revenue, 5 March 1798, NAB Dhaka DR, vol. 298, pp. 29–47.
36. Wright to Board of Revenue, 19 April 1798, 18 May 1798, 7 January 1799, NAB Dhaka DR, vol. 298, pp. 58, 83, vol. 299, p. 3; 'Account Sale of Land Sold for Arrears of Revenue', Rangpur, 1795–1815, WBSA, Board of Revenue, Misc. Records, vol. 493.
37. Islam, *The Permanent Settlement in Bengal*; Ratnalekha Ray, *Change in Agrarian Bengal* (1979), pp. 275–83.
38. Sugata Bose, *Peasant Labour and Colonial Capital: Rural Bengal Since 1770* (Cambridge, 1993), p. 117.
39. See Ratnalekha Ray's discussion of the process by which the new purchasers of Surul consolidated their authority after 1799. Two Bishnupur style *mathas* (temples) had been constructed in Surul by 1831, one dedicated to Siva, the other Vishnu. The family also lent money to their tenants, maintained a school in the village and arbitrated local disputes. Ray, *Change in Agrarian Bengal*, p. 112.

40. For instances of litigation between the two, see William Armstrong, Collector of Dhaka to J.D. Paterson, Judge of Dhaka, Letters of 23, 25 and 26 June 1795, NAB Dhaka DR, vol. 130, pp. 56–60; William Massie, Collector of Dhaka to Board of Revenue, n.d. [September 1798], NAB Dhaka DR, vol. 133, p. 317.
41. *Zebanbandi* of Mahommed Fakhir Chaprasi, with E. Moore, Collector Dhaka to Samuel Middleton, Judge Bakarganj, 29 August 1799, NAB Dhaka, vol. 134, pp. 409–11. See also the numerous *arzis* of Lala Rama Bakshi, *kharach amin* of *pargana* Chandradvip, for example, enclosed with William Massie to Board of Revenue, 22 September 1800, vol. 136, pp. 261–2; *arzis* of Mirza Gholas Ali, government pleader, with William Massie to Board of Revenue, 16 April 1804, ibid., vol. 136, p. 323 and with Massie to Board of Revenue, 14 January 1801, ibid., vol. 137, pp. 59–60.
42. See also letters from Alexander Wright to Board of Revenue, 30 September 1796 and 4 August 1798, NAB, Rangpur DR, vol. 296 p. 196; vol. 298, p. 113.
43. Alexander Wright, Collector Rangpur to James Wordsworth, Judge Rangpur, 13 January 1796 and 15 June 1796, NAB Rangpur DR, vol. 296, pp. 31, 147; Proceedings of the SDA, 27 June 1799, no.35, IOR P/154/6; Enclosures with C. D'Oyly, Collector of Dhaka to Board of Revenue, 31 January 1810, NAB Dhaka DR, vol. 150, pp. 32–9. J.A. Vas, *Rangpur: East Bengal and Assam District Gazetteers* (Allahabad, 1911), p. 112 discusses the *upanchauki* tenure that was the focus of the controversy, and Wilson, 'Governing Property, Making Law'.
44. Kali Narayan (appellant) versus Ram Rudr Chaudhuri (respondent), Translation of decision of Murshidabad Court of Appeal, 13 June 1800, NAB Rangpur DR, vol. 302, pp. 48–9.
45. Strachey, 'Answers to Interrogatories', II, p. 610.
46. Mclane, *Land and Local Kingship in 18th Century Bengal*, p. 264.
47. Regulation VII, 'A Regulation for Enabling Proprietors and Farmers of Land to Realize Their Rents with Greater Punctuality; for Providing against Unnecessary Delay in the Payment of the Public Revenue Assessed upon Lands', passed 29 August 1799; Regulation V, 1812, 'A Regulation for Amending Some of the Rules at Present in Force for the Collection of the Land Revenue', passed 1 May 1812.
48. VII, 1799, s. 1.
49. Mclane, *Land and Local Kingship in 18th Century Bengal*, pp. 287–305 and Shinkichu Taniguchi, 'The Patni System – A Modern Origin of the "Sub-Infeudation" of Bengal in the Nineteenth Century', *Hitotsubashi Journal of Economics* (1981).
50. These details are all contained within H.T. Prinsep, Memorandum, 12 July 1819, Bengal Judicial Consultations (BJC) (Civil, Lower Provinces), 8 October 1819, no.36, IOR P/149/67.
51. For an account of the re-emergence of custom in the discussion of the 1885 Tenant Bill for Bihar and Bengal, see Robb, *Ancient Rights and Future Comfort: Bihar, the Bengal Tenancy Act of 1885, and British Rule in India*, pp. 123–8.
52. Mclane, *Land and Local Kingship in 18th Century Bengal*, p. 301. The regulation became VIII, 1819.
53. Ibid., pp. 267–9.
54. See the correspondence relating to the Burdwan estate in the Ducarel papers, Gloucestershire County Record Office.
55. Samuel Davies, 'Rights of Zemindars and Ryots', p. 343.
56. For example, *Bhumadhikari Sabha, Britrantra* (Kalikata, 1838) [Rules of the Landowners' Society]. The Hinduisation of the landholder can also be traced in Bhabanicharan Bandopadhyay's writings, for example, Bhabanicharan Bandopadhyay, *Kalikata Kamalalay* (Calcutta, 1823).

57. In particular Grand, *Summary Remarks*.
58. Burton Stein, *Thomas Munro. The Origins of the Colonial State and His Vision of Empire* (Delhi, 1989); Eric Stokes, *The English Utilitarians and India* (Oxford, 1959).
59. D.A. Washbrook, 'South India 1770–1840: The Colonial Transition', *Modern Asian Studies* 38, 3 (2004), p. 491.
60. For different arguments about the degree to which Munro's system was a peculiarly southern phenomenon, or a response to events in Bengal, see Burton Stein, *The Making of Agrarian Policy in British India, 1770–1900* (Delhi, 1992) and Washbrook, 'South India 1770–1840: The Colonial Transition'.
61. Thomas Munro, 'Memo on Rayotwar and Village Settlements', *Mss Eur* F/151/125, f.5; Stein, *Thomas Munro*, pp. 123–4.
62. Thomas Munro to William Bentinck, 17 July 1804, Wellesley Papers, BL *Add Mss* 13678, f.73.
63. Fifth Report of the Select Committee on Affairs of East India Company, 181 (377).
64. 'Memoir of James Cumming', *The Asiatic Journal* 24, 140 (1827), pp. 1–168.
65. Stein, *Thomas Munro*, p. 319.
66. Calcutta Finance Committee to Governor-General in Council, 12 July 1830, quoted again in 'Report from the Select Committee', *PP*, 1831–1832 (735-III), p. 63 and Appendix 1, p. 208.
67. J.H. Harington, 'Regulation Proposed for Securing the Rights of *Khodkhast, Chupperbund* and Other Resident Ryots', *PP*, 1831–1832 (735-III), Appendix 21, pp. 117–26.
68. W. Leycester, Minute, 6 March 1827, Ibid., p. 123.
69. Alexander Ross, Minute, 22 March 1827, Ibid., p. 125.
70. Chitta Panda, *The Decline of the Bengal Zamindars, 1870–1920* (Delhi, 1997); Ray, *Change in Agrarian Bengal*.
71. Magniac to Board of Revenue, 24 March 1825, NAB Dhaka DR, vol. 164, p. 21; for a similar complaint relating to the settlement of land occupied after the first Anglo-Nepalese war, see Nathaniel Smith to Board of Revenue, 20 February 1827, NAB Rangpur DR, vol. 321, p. 78.
72. Carl Schmitt, *Political Theology: Four Chapters on the Concept of Sovereignty* (Cambridge, MA, 1985), p. 19.

6   The state as machine and the ambivalent origins of colonial utilitarianism

1. Charles Grant to Lord Bentinck, 25 December 1833, Bentinck Papers, Nottingham University Library.
2. Bentinck to Charles Grant, 3 May 1831, C.H. Philips (ed.), *The Correspondence of Lord William Cavendish Bentinck, Governor-General of India, 1828–1835* (Oxford, 1977), p. 311.
3. Eric Stokes, *The English Utilitarians and India* (Oxford, 1959), p. 94.
4. Holt Mackenzie, Minute, 1 October 1830, East India Select Committee Report, *PP*, 1831–1832 (735), III, General Appendix, pp. 136–7.
5. James Mill, *The History of British India*, edited and with comments by H.H. Wilson, 10 vols (5th edn, London, 1858), I, pp. xi, xiii.
6. For a sketch of the importance of such a bureaucratic state in Bentham's work, see Leonard Hume, *Bentham and Bureaucracy* (Cambridge, 1981).
7. Mill, *History*, I, p. xii. See Javed Majeed, *Ungoverned Imaginings* (Oxford, 1992) for a discussion of these themes.

8. Mill, *History*, I, p. xxi.
9. Said, *Orientalism*, pp. 176–7.
10. William Tennant, *Indian Recreations. Consisting of Thoughts and Strictures on the Effects of the British Government on the State of India* (Edinburgh, 1808); Francis Hamilton, *A Journey from Madras Through the Countries of Mysore, Canara, and Malabar* (London, 1807); Alexander Fraser Tytler, *Considerations on the Present Political State of India* (London, 1815); William Ward, *A View of the History, Literature, and Religion of the Hindoos: Including a Minute Description of Their Manners and Customs, and Translations from Their Principal Works* (Serampore, 1815).
11. Tennant, *Indian Recreations*, III, p. 67; Robert Patton, *The Effects of Property Upon Society and Government Investigated* (London, 1797) also articulated this new interest in despotism.
12. Tennant, *Indian Recreations*, III, p. 255; Tytler, *Considerations*, I, p. 222.
13. Mill, *History*, II, p. 51.
14. Tennant, *Indian Recreations*, III, pp. 105, 81–2.
15. Tytler, *Considerations*, p. 192. Compare with Stokes, *English Utilitarians*, pp. 14–25, who argued that colonial utilitarianism and the kind of paternalism articulated here had common roots. For the influence of such ideas in the 'Punjab School' later in the nineteenth century, see Stokes, *English Utilitarians*, pp. 245–8; Clive Dewey, *Anglo-Indian Attitudes: The Mind of the Indian Civil Service* (London, 1993), pp. 43, 219.
16. Mill, *History*, pp. 1, 176.
17. Ibid., pp. 1, 326.
18. J.G.A. Pocock, *Barbarism and Religion, Vol. IV. Barbarians, Savages and Empires* (Cambridge, 2005).
19. 'Government of India', 10 July 1833, G.M. Young (ed.), *Speeches by Lord Macaulay, with His Minute on Indian Education* (London, 1935), p. 163.
20. Knud Haakonssen, 'James Mill and Scottish Moral Philosophy', *Political Studies* 33 (1985), pp. 628–41; Pitts, *A Turn to Empire*, p. 127.
21. Mill, *History*, I, p. 147; I, p. 286; V, p. 79; V, pp. 432–4; V, pp. 475–6 and V, p. 520.
22. James Mill to David Ricardo, quoted in Stefan Collini, Donald Winch and J.W. Burrow, *That Noble Science of Politics: A Study in Nineteenth-Century Intellectual History* (Cambridge, 1983), p. 121.
23. Ibid., p. 121.
24. Pitts, *A Turn to Empire*, p. 128; Haakonssen, 'James Mill and Scottish Moral Philosophy', pp. 631–2.
25. Evidence 21 February 1832, East India Select Committee, *PP*, 1831–1832 (735), I, p. 43.
26. Mill, *History*, V, p. 513.
27. James Mill, *The History of British India with Notes and Continuation, by Horace Hayman Wilson* (London, 1858).
28. Edward Strachey, *Bija Ganita of Bhaskara Acharya: Or the Algebra of the Hindus. Tr. By E. Strachey* (London, 1813).
29. 'Of the Moral Character of the Hindoos as Described in Mill's British India', *Mss Eur* F/128/218.
30. *Mss Eur* F/128/193, n.d. See Strachey to W.B. Bayly, 22 April 1800, *Mss Eur* F/128/180 for instances of his perplexity in court.
31. William Hazlitt, 'The Spirit of the Age III: Mr Horne Tooke', *The New Monthly Magazine* 7, 43 (1824), p. 252.
32. Majeed, *Ungoverned Imaginings*; for the importance of the idea of fiction in Bentham's writing, see Ross Harrison, *Bentham* (London, 1983), pp. 24–46.

33. Mill, *History*, V, p. 434 and V, p. 476.
34. John James Park, *A Contre-Projet to the Humphreysian Code* (London, 1828), p. 58.
35. T.B. Macaulay, 'Mill on Government' in James Mill, *Political Writings* (Cambridge, 1992), pp. 271–303.
36. J.W. Burrow, *Whigs and Liberals. Continuity and Change in English Political Thought* (Oxford, 1988), pp. 105–21.
37. 'Government of India', 10 July 1833 in Macaulay, *Speeches of Lord Macaulay*, p. 135.
38. Holt Mackenzie, Minute, 1 October 1830, *PP*, 1831–1832, (735) III, General Appendix, p. 136.
39. Note by Holt Mackenzie, April 1829, *PP*, 1831 (320E), V, Appendix, pp. 30–1.
40. Holt Mackenzie, 'To the Independent Electors of the Burghs of Elgin, Cullen &ca.', Aberdeen University, Local Collection, RAD051.
41. Travers, *Ideology and Empire*, pp. 181–206.
42. Stokes, *English Utilitarians*, p. 168; 'In re: the Justices of the Bombay Supreme Court of Judicature', 14 May 1829, 1 *Knapp*, p. 1 (12 *English Reports*, p. 222).
43. Evidence of Holt Mackenzie, 6 March 1832, East India Select Committee, *PP*, 1831–1832 (735), General Appendix, p. 95; Note by C.T. Metcalfe, Appendix to East India Select Committee Report, *PP*, 1831 (320E), Appendix V, p. 17.
44. 'Letter from the Judges of the Supreme Court', 28 December 1830, *PP*, 1831 (320E), Appendix V, p. 181.
45. Metcalf, Minute, 15 April 1829, *PP*, 1831 (320E), Appendix V, p. 13.
46. Search conducted using House of Commons *PP* at parlipapers.chadwyk.co.uk, accessed on 1 June 2007.
47. C.D. Dharker, *Lord Macaulay's Legislative Minutes* (London, 1946), p. 2.
48. Government of India Act, 1833, 3 and 4 Will IV, *c*.85.
49. Henry Tucker to Bentinck, 7 November 1833, p. 1127.
50. Colin Gordon, 'Governmental Rationality. An Introduction' in Gordon, Miller and Burchell (ed.), *The Foucault Effect* p. 15.
51. Mill, *History*, I, p. 4.
52. 'Government of India', 10 July 1833 in Macaulay, *Speeches of Lord Macaulay*, p. 157.
53. C.H. Philips, *The East India Company, 1784–1834* (Manchester, 1940).
54. C.T. Metcalfe, Minute, 15 April 1829, *PP*, 1830 (320E), Appendix, p. 17.
55. Penal Code prepared by Indian Law Commissioners, published by Governor-General, 14 October 1837, *PP*, 1837–1838 (673), pp. 1–11.
56. Lynn Zastoupil and Martin Moir, *The Great Indian Education Debate: Documents Relating to the Orientalist-Anglicist Controversy, 1781–1843* (Richmond, 1999), p. 165.
57. Ibid., p. 5.
58. Lord Wellesley, Minute Relative to the College at Fort William, 18 August 1800, *PP*, 1813 (276), p. 4.
59. Ibid., pp. 7–8, 11.
60. Zastoupil and Moir, *Great Education Debate*, pp. 121–2.
61. Mackenzie, Notes, 27 September 1825, Proceedings of the General Committee on Public Instruction, III, 2, *WBSA*, pp. 487, 550.
62. Minute of Officiating Judge, C. Smith, 26 August 1825, General Committee of Public Instruction Proceeding, III (2) pp. 468–72, WBSA.
63. Zastoupil and Moir, *Great Education Debate*, p. 160.
64. See, for example, James Mill, *The History of British India*, edited and with comments by H.H, Wilson, I, pp. i–xiii.
65. Thomas Pinney (ed.), *The Letters of Thomas Babington Macaulay* (London, 1974), III, p. 103.

66. Macaulay, 'Minute on Education' in H. Sharp, *Selections from Education Records* (Calcutta, 1920), pp. 111, 114.
67. Dodson, *Orientalism, Empire and National Culture* for a discussion of these concerns in Benares Hindu College during later decades.
68. Zastoupil and Moir, *Great Education Debate*, p. 158.
69. Miles Taylor, 'Empire and Parliamentary Reform: The 1832 Reform Act Revisited' in Arthur Burns *et al.* (eds), *Rethinking the Age of Reform. Britain, 1780–1850* (Cambridge, 2003).
70. Representation of the People Act 1832, 2 & 3 Will IV, *c.*45 and Slavery Abolition Act 1833, 3 & 4 Will IV, *c.*73.
71. Asa Briggs, *The Age of Improvement, 1783–1867* (London, 1959); J.C.D. Clark, *English Society 1688–1832: Ideology, Social Structure and Political Practice During the Ancien Regime* (Cambridge, 1985); Scott, 'Colonial Governmentality'.
72. Mary Reckord, 'The Jamaica Slave Rebellion of 1831', *Past and Present* 40 (1968); Robin Blackburn, *The Overthrow of Colonial Slavery, 1776–1848* (London, 1988), pp. 437–60.
73. 'Commission of Inquiry into Grievances in Lower Canada', *PP*, 1837 (50), p. 184; 'Report of Earl of Durham on Affairs of British N. America', *PP*, 1839 (3), p. 8.
74. For different perspectives on reform which nonetheless share a common sense of the importance of historical continuity, see M.G. Brock, *The Great Reform Act* (London, 1973); Peter Mandler, *Aristocratic Government in the Age of Reform: Whigs and Liberals 1830–1852* (Oxford, 1990); Arthur Burns, *The Diocesan Revival in the Church of England, C. 1800–1870* (Oxford, 1999); Arthur Burns and Joanna Innes (eds), *Rethinking the Age of Reform. Britain, 1780–1850* (Cambridge, 2003).
75. Collini, Winch and Burrow, *That Noble Science*.
76. Young (ed.), *Speeches by Lord Macaulay*, pp. 125–6. For a discussion of the relationship between history and the study of politics in the nineteenth century, see Collini, Winch and Burrow, *That Noble Science*.

7 Indian liberalism and colonial utilitarianism

1. 'Samaj bahirer sahajyer apekka rakhe nai ebong bahirer upadrabe sribhrashta hai na', 'Swadeshi Samaj' in Rabindranath Tagore, *Sangkalam* (Kolkata, 1332 BS [1925]), p. 55; translated in Rabindranath Tagore, *Greater India* (1921), p. 2.
2. Sumit Sarkar, *The Swadeshi Movement in Bengal, 1903–1908* (Delhi, 1973).
3. For some of these tendencies, see J.W. Burrow, *The Crisis of Reason: European Thought, 1848–1914* (New Haven, CT, 2000); Daniel Pick, *Faces of Degeneration: A European Disorder, C.1848–C.1918* (Cambridge, 1989).
4. Andrew Sartori, 'Emancipation as Heteronomy'.
5. Bayly, *Origins of Nationality in South Asia*, pp. 63–97; see also Ray, *The Felt Community* and the discussion in Chapter 2 above.
6. For a discussion of this idea of *inquilab*, see Kumkum Chatterjee, 'History as Self-Representation. The Recasting of a Political Tradition in Late Eighteenth-Century India', *MAS* 34, 4 (1998).
7. 'Swadeshi Samaj' in Tagore, *Sangkalam*, pp. 55–67; translated in Tagore, *Greater India*, pp. 1–30.
8. 'In Search of Civil Society' in Kaviraj and Khilnani, *Civil Society*, p. 289.
9. For a discussion and definition of liberalism along these lines, see Quentin Skinner, *Liberty before Liberalism* (Cambridge, 1998) and Graham Burchell, 'Peculiar

Interests: Civil Society and Governing "the System of Natural Liberty"' in Graham Burchell *et al.* (eds), *The Foucault Effect. Studies in Governmentality* (Hemel Hemstead, 1991).

10. C.A. Bayly offered a larger scale account of nineteenth-century Indian liberalism at his 2007 Queen University Wiles lectures, 'Liberalism at Large: South Asian and Britain, c.1800–1947'.

11. Bayly, *The Birth of the Modern World*, p. 40. The best introductions to Rammohan's thought are Bruce Robertson, *Raja Rammohan Roy: The Father of Modern India* (Delhi, 1995) and Bimanbehari Majumdar, *History of Indian Social and Political Ideas, from Rammohan to Dayananda* (Calcutta, 1967). See also C.A. Bayly, 'Rammohan Roy and the Advent of Constitutional Liberalism in India, 1800–1830', *Modern Intellectual History* 4, 1 (2007), pp. 25–41.

12. Michel Foucault, *Security, Territory, Population. Lectures at the College de France, 1977–1978* (Basingstoke, 2007), p. 48.

13. Robertson, *Raja Rammohan Roy*, pp. 176–80.

14. Rammohan Roy, 'Brief Remarks Regarding Modern Encroachments on the Ancient Rights of Females' in Kalidas Nag *et al.* (eds), *The English Works of Raja Rammohan Roy* (Calcutta, 1945–1958), pp. 2–3.

15. Raja Rammohan Roy, 'Conference between an Advocate for and an Opponent of, the Practice of Burning Widows Alive' in Ibid., p. 105.

16. 'Minute on *sati*', 8 November 1829, C.H. Philips (ed.), *The Correspondence of Lord William Cavendish Bentinck, Governor-General of India, 1828–1835* (Oxford, 1977), p. 335.

17. The story can be found in Swarupa Gupta, 'Notions of Nationhood in Bengal: Perspectives on *Samaj*, 1867–1905', *MAS* 40, 2 (2006), pp. 16–17.

18. Roy, 'Brief Remarks', p. 1.

19. Bayly, 'Rammohan Roy and the Advent of Constitutional Liberalism in India', p. 30.

20. Roy, 'Brief Remarks', p. 9.

21. Ibid., p. 9; Rammohan Roy 1945–1958, 'Questions and Answers on Judicial and Revenue Systems' in Kalidas Nag *et al.* (eds), *The English Works of Raja Rammohan Roy* (Calcutta, 1945–1958), p. 16.

22. Roy, 'Questions and Answers on Judicial and Revenue Systems', pp. 35–7.

23. For details of these disputes, see Ramprasad Chanda and J.K. Majumdar, *Letters and Documents Relating to the Life of Raja Rammohan Roy* (Calcutta, 1938).

24. Rammohan Roy, 'The Rights of Hindus over Ancestral Property According to the Law of Bengal' in Kalidas Nag *et al.* (eds),*The English Works of Raja Rammohan Roy* (Calcutta, 1945–1958), p. 24.

25. Ibid., p. 22.

26. Ibid., p. 35.

27. Bose, *Peasant Labour and Colonial Capital*.

28. Blair B. Kling, *Partner in Empire: Dwarkanath Tagore and the Age of Enterprise in Eastern India* (Berkeley, 1976), pp. 30–3.

29. For example, David L. Curley, '"Voluntary" Relations and Royal Gifts of *Pan* in Mughal Bengal' in Stewart Gordon (ed.), *Robes of Honour: Khil'at in Pre-Colonial and Colonial Bengal* (Delhi, 2003).

30. Abu Hena Mustafa Kamal, *The Bengali Press and Literary Writing, 1818–31* (Dacca, 1977).

31. Anderson, *Imagined Communities*; for this critique, see John Breuilly, 'Reflections on Nationalism', *Philosophy and Social Science*, 15, 1 (1985).

32. Bhabanicharan Bandopadhaya, *Kalikata Kamalalay* (Calcutta, 1823) translated as Bhawanicharan Bandopadhyay, *Kalikata Kamalalay* (Calcutta, 1990). See also Hans Harder, 'The Modern Babu and the Metropolis: Reassessing Early Bengali Narrative Prose (1821–1862)' in Stuart Blackburn *et al.* (eds), *India's Literary History: Essays on the Nineteenth Century* (Delhi, 2004), pp. 358–401 and Dipesh Chakrabarty, *Provincialising Europe. Postcolonial Thought and Historical Difference* (Princeton, NJ, 2000), pp. 219–24.
33. Brian K. Pennington, 'Constructing Colonial Dharma: A Chronicle of Emergent Hinduism, 1830–1831', *Journal of the American Academy of Religion* 69, 3 (2001).
34. Binay Ghosh, *Samayika Patre Bangla Samaj Jacitra* (Kalikata, 1966).
35. Satyendranath Pal, *The Rise of Radicalism in Bengal in the Nineteenth Century* (Calcutta, 1991), p. 163.
36. Susobhan C. Sarkar, 'Derozio and Young Bengal' in A.C. Gupta (ed.), *Studies in Bengal Renaissance* (Calcutta, 1958), p. 486; Sushil Kumar De, *Bengali Literature in the Nineteenth Century, 1757–1857* (Calcutta, 1962); Rosinka Chaudhuri, 'An Ideology of Indianness: The Construction of Colonial/Communal Stereotypes in the Poems of Henry Derozio', *Studies in History* 20, 2 (2004), pp. 167–87.
37. Pal, *Rise of Radicalism*, p. 172.
38. 'The Confession of a Young Bengal', Jogesh Chandra Bagal (ed.), *Bankim Rachanavali* (Calcutta, 1969), pp. 137–41.
39. For Rammohan's complicity in the global circulation of biological ideas of racial difference, see Shruti Kapila, 'Race Matters: Orientalism and Religion, India and Beyond, C.1770–1880', *MAS* 41 (2007), pp. 471–513. For the most part though, as Amitav Ghosh notes in a thoughtful exchange with Dipesh Chakrabarty, ideas of Hindu superiority are rooted in a sense of the superiority of social practice not a scientific notion of physical racial difference, Amitav Ghosh and Dipesh Chakrabarty, 'A Conversation on *Provincialising Europe*', *Radical History Review* 83 (2002), p. 158.
40. For the role of Comptean positivism in Bengal, see Geraldine Hancock Forbes, *Positivism in Bengal: A Case Study in the Transmission and Assimilation of an Ideology* (Colombia, 1975); for the relationship between Indian thought and another branch of European sociology, see Shruti Kapila, 'Self, Spencer and *Swaraj*. Nationalist Thought and Critiques of Liberalism, 1890–1920', *Modern Intellectual History* 4, 1 (2007), pp. 109–27.
41. Sudipta Kaviraj, *The Unhappy Consciousness: Bankimchandra Chattopadhyay and the Formation of Nationalist Discourse in India* (Delhi, 1995); Hegel, *Phenomenology of Spirit*, pp. 124–5.
42. Stephen Blore, 'Miss Martineau Speaks Out', *New England Quarterly* 9, 3 (1936), pp. 403–16.
43. Raj Jogeshur Mitter (ed.), *Speeches by Mr. George Thompson (Father of Political Education in India)* (Calcutta, 1895), pp. 144, 154.
44. For the relationship between political protest and social reform in the *Swadeshi* campaign, see Tagore's *Ghore-Bhahire* translated as Rabindranath Tagore, *The Home and the World* (London, 1919). The best account of the *swadeshi* movement remains Sarkar, *The Swadeshi Movement in Bengal, 1903–1908*, pp. 47–63.
45. Peter Mandler, ' "Race" and "Nation" in Mid-Victorian Thought' in Stefan Collini *et al.* (eds), *History, Religion and Culture. British Intellectual History, 1750–1950* (Cambridge, 2000) and Peter Mandler, 'What is National Identity? Definitions and Applications in Modern British Historiography', *Modern Intellectual History* 3 (2006), pp. 271–97.
46. The first set of lectures were on Hindu law, Herbert Cowell, *The Hindu Law: Being a Treatise on the Law Administered Exclusively to Hindus by the British Courts in India* (Calcutta, 1871).
47. Chakrabarty, *Provincialising Europe*, pp. 220–1.

8 Reflections

1. Matthew Taylor, *England's Bloody Tribunal: Or, Popish Cruelty Displayed* (London, 1771); 'Opening of the Congress', *The Political Examiner*, 16 October 1814, p. 2; 'Netherlands India', *Asiatic Journal and Annual Miscellany*, July 1825, p. 97; 'Health of Towns Bill', *The Chronicle*, Preston, 8 May 1847; 'Irish Unity', *Leeds Mercury*, 17 March 1899; Henry Smith Williams, *The Historians' History of the World* (New York, NY, 1904), pp. xvi, 647.
2. Minute by the acting Governor-General of India, 16 May 1835, C.T. Metcalfe, Military Department, *PP*, 1867 (500), p. 158.
3. 'Minute on Press Regulation', IOR H/532 quoted in Burton Stein, *Thomas Munro. The Origins of the Colonial State and His Vision of Empire* (Delhi, 1989), p. 285.
4. The literature on Bankim is extensive. In English, see in particular Partha Chatterjee, *Nationalist Thought and the Colonial World: A Derivative Discourse?* (London, 1986), pp. 54–84; Tapan Raychaudhuri, *Europe Reconsidered: Perceptions of the West in Nineteenth Century Bengal* (Delhi, 1988), Chapter 2; Sudipta Kaviraj, *The Unhappy Consciousness: Bankimchandra Chattopadhyay and the Formation of Nationalist Discourse in India* (Delhi, 1995).
5. Jogesh Chandra Bagal (ed.), *Bankim Rachanavali* (Calcutta, 1969), III, pp. 140–1.
6. Ibid., pp. 147–8.
7. Chatterjee, *The Nation and Its Fragments*, p. 225; Kaviraj, *Unhappy Consciousness*.
8. Kaviraj, *Unhappy Consciousness*, p. 2; despite scanty references to the passage of the *Phenomenology of Spirit* concerned with this oscillation in the text, the relationship to Hegel is explicit in the title and implicit throughout Kaviraj's text.
9. Jack P. Greene, *Peripheries and Center: Constitutional Development in the Extended Polities of the British Empire and the United States, 1607–1788* (Athens, 1986); Daniel J. Hulsebosch, 'Writs to Rights. "Navigability" and the Transformation of the Common Law in the Nineteenth Century', *Cardozo Law Review* 23, 3 (2002); Afaf Lutfi Sayyid-Marsot, *Egypt in the Reign of Muhammad Ali* (Cambridge, 1984).
10. For this argument, see Peter Mandler, '"Race" and "Nation" in Mid-Victorian Thought' in Stefan Collini *et al.* (eds), *History, Religion and Culture. British Intellectual History, 1750–1950* (Cambridge, 2000), Peter Mandler, 'Nation and Power in the Liberal State: Britain, c.1800–c.1914' in Len Scales *et al.* (eds), *Power and the Nation in European History* (Cambridge, 2005), pp. 354–69 and Peter Mandler, 'What is National Identity? Definitions and Applications in Modern British Historiography', *Modern Intellectual History* 3, 2 (2006), pp. 271–91.
11. Langford, *Public Life and the Propertied Englishman*; contrast with Lynn Hunt, *Politics, Culture, and Class in the French Revolution* (Berkeley, CA, 1984) and William Scott, 'The Pursuit of "Interests" in the French Revolution. A Preliminary Survey', *French Historical Studies* 19, 3 (1996). The importance of Langford's argument in relation to arguments made about the British slave trade was suggested to me by Ian Barrett, whose PhD thesis will discuss the issue.
12. Bayly, *The Birth of the Modern World*, p. 86.
13. Ibid., p. 100.
14. William M. Reddy, *The Navigation of Feeling: A Framework for the History of Emotions* (Cambridge, 2001), pp. 109–52.
15. Chatterjee, *The Nation and Its Fragments*, p. 5.
16. John Davis, 'The Many Faces of Modernity: French Rule in Southern Italy, 1806–1815' in Michael Rowe (ed.), *Collaboration and Resistance in Napoleonic Europe: State-Formation in an Age of Upheaval, c.1800–1815* (Basingstoke, 2003).

17. Michael Rowe, *From Reich to State: The Rhineland in the Revolutionary Age, 1780–1830* (Cambridge, 2003), pp. 114, 258–63.
18. For a discussion of the bodily separation of British officers from Indian society, see E.M. Collingham, *Imperial Bodies: The Physical Experience of the Raj, c.1800–1947* (London, 2001).
19. For an account of such an abstract model in British famine policy, see David Hall-Matthews, *Peasants, Famine and the State in Colonial Western India* (Basingstoke, 2005).
20. The elite utopian knowledge discussed here can be contrasted with the forms of insurgent knowledge in nineteenth-century India discussed in the ongoing work of Shruti Kapila.
21. Matthew Beaumont, '*News from Nowhere* and the Here and Now: Reification and the Representation of the Present in Utopian Fiction', *Victorian Studies* 47, 1 (2004).
22. Quoted in Ibid., p. 33.
23. Bandopadhaya, *Kalikata Kamalalay*.
24. Beaumont, '*News from Nowhere* and the Here and Now', p. 37.
25. For utopianism in the creation of Pakistan, see Taj Ul-Islam Hashmi, *Pakistan as a Peasant Utopia: The Communalization of Class Politics in East Bengal, 1920–1947* (Boulder, CO, 1992).

Bibliography

Manuscript Sources

Aberdeen University Library
  Local Collection

Africa, Asia and Pacific Collections, British Library
European Manuscripts
  Barlow Collection
  Munro Collection
  Smith Collection
  Sutton Court Collection
  Wilson Collection
India Office Records
  Bengal Judicial Consultations
  Bengal Law Consultations
  Bengal Revenue Consultations
  Board of Revenue Consultations
  Board's Collections
  Committee of Revenue Consultations
  Home Miscellaneous
  Sudder Dewanny Adawlut

Barisal District Record Room, Barisal, Bangladesh
  Mouza Notes

British Library of Political and Economic Science, London
  Mill-Taylor Collection

Gloucestershire County Record Office
  Ducarel Papers

Manuscript Collections, British Library
  David Anderson papers
  Warren Hastings papers
  Wellesley Papers

National Archives of Bangladesh
  Comilla District Records
  Dhaka District Records
  Rangpur District Records
  Sylhet District Records

Rangpur District Record Room, Rangpur, Bangladesh
  Quinquennial Register
  Revenue Survey Maps, 1855–6

West Bengal State Archives, Kolkata
Board of Revenue Consultations
General Committee of Public Instruction Proceedings

Published manuscripts and other sources

Cannon, Garland (ed.), *The Letters of William Jones* (Oxford, 1970).
Colebrooke, Thomas Edward, *Life of the Honourable Mountstuart Elphinstone* (London, 1884).
Dharker, C.D., *Lord Macaulay's Legislative Minutes* (London, 1946).
Firminger, Walter K. (ed.), *Bengal District Records. Rungpore* (Calcutta, 1914).
Firminger, Walter K. (ed.), *The Fifth Report on the Affairs of the East India Company* (Calcutta, 1917), II, p. 512.
Forrest, G.W., *Selections from the State Papers of the Governors-General of India: Warren Hastings*, 4 vols (Oxford, 1910).
Fort William-India House Correspondence, 21 vols (Indian Records Series, Delhi, 1949).
Furber, Holder (ed.), *The Private Record of an Indian Governor-Generalship. The Correspondence of John Shore with Henry Dundas, 1793–1798* (Cambridge MA, 1933).
Gangarama, *The Maharashta Purana: An Eighteenth-Century Bengali Historical Text*, trans. Edward C. Dimock and Pratulacandra Gupta (Honolulu, HA, 1965).
Gleig, G.R., *Memoirs of the Life of the Right Hon. Warren Hastings*, 3 vols (London, 1841).
Langford, Paul *et al.* (eds), *The Writings and Speeches of Edmund Burke*, 9 vols (Oxford, 1981–1991).
Oldham, James, *The Mansfield Manuscripts and the Growth of English Law in the Eighteenth Century*, 2 vols (Chapel Hill, NC, 1992).
Philips, C.H. (ed.), *The Correspondence of Lord William Cavendish Bentinck, Governor-General of India, 1828–1835*, 2 vols (Oxford, 1977).
Pinney, Thomas (ed.), *The Letters of Thomas Babington Macaulay*, 6 vols (London, 1974).
Ross, Charles (ed.), *Correspondence of Charles, First Marquis Cornwallis*, 3 vols (London, 1859).
Sharp, H., *Selections from Education Records* (Calcutta, 1920).
Teignmouth, Charles John Shore, *Memoir of the Life and Correspondence of John, Lord Teignmouth*, 2 vols (London, 1843).
Zastoupil, Lynn and Moir, Martin, *The Great Indian Education Debate: Documents Relating to the Orientalist-Anglicist Controversy, 1781–1843* (Richmond, 1999).

Texts written before 1914

Anon., 'Memoir of James Cumming', *The Asiatic Journal* 24, 140 (1827), pp. 185–6.
Bagal, Jogesh Chandra (ed.), *Bankim Rachanavali* (Calcutta, 1969), vol. III, *English Works*.
Bandopadhyay, Bhabanicharan, *Kalikata Kamalalay* (1952 edn, Calcutta, 1823).
Bandopadhyay, Bhawanicharan, *Kalikata Kamalalay*, trans. Satyabrata Dutta (1st English edn, Calcutta, 1990).
Beveridge, Henry, *The District of Bakarganj, Its History and Statistics* (London, 1876).
Bhattacharya, Jogendra Nath, *A Commentary on the Hindu Law of Inheritance* (Calcutta, 1885).

Bhattacharyya, Krishna Kamal, *The Law Relating to the Joint Hindu Family* (Calcutta, 1885).

Blore, Stephen, 'Miss Martineau Speaks Out', *New England Quarterly* 9, 3 (1936), pp. 413–6.

Bolts, William, *Considerations on India Affairs* (London, 1772).

Caraccioli, Charles, *The Life of Robert Lord Clive, Baron Plassey* (London, 1775).

Castiglione, Baldassarre, *The Book of the Courtier* (Harmondsworth, 1967).

Cawthorne, Joseph, *The Crisis: Or, A Defence of Administration against the Imaginary Victory and Ill-Grounded Triumph of Opposition* (London, 1785).

Chanda, Ramprasad and Majumdar, J.K., *Letters and Documents Relating to the Life of Raja Rammohan Roy* (Calcutta, 1938).

Cobbett, William (ed.), *The Parliamentary History of England* (London, 1806).

Cochrane, John, *A Defence of the Daya-Bhaga* (London, 1872).

Colebrooke, H.T. (ed.), *A Digest of Hindu Law on Contracts and Successions, with a Commentary*, 4 vols (Calcutta, 1798).

Colebrooke, H.T. (ed.), *A Digest of Hindu Law on Contracts and Successions, with a Commentary* (London, 1801).

Colebrooke, H.T., *Remarks on the Husbandry and Internal Commerce of Bengal* (Calcutta, 1804).

Colebrooke, H.T. (ed.), *Two Treatises on the Hindu Law of Inheritance* (Calcutta, 1810).

Colebrooke, T.E. (ed.), *Miscellaneous Essays [of H.T. Colebrooke], with Life of the Author* (London, 1873).

Cowell, Herbert, *The Hindu Law, Being a Treatise on the Law Administered Exclusively to Hindus in the British Courts in India* (Calcutta, 1870–1871).

Day, Lal Behari, *Bengal Peasant Life* (London, 1878).

Dimock, Edward C., *The Thief of Love: Bengali Tales from Court and Village* (Chicago, 1963), pp. 140–68.

Erskine, Thomas, *Resolutions of the First Meeting of the Friends to the Liberty to the Press, to Which is Added a Letter by Thomas Law* (London, 1793).

Francis, Philip, *Original Minutes of the Governor-General and Council of Fort William* (London, 1782).

Ghosh, Binay, *Samayika Patre Bangla Samaj Jacitra*, 4 vols (Kalikata, 1978).

Gisborne, Thomas, *An Enquiry into the Duties of Men in the Higher and Middle Classes of Society in Great Britain* (London, 1794).

Grand, George Francis, *Summary Remarks on the Resources of the East Indies … Intended as a Contrast to the Pamphlet of Mr. Thomas Law, Entitled 'Rising Resources'* (London, 1792).

Hamilton, Francis, *A Journey from Madras Through the Countries of Mysore, Canara, and Malabar*, 3 vols (London, 1807).

Hastings, Warren, *Memoirs Relative to the State of India* (London, 1787).

Hastings, Warren, *The Present State of the East Indies* (London, 1786).

Hazlitt, William, 'The Spirit of the Age III: Mr Horne Tooke', *The New Monthly Magazine* 7, 43 (1824), pp. 246–52.

Hegel, G.W.F., *The Subjective Logic of Hegel* (London, 1855).

Hegel, G.W.F., *Phenomenology of Spirit*, trans. A.V. Miller (Oxford, 1977).

Hossein Khan Tabatabai, Ghulam, *The Seir Mutaquerin, or Review of Modern Times*, trans. Haji Mustafa, 4 vols (Delhi, 1926).

Hume, David, *A Treatise of Human Nature*, L.A. Selby-Bugge and P.H. Nesbit (eds), (Oxford, 1978).

Iyer, Raghuvan (ed.), *The Essential Writings of Mahatma Gandhi* (Delhi, 1990).

Johnson, Samuel, *A Dictionary of the English Language*, 2 vols (2nd edn, London, 1756).

Kalidas Nag and Debajyoti Burman (eds), *The English Works of Raja Rammohan Roy* (Calcutta, 1945–1958).

Kavyatirtha, Gadadhar, *Harishchandra* (Calcutta, 1898).

Knox, T.M. and Pelcyzynski, Z.A. (eds), *Hegel's Political Writings* (Oxford, 1964).

Law, Thomas, *A Sketch of Some Late Arrangements, and a View of the Rising Resources, in Bengal* (London, 1792).

Law, Thomas, *Remarks on the Ryotwaree and Mocurrey Systems* (London, 1820).

Locke, John, *Two Treatises of Government* Peter Laslett (ed.), (Cambridge, 1988).

Lyall, Alfred C., *Warren Hastings* (London, 1889).

Macaulay, Thomas Babington, *Critical and Historical Essays: Contributed to the Edinburgh Review*, 3 vols (London, 1860).

Macaulay, Thomas Babington, *Speeches of Lord Macaulay* (London, 1860).

Machiavelli, Niccolo, *The Prince*, Quentin Skinner (ed.), (Cambridge, 1988).

MacNaghten, Francis Workman, *Considerations on the Hindoo Law, as it is Current in Bengal* (Serampore, 1824).

MacNaghten, William Hay, *Reports of Cases Determined in the Court of Sudder Dewanny Adawlut* (Calcutta, 1827).

MacNaghten, William Hay, *Principles and Precedents of Hindu Law*, 2 vols (Calcutta, 1828).

Maine, Henry, *Ancient Law* (Tucson, AZ, 1986 reprint of 1864 edn).

Mayne, John D., *A Treatise on Hindu Law and Usage* (Madras, 1878).

Mill, James, *The History of British India*, 6 vols (3rd edn, London, 1826).

Mill, James, *The History of British India*, edited with comments by H.H. Wilson, 10 vols (5th edn, London, 1858).

Mill, James, *Political Writings*, Terence Ball, (ed.) (Cambridge 1992).

Millar, John, *Observations Concerning the Distinction of Ranks in Society* (London, 1771).

Mitter, Raj Jogeshur (ed.), *Speeches by Mr. George Thompson (Father of Political Education in India)* (Calcutta, 1895).

Paley, William, *The Principles of Moral and Political Philosophy* (Indianapolis, IN, 2002).

Park, John James, *A Contre-Projet to the Humphreysian Code* (London, 1828).

Patton, Robert, *The Effects of Property upon Society and Government Investigated* (London, 1797).

Prinsep, John, *Strictures and Observations on the Mocurrey System of Landed Property in Bengal* (London, 1794).

Rouse, Charles William Boughton, *Dissertation Concerning the Landed Property of Bengal* (Calcutta, 1791).

Simmel, Georg, *On Individuality and Social Forms* (Chicago, IL, 1971).

Smith, Adam, *An Inquiry into the Nature and Causes of the Wealth of Nations*, R.H. Campbell and A.S. Skinner (eds), 2 vols (Oxford, 1976 edn).

Smith, Adam, *The Theory of Moral Sentiments*, D.D. Raphael and A.L. Macfie (eds) (Oxford, 1976 edn).

Smith, Adam, *The Correspondence of Adam Smith*, Ian Simpson Ross and Ernest Campbell Mossner (eds) (Oxford, 1977).

Smyth, David Carmichael, *Original Bengalese Zumeendaree Accounts* (Calcutta, 1823).

Steingass, Francis, *A Comprehensive Persian–English Dictionary* (London, 1892).

Strachey, Edward (tr.), *Bija Ganita of Bhaskara Acharya: Or the Algebra of the Hindus.* (London, 1813).

Stuart, Gilbert, *An Historical Dissertation Concerning the Antiquity of the English Constitution* (2nd edn, London, 1770).

Sullivan, Richard Sir, *An Analysis of the Political History of India* (London, 1784).

Tagore, Rabindranath, *The Home and the World* (London, 1919).

Tagore, Rabindranath, *Greater India* (Calcutta, 1921).

Tagore, Rabindranath, *Sangkalam* (Kolkata, 1332 BS [1925]).

Tarkalankara, Jaganmohan, *Harishchandra-charitra* (Calcutta, 1869).

Taylor, Matthew, *England's Bloody Tribunal: Or, Popish Cruelty Displayed* (London, 1771).

Tennant, William, *Indian Recreations. Consisting of Thoughts and Strictures on the Effects of the British Government on the State of India*, 3 vols (2nd edn, Edinburgh, 1808).

Thompson, W.F., *Practical Philosophy of the Muhammedan People, Being a Translation of the Akhlak-I-Jalaly, from the Persian of Fakir Jany Muhammad Asaad* (London, 1839).

Tytler, Alexander Fraser, *Considerations on the Present Political State of India*, 2 vols (London, 1815).

Vas, J.A., *Rangpur: East Bengal and Assam District Gazetteers* (Allahabad, 1911).

Ward, William, *A View of the History, Literature, and Religion of the Hindoos: Including a Minute Description of Their Manners and Customs, and Translations from Their Principal Works*, 2 vols (2nd edn, Serampore, 1815).

Weber, Max, *Economy and Society*, 2 vols (Berkeley, CA, 1978).

Wilkins, Charles, *The Bhagvat-Geeta, or Dialogues of Kreeshna and Arjoon: In Eighteen Lectures* (London, 1785).

Williams, Henry Smith, *The Historians' History of the World*, 16 vols (New York, NY, 1904).

Young, G.M., *Speeches by Lord Macaulay, with His Minute on Indian Education* (London, 1935).

Texts written after 1914

Abrams, Philip, 'Notes on the Difficulty of Studying the State', *Journal of Historical Sociology* 1, 1 (1988), pp. 58–89.

Adas, Michael, '"Moral Economy" or "Contest State"?: Elite Demands and the Origins of Peasant Protest in Southeast Asia', *Journal of Social History*, 13, 4 (1980), pp. 521–46.

Alam, Muzaffar, *The Languages of Political Islam: India, 1200–1800* (London, 2004).

Alam, Muzaffar and Subrahmanyam, Sanjay, *The Mughal Empire* (Delhi, 1998).

Armitage, David, *The Ideological Origins of the British Empire* (Cambridge, 2000).

Asad, Talal, *Genealogies of Religion. Discipline and Reasons of Power in Christianity and Islam* (Baltimore, 1993).

Asad, Talal, *Formations of the Secular: Christianity, Islam, Modernity* (Stanford, CA, 2003).

Ashcraft, Richard, *Revolutionary Politics and Locke's Two Treatises of Government* (Princeton, NJ, 1986).

Bagchi, Amiya Kumar, *The Evolution of the State Bank of India: The Roots, 1806–1876*, 2 vols (Bombay, 1987).

Barua, Pradeep, *The State at War in South Asia* (Lincoln, NE, 2005).

Bauman, Zygmunt, *Modernity and Ambivalence* (Oxford, 1991).

Bayly, C.A., *Rulers, Townsmen and Bazaars: North Indian Society in the Age of British Expansion 1770–1870* (Cambridge, 1983).

Bayly, C.A., *Indian Society and the Making of the British Empire* (Cambridge, 1988).

Bayly, C.A., *Imperial Meridian. The British Empire and the World, 1780–1830* (London, 1989).

Bayly, C.A., *Empire and Information. Intelligence Gathering and Social Communication in India, 1780–1870* (Cambridge, 1996).

Bayly, C.A., *Origins of Nationality in South Asia: Patriotism and Ethical Government in the Making of Modern India* (Delhi, 2001).

Bayly, C.A., 'Rammohan Roy and the Advent of Constitutional Liberalism in India, 1800–1830', *Modern Intellectual History* 4, 1 (2007), pp. 25–41.

Beaumont, Matthew, '*News from Nowhere* and the Here and Now: Reification and the Representation of the Present in Utopian Fiction', *Victorian Studies* 47, 1 (2004), pp. 33–54.

Beckett, J.V., 'Land Tax or Excise: The Levying of Taxation in Seventeenth- and Eighteenth-Century England', *English Historical Review* 100 (1985), pp. 285–308.

Benjamin, Walter, 'Theses on the Philosophy of History', *Illuminations* (London, 1973).

Bhabha, Homi K., *The Location of Culture: Critical Theory and the Postcolonial Perspective* (London, 1991).

Bhadra, Gautam, 'The Mentality of Subalternity. *Kantanama* or *Rajdharma*', in Ranajit Guha (ed.), *Subaltern Studies VI* (Delhi, 1989).

Blackburn, Robin, *The Overthrow of Colonial Slavery, 1776–1848* (London, 1988).

Bose, Sugata, *Peasant Labour and Colonial Capita: Rural Bengal since 1770* (Cambridge, 1993).

Bourke, Richard, 'Liberty, Authority, and Trust in Burke's Idea of Empire', *Journal of the History of Ideas* 61, 3 (2000), pp. 453–71.

Bowen, H.V., *The Business of Empire: The East India Company and Imperial Britain, 1756–1833* (Cambridge, 2006).

Breuilly, John, 'Reflections on Nationalism', *Philosophy and Social Science* 15, 1 (1985), pp. 65–75.

Brewer, John and Styles, John A., *An Ungovernable People: The English and Their Law in the Seventeenth and Eighteenth Centuries* (New Brunswick, NJ, 1980).

Briggs, Asa, *The Age of Improvement, 1783–1867* (London, 1959).

Brock, Michael, *Great Reform Act* (London, 1973).

Burchell, Graham, 'Peculiar Interests: Civil Society and Governing "the System of Natural Liberty" ', in Graham Burchell, Colin Gordon and Peter Miller (eds), *The Foucault Effect. Studies in Governmentality* (Hemel Hemstead, 1991).

Burgess, Glenn, *The Politics of the Ancient Constitution: An Introduction to English Political Thought, 1603–1642* (Basingstoke, 1992).

Burns, Arthur, *The Diocesan Revival in the Church of England, C. 1800–1870* (Oxford, 1999).

Burns, Arthur and Innes, Joanna (eds), *Rethinking the Age of Reform: Britain, 1780–1850* (Cambridge, 2003).

Burrow, J.W., *Whigs and Liberals. Continuity and Change in English Political Thought* (Oxford, 1988).

Burrow, J.W., *The Crisis of Reason: European Thought, 1848–1914* (New Haven, CT, 2000).

Butler, Judith, *Subjects of Desire: Hegelian Reflections in Twentieth-Century France* (New York, 1987).

Cannadine, David, *Class in Britain* (New Haven, 1998).

Cannon, Garland (ed.), *The Letters of William Jones* (Oxford, 1970).

Cannon, John, *The Fox-North Coalition: Crisis of the Constitution, 1782–4* (Cambridge, 1969).

Chakrabarty, Dipesh, *Provincialising Europe. Postcolonial Thought and Historical Difference* (Princeton, NJ, 2000).

Chandrasekhar, S., 'The Hindu Joint Family', *Social Forces* 21, 3 (1943), pp. 327–33.

Chatterjee, Amal, *Representations of India, 1740–1840: The Creation of India in the Colonial Imagination* (Basingstoke, 1998).

Chatterjee, Indrani, *Gender, Slavery and Law in Colonial India* (New Delhi, 1999).

Chatterjee, Indrani, *Unfamiliar Relations: Family and History in South Asia* (New Brunswick, NJ, 2004).

Chatterjee, Kumkum, 'History as Self-Representation. The Recasting of a Political Tradition in Late Eighteenth-Century India', *MAS* 34, 4 (1998), pp. 913–48.

Chatterjee, Partha, *Nationalist Thought and the Colonial World: A Derivative Discourse?* (London, 1986).

Chatterjee, Partha, *The Nation and its Fragments. Colonial and Postcolonial Histories* (Princeton, NJ, 1993).

Chatterji, Roma, 'The Nationalist Sociology of Benoy Kumar Sarkar', in Patricia Uberoi, Nandini Sundar and Satish Deshpande (eds), *Anthropology in the East: Founders of Indian Sociology and Anthropology* (Kolkata, 2007).

Chaudhuri, Rosinka, 'An Ideology of Indianness: The Construction of Colonial/Communal Stereotypes in the Poems of Henry Derozio', *Studies in History* 20, 2 (2004), pp. 167–87.

Çirakman, Asli, 'From Tyranny to Despotism: The Enlightenment's Unenlightened Image of the Turks', *International Journal of Middle Eastern Studies* 33, (2001), pp. 49–68.

Clark, J.C.D., *English Society 1688–1832: Ideology, Social Structure and Political Practice During the Ancien Regime* (Cambridge, 1985).

Cohn, Bernard S., 'Anthropological Notes on Law and Disputes in India', *American Anthropologist* 67, 6 (1965), pp. 82–122.

Cohn, Bernard S., 'Law and the State in Colonial India', *Colonialism and Its Forms of Knowledge* (Princeton, NJ, 1996).

Collingham, E.M., *Imperial Bodies: The Physical Experience of the Raj, C.1800–1947* (London, 2001).

Collini, Stefan, Winch, Donald and Burrow, J.W. *That Noble Science of Politics. A Study in Nineteenth-Century Intellectual History* (Cambridge, 1983).

Cornish, H.D., *A Short Manual of Hindu Law* (London, 1937).

Cross, Rupert and Harris, J.W., *Precedent in English Law* (4th edn, Oxford, 1991).

Curley, David L., ' "Voluntary" Relations and Royal Gifts of *Pan* in Mughal Bengal', in Stewart Gordon (ed.), *Robes of Honour: Khil'at in Pre-Colonial and Colonial Bengal* (Delhi, 2003).

Das, Veena and Poole, Deborah, *Anthropology in the Margins of the State* (Oxford, 2004).

Dasgupta, Atis K., *The Fakir and Sannyasi Uprisings* (Calcutta, 1992).

Davis, John, 'The Many Faces of Modernity: French Rule in Southern Italy, 1806–1815', in Michael Rowe (ed.), *Collaboration and Resistance in Napoleonic Europe: State-Formation in an Age of Upheaval, C.1800–1815* (Basingstoke, 2003).

De, Sushil Kumar, *Bengali Literature in the Nineteenth Century, 1757–1857* (Calcutta, 1962).

Deleuze, Gilles, *Foucault*, trans. Sean Hand (London, 1988).

Derrett, J.D.M., *Religion, Law and the State in India* (London, 1968).

Dewey, Clive, *Anglo-Indian Attitudes: The Mind of the Indian Civil Service* (London, 1993).

Dirks, Nicholas B., 'From Little King to Landlord. Property, Law and the Gift under the Madras Permanent Settlement', *CSSH* 28, 2 (1986), pp. 307–33.

Dirks, Nicholas B., 'The Invention of Caste: Civil Society in Colonial India', *Social Analysis* 25 (1993).

Dodson, Michael S., *Orientalism, Empire and National Culture: India, 1770–1880* (Basingstoke, 2007).

Dreyfus, Hubert, *Being-in-the-World: A Commentary on Heidegger's Being and Time, Division I* (Cambridge, MA, 1991).

Driver, Felix, *Power and Pauperism. The Workhouse System, 1834–1884* (Cambridge, 1993).

Dumont, Louis, *Homo Hierarchicus: The Caste System and Its Implications* (London, 1970).

Eastwood, David, *Governing Rural England. Tradition and Transformation in Local Government, 1780–1840* (Oxford, 1994).

Eastwood, David, 'The Age of Uncertainty. Britain in the Early-Ninenteenth Century', *Transactions of the Royal Historical Society* 6th ser., 8 (1998), pp. 91–115.

Eaton, Richard, *The Rise of Islam and the Bengal Frontier, 1204–1760* (Berkeley, 1993).

Edwardes, Michael, *The Nabobs at Home* (London, 1991).

Esteban, Javier Cuenca, 'The British Balance of Payments, 1772–1820: India Transfers and War Finance', *Economic History Review* 54 (2001), pp. 56–86.

Finn, Margot, 'Colonial Gifts: Family Politics and the Exchange of Goods in British India, C.1780–1820', *MAS* 40, 1 (2006), 203–31.

Fisher, Michael H., 'The Office of Akhbar Nawis: The Transition from Mughal to British Forms', *MAS* 27, 1 (1993), pp. 45–82.

Forbes, Duncan, *Hume's Philosophical Politics* (Cambridge, 1975).

Forbes, Geraldine Hancock, *Positivism in Bengal: A Case Study in the Transmission and Assimilation of an Ideology* (Colombia, 1975).

Foucault, Michel, *The Archaeology of Knowledge*, trans. Alan Sheridan (London, 1972).

Foucault, Michel, 'Governmentality', in Graham Burchell, Colin Gordon, and Peter Miller (eds), *The Foucault Effect* (Hemel Hempstead, 1991).

Foucault, Michel, *Security, Territory, Population. Lectures at the College de France, 1977–1978*, trans. Graham Burchell (Basingstoke, 2007).

Fuller, C.J. and Bénéï, Veronique (eds), *The Everyday State and Society in Modern India* (New Delhi, 2001).

Gallagher, John, Robinson, Ronald and Denny, Alice, *Africa and the Victorians: The Official Mind of Imperialism* (London, 1961).

Ghosh, Amitav and Chakrabarty, Dipesh, 'A Conversation on *Provincialising Europe*', *Radical History Review* 83, 1 (2002) pp. 146–72.

Goswami, Manu, *Producing India: From Colonial Economy to National Space* (Chicago, IL, 2004).

Gould, Eliga H., 'To Strengthen the King's Hands: Dynastic Legitimacy, Militia Reform and Ideas of National Unity in England 1745–1760', *Historical Journal* 34, 2 (1991), pp. 329–48.

Greene, Jack P., *Peripheries and Center: Constitutional Development in the Extended Polities of the British Empire and the United States, 1607–1788* (Athens, 1986).

Griffin, Dustin, *Literary Patronage in England, 1650–1800* (Cambridge, 1996).

Guha, Ranajit, *A Rule of Property for Bengal: An Essay on the Idea of Permanent Settlement* (3rd edition, Durham, NC, 1996).

Guha, Ranajit, 'Not at Home in Empire', *Critical Inquiry* 23, 3 (1997), pp. 482–93.

Gupta, 'Blurred Boundaries: The Discourse of Corruption, the Culture of Politics, and the Imagined State', *American Ethnologist* 22, 2 (1995), p. 375.

Gupta, Ranjan Kumar, *The Economic Life of a Bengal District, Birbhum, 1770–1857* (Burdwan, 1984).

Gupta, Swarupa, 'Notions of Nationhood in Bengal: Perspectives on *Samaj*, 1867–1905', *Modern Asian Studies* 40, 2 (2006), pp. 273–302.

Haakonssen, Knud, 'James Mill and Scottish Moral Philosophy', *Political Studies* 33, (1985), pp. 628–41.

Habib, Irfan, *The Agrarian System of Mughal India* (2nd edn, New Delhi, 2000).

Hall-Matthews, David, *Peasants, Famine and the State in Colonial Western India* (Basingstoke, 2005).

Harder, Hans, 'The Modern Babu and the Metropolis: Reassessing Early Bengali Narrative Prose (1821–1862)', in Stuart Blackburn and Vasudha Dalmia (eds), *India's Literary History: Essays on the Nineteenth Century* (Delhi, 2004), pp. 358–401.

Harling, Philip, *The Waning of 'Old Corruption': The Politics of Economical Reform in Britain, 1779–1846* (Oxford, 1996).

Harris, Bob, ' "American Idols". Empire, War and the Middling Ranks in Eighteenth-Century England', *Past and Present* 150 (1996), pp. 111–41.

Harrison, Ross, *Bentham* (London, 1983).

Harrison, Ross, *Hobbes, Locke and Confusion's Masterpiece: An Examination of Seventeenth Century Philosophy* (Cambridge, 2002).

Hashmi, Taj Ul-Islam, *Pakistan as a Peasant Utopia: The Communalization of Class Politics in East Bengal, 1920–1947* (Boulder, CO, 1992).

Heidegger, Martin, *Being and Time*, trans. John Macquarrie and Edward Robinson (Oxford, 1962).

Heidegger, Martin, *Basic Writings: Martin Heidegger*, David Krell (ed.) (London, 1993).

Heidegger, Martin, *Off the Beaten Track*, trans. Julian Young and Kenneth Haynes (New York, 2002).

Hilton, Boyd, *The Age of Atonement: The Influence of Evangelicalism on Social and Economic Thought, 1795–1865* (Oxford, 1988).

Hilton, Boyd, *A Mad, Bad and Dangerous People? England 1783–1846* (Oxford, 2006).

Hulsebosch, Daniel J., 'Writs to Rights. "Navigability" and the Transformation of the Common Law in the Nineteenth Century', *Cardozo Law Review* 23, 3 (2002) 1049–1106.

Hume, Leonard, *Bentham and Bureaucracy* (Cambridge, 1981).

Hunt, Lynn, *Politics, Culture, and Class in the French Revolution* (Berkeley, CA, 1984).

Inden, Ronald B., *Marriage and Rank in Bengali Culture: A History of Caste and Clan in Middle Period Bengal* (Berkeley, CA, 1976).

Inden, Ronald B., *Imagining India* (Oxford, 1990).

Innes, Joanna, 'Parliament and the Shaping of Eighteenth-Century English Social Policy', *Transactions of the Royal Historical Society* 5th ser., 40 (1990), pp. 63–92.

Innes, Joanna, 'Legislation and Public Participation 1760–1830', in D. Lemmings (ed.), *The British and Their Laws* (Woodbridge, 2005), pp. 102–32.

Islam, Sirajul, *The Permanent Settlement in Bengal: A Study of Its Operation, 1790–1819* (Dacca, 1979).

Jack, J.C., *Final Report of the Survey and Settlement Operations in the Bakarganj District* (Calcutta, 1915).

Kamal, Abu Hena Mustafa, *The Bengali Press and Literary Writing, 1818–31* (Dacca, 1977).

Kane, Pandurang Vaman, *History of Dharmasastra: Ancient and Medieval Religious and Civil Law in India* (2nd edn. Poona, 1968).

Kapila, Shruti, 'Race Matters: Orientalism and Religion, India and Beyond, C.1770–1880', *Modern Asian Studies* 41 (2007), pp. 169–97.

Kapila, Shruti, 'Self, Spencer and *Swaraj*. Nationalist Thought and Critiques of Liberalism, 1890–1920', *Modern Intellectual History* 4, 1 (2007), pp. 109–27.

Kaviraj, Sudipta, *The Unhappy Consciousness: Bankimchandra Chattopadhyay and the Formation of Nationalist Discourse in India* (Delhi, 1995).

Kaviraj, Sudipta and Khilnani, Sunil, *Civil Society: History and Possibilities* (Cambridge, 2001).

Kenyon, J.P., *Revolution Principles: The Politics of Party, 1689–1720* (Oxford, 1977).

Khan, Gulfishan, *Indian Muslim Perceptions of the West During the Eighteenth Century* (Karachi, 1998).

Kidd, Colin, *British Identities before Nationalism. Ethnicity and Nationhood in the Atlantic World, 1600–1800* (Cambridge, 1999).

Kling, Blair B., *Partner in Empire: Dwarkanath Tagore and the Age of Enterprise in Eastern India* (Berkeley, CA, 1976).

Kopf, David, *British Orientalism and the Bengal Renaissance: The Dynamics of Indian Modernization 1773–1835* (Berkeley, 1969).

Koselleck, Reinhart, *Futures Past: On the Semantics of Historical Time* (Cambridge, MA, 1985).

Koselleck, Reinhart, *Critique and Crisis: Enlightenment and the Pathogenesis of Modern Society* (Cambridge, MA, 1988).

Kozlowski, Gregory C., 'Loyalty, Locality and Authority in Several Opinions (Fatawa) Delivered by the Mufti of the Jami'ah Nizamiyyah Madrasah, Hyderabad, India', *MAS* 29, 4 (1995), pp. 893–923.

Langford, Paul, *Public Life and the Propertied Englishman, 1689–1798* (Oxford, 1991).

Lariviere, Richard W., 'Justices and Panditas: Some Ironies in Contemporary Readings of the Hindu Legal Past', *Journal of Asian Studies* 48, 4 (1989), pp. 759–69.

Lieberman, David, *The Province of Legislation Determined: Legal Theory in Eighteenth-Century Britain* (Cambridge, 1989).

Lieberman, Victor, 'Transcending East-West Dichotomies: State and Culture Formation in Six Ostrensibly Disparate Areas', *MAS* 21, 3 (1997), pp. 463–546.

Lobban, Michael, *The Common Law and English Jurisprudence, 1760–1850* (Oxford, 1991).

Lucas, Paul, 'On Edmund Burke's Doctrine of Prescription; or, an Appeal from the New to the Old Lawyers', *Historical Journal* 11, 1 (1968), 35–63.

Macdonagh, Oliver, 'The Nineteenth-Century Revolution in Government: A Reappraisal', *Historical Journal* 1, 1 (1958), pp. 52–67.

Macintyre, Alasdair, 'Hegel on Faces and Skulls', in Alasdair MacIntyre (ed.), *Hegel: A Collection of Critical Essays* (Garden City, NY, 1972).

Macintyre, Alasdair, *After Virtue: A Study in Moral Theory* (London, 1981).

Madelung, Wilferd, 'Nasir Al-Din Tusi's Ethics between Philosophy, Shi'ism, and Sufism', in Richard G. Hovannisian (ed.), *Ethics in Islam* (Lancaster, CA, 1985).

Madhavi Kale, 'Subject to Question: Empire and Catherine Hall's *Civilising Subjects*', *Small Axe* 7, 2 (2003), pp. 127–36.

Majeed, Javed, *Ungoverned Imaginings* (Oxford, 1992).

Majeed, Javed, 'Bathos, Architecture and Knowing India: E.M. Forster's *A Passage to India* and Nineteenth-Century British Ethnology and the Romance Quest', *Journal of Commonwealth Literature* 40, 1 (2005), pp. 21–36.

Majumdar, Bimanbehari, *History of Indian Social and Political Ideas, from Rammohan to Dayananda* (2nd edn, Calcutta, 1967).

Mandler, Peter, *Aristocratic Government in the Age of Reform: Whigs and Liberals 1830–1852* (Oxford, 1990).

Mandler, Peter, '"Race" and "Nation" in Mid-Victorian Thought', in Stefan Collini, Richard Whatmore and Brian Young (eds), *History, Religion and Culture. British Intellectual History, 1750–1950* (Cambridge, 2000), pp. 224–44.

Mandler, Peter, 'The Problem with Cultural History', *Cultural and Social History* 1, 1 (2004), pp. 94–117.

Mandler, Peter, 'Nation and Power in the Liberal State: Britain, c.1800–c.1914' in Len Scales *et.al.* (eds), *Power and the Nation in European History* (Cambridge, 2005), pp. 354–69.

Mandler, Peter, 'What is National Identity? Definitions and Applications in Modern British Historiography', *Modern Intellectual History* 3 (2006), pp. 271–97.

Marriott, John, *The Other Empire: Metropolis, India and Progress in the Colonial Imagination* (Manchester, 2003).

Marshall, P.J., 'Indian Officials under the East India Company in Eighteenth-Century Bengal', *Bengal Past and Present* 84 (1965), pp. 95–120.

Marshall, P.J., *British Discovery of Hinduism in the Eighteenth Century* (Cambridge, 1970).

Marshall, P.J., '*A Free Though Conquering People': Britain and Asia in the Eighteenth Century*, Inaugural Lecture in the Rhodes Chair of Imperial History, Delivered at King's College London (London, 1981).

Marshall, P.J., *The Making and Unmaking of Empires: Britain, India, and America, 1750–1783* (Oxford, 2005).

McDermott, Rachel, *Mother of My Heart, Daughter of My Dreams: Kalai and Uma in the Devotional Poetry of Bengal* (Oxford, 2001).

Mclane, John R., *Land and Local Kingship in 18th Century Bengal* (Cambridge, 1993).

Megill, A.D., 'Theory and Experience in Adam Smith', *Journal of the History of Ideas* 36, 1 (1975), pp. 79–94.

Mehta, Uday Singh, *The Anxiety of Freedom: Imagination and Individuality in Locke's Political Thought* (Ithaca, NY, 1992).

Mehta, Uday Singh, *Liberalism and Empire: A Study in Nineteenth-Century British Liberal Thought* (Chicago, IL, 1999).

Menski, Werner, *Hindu Law. Beyond Tradition and Modernity* (New Delhi, 2003).

Michell, George (ed.), *Brick Temples of Bengal: From the Archives of David Mccutchion* (Princeton, 1983).

Mingay, G.E., *English Landed Society in the Eighteenth Century* (London, 1964).

Mink, Louis O, 'History and Fiction as Modes of Comprehension', *New Literary History* 1, 3 (1970), pp. 541–58.

Mukherjee, Tillotama, 'The Co-ordinating State and the Economy: The Nizamat in Eighteenth-Century Bengal', *MAS* 42, 1 (2008), pp. 1–48.

Mukhopaddhyay, Nirmalendru (ed.), *Bharatcandrer Annadamangal* (Kalikata, 1978).

Muldrew, Craig, 'Rural Credit and Legal Institutions in the Countryside in England 1550–1700', in Christopher Brooks and Michael Lobban (eds), *Communities and Courts in Britain, 1450–1900* (London, 1997), pp. 155–78.

Mulhall, Stephen, *Heidegger and Being and Time* (London, 1996).

Nag Chowdhury-Zilly, Aditee, *The Vagrant Peasant: Agrarian Distress and Desertion in Bengal, 1770–1830* (Wiesbaden, 1982).

Nandy, Somendra Chandra, *History of the Cossimbazar Raj in the Nineteenth-Century* (Calcutta, 1986).

Narayana Rao, Velcheru, Shulman, David and Subrahmanyam, Sanjay, *Textures of Time: Writing History in South India, 1600–1800* (Delhi, 2001).

O'Brien, Patrick K., 'The Political Economy of British Taxation, 1660–1815', *Economic History Review* New ser., 41, 1 (1988), pp. 1–32.

O'Gorman, Frank, *Voters, Patrons and Parties: The Unreformed Electorate in England, 1734–1832* (Oxford, 1989).

Oldham, James, *The Mansfield Manuscripts and the Growth of English Law in the Eighteenth Century*, 2 vols (Chapel Hill, NC, 1992).

Packham, Catherine, 'The Physiology of Political Economy: Vitalism and Adam Smith's *Wealth of Nations'*, *Journal of the History of Ideas* 63, 3 (2002), pp. 465–81.

Pal, Satyendranath, *The Rise of Radicalism in Bengal in the Nineteenth Century* (Calcutta, 1991).

Panda, Chitta, *The Decline of the Bengal Zamindars, 1870–1920* (Delhi, 1997).

Parkin, Jonathan, 'The Reception of Hobbes' *Leviathan'*, in Patricia Springborg (ed.), *The Cambridge Companion to Hobbes's Leviathan* (Cambridge, 2007), pp. 441–55.

Peers, Douglas M., 'War and Public Finance in Early Nineteenth-Century British India: The First Burma War', *International History Review* 11 (1989), pp. 627–48.

Peers, Douglas M., *Between Mars and Mammon. Colonial Armies and the Garrison State in India 1819–1835* (London, 1995).

Pennington, Brian K., 'Constructing Colonial Dharma: A Chronicle of Emergent Hinduism, 1830–1831', *Journal of the American Academy of Religion* 69, 3 (2001), pp. 577–603.

Philips, C.H., *The East India Company, 1784–1834* (Manchester, 1940).

Pick, Daniel, *Faces of Degeneration: A European Disorder, C.1848–C.1918* (Cambridge, 1989).

Pitts, Jennifer, *A Turn to Empire: The Rise of Imperial Liberalism in Britain and France* (Princeton, NJ, 2005).

Pocock, J.G.A., *The Ancient Constitution and the Feudal Law: A Study of English Historical Thought in the Seventeenth Century* (Cambridge, 1957).

Pocock, J.G.A., *The Machiavellian Moment: Florentine Political Thought and the Atlantic Republican Tradition* (Princeton, 1975).

Pocock, J.G.A., 'The Classical Theory of Deference', *American Historical Review* 81, 3 (1976), pp. 516–23.

Pocock, J.G.A., 'Modes of Political and Historical Time in Early Eighteenth-Century Britain', *Virtue, Commerce and History* (Cambridge, 1985).

Pocock, J.G.A., *Barbarism and Religion, Vol. IV. Barbarians, Savages and Empires* (Cambridge, 2005).

Pollock, Sheldon, 'The Theory of Practice and the Practice of Theory in Indian Intellectual History', *Journal of the American Oriental Society* 105, 3 (1984), pp. 499–519.

Postema, Gerald J., *Bentham and the Common Law Tradition* (Oxford, 1986).

Prakash, Gyan, *Another Reason: Science and the Imagination of Modern India* (Princeton, NJ, 1999).

Prior, Katherine, 'MacNaghten, Sir William Hay, Baronet (1793–1841)', *Oxford Dictionary of National Biography* http://www.oxforddnb.com/view/article/17705, accessed 29 July 2005.

Ray, Rajat Kanta, *The Felt Community: Commonalty and Mentality before the Emergence of Indian Nationalism* (Delhi, 2003).

Ray, Ratnalekha, *Change in Agrarian Bengal* (Delhi, 1979).

Raychaudhuri, Tapan, *Europe Reconsidered: Perceptions of the West in Nineteenth Century Bengal* (Delhi, 1988).

Reckord, Mary, 'The Jamaica Slave Rebellion of 1831', *Past and Present* 40 (1968), pp. 108–25.

Reddy, William M., *The Navigation of Feeling: A Framework for the History of Emotions* (Cambridge, 2001).

Ricoeur, Paul, *Time and Narrative* (Chicago, IL, 1984).

Rizvi, Sajjad H., 'Mysticism and Philosophy: Ibn Arabi and Mulla Sadra', in Peter Adamson and Richard C. Taylor (eds), *The Cambridge Companion to Arabic Philosophy* (Cambridge, 2005).

Robb, Peter, *Ancient Rights and Future Comfort: Bihar, the Bengal Tenancy Act of 1885, and British Rule in India* (Richmond, Surrey, 1997).

Robertson, Bruce, *Raja Rammohan Roy: The Father of Modern India* (Delhi, 1995).

Robertson, John, *The Scottish Enlightenment and the Militia Issue* (Edinburgh, 1985).

Rocher, Ludo, *Jimutavahana's Dayabhaga. The Hindu Law of Inheritance in Bengal* (New York, NY, 2002).

Rocher, Rosane, *Orientalism, Poetry, and the Millennium: The Checkered Life of Nathaniel Brassey Halhed, 1751–1830* (Delhi, 1983).

Rocher, Rosane, 'The Career of Radhakanta Tarkavisaga, an Eighteenth-Century Pandit in British Employ', *Journal of the American Oriental Society* 109, 4 (1989), pp. 627–33.

Rocher, Rosane, 'British Orientalism in the Eighteenth Century: The Dialectics of Knowledge and Government', in Carol Breckenbridge and Peter van der Veer (eds), *Orientalism and the Postcolonial Predicament* (Philadelphia, 1993).

Rocher, Rosane, 'Weaving Knowledge: William Jones and the *Pandits*', in Garland Cannon and Kevin Brine (eds), *Objects of Inquiry: The Life, Contribution and Influence of Sir William Jones (1746–1794)* (New York, 1995), pp. 51–82.

Ross, Charles (ed.), *Correspondence of Charles, First Marquis Cornwallis*, 3 vols (London, 1859).

Rosselli, John, *Lord William Bentinck: The Making of a Liberal Imperialist, 1774–1839* (Berkeley, CA, 1974).

Rothschild, Emma, *Economic Sentiments: Adam Smith, Condorcet and the Enlightenment* (Harvard, 2001).

Rowe, Michael, *From Reich to State: The Rhineland in the Revolutionary Age, 1780–1830* (Cambridge, 2003).

Rubiés, Joan Pau, 'Oriental Despotism and European Orientalism: Botero to Montesquieu'. *The Journal of Early Modern History: Contacts, Comparisons, Contrasts* 9, 1–2 (2005), pp. 109–80.

Said, Edward W., *Orientalism. Western Conceptions of the Orient* (Harmondsworth, 1978).

Sarkar, Benoy Kumar, 'The Futurism of Young Asia', *International Journal of Ethics* 28, 4 (1918), pp. 521–41.

Sarkar, Benoy Kumar, *The Positive Background of Hindu Sociology: Book 1, Introduction to Hindu Positivism* (Allahabad, 1937).

Sarkar, Sumit, *The Swadeshi Movement in Bengal, 1903–1908* (Delhi, 1973).

Sarkar, Susobhan, 'Derozio and Young Bengal', in A.C. Gupta (ed.), *Studies in Bengal Renaissance* (Calcutta, 1958).

Sartori, Andrew, 'Emancipation as Heteronomy: The Crisis of Liberalism in Later Nineteenth-Century Bengal', *Journal of Historical Sociology* 17, 1 (2004), pp. 56–86.

Sartori, Andrew, 'The British Empire and its Liberal Mission', *Journal of Modern History* 78 (2006), pp. 623–42.

Sayyid-Marsot, Afaf Lutfi, *Egypt in the Reign of Muhammad Ali* (Cambridge, 1984).

Schmitt, Carl, *Political Theology: Four Chapters on the Concept of Sovereignty* (Cambridge, Mass, 1985).

Scott, David, 'Colonial Governmentality', *Social Text* 43 (1995), pp. 191–220.

Scott, William, 'The Pursuit of "Interests" in the French Revolution. A Preliminary Survey', *French Historical Studies* 19, 3 (1996), pp. 811–51.

Sen, Amartya and Williams, Bernard, *Utilitarianism and Beyond* (Cambridge, 1982).

Sen, Dinesh Chandra, *History of Bengali Language and Literature* (Calcutta, 1911), pp. 168–71.

Sen, Dinesh Chandra, *The Bengali Ramayanas* (Calcutta, 1920), p.84.

Sen, Ranajit, 'A Note on Land Resumption in Bengal in the Second Half of the 18th Century', *Quarterly Review of Historical Studies* (1986), pp.23–34.

Sen, Sudipta, *Empire of Free Trade: The East India Company and Making of the Colonial Marketplace* (Philadelphia, PA, 1998).

Sen, Sudipta, *A Distant Sovereignty: National Imperialism and the Origins of British India* (New York, 2002).

Sen, Sukumar, *History of Bengali Literature* (New Delhi, 1960).

Serajuddin, A.M., 'The Origin on the Rajas of the Chittagong Hill Tracts and Their Relations with the Mughals and the East India Company in the Eighteenth Century', *Journal of the Pakistan Historical Society* 19, 1 (1971), pp. 51–60.

Sharma, Aradhana and Gupta, Akhil, *The Anthropology of the State: A Reader* (Oxford, 2006).

Singha, Radhika, *A Despotism of Law. Crime and Justice in Early Colonial India* (New Delhi, 1998).

Sinha, Chittaranjan, 'Doctrinal Influences on the Judicial Policy of the East India Company's Administration in Bengal, 1772–1833', *Historical Journal* 12, 2 (1969), pp. 240–8.

Sinha, Samita, *Pandits in a Changing Environment: Centres of Sanskrit Learning in Nineteenth Century Bengal* (Calcutta, 1993).

Skinner, Quentin, *The Foundations of Modern Political Thought*, 2 vols (Cambridge, 1978).

Skinner, Quentin, *Liberty before Liberalism* (Cambridge, 1998).

Skinner, Quentin, *Visions of Politics*. Vol. I, *Regarding Method* (Cambridge, 2002).

Skinner, Quentin, *Visions of Politics*. Vol. III, *Hobbes and Civil Science* (Cambridge, 2002).

Spear, Percival, *The Nabobs: A Study of the Social Life of the English in Eighteenth Century India* (London; New York, 1932).

Stedman-Jones, Gareth, *Languages of Class. Studies in English Working-Class History* (Cambridge, 1984).

Stein, Burton, *Thomas Munro. The Origins of the Colonial State and His Vision of Empire* (Delhi, 1989).

Stein, Burton, *The Making of Agrarian Policy in British India, 1770–1900* (Delhi, 1992).

Stokes, Eric, *The English Utilitarians and India* (Oxford, 1959).

Subrahmanyam, Sanjay, *Penumbral Visions: Making Polities in Early Modern South India* (Ann Arbor, 2001).

Subrahmanyam, Sanjay, 'Frank Submissions: The Company and the Mughals between Sir Thomas Roe and Sir William Norris', in H.V. Bowen, Margarette Lincoln and Nigel Rigby (eds), *The Worlds of the East India Company* (Woodbridge, 2006).

Sutherland, Lucy, *The East India Company in Eighteenth Century Politics* (Oxford, 1952).

Taniguchi, Shinkichu, 'The Patni System – A Modern Origin of the "Sub-Infeudation" of Bengal in the Nineteenth Century', *Hitotsubashi Journal of Economics*, 22, 1 (1981), pp. 40–61.

Taylor, Charles, *A Secular Age* (Cambridge, MA, 2007).

Taylor, Miles, 'Empire and Parliamentary Reform: The 1832 Reform Act Revisited', in Arthur Burns and Joanna Innes (eds), *Rethinking the Age of Reform. Britain, 1780–1850* (Cambridge, 2003).

Thapar, Romila, *Time as a Metaphor of History: Early India* (Delhi, 1996).

Thompson, E.P., *Customs in Common* (London, 1993).

Travers, Robert, ' "The Real Value of the Lands": The *Nawabs*, the British and the Land Tax in Eighteenth-Century Bengal', *MAS* 38, 3 (2004), pp. 517–58.

Travers, Robert, 'Ideology and British Expansion in Bengal', *Journal of Imperial and Commonwealth History* 33, 1 (2005), pp. 7–27.

Travers, Robert, *Ideology and Empire in Eighteenth-Century India. The British in Bengal* (Cambridge, 2007).

Tribe, Keith, *Land, Labour and Economic Discourse* (London, 1978).

Tripathi, Amales, *Trade and Finance in the Bengal Presidency, 1793–1833* (2nd edn, Calcutta, 1979).

Tuck, Richard, *Natural Rights Theories: Their Origin and Development* (Cambridge, 1979).

Tully, James and Skinner, Quentin (eds), *Meaning and Context: Quentin Skinner and His Critics* (Cambridge, 1988).

Wahrman, Dror, *Imagining the Middle Class: The Political Representation of Class in Britain, C. 1780–1840* (Cambridge, 1995).

Ward, J.R., 'The Industrial Revolution and British Imperialism, 1750–1850', *The Economic History Review* 47, 1 (1994), pp. 44–65.

Washbrook, D.A., 'Law, State and Agrarian Society in Colonial India', *MAS*, 15, 3 (1981), pp. 649–721.

Washbrook, D.A., 'Land and Labour in late Eighteenth-Century South India: The Golden Age of the Pariah', in Peter Robb (ed.), *Dalit Movements and the Meanings of Labour in India* (New Delhi, 1997), pp. 68–87.

Washbrook, D.A., 'South India 1770–1840: The Colonial Transition', *MAS* 38, 3 (2004), pp. 479–516.

Webster, Anthony, 'An Early Global Business in a Colonial Context: The Strategies, Management, and Failure of John Palmer and Company of Calcutta, 1780–1830', *Enterprise and Society* 6, 1 (2005), pp. 98–133.

Weil, Frederick D., 'The Stranger, Prudence and Trust in Hobbes's Theory', *Theory and Society* 15, 5 (1986), pp. 759–88.

Williams, Bernard, *Morality: An Introduction to Ethics* (Harmondsworth, 1973).

Wilson, Jon E., ' "A Thousand Countries to Go to": Peasants and Rulers in Late Eighteenth-Century Bengal', *Past and Present* 189 (2005), pp. 81–110.

Wink, André, *Land and Sovereignty in India: Agrarian Society and Politics under the Eighteenth-Century Maratha Svarâajya* (Cambridge, 1986).

Unpublished works

Iqbal, Khondker Iftekhar 'Society and Ecology in Nineteenth and Early Twentieth Century Bengal Delta' (PhD, University of Cambridge, 2005).

Stern, Philip, ' "One Body Corporate and Politick": The Growth of the East India Company-State in the Later Seventeenth Century' (PhD, Columbia University, 2004).

Wilson, Jon E., 'Governing Property, Making Law: Land, Local Society & Colonial Discourse in Agrarian Bengal, C.1785–1830' (D Phil, University of Oxford, 2000).

Index

This index is intended to work in part as a glossary. Passages are indicated in bold where the meaning of a particular term, the use of a concept, the biography of an individual or significant details about a place are discussed.

achara (custom), 38, **85**
adoption, 98
affection, *see* sentiment
Alam, Muzaffar, 21–2, 112
al-Dawani, Jalal al-din (1426–1502), 22–3
Alivardi Khan, *Nawab* of Bengal (1671–1756), 39, 41, 171
al-Shirazi, Sadr al-din (Mulla Sadra) (1571/2–1640), 22
ancient constitution, 46, **51–4**, 64, 71, 93, 168–9
ancient law, 53, 76, 92–3, 102–3, 104, 126–31
anxiety, 1, 8, 10, 43, **47**, 60, 65–9, 76, 90–2, 105, 159–60, 189–92
Aristotle, 6
Asad, Talal, 15, 36
Austin, John (1790–1859), 12

Bakarganj, 25, **27–8**, 42, 109–10, 117
Bankimchandra Chattopadhyay (1838–1894), 176–7, 183–4, 187, 194
Barisal (Bakarganj), **42–4**
Barlow, George Hilario, 56, **59–65**, 72–3, 107, 124
Bauman, Zygmunt, 15–16, 195 n.3
Bayley, William Butterworth (1781–1860), 101, 150
Bayly, C.A., 7, 17, 22, 29, 162, 168, 188–9
'Bengal system' of government, 46–7, 59–62, 69, 73, 76, 104, 106–8, 111, 120, 124–5, 127–8
Benjamin, Walter, 36
Bentham, Jeremy (1748–1832), 75, 95, 101, 123, 133, 135–6, 143, 181

Bentinck, Lord William Cavendish (1774–1839), 8, 74, 133, 150, 167–9
Beveridge, Henry (1837–1929), 25
Bhabanicharan Bandopadhyay (1787–1848), 17, **174–5**, 180–1, 194
bhadralok, 122, 146, **161–81**
Bharatchandra Ray (1712–1760), 23, 28, 40
Bimala Dasaya, 86–91
Birbhum, 27–8, 54, 104–5, 111, 181
Blackstone, Willliam (1723–1780), 81
Bolts, William (1739–1808), 64–5, 70
Bombay Presidency, 94, 145–7
Bose, Sugata, 173
Boughton-Rouse, Charles William (1747–1821), 65, 70–1
Britain, *see* custom–common law as; law; politics, history of political thought
Brooke, Thomas, 104–5, 107–8, 111
Burdwan, **23–4**, 34, 69, 108–9, 120, 165
Burdwan, *Raja / Rani* of, 24, 38, 108–9, 117–22, 172
Burke, Edmund (f.1729–1797), 1, 7, 33–4, 38, 53–7, 65, 146, 188

Calcutta, as colonial metropolis, 2–3, 16, 50, 64, 74, 76–7, 94, 104–8, 115, 122, 146–8, 155–7, 171–5, 178–9
Chakmas, 27–8
Chandradwip (Bakarganj), 42–4, 117
Chatterjee, Partha, 3, 36–7, 184, 191
civil society, 6, 19, 29, 30–1, 76, 129, 134–5, **163–7**, 178–80, 186
Clive, Robert, first Baron Clive of Plassey (1725–1774), 68
Code of Gentoo Law, 52, 78
codification, *see* law

Cohn, Bernard, 92–3
Colebrooke, Henry Thomas (1765–1837), **80**, 82–3, 92–3, 108, 140, 193
colonialism, 5–11, **190**, 191–4
common law, *see* law
comparative history, 19, 36, 41
Cornwallis, Charles, first Marquess (1738–1805), 16, 25, 45–6, 52, **55–63**, 66, 71–4, 106–7, 136–7, 149, 156–7, 185, 189
crises, financial and epistemic, 47, **49**, 50–4, 92, 109, 117
Cumming, James, 127
custom
  common law as, 33, 75, 88
  family, 88
  as principle of governance, 51, 56, 70–1, 75, 79–83
  in resolution of property disputes, 26, 51, 56, 88, 90–3, 96–9, 104–6, 118
  see also law

Davies, Samuel, 108, 123, 127
Derozio, Henry, 167, 176
Despotism, 55, **63–6**, 67, 70, 137–8, 140
Dhaka, 42, 109
Digest of Hindu Law, 79–82, 140
disputes
  Badr uddin Khan (Bakarganj), 210 n.30
  Bhola Dhami *vs* Nawazu (Gaya), 98–9
  Bimala vs Gokul Nath Ray (Rangpur), 86–91, 97
  Khardah *goswami*s (24 Parganas), 90–1
  Mirza Ali Naki vs. Ram Rudr Chaudhuri (Rangpur), 118–19
  Paniottys vs Durga Kuar Narayan (Bakarganj), 42, 117–18
  Prasanna Kumar Tagore (Calcutta), 100–1
  Rammohan Roy (Burdwan), 171
  Wames Chandra Pal Chaudhuri vs. Ratanchandra Pal Chaudhuri (Calcutta), 146–7, 171
  widow of Joy Narayan Qanungu vs Devi Prasad (Sylhet), 89–90
Dodson, Michael, 93, 210 n.36, 218 n.66
Dow, Alexander, 64–5, 70
Ducarel, George, 69
duty, differing conceptions of, 31

economy, as separate sphere of human activity, 52, 72
education, of British and Indian officials, 150–7
Elphinestone, Mountstuart (1779–1859), 91–2, 94
ethical practice, governance as, 2, 6, 28, 38–9
experience
  colonial rejection of, 137, 141–2, 60–1, 66–70
  defence of, 4–6, 67
  and expectation, 74, 111, 126, 192–4

Fakhir Mohammed Chaprasi, 24, 117–18
Fort Willliam College, 92
Foucault, Michel (1926–1984), 3, 9–10, 164, 183
Francis, Sir Philip (1740–1818), 51–2, 59

Ganga Govinda Sinha, 70
Gangaram, 39–40
Gaya, 59, 98, 107
Genealogy, 37
Ghulam Hussein Khan (1727–1797), 4–6, 10–13, 22, 28, 33, 40–1, 162–3, 190
Gibbon, Edward (1737–1794), 139, 144
Gisborne, Thomas (1758–1846), 31–2
Gokul Nath Ray, 24, 86–91
Goodlad, Richard, 26
Goswami, Manu, 36
*goswami*s (*vaisnava* ascetics), 90
governance
  as ethical practice, *see* politics
  as management of population, governmentality, 106, 119–20, 129, 158–9
Graham, Thomas, 107
Grant, Charles, 68
Guha, Ranajit, 8, 46, 47, 106–7
Gupta, Akhil, 14–15

Haileybury College, 151
Halhed, Nathaniel Brassey (1751–1830), 52, 78–80
Harington, J.H., 127–8
Harishchandra, story of Maharaja, 20–2
Hastings, Francis Rawdon, Marquess of (1754–1826), 100, 127

Hastings, Warren (1732–1818), 38, 47–57, 78, 146
Hegel, Georg Wilhelm Friedrich (1770–1831), 30–2, 72, 134, 146, 178, 180, 185, 187, 189
Heidegger, Martin (1889–1976), 9–13, 47, 76, 162
Hindu Code Bill, 101
Hinduism, attempts to define with rules, 183–5
Hindu law, *see* law
Hobbes, Thomas (1588–1679), 1, 30, 34–5
Hume, David (1711–1776), 39, 139, 144

Idilpur (Dhaka), 26
Idrakpur (Rangpur), 24, 86–91, 97, 117
ijaradars (revenue farmers), *ijaradar* system, 23, 53–4
indexing, 96–7
Iqbal, Iftekhar, 28, 46
Islam, Sirajul, 116

Jacobite rebellion (1745), 38
Jagannatha Tarkapancanana, 24, 80, 82–3, 169
Jones, William (1746–1794), 67–9, **79–83**, 92, 137, 140, 166
jotdar thesis, 128

kachchari (office), 109–15
Kale, Madhavi, ix
Kapila, Shruti, 191–2, 197 n.40
Kaviraj, Sudipta, 163
Koselleck, Reinhardt, 73–4
Krishna Chandra, *Raja* of Nadia, 24

Landholders, *see* zamindars
Langford, Paul, 32
law
    codification, 75–7, 92–102, **97**, 143, 150, 167, 187
    common, 81–4, 93–6, 143; *see also* custom–common law as
    Hindu, 75–103
    Indian Law Commission, 101, 150
    legislation, 4, 62–3, 100, 149–51; *see also* Parliament
    Muslim, **77–8**, 91, 96, 102
    precedent, 96–7
Law, Thomas (1756–1834), 59, 107, 124

Liberalism, 7–8, 181, 132–6, 163–4, 167–9, 175–8
Lobban, Michael, 33
Locke, John (1632–1704), 34–5
London, role in imperial policy-making, 49–54, 106–8, 178, 181

Macaulay, Thomas Babington (1800–1859), 97, 139, 143–4, 140, 148–50, 155–6, 159–60
MacDonagh, Oliver (1924–2002), 3
Machiavelli, Niccollo, 1, 38
Mackenzie, Holt, 133–5, 144–8, 150–4
MacNaghtem Sir Francis (1763–1843), 95, 141
MacNaghten, William Hay (1793–1841), 95–7, 141
MacPherson, John, 48–9
Madhabpasha (Barisal), 42
Madras Presidency, 124–7
Maine, Sir Henry Sumner (1822–1888), 81, 87, 104, **129–32**
Majeed, Javed, 142–3
Mandler, Peter, 189
mapping, 129
Maratha raids (1742–51), 39–41
Mehta, Uday Singh, 7–8, 37, 185
Metcalfe, Charles, 147–9, 182
Mill, James (1773–1836), 8, 76, 101, **135–44**, 148–51, 155, 169, 184
Mink, Louis O, 17, 197 n.41
Mritunjoy Vidyalankar, 18, 167
Mughal state, 112–13
Munro, Sir Thomas, 124–8, 182
Murshidabad, 2, 23, 28, 59, 65–6, 88
Muslim law, *see* law

Nabadwip (Nadia), 29, 80–2
Nadia, 24, 26
Napoleon Bonaparte, 186, 191–2
narrative
    of Bengali litigants, 28, 37, 87–8
    history as, 17–18, 36
Nietzsche, Friedrich, 185

objectification, **12–13**, 16, **76**, 85, 122–7, 143

Packham, Catherine, 34
Paley, William, 1, 34

pandits, 28–9, 78, 86–8, 98–9, 101, 152–4, 170
Paniotty, Alexander and George, 42, 117, 119
Park, John James (1793–1833), 143
Parliament, 29, 49–51, 63, 70, 144, 156, 158
patni tenure, 120–1
patronage, 23–6, 32, 69, 87, 117, 165
pattas, **113–15**
peasants
  action in constituting polity, 25–9, 32–5, 105–6, 114–15
  mobility, 25–8
  objectification, within colonial agrarian discourse, 124–9
  resistance, 27–9, 35, 114–15, 125
  see also raiyatwari settlement
permanent settlement, *see* 'Bengal system' of government
pirs, 23
Pitt, William the Younger (1759–1806), 45, 56, 62
Plassey / Polashi, Battle of, 51
Pocock, J.G.A., 31, 37–40
politics
  history of political thought, 19
  as practical, inter-subjective art, 4–6, 19–41, 84–5, 184, 190
Principles and Precedents of Hindoo Law, 96, 100–1
Prinsep, Henry Thoby (1792–1878), 96, 100
Prinsep, John (1746–1830), 108–9, 150
property, idea of, 32–3, 55–64, 72–3, 85–7, 100–2, 105–8, 166–7

qanungus, 113, 70–2
qazis, 28–9, 152–4

race, racism, 191–2
Radhanagar (Rangpur), 25
raiyats, see peasants
raiyatwari settlement, **125–6**
Rammohan Roy (1772–1833), 17, 23, 163–77, 186
Rangpur, 24–7, 40, 54, 86–91, 109–10, 115–16
Rath Jatra procession, 90
Ray, Rajat Kanta, 22

record-keeping, 61, 81, 83–4, 109–12
regulations
  I of 1793, *see* 'Bengal system' of government
  V of 1812, 120–1
  VII of 1799, 120–1
  VIII of 1816, 122
  X of 1859, 128
revenue, collection of, 47–8, 53–6, 59–62, 73–4, 105–7, 112–27, 131
Revolution
  American, 185
  French, 36, 37, 185
Robertson, Bruce, 165–6
rules of law, *see* codification

Sadr Diwani Adalat, 84, 153
Said, Edward, 6
samaj (society), 29, 32, 36, **162–5**, 181
  see also civil society
Sarkar, Benoy Kumar (1887–1949), 19, 36
sati, 165–8
semantic coherence, search for, 7, 15–16, 103, 105, 120–1, 132, 193–4 and *passim*
sentiment, role in politics, **22–3**, 28, **30–5**, 42, 52–3, 57, 67–9, 111, 117, 160, 166–9, 182, 189
  see also politics
Shore, John (Lord Teighmouth) (1751–1834), 45, **56–66**, 69, 72–4, 75–9, 89, 112, 126, 137
Simmel, Georg (1858–1918), 1–2, 194
Siraj ad Daula, *nawab* of Bengal (1733–1757), 51
Smith, Adam (1723–1790), 33–4, 139, 144, 153–4
Smith, Courtney, 98–9, 153–4
State
  as agent of transformation, 14–15, 133–60
  as network, 2, 19–44, 50, 69, 117, 143, 146, 179, 189–90
  see also law *and* time
Stokes, Eric (1924–1981), 3, 16, 135
story-telling, *see narrative*
Strachey, Edward, 1774–1832), 91, 155
Strachey, Henry, 91, 119, 121, 141–2
stranger, figure of, 1–2, 193–4

Sudder Dewanny *Adawlut, see Sadr*
    Diwani Adalat
Supreme Court, Calcutta, 69, 95, 133–4,
    146–9, 172
systems, attempts to systematize, 31, 45,
    66, 73, 96, 133–4, 140, 183–4, 186–7

Tagore, Dwarkanath, 172–3
Tagore, Prasanna Kumar, 100
Tagore, Rabindranath, 36, 161–3, 181
Tara Chandra Chakrabarty, 176–8
temple-building, 24
temporality, *see* time
Tennant, William, 137–8
texts
    different roles in governance, 5, 52,
        76, 80–1, 92–9, 123, 127, 168–9,
        174, 184; *see also* record-keeping
    self-referential web of, 99, 127
    as source of law, *see* law, *codification*
Thompson, George, 178–80
time
    contingent mode of, **38–40**
    customary mode of, **37–8**, 63
    frozen bureaucratic, 110–11
    modern state and, 14–15, 36, 41–4,
        135, 140, 159–60, 190–4
    nation and, 164–5, 171–5
    puranic, 36
Tipu Sultan, 124

Travers, Robert, 46, 51, 64
Trevelyan, Charles, 150, 155–7
Two Treatises on the Hindoo Law of
    Inheritance, 92–3, 98
Tytler, Alexander Fraser, 91, 137–8, 141

uncultivated land, 'waste', 25–6
utilitarianism
    British, 16–17, 142–4
    Colonial, 3, 7–8, 133–60
utopia, 193–4

vagueness, 76, 79, 91, 100, 139–41
vyavahara (arrangement, resolution),
    85, 97

war, 8, 47–8, 54–6, 58
Ward, William (1766–1826), 137–8
Washbrook, David, 100, 124
waste, *see* uncultivated land
Wellesley, Richard, Marquess
    (1760–1842), 148, 151–3, 157
Wilkins, Charles (f.1749–1836), 52
Wilson, Horace Hayman (1786–1860),
    94, 136, 141, 193

zamindari settlement, *see* Bengal system'
    of government
zamindars, 2, **23–9**, 37–8, 45–6, 52–4,
    60, 85–7, 104–32, **122–3**
zimma (protection), 25